Pursuing
John Brown

SERIES ON OHIO HISTORY AND CULTURE

Series on Ohio History and Culture
 Kevin Kern, Editor

For a complete listing of titles published in the series, go to
 www.uakron.edu/uapress.

Pursuing
John Brown
On the Trail of a Radical Abolitionist

JOYCE DYER

The University of Akron Press
Akron, Ohio

ISBN: 978-1-629221-36-6 (paper)

A catalog record for this title is available from the Library of Congress.

∞ The paper used in this publication meets the minimum requirements of ANSI/NISO z39.48–1992 (Permanence of Paper).

Cover image: (Item: UTB-6, 5.4, broj (no. 1). John Brown, 1 photograph : sixth plate daguerreotype, b&w, [ca. 1856]). Reproduced by permission of the Boston Athenæum.

Cover design by Amy Freels.

Pursuing John Brown was designed and typeset in Garamond Premier Pro by Amy Freels and printed on sixty-pound white and bound by Bookmasters of Ashland, Ohio.

All images, unless otherwise indicated, were taken by Joyce Dyer or Daniel Dyer. For the full list of photo credits see page 512.

Most original spelling, grammar, and punctuation retained in quoted material unless otherwise indicated.

Affordable Learning Initiative
THE UNIVERSITY OF AKRON

Produced in conjunction with the University of Akron Affordable Learning Initiative. More information is available at www.uakron.edu/affordablelearning/.

Daniel

Assent - and you are sane -
Demur - you're straightway dangerous -
And handled with a Chain -

Emily Dickinson

Contents

Preface

It's difficult to know what to call *Pursuing John Brown*. It's a work of non-fiction, of course, but what sort? In some ways it resembles biography. Although it's not always strictly chronological, the book accounts for most of the years John Brown lived on earth. But I never set out to capture every detail of John Brown's life. The scenes and images I researched most intensely were often ones that emerged unexpectedly during my pursuit.

The book veers from traditional biography in other ways. At one point I thought it was a travel book. Returning to the physical places a person once occupied always seems such a private and mysterious act, a way of finding something out that reading alone can't supply. Biographer Richard Holmes called this approach the *footsteps principle*—pursuing people from the past by following them to the places of their lives, including "the temporary places, the passing places, the lost places, the dream places."¹ I owed Holmes a great debt for language like that. Repeatedly, I packed a bag and hopped in the car, my husband often beside me, and off we'd go.

Frequently, when I was on the road or sitting in the marvelous archives of the Hudson Library & Historical Society, troubling questions began to form that kept me awake at night. Questions I knew I'd have to answer. After all, John Brown was my neighbor—just from a different century. He'd grown up in Hudson, Ohio, where I'd lived for over thirty years, resided in a cabin around the corner from me, and in 1837 taken his first public vow to destroy slavery in a church that had stood one hundred feet from my porch steps. Why did I think I could just observe him, and we wouldn't have to talk?

I asked hard questions of him, but before long, he began asking even harder questions of me. Who was pursuing whom? Our growing intimacy and colloquy led, inevitably, to a mix of memoir and nonfiction.

Perhaps more than anything, this is a story of a difficult friendship that changed me in irrevocable ways.

List of John Brown's Contemporaries

THE BROWN FAMILY
The Parents of John Brown

Owen Brown — John Brown's father; born in West Simsbury, Connecticut, 1771; died in Hudson, Ohio, 1856

Ruth Mills Brown — John Brown's mother; born in 1772; died in Hudson, Ohio, 1808

Sally Root Brown — John Brown's first stepmother; born in 1789; died in Hudson, Ohio, 1840

Lucy Drake Hinsdale Brown — John Brown's second stepmother; born in Torrington, Connecticut, 1796; died in Hudson, Ohio, 1876

The Wives of John Brown

Dianthe Lusk Brown — John Brown's first wife; born in Hudson, Ohio, 1801; died in New Richmond, Pennsylvania, 1832

Mary Ann Day Brown — John Brown's second wife; born in Granville, New York, 1816; died in Saratoga, California, 1884

The Children of John Brown and Dianthe Lusk Brown

1) John Brown Jr. — Born in Hudson, Ohio, 1821; died in Put-in-Bay, Ohio, 1895; married Wealthy Hotchkiss

2) Jason Brown — Born in Hudson, Ohio, 1823; died in Akron, Ohio, 1912; married Ellen Sherbondy

3) Owen Brown — Born in Hudson, Ohio, 1824; died in Pasadena, California, 1889

4) Frederick Brown   Born in New Richmond,
                                     Pennsylvania, 1827; died in New
                                     Richmond, Pennsylvania, 1831

5) Ruth Brown   Born in New Richmond,
                                     Pennsylvania, 1829; died in Pasadena,
                                     California, 1904; married Henry
                                     Thompson

6) Frederick Brown   Born in New Richmond,
                                     Pennsylvania, 1830; died in
                                     Osawatomie, Kansas, 1856

7) Unnamed Son   Born in New Richmond,
                                     Pennsylvania, 1832; died at birth,
                                     along with mother

The Children of John Brown and Mary Ann Day Brown

8) Sarah Brown   Born in New Richmond,
                                     Pennsylvania, 1834; died in Richfield,
                                     Ohio, 1843

9) Watson Brown   Born in Franklin Mills, Ohio, 1835;
                                     died at Harpers Ferry, Virginia, 1859;
                                     married Isabella Thompson

10) Salmon Brown   Born in Hudson, Ohio, 1836; died in
                                     Portland, Oregon, 1919; married
                                     Abbie C. Hinckley

11) Charles Brown   Born in Hudson, Ohio, 1837; died in
                                     Richfield, Ohio, 1843

12) Oliver Brown   Born in Franklin Mills, Ohio, 1839;
                                     died at Harpers Ferry, Virginia, 1859;
                                     married Martha Evelyn Brewster

13) Peter Brown   Born in Hudson, Ohio, 1840; died in
                                     Richfield, Ohio, 1843

14) Austin Brown   Born in Richfield, Ohio, 1842; died in
                                     Richfield, Ohio, 1843

15) Annie Brown

Born in Richfield, Ohio, 1843; died in Shively, California, 1926; married Samuel Adams

16) Amelia Brown

Born in Akron, Ohio, 1845; died in Akron, Ohio, 1846

17) Sarah Brown

Born in Akron, Ohio, 1846; died in Saratoga, California, 1916

18) Ellen Brown

Born in Springfield, Massachusetts, 1848; died in Springfield, Massachusetts, 1849

19) Unnamed Son

Born in Akron, Ohio, 1852; died in Akron, Ohio, 1852

20) Ellen Brown

Born in Akron, Ohio, 1854; died in Saratoga, California, 1916; married James Fablinger

In-laws of John Brown

Rev. Samuel Lyle Adair

Brother-in-law of John Brown who married Florella Brown and preceded the Brown boys to Kansas

Henry Thompson

Son-in-law of John Brown who married Ruth Brown in 1850 at North Elba and fought with John Brown in Kansas

HUDSON NEIGHBORS

John Buss

Hudson storekeeper who kept a daily journal

Christian Cackler

Early settler in the Western Reserve who lived in both Hudson and Franklin Townships and knew John Brown for forty years, recording his memories of the Reserve and of John Brown in *Recollections of an Old Settler* (1874)

Lora Case

Sunday School student and adoring disciple of John Brown who was active in the Underground Railroad

Amos Chamberlin

Hudson resident who bought Westlands, John Brown's farm, after it foreclosed and was auctioned off

William Dawes

Abolitionist who lived in Hudson during the 1830s and worked at Western Reserve College; best remembered for raising money for Oberlin Collegiate Institute and attending the 1840 World Anti-Slavery Convention in London

Edgar Birge Ellsworth

Owner of a feed store on East Main in Hudson and father of James W. Ellsworth

James W. Ellsworth

Son of Edgar Birge Ellsworth; made a fortune in coal and returned to Hudson to modernize the town and invest in Western Reserve Academy

Jesse Root Grant

Randolph, Ohio, resident who apprenticed with Owen Brown at his tannery on Brown Street, living with the Browns during that time; father of Civil War general Ulysses S. Grant

Beriah Green

Professor of Sacred Literature who delivered antislavery lectures during the controversy over abolitionism at Western Reserve College in Hudson in the early 1830s

David Hudson

Founder of Hudson, Ohio

Judge Van Rensselaer Humphrey

Hudson resident who destroyed the town's printing press in 1836 and was hanged in effigy on the village Green during the Civil War for being a Copperhead

John Markillie	Photographer, artist, and abolitionist who founded the Hudson Cemetery on Main Street (later named Markillie Cemetery) and most likely photographed John Brown in Hudson in 1856
Emily Metcalf	Principal of a female seminary in Hudson, Ohio, and writer of church history (First Congregational Church)
Heman Oviatt	Wealthy Hudson landowner who opened general stores in sixteen townships, became the first mayor of the Village of Hudson, and employed John Brown as a tanner and sheep expert in Richfield, where Oviatt moved in the late 1830s
Elizur Wright	Mathematics professor at Western Reserve College who wrote strongly worded articles supporting emancipation in Hudson's paper *Observer and Telegraph*, sending them to *The Liberator* when his column was shut down; traveled to New York to become secretary of the American Anti-Slavery Society after the controversy at the school between abolitionists and colonizationists

NATIONAL PARTICIPANTS IN THE JOHN BROWN STORY

Eli Baptist	Free Black from Springfield, Massachusetts, who was a soap peddler and friend of John Brown, as well as a charter member of the Sanford Street Church; lived to see his church become St. John's Congregational

Lucius V. Bierce	Brigadier-general from Akron, Ohio, who fought in the Canada Patriot War of 1837–39 and helped supply John Brown with weapons in Kansas, including swords
John Wilkes Booth	A soldier who insinuated himself into the Richmond Grays to guard Charles Town during the time of John Brown's execution; the assassin of Abraham Lincoln at Ford's Theatre
William Wells Brown	Fugitive from Kentucky who escaped to Ohio and became an activist, lecturer, and prolific writer; published *Clotel* in 1853, the first novel by a Black American
John Copeland Sr.	Oberlin resident and father of Black raider John Copeland Jr.; tried to retrieve his son's body after he was hanged in Charles Town on December 16, 1859
Jim Daniels	Enslaved man from Missouri who crossed into Kansas, supposedly to sell brooms, but instead found George Gill and told him about an impending auction where he, his family, and his friends were soon to be sold
John Brown Daniels	Infant born to fugitive Jim Daniels and his wife shortly after John Brown's raid to free enslaved people in Missouri
Frederick Douglass	Black abolitionist, orator, writer, and friend of John Brown
Lyman Epps Sr.	Black resident of Timbucto, a community established near North Elba, New York, who became John Brown's close friend and neighbor

Kate Field	Journalist who founded the John Brown Association and saved the Engine House
James A. Garfield	Student, and later, principal of the Western Reserve Eclectic Institute (which became Hiram College), member of the Ohio State Senate (1859–1861), and twentieth president of the United States (served March-September of 1881 and died from an assassin's bullet)
Henry Highland Garnet	Militant Black abolitionist to whom John Brown unfolded his plan for Harpers Ferry
George B. Gill	Iowan who was with John Brown in Kansas, on his journey with enslaved people from Missouri across Iowa, and at the Chatham Convention in Ontario
Josiah Bushnell Grinnell	Congregational minister in Grinnell, Iowa
Benjamin F. Gue	Abolitionist, newspaper editor, and Republican Lieutenant Governor of Iowa after the Civil War who, along with his brother David J. Gue, warned the Secretary of War about the raid on Harpers Ferry
Dr. Jarvis J. Johnson	Surgeon in the 27th Regiment, Indiana Volunteers, who was given permission by General Banks to remove the preserved remains of Watson Brown from Winchester Medical College during the Civil War before the building was burned to the ground by Union troops

Zenas Kent	Businessman from Franklin Mills who invited John Brown to return from New Richmond, Pennsylvania, in 1835 to run a tannery business with him
Samuel L. Lane	Summit County sheriff, newspaper editor, and mayor of Akron who wrote a detailed history of Akron and Summit County
Robert E. Lee	Colonel at Harpers Ferry who led the marines in the defeat of John Brown; general of the Confederate army during the Civil War
Abraham Lincoln	Sixteenth president of the United States from rural Kentucky, assassinated in 1865
Elijah Parish Lovejoy	Abolitionist editor murdered in Alton, Illinois, during an attack by a proslavery mob to destroy his printing press
William Maxson	Springdale, Iowa, farmer and abolitionist who provided lodging for John Brown's men in 1858 when they came to the town for military training
J. Miller McKim	Philadelphia abolitionist and Presbyterian minister who accompanied John Brown's body from Harpers Ferry to North Elba, New York; one of the founders of *The Nation*
James Monroe	Oberlin professor and, later, US Congressman; went to Harpers Ferry at the request of John Copeland Sr. to try to recover the body of raider John Copeland Jr.

Col. Simon Perkins	Son of Akron founder General Simon Perkins; formed a wool partnership with John Brown (Perkins & Brown), renting him a small frame house across the street from his Akron mansion
W. A. Phillips	Antislavery journalist for the *Tribune* who interviewed John Brown on several occasions
Wendell Phillips	Wealthy Boston orator and abolitionist
James Redpath	Free Soil reporter who covered the dispute over slavery in Kansas Territory and wrote a sympathetic biography of John Brown published in 1860
David Ruggles	Freeborn antislavery activist and secretary of the biracial New York Committee of Vigilance who became a self-trained doctor of hydrotherapy near Northampton, Massachusetts
Samuel E. Sewall	Director of a Boston committee that raised relief funds for the Brown family after the execution of John Brown
Heyward Shepherd	First casualty of Harpers Ferry, a porter and free Black shot by raiders when he began running toward the railroad office after confronting them on a railroad bridge
The Secret Six	Six East Coast aristocrats who helped fund John Brown's military ventures: Gerrit Smith, George Luther Stearns, Samuel Gridley Howe, Franklin Sanborn, Theodore Parker, and Thomas Wentworth Higginson

Rebecca Buffum Spring	Prominent Quaker from Perth Amboy, New Jersey, who visited John Brown in his jail cell
Thaddeus Stevens	Pennsylvania member of the US House of Representatives who chided Lincoln for not supporting full emancipation soon enough and argued for the distribution of land to people freed after the Civil War
Charles Sumner	Republican senator from Massachusetts who was severely beaten in 1856 on the Senate floor by Preston Brooks two days after Sumner delivered an antislavery speech called "The Crime Against Kansas," and just days before the Pottawatomie Massacre
Thomas Thomas	Former fugitive, prominent member of the Sanford Street Church, and employee of John Brown at his wool warehouse in Springfield, Massachusetts
Hon. Daniel R. Tilden	Personal friend of John Brown who lived in the Ohio towns of Garrettsville, Warren, and Ravenna before moving to Cleveland, where he served as probate judge of Cuyahoga County, Ohio, from 1855–1888
Rev. John Todd	First minister of the Congregational Church in Tabor, Iowa; educated at Oberlin
James Townsend	Abolitionist and Quaker who lived in West Branch, Iowa, and ran an inn called Traveler's Rest

Harriet Tubman	Former fugitive from Maryland who became a political activist and famous conductor on the Underground Railroad; friend of John Brown, privy to plans and conversations about Harpers Ferry
Nat Turner	Enslaved man (born the same year as John Brown) who led a rebellion in 1831 in Southampton County, Virginia, that led to the deaths of nearly sixty whites and to his own hanging
Hector Tyndale	Philadelphia lawyer who accompanied the body of John Brown to North Elba and became a Union general in the Civil War
C. L. Vallandigham	Democratic congressman from Ohio who participated in the interview of John Brown immediately after his capture
Col. Lewis W. Washington	Great-grandnephew of George Washington who, along with the enslaved people he held, was kidnapped during the Harpers Ferry raid
Rev. Martin White	Kansan minister who guided General Reid's proslavery troops into Osawatomie, where he shot and killed Frederick Brown on the morning of August 30, 1856
Henry A. Wise	Governor of Virginia who signed the death warrant of John Brown and conducted state business during and after Harpers Ferry
Rev. Joshua Young	Minister of the Unitarian Church in Burlington, Vermont, who officiated at John Brown's funeral

THE HARPERS FERRY RAIDERS
Those Who Died at Harpers Ferry (10)

Jeremiah Goldsmith Anderson

Oliver Brown

Watson Brown

John Henry Kagi

Lewis Sheridan Leary

William H. Leeman

Dangerfield Newby

Stewart Taylor

Dauphin Thompson

William Thompson

Those Who Were Hanged (7)

John Brown	Hanged December 2, 1859
John E. Cook	Hanged December 16, 1859
John Anthony Copeland Jr.	Hanged December 16, 1859
Edwin Coppoc	Hanged December 16, 1859
Shields Green	Hanged December 16, 1859
Albert Hazlett	Hanged March 16, 1860
Aaron D. Stevens	Hanged March 16, 1860

Those Who Escaped (5)

Osborne Perry Anderson

Owen Brown

Barclay Coppoc

Francis Jackson Meriam

Charles Plummer Tidd

GLIMPSES OF JOHN BROWN IN HUDSON, OHIO

The Learnéd Owl Book Shop, Hudson, Ohio

I.

It was shame that first drove me to John Brown, I suppose.

Before Robert Sullivan appeared, the town to me was a simple, lovely place with pretty buildings, still called a "village" by those of us who moved there before 1993, the year the village and township merged into a small city of twenty-five square miles.[1] My husband and I arrived in 1979 to teach English at Western Reserve Academy, a private school up the hill from town center. He left the school in the '80s, and I in the '90s, but we continued to live in Hudson.

In 2007, Robert Sullivan stopped at The Learnéd Owl Book Shop on Main Street to promote the release of his paperback edition of *Cross Country*, a book about driving from coast to coast.

We couldn't imagine anything more pleasant than crossing East Main (the little street that intersects Church on the west), cutting across the Green, hiking a block or so up North Main to hear someone like Robert Sullivan, and then strolling back home with an autographed book under our arms, night softly descending and the sound of spring peepers rising like bells.

The author spun through the front door, as if a high wind had carried him, his feet barely touching ground, though I didn't remember any wind striking my face on the walk over just minutes before. Sullivan might have flown, for all I knew, then quickly folded his little wings under his dark sport coat.

He looked directly at me, perhaps because I was closest to the door and there were only three patrons to choose from. "Do you know where his house was?" Robert Sullivan asked. No "hello," no greeting at all.

My husband was standing a little farther back, as was a colleague of mine from the college where I taught after I left the Academy.

There would be hundreds of people in this room when the new Harry Potter book would be released in a couple of weeks, but no one seemed particularly interested in Robert Sullivan—except for the three of us and a couple of students my colleague had brought with her who were exploring Main Street but would soon come inside.

In retrospect, I want to read significance in the fact that he fielded his question in my direction, though I know there wasn't any.

"Whose house?" I asked.

"John Brown," he said, looking at me strangely, as if those words shouldn't have to be spoken.

It had taken him only seconds after he parked his car to locate the historical marker on the Green about the Underground Railroad and the antislavery community in Hudson, a marker I hadn't even read at the time of his visit.

His question seemed to continue the dialogue he'd been having with himself about the sign. He'd spotted John Brown's name on it, and the names of other Browns. He was working on a new book about Thoreau, he said, so mention on the plaque of John Brown, a man Thoreau idolized, was irresistible to him.

He was, after all, in the town where John Brown was raised, so why wouldn't a resident standing in a local bookstore know something about him? He asked if a house or a site was marked, or maybe there was some historic building he could wander through—with a fee for admittance, which he would be glad to pay—and perhaps a little tour to go along with it or a brochure or postcard on a rack? It wouldn't have taken him long to see that Hudson believed in historic preservation and had an abundance of old houses lining its streets, so his assumption was a fair one.

All I knew about the years John Brown spent in Hudson was that he grew up there. I said, "I don't know."

I could tell that he was disappointed. My neck was burning, but even before the color crept too high, Robert Sullivan stopped asking questions and let me relax. He returned to the subject of the Underground Railroad marker and told me how wonderful and strange it was that the plaque had text carved on both sides of the bronze. It was as if he'd found Egyptian hieroglyphs on the Hudson Green.

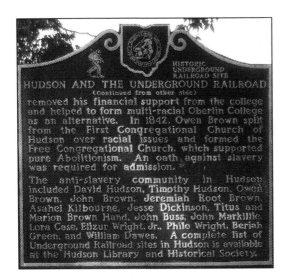

Underground Railroad marker on the Hudson Green

"The street after Clinton, just north of the bookstore, is named Owen Brown Street," I said, surprised to hear the words jump out. "Maybe his house is there, or was. I'm not sure."

I didn't have any idea who Owen Brown was when I told him this. I'd simply guessed there was a relationship between John Brown and Owen. I saw my husband look at me with suspicion.

"I don't really know," I told Robert Sullivan. I'd wanted so much to alter his impression of me, but it hadn't worked. All I could do now was change the subject, so I told him about the David Hudson house farther north on Main Street—the oldest house in town, built in 1806. Most residents knew about David Hudson, the man from Goshen, Connecticut, who drove the first stake in Hudson ground when he laid out the town in 1799, and then arrived the next year with his family and twenty-nine settlers.

The visitor was polite at first and nodded his head, so I continued to talk, believing that my authority as the town's spokesperson was increasing. I told him about the old marker on Baldwin Street near the site of David Hudson's first log house, with its strange claim that Hudson's daughter was "the first white child" in Summit County—Anner Maria Hudson.[2] Seven years later Hudson built the frame house that still stands, and since he was the only man in town with a license to serve alcohol, opened it after the War of 1812 as a tavern and inn and cut a new road that spilled directly into his front yard so

David Hudson House. (Courtesy Hudson
Library & Historical Society)

Owen Brown Street

teamsters could bring passengers to his establishment instead of Mansion
House, the town's most popular hotel on Main Street.[3] Hudson's house stayed
in the family until 1967, when it was purchased by Western Reserve Academy.[4]

Sullivan began to wander toward the back of the bookstore, where a
reading space had been set up for him, so I stopped talking and followed. He
handed out a sort of bookmark for members of the audience with lyrics from
three tunes he associated with family road trips, then pulled out his harmon-
ica from a backpack and led with "Don't Fence Me In." He read from his book,
and after that we sang again.

The final tune, "Farther Along," was less familiar to me, but I tried to keep
up: "Farther along / We'll know all about it / Farther along / We'll understand
why / Cheer up my brother / Live in the sunshine / We'll understand it / All,
by and by."

I didn't look up from the page until the final refrain of the gospel song
had ended. I wanted to get the words right, but I also wanted to avoid Robert
Sullivan's glance. I feared it would hold a reprimand. My knowledge of David
Hudson and Western Reserve Academy was no substitute for my ignorance
about Hudson's most famous citizen.

I'd see it in his eyes, and realize he was right. I knew even less about John
Brown than a stranger who blew into town.

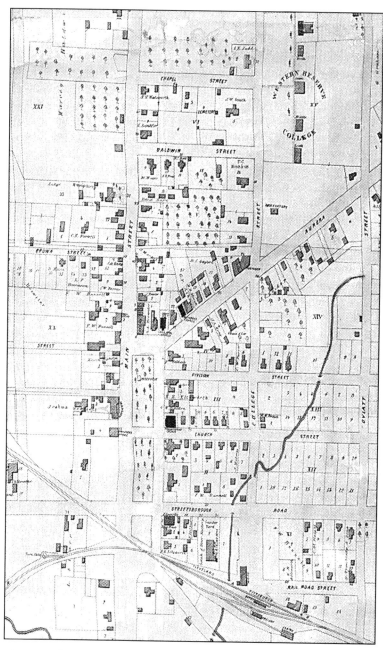

1855 map of Hudson, Ohio, drawn by John Bevan of Bevan & Boell. (Photo by Jamie Newhall, used with the permission of Hudson Library & Historical Society)

2.

In the bookstore I began to feel some new obligation to my town, as if I'd run for city council on a pledge. My job, I sensed, would be to search for a missing person—a neighbor who had disappeared.

After the reading, my husband and I once again cut across the Hudson Green, but this time I stopped to read the marker Robert Sullivan had drawn my attention to:

> The anti-slavery community in Hudson included David Hudson, Timothy Hudson, Owen Brown, John Brown, Jeremiah Root Brown, Asahel Kilbourne, Jesse Dickinson, Titus and Marion Brown Hand, John Buss, John Markillie, Lora Case, Elizur Wright, Jr., Philo Wright, Beriah Green, and William Dawes.

It wouldn't be until morning that I'd be sitting on my porch on Church Street and spot a second bronze sign I'd also managed to miss—right across the street from me, just a hundred feet away. It was an Ohio bicentennial sign installed in 2003 to mark an earlier site of Hudson's historic First Congregational Church (at times in its history referred to as the Presbyterian Church). *Of course.* That explained the name of my street, something I'd often wondered about. Just because there wasn't a church on it anymore didn't mean there never had been.

Town Hall, opened in 1879, was now on the corner where the church had been. Its first floor was being converted into a Visitors Center and Fire Museum, so, in a way, the building was changing once more, though not as dramatically this time.[5]

Town Hall

The inscription on the sign was mainly about the founding of the church (also called the meetinghouse), but there was also this: "At a November 1837 prayer meeting, church member and anti-slavery leader John Brown made his first public vow to destroy slavery."[6]

I'd soon learn that the meeting the sign referred to was organized to protest the murder in Illinois of abolitionist editor Elijah Lovejoy on November 7, 1837, and that most of antislavery Hudson was in that building when John Brown took his vow. Three of Lovejoy's printing presses were destroyed before a fourth was tossed into the Mississippi River by a proslavery mob, and Lovejoy shot.

This was not the first time in antebellum America, nor the last, that printing presses fell victim to violence or heralded greater trouble on the way. Even in Hudson, Judge Van Rensselaer Humphrey destroyed the press of a local abolitionist newspaper in June of 1836.[7] Some people thought he was trying to stop the dissemination of information about his relationship with a married woman, but others felt his opposition to full emancipation was the cause.[8]

I began to wonder if my own house, so close to the former church, had any connection to John Brown. I knew something about its history, so I suspected that it might. Over the next months, and then years, I sometimes thought I heard his voice in my Church Street house—a phantasm, I realized, but not just that.

Ohio bicentennial marker for First Congregational Church

Honorable Van Rensselaer Humphrey residence, Hudson, Ohio, detail from 1855 map drawn by John Bevan of Bevan & Boell. (Photo by Jamie Newhall, used with the permission of Hudson Library & Historical Society)

Wasn't it likely that he'd been inside as a boy when a cabin stood on the property? One feature that architectural historians have confirmed about our house from tax records is that the original 1814 cabin built on the site was incorporated into the current structure, so even though the cabin isn't visible, I know it's there.[9]

It also seemed possible that I was hearing the echoes of the vow he made that November day in 1837, for some of the lower story of our house had once been a wing of the Israel Town House, which stood a few feet south of the church—a stately house that began to function as a funeral home in 1930, and remains one to this day. The sound might have traveled in November of 1837 from the meetinghouse into the wing of the Israel Town House—a wing removed in the late 1800s when the house was remodeled, and eventually seamed into our house on Church Street.[10]

When that happened, our house started to become the "composite" home it is today, made up of multiple additions and pieces of other buildings—long and narrow, like a series of small railroad cars hitched together with mortar.

Since Church Street wasn't cut until 1840, I imagined only a narrow path, or perhaps just dirt and grass, between the Israel Town House and the meetinghouse, a structure with massive columns, circular pews in the middle section, and square pews around the sides.[11] I pictured a window open or a door left ajar in both the church and in the wing nearby, and heard the sound of John Brown's voice rushing through.

Century homes (which in the case of Hudson could mean two centuries, not just one), including our own, began to seem like characters in history books, since they'd held and witnessed so much of the past. John Brown's touch might have been on the logs of the old cabin, his voice in the molecules of ancient air in the lost wing we occupy.

"All houses wherein men have lived and died / Are haunted houses," Longfellow said, understanding the past. "Impalpable impressions on the air."[12]

The idea that I lived in a haunted house grew whenever I glanced through the upstairs window behind my computer screen and saw the funeral home next door. The sound of John Brown's vow to destroy slavery, which would end what had begun with the arrival of "20. and odd Negroes" on the Virginia coast in 1619,[13] could have drifted into a room now positioned somewhere below me. His fingerprints or a strand of his hair might be lodged in a ridge of wood behind a plaster wall.

The sheer proximity of my life to John Brown's—this strange tangle of beams and words and streets from different times—only intensified the spell first cast in a local bookstore right across the Hudson Green.

Israel Town House, with wings. (Courtesy Hudson Library & Historical Society)

Remodeled Israel Town House, without wings. (Courtesy Hudson Library & Historical Society)

3.

I was John Brown's neighbor, and at first that fact seemed to protect me from the danger I suspected was in the man. The stories of his killing of people in Kansas and his storming of a federal arsenal in Harpers Ferry were familiar to me. I'd learned them in high school, and although John Brown always remained a minor character in history books, his shadow was long and ominous. Being just a neighbor seemed a safer stance.

I found a letter early in my research that he'd written in Kansas Territory to the editor of the *Summit County Beacon*, a paper begun by Whigs as a weekly in 1839. That same paper, a daily now renamed the *Akron Beacon Journal*, arrives in my driveway every morning. My son spent ten years of his life reporting its news.

John Brown walked the same ground I walk today and knew its streets and buildings. He paid attention to his neighbors. Many of his letters were addressed to people in the Western Reserve and bore the closing, "Your friend, John Brown." He often told recipients to remember him to individuals he was thinking about—to "Mr. Griswold, and to all others who love their neighbors," "Mrs. Woodruff & her son George," and "my old friends from Akron."[14]

I felt obliged to spend at least as much time with him as I had my other neighbors. Felt it would be rude to do anything less. I was sure I could keep any threat he posed away from me and pursue the casual attachments to him that I had with other people in town.

The first personal fact I learned about him made me think our relationship could be simple: he was born in 1800. I could calculate his life so easily with a date like that, and it made me happy. He was five when his family arrived from

(*Left*) Marker on Bandstand Green, with younger grandson, Carson, atop, and Israel Town House behind on corner of Church Street

Hudson Library & Historical Society on Library Street

Connecticut, twelve when the War of 1812 began, fifty when the Fugitive Slave Act was passed, fifty-seven when the Supreme Court handed down the Dred Scott decision (pronouncing that Black people were not citizens and had no rights[15]), and fifty-nine when he raided Harpers Ferry and was hanged.

But nothing else about John Brown would be easy.

Even the matter of finding other markers in town was difficult. On my own, I only located his name one more time—on a large stone close to a bandstand built on the Green in 1975. The stone was dedicated on September 4, 1952, in honor of the sesquicentennial of First Congregational Church, but, just like the two more recent markers I found after the visit of Robert Sullivan, only named him briefly.

The words on the stone were etched into a bronze tablet whose patina was as green as the Statue of Liberty, and difficult to read. The plaque mainly commemorated the location of the first schoolhouse and church in the village, but the name of John Brown sneaked in—a skill he always seemed to have:

> On this site stood a log schoolhouse built in 1801, the first in Summit County. It was used as a meeting-place by the Hudson Congregational Church formed by David Hudson, its lifetime Deacon and organized Sept. 4, 1802, by Rev. Joseph Badger. It was the first church in this county, and the second in the Western Reserve. John Brown became a member in 1816.

Seven words. That's all. Written fifty years before his name would appear on a second plaque—the one Robert Sullivan found on the Green.

Surely this couldn't be correct. I wound my way to the archives in the Hudson Library & Historical Society, a space which soon became my second home.

If John Brown was alive anywhere in town, it was in the archives, with caretaker Gwen Mayer. An interior vault off the central room housed one of the most impressive Brown collections in the country.

John Brown didn't exactly have the rule of the house in the library, but he wasn't scolded or reprimanded for bad behavior, the way he often was in other places. He wasn't idolized, either. He was just allowed to exist, on his own terms and in his own right.

In that mysterious place were manuscripts with John Brown's original signature, clippings about local research into John Brown's life, obscure and prominent biographies and histories, original wills and letters of Owen Brown, the Adair family papers, Jeremiah Root Brown and Clark family records (1809–1971), the Oliver O. Brown Collection (1828–1897), the Brown Family Association reunion information (1903–1966), the Oswald Garrison Villard Ohio interviews (1908), John Brown's Bible, genealogies of John Brown,[16] first editions of books relating to John Brown (including a collection of poetry by Richard Realf, who was present at the Chatham Convention in Canada West, where a new Constitution was approved and Realf was named "Secretary of State"), a piece of rope and a piece of wood from John Brown's gallows. Box after box of rare documents and relics that biographers and historians from all over the world came to see.

In the archives—originally located in the basement of the old downtown library on the corner of East Main and Aurora Street—John Brown had met David S. Reynolds, Louis A. DeCaro Jr., Tracy Chevalier, Jean Libby, Gerald McFarland, Robert McGlone, Paul Finkelman, Tony Horwitz, and many other writers and scholars who'd come to visit him.[17] The library's name was prolific on acknowledgments pages of scholarly books about John Brown. The names of Tom Vince, who was the former director of the Hudson Library & Historical Society and is now archivist at Western Reserve Academy, and Gwen Mayer, the massive building's present archivist, were especially familiar ones. All of this was essentially just across the street from me. *Lucky, lucky me.*

4.

I continued my search for stones in a room full of documents that held the town's history.

A man who started a tree company in Kent in 1880, John Davey, had tried at the turn of the century to raise money to build a monument to John Brown in Hudson, but nothing came of it.[18]

In 1930, Western Reserve Academy discussed marking the site of Hudson's first church and schoolhouse. One of the Academy's trustees wanted to commemorate Hudson's leading citizens—most especially, John Brown. About the same time, the Historical Society and descendants of the Brown family expressed interest in a marker of some sort to document John Brown and his Hudson years.[19]

Before the town knew it, it was 1940 and still nothing had been done.

And then it was the 1950s, when the monument on the Green in honor of the sesquicentennial of First Congregational Church would devote seven words to John Brown.

But there was a marker I'd missed—from the 1980s. Members of the town, inspired by librarian archivist James F. Caccamo and library director Tom Vince, had dedicated a monument exclusively to John Brown.

A small commemorative ceremony occurred on May 9, 1985—John Brown's birthday. Later, in July, the community celebrated again during an event sponsored by the Retail Merchants Association—something dubbed "John Brown Days." It was mounted primarily to recreate the period of the

Author standing beside John Brown
Memorial

Civil War and promote business.[20] I have no memory of either event. John
Brown wasn't of interest to me then.

The John Brown Memorial, a clipping said, was located on the "South
Green." I'd never heard that term. I was familiar with the clock tower rectangle and the bandstand rectangle, but town officials apparently considered
a third patch of public land across Streetsboro Street, on a little elbow of East
Main, the South Green.

A Green Plan, I'd later learn, had been approved through bond levies in
1976 to make better use of two squares of green southeast of town center—"a
meat-cleaver-shaped" parcel of land that wasn't new at all but appeared on old
maps. In the 1840s it had even included a right of way for the Cleveland and
Pittsburgh Railroad.[21] I was familiar with the most eastern end of the parcel—
the police center and community center stood on the property and were part
of the renovation—but only the tip of the South Green, where the parcel
began, was visible from downtown. Although an annual arts festival was held
there every fall, it still felt remote to me.

Before reading about the development of this patch of land, I knew of it
mainly through my husband, a veteran biker who used it as a cut-through to
his barbershop, though he told me he'd never noticed the John Brown marker
in all the years he'd wheeled by.

I left the library and walked to the site. The stone was rather large, a gift from the Hudson Questers, a group interested in studying, restoring, and preserving historical objects. On it was a plaque labeled "Boyhood Home of John Brown (1800–1859)," with these words inscribed:

> Abolitionist John Brown came to Hudson in 1805 and lived here until 1826. A frequent visitor to Hudson in the ensuing years, Brown attended services at the Free Congregational Church which was a rallying point for the Abolitionist cause in Hudson. Gift of Hudson Quester Chapters: James Ellsworth, David Hudson, Ann Lee, May 9, 1985.

There was an intended association between the marker and a church, but I knew the Congregational Church only by the name "First" Congregational, not "Free." I'd read the word "Free" on the marker Robert Sullivan pointed out, but I never connected it with a building.

The memorial, nearly hidden by lush blossoms of lilac, rested on a base of stone from the house of Frederick Brown (John Brown's younger brother), which once sat at the northwest corner of Hines Hill and Darrow Road—not far from a wooded site on his property that supposedly served as an encampment for fugitives.[22]

Tom Vince spoke at the dedication. I learned later from Tom that trustees were opposed to placing the memorial on either the Clocktower Green or the Bandstand Green due to the controversial nature of John Brown's life.

I returned to the archives to ask Gwen about the "Free" church and the "First" church to try to resolve my confusion. She told me that the building the John Brown marker referred to—Free Congregational Church—was the structure catty-corner from the marker itself, on the corner of East Main and Streetsboro Street. It was originally the dissident church begun by Owen Brown and other abolitionist defectors from First Congregational Church, but its history was unmarked. To me it remained the Conn Insurance Agency, and a knit shop before that, though recently a For Lease sign had gone up in the yard.[23] The white building was three stories high, set on concrete blocks, a structure so tall I could see it out an upstairs window of my house in the wintertime. In Owen Brown's day, it was a single story. Just a simple village church.

Gwen handed me folders about the Dissident Church and First Congregational, and then disappeared into her office.

She leaves people alone when they work in the archives, but sometimes stops to check on them or say something she senses they need to hear. Tired from my field trip, I removed my glasses and leaned back to stretch.

Former Free Congregational Church
(Dissident Church)

Gwen Mayer, archivist, Hudson
Library & Historical Society

There she was, standing beside me with an impish smile on her face. If she could ask two questions when she got to heaven, Gwen said, the first would be, "What do you think, God, of John Brown?" The second, "John Brown, what do you think of us?" She knew John Brown should be judged, but she also knew that he might have something to say to the world.

Gwen lived beside John Brown in the archives, but she never lost patience with me as I struggled to learn a fraction of what she already knew. She loved all the John Brown details in the boxes and folders the library owned, but she also loved to watch people work to make sense of them.

In the library that day, Gwen made me consider that perhaps I would need to ask other questions about John Brown than the date of his birth. Larger questions than a neighbor carelessly tosses over a hedge or, as in my case, a cedar fence that separates my house from a funeral home—formerly the residence of Dr. Israel Town.

I knew she was right. What I could not have known was how long it would take me to learn how to ask them.

5.

I gave up markers and turned my attention to the landscape that was here when John Brown was. If I saw the Conn Insurance Agency instead of a radical church when I looked at the historic building on the corner of Streetsboro and East Main, my gaze was surely impaired. History was everywhere in this town, its buildings period instruments whose beams and rafters were waiting to be plucked so the old tunes could be heard again. The Connecticut Western Reserve and Hudson's architecture were not just mine, but his.

The Reserve—a 120-mile strip of northeastern Ohio land that borders Lake Erie and extends just a little south of Akron[24]—was the common ground I shared with John Brown. The thing that irreversibly made us neighbors. People typically think of Kansas and Virginia when they think of him, as I did when I started out, but he spent the greatest part of his life near my town. In the late eighteenth century, Ohio land in the Reserve was sold by lottery in townships of twenty-five miles to rich Connecticut developers, and David Hudson drew 10th range/4th township—Hudson.[25] He spent several months of 1799 exploring and preparing the parcel that surveyors had marked off for him, hoping "to found a utopian colony."[26]

No swath of land in America was more famous for its fierce abolitionist spirit than the Connecticut Western Reserve, and Hudson was an important piece of it.[27] I didn't grow up in John Brown's town, but I'd lived nearly my whole life somewhere in the Reserve. My girlhood home was nearby Akron, the Western Reserve site where John Brown tended sheep. Franklin Mills,

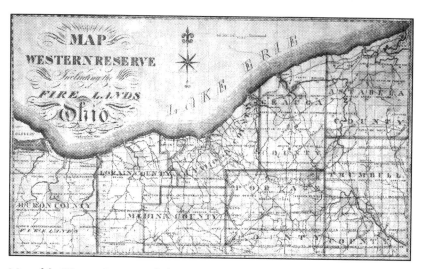

Map of the Western Reserve including the Fire Lands in Ohio, 1826. (Courtesy The Western Reserve Historical Society, Cleveland, Ohio)

renamed Kent in honor of Marvin Kent, who made sure railroads were welcome in his town, was another place in the Reserve where we had both lived.[28] The region was still called the Connecticut Western Reserve, and Hudson still looked much as it had after early settlers began to build frame homes.

The town looked different, of course, when Owen Brown arrived in 1805 from Torrington, Connecticut, with his family—rolling across Pennsylvania in wagons drawn by oxen.[29] Just founded, it had only a few settlers and cabins, large numbers of Native Americans, massive trees, elk, panthers, bear, wild turkeys, and deer.

Not even a cemetery yet, since no one had had time to die.

The Browns, like other Western Reserve settlers, most likely brought food to begin a new cuisine in Ohio: poultry, hogs, cattle; root vegetables like potatoes, turnips, and salsify; herbs and spices for seasoning and for medicine— tansy, pennyroyal, catnip, and perhaps a whole nutmeg in a tiny traveling box for "fancy food."[30]

Western Reserve Academy, where I taught for twelve years and where our son went to school, was originally Western Reserve College, and Owen Brown was appointed by its trustees to assist with the erection of its first buildings in the late 1820s. Other buildings followed, and my husband, our son, and I all had the honor of speaking in one of them—the school's Chapel, a beautiful Federal

Bas-relief in Kent, Ohio, showing
John Brown, with John Davey to
right with beard

Clarence S. Gee, photo by
Grace Goulder Izant. (Courtesy
Hudson Library & Historical
Society)

and Greek Revival structure built in 1836,[31] where luminaries such as Frederick Douglass, Ralph Waldo Emerson, and James A. Garfield had lectured long ago.[32]

Still uncertain where to find John Brown's boyhood home, I called Tom Vince, a man who knows more Hudson history than anyone alive. He was largely responsible for Hudson becoming the prominent center of John Brown research it is today through his efforts to secure the Clarence S. Gee Collection as a donation to the Hudson Library & Historical Society. Gee, a former minister of Hudson's First Congregational Church turned lifelong John Brown fanatic, had focused on John Brown's genealogy, collecting and transcribing invaluable letters and documents, sometimes appending priceless notations to them.

I'd known Tom for years. He knew all about Hudson's ghosts, and before my question was finished, he mentioned the log cabin that Owen Brown had built about where the Brewster Mansion stands today, two short blocks from my house. He told me that the cabin and small farm of the Browns ran approximately from Main Street to the lot where the Episcopalians built a church in 1846, on what's now Aurora Street—formerly called Chillicothe.

I began walking to the mansion every day and sometimes sat on its stone stairs, thinking about a yellow marble that might be hidden under the building behind me, lodged somewhere in an old foundation stone. I'd read about the marble in a famous letter that John Brown wrote late in his life to Henry L. Stearns, the son of George Stearns, one of John Brown's wealthy Eastern

Brewster Mansion, built 1853

Titus Hand House, built by Owen Brown in 1834

supporters known as the Secret Six—a letter that some scholars refer to as John Brown's autobiography.[33] He wrote about losing a "Yellow Marble" an "*Indian boy*" had given him in Hudson when he was only six.

Sometimes I thought of Beethoven's *Rage Over a Lost Penny* when I thought of the marble John Brown lost, though I had to remind myself that it was sorrow, not rage, that John Brown felt. He remembered the loss over fifty years after it occurred, calling it in the letter one "beyound recovery" that "*took years to heal*" and had caused him to cry.

After the cabin was razed, a second structure was built on the site, but it was gone too. There are different opinions in town about when Owen replaced his cabin with a frame house. Some say 1825,[34] others, as early as 1810.[35] The lumber for the prominent house Owen Brown eventually built on Aurora Street might have come from great chunks of chestnut and oak, planks as sacred to New England settlers as the bedpost Odysseus rived from the trunk of an olive tree. Owen and his sons may have cut the planks themselves, or purchased boards from Ezra Wyatt, who opened a sawmill in the area in 1808.

There are frame houses Owen Brown built that still remain. Although the first block of Main Street was destroyed in 1892 by a fire that began in the Lockhart Saloon,[36] the two blocks north escaped the flames, and on them stand houses Owen Brown erected in 1834 for a daughter—Marian Brown Hand—and for a son—Oliver.

Owen sold his own frame house in 1830 to Anson A. Brewster, who, along with his partner Zenas Kent, later constructed a Federal building on the corner right beside it, where he established Brewster's Dry Goods (1839). The Brown/Brewster house burned down in 1842 and Brewster built a second

Two children standing in unpaved street of downtown Hudson in front of R. H. Grimm Hardware, the Federal building that was originally Brewster's Dry Goods, ca. 1880–1900. (Courtesy Hudson Library & Historical Society)

Spring Hill Farm. (Courtesy Hudson Library & Historical Society)

Whedon-Hinsdale House. (Courtesy Hudson Library & Historical Society)

frame on the site, but he was so successful in business that by 1853 he could afford to live in a Gothic mansion—so he built again, this time with stone.[37]

After the sale, Owen Brown moved from town center with his second wife, Sally Root Brown, to Spring Hill Farm, a couple of miles east on Aurora Street, another property that still stands. When Sally died, Owen moved from Spring Hill to the house next door, the home of his neighbor Lucy Hinsdale— who had become his third wife. That structure remains as well.

I see both houses whenever I drive east out of town toward Streetsboro or Aurora. In an undated letter written about 1850 in Lorain County at the later home of his daughter Marian Brown Hand, a narrative now known as *Owen Brown's Autobiography*, Owen called Lucy's house "my favirite House and Farm,"[38] and I can understand why. Spring Hill was a formal house, a Federal/Greek Revival, but Lucy Hinsdale's house (known today as the Whedon-Hinsdale House) was modeled on Connecticut farmhouses, full of large-planked warmth that must have pleased Owen Brown.

Old Tannery Farm, in winter.
(Courtesy Hudson Library &
Historical Society)

In 1843, according to Tom Vince, Owen did build a house in the center of town on Owen Brown Street—called just "Brown Street" then. John Brown didn't grow up in a house on that street, as I'd proposed to Robert Sullivan, but Owen Brown eventually built one there after his family began to scatter, so I'd accidentally been half-right. Within three years of his move back to town, Owen's widowed sister and a son-in-law who was suffering from consumption moved in with Owen Brown and his third wife.

There are other houses on the outskirts of town that have importance in the story of John Brown. Just north of town, off old Chapman Road—now Hines Hill—John Brown built his first tannery near Brandywine Creek on property his father owned. The structure was destroyed in 1872, but the house he lived in while running it stands. John Brown built a cabin there in 1819, when he left home. Later, Herman Peck—John Brown's carpenter—constructed a house on the site for him and his new wife, Dianthe Lusk. They lived there until John Brown sold his tannery to his brother Oliver in 1826 and headed to Pennsylvania.

I went through that house one year when it was on the House and Garden Tour, an annual June event in Hudson. There's a sign at the entrance (Old Tannery Farm, Home of John Brown, 1818–1826), and then a long driveway that winds back toward the house. The homeowner, Carole Smith, is generous with the building, always welcoming people who have an interest in John Brown. There have been three major additions to the house over the years. A foyer, originally a porch, is a sort of John Brown shrine now, and visitors can sign their names and leave comments.

I was glad that Old Tannery Farm and the houses in the "country" that Owen Brown and his wives had lived in remained, but the downtown houses and stores—those John Brown saw every day as a boy, or those he might have

Downtown Hudson, south to north, showing Buss General Store and Mansion House Hotel.
(Courtesy Hudson Library & Historical Society)

entered during later visits—interested me more. I constructed a diorama in
my brain of the old Hudson village, bringing buildings back that had disappeared, learning about them and then clumsily flying them in with my imagination so that they stood beside those that had survived.

There they were: the Buss General Store; Mansion House Hotel, built by
Judge Van Rensselaer Humphrey; another building constructed by Julian
Lusk in 1832 as a private home and store, which was later turned into the
American House Hotel and then expanded into Adelphian Hall; the feed
store, a shoe shop, the drug store.[39]

The architecture of this town made it easier for me to imagine John
Brown alive in the twenty-first century, or to imagine myself alive in the nineteenth. Maybe, even, made those things possible.

I might have passed him on the wooden sidewalks of the town or been invited
to his wedding in the old meetinghouse on my corner. At the very least, I would
have heard the church bell ring that day in the key of B,[40] for Hudson's First Congregational Church was supposedly the first church in the Western Reserve with
a bell.[41] Maybe we would have met on the Green, stood in lines together waiting
for the mail to come in and talked a little about weather and health, greeted each
other while buying spices, chicken wire, prunes, calomel, or pickles from a barrel
at Buss General Store, where the Hudson Square Building stands today.

But other times I wondered if two people as different as John Brown and
I would have spent any time at all together or even said "hello" on Main Street
if we passed.

6.

According to his neighbor Benjamin Waite, Owen's tannery sat on Brown Street, though the cut for the street wasn't made until many years after the tannery was built. Owen Brown's livelihood, like John Brown's for a long while, depended on a tannery, so its construction probably occurred shortly after he and his family unloaded their wagons from Connecticut.

A tannery can't thrive without a water source, since hides need to soak up to two days before tanning can begin, so after buildings, I began my search for streams.

I'd never noticed bodies of water in Hudson before the Browns and their tanneries entered my imagination, except little pools on the outskirts of town in the swampy land that even early settlers didn't want, land that only ducks and herons find of interest. David Hudson had scouted out the streams of the Reserve before he moved from Connecticut, as had Moses Cleaveland.

Brandywine Creek has its headwaters in Hudson, starting at a spring north of town. The water flows through the ground of John Brown's Tannery and then heads south toward the village. One branch of the Brandywine bends west, beginning its trip to the Cuyahoga River in the Cuyahoga Valley National Park, but near West Prospect Street another branch shoots east for a short while and then starts a sharp perpendicular descent, cutting across Owen Brown and Streetsboro Street before bending east. On Owen Brown, you might not even know the stream is there, it's so narrow and so quiet, but you can see it when you walk across a little bridge. When you drive, the bridge blocks the view, and the water disappears.

The stream is typically not much more than a trickle and calls no attention to itself, but in the summer of 2003, this quiet little stream spilled over its banks and raced down roads and up porch steps. Someone who lived in an apartment right in the path of the creek died trying to rescue his car from a lower-level garage. My son's former pediatrician was trapped in a building where his office was, a building in the same low area of town, and had to jump out a window and swim across Streetsboro Street to safety. The building was so damaged that it was recently bulldozed and replaced with townhouses raised high on concrete pedestals like island property.

John Brown had to swim across rivers and streams when he fought in Kansas, but I didn't know if the Brandywine, loose and swift-moving in his day, ever flooded while he was here, forcing him to battle it.[42] Now it's so narrow that the image of anyone having to fight its waters to reach safety seems silly—except it happened once in my own lifetime. Even though the Brandywine is locked in a culvert, it can still roar up at flood time, the way the past can too.

7.

Houses and buildings and streams are not the whole of it. Bones of some of the Browns are buried in Hudson ground for all eternity. The first summer I lived as John Brown's neighbor, I took walks up North Main to the Old Hudson Township Burying Ground almost every day to visit his family. I carried flowers from my garden and laid them on the graves of Owen Brown and Ruth Mills Brown, John Brown's parents. His mother was the first person buried in that ground, land that had been David Hudson's apple orchard until he donated it to the town in 1808, when Ruth died and needed a place to rest.[43]

If I happened to forget daisies or loosestrife from my backyard, I'd pick a sprig of orange trumpet creeper from the rail fence of the cemetery and place it on one of the headstones in the family plot.

Gwen Mayer told me that every year thirty to fifty people visit the cemetery—the oldest one in Summit County. I didn't know if they traveled to see the Browns or someone else (there were four Revolutionary War veterans buried here), but I did know that I never saw flowers or tokens on the graves of the Brown family and I never saw other people there when I visited. The cemetery might have been a greater attraction if John Brown himself had been buried there, but his body was in North Elba, New York, about five hours north of New York City.

My husband and I always stop at famous graves of writers whenever we travel. The gravestones and monuments of Louisa May Alcott, Nathaniel Hawthorne, Ralph Waldo Emerson, and Henry David Thoreau—all buried

Entrance to Old Hudson Township Burying Ground

Graves of Sally Brown, Owen Brown, and Ruth Mills Brown in Old Hudson Township
Burying Ground

on Authors Ridge in Concord, Massachusetts—had poems and pennies and pebbles on them no matter when we visited, and we were seldom the only people inching up that quiet hill.

It had been different, once, in Hudson. After Harpers Ferry, when everyone knew the name of John Brown, cones from a spruce tree planted beside the grave of Ruth Mills Brown were gathered and then sent across the country as souvenirs.[++] That tree was long gone.

A silver maple stood by the gravesite when I first started going to the cemetery, but one day I noticed a red X on its trunk. It had grown sickly, and the city arborist had ordered its removal. Several summers passed before I visited the cemetery again, but when I did, the maple had disappeared. Only a stump remained.

Trees were so thick and abundant in the early days of Hudson that they blocked out the sky. Ruth Brown didn't live long enough in this town to have known it otherwise. She would have wanted a tree always hovering over her remains, a cool canopy, I thought. And trees offered more than shade. To a family of tanners like the Browns, the bark of trees—the source of tannin needed to cure hides—must have been as comforting and redolent as apples to an orchardist. A stump with crabgrass and clover winding through its crevices didn't seem enough for a woman like Ruth.

But what business of mine was this matter of trees and graves? Why did I climb that hill day after day in the hot Ohio sun the summer of the first year, and then the summers of later years, and worry about the dead?

Old Hudson Township Burying Ground had begun to feel as real as my own street did, feel just like another place where people lived, a subdivision well within city limits. I was only calling on them the way a neighbor would.

A LINCOLN LOOK-ALIKE

Abraham Lincoln, candidate for US president, before delivering his Cooper Union address, New York, NY, on Feb. 27, 1860, photo by Mathew Brady. (Courtesy Library of Congress)

I.

If someone's your neighbor, you know what they look like. If you share recipes over a cedar fence, much less secrets, you need to recognize the person you're becoming familiar with. Maybe it was natural that soon after I realized John Brown was my neighbor, I started collecting images of him. I xeroxed copies of photographs from books and taped them to the file cabinet beside my computer and bought postcards in museums, displaying them in empty corners of shelves.

Which was the real John Brown? I'd rest my chin in my palm and look at the pictures in front of me.

Curator Jean Libby assembled fourteen portraits of John Brown, most of them daguerreotypes, for an exhibit at Harpers Ferry in 2009 and later published them in a book. They were taken between the late 1840s and 1858 by photographers in various cities who used an array of early methods. She said John Brown loved technology and understood its necessity and power—in photography, but in weapons and transportation too.[1] He ordered Sharps rifles for his men, for instance—breechloaders that could fire ten shots a minute, not muzzleloaders that were slower and had only half the range.[2]

He knew, as Lincoln did, that reputation could spread more quickly through photography, even though it was a time-consuming process in early days. He gave out prints as souvenirs to raise money for his cause and often inscribed them in the simple manner of his letters. "Your Friend, John Brown."

One famous picture (1847/48)—made by Black daguerreotypist Augustus Washington in his Hartford studio and purchased by the National Portrait

John Brown holding Subterranean
Pass banner. (Courtesy Boyd B.
Stutler Collection of John Brown,
West Virginia State Archives)

Gallery in Washington in 1996 for $115,000—shows John Brown with one
hand raised in a pledge and the other holding an abolition flag, sometimes
referred to as the Subterranean Pass Way banner. Another popular image is
a daguerreotype by John Bowles from 1856, during the time the photographer
himself was active in the fight for Kansas Territory. The Bowles image, taken
in Lawrence, Kansas, records what the photographer saw that day in his
studio—John Brown sitting in a chair, one hand wrapped around the barrel
of an upright Sharps rifle, boots on (spurs attached), a coat buttoned up
partway, a squashed and well-worn fedora on a table right beside him.

Most of the photographs I'd collected of John Brown showed him hatless,
so the detail of the fedora confused me a little, but over time I found other ref-
erences to his hats. James Townsend, the innkeeper of Traveler's Rest near Iowa
City, who lodged John Brown in 1858 when he brought his men to train in
Springdale, supposedly drew a large X on a hat John Brown was wearing. The
popular story was that John Brown, on his first visit to the inn in 1856, devi-
ously asked the abolitionist innkeeper if he had ever heard of John Brown.
Townsend said nothing, but "took...a piece of chalk and, removing Brown's
hat, marked it with a large X; he then replaced the hat and solemnly decorated
the back of Brown's coat with two large X marks; lastly he placed an X on the
back of the mule." The story was improbable, and even John Brown's daughter
Annie said it was a lie, but the image stayed in John Brown lore as a symbol of
the innkeeper's sentiment that John Brown had a free pass.[3]

Painting of John Brown in Kansas
by Daniel Beard from a photo taken
by Colonel John Bowles. (Courtesy
Boyd B. Stutler Collection of John
Brown, West Virginia State Archives)

Akron portrait of John Brown.
(Courtesy Chicago History Museum)

The story of a wide-brimmed hat also circulated. Currier & Ives produced a lithograph called *Brown of Osawatomie* that showed it,[4] and biographers sometimes mentioned the "wide straw hat" he wore when he waded across the Marais des Cygnes (Marsh of the Swans) to escape certain death from Missourians at the Battle of Osawatomie, looking nothing like the graceful trumpeter swans the river was named for.[5] But he seldom chose to be photographed in a hat, removing the one he apparently had with him when he sat for John Bowles and placing it on a table, so it was a maelstrom of hair I generally pictured when I thought of him.

My favorite photos were ones taken in Summit County, though I liked them best for largely selfish reasons. The Akron photo, completed in 1855, reminded me of my Akron roots.[6] It had been turned into painted photographs, one on display in the Summit County Historical Society (originally the Simon Perkins mansion, where the painting was discovered), and one housed in the Akron-Summit County Library. It's attributed to Benjamin Battels, whose studio stood at 106 Market Street, a street I walked as a girl with my aunt Ruth on the way to swimming lessons. In January 1858, Battels married

Images taken by John Markillie. The one on the right shows his house and business on Main Street. (Courtesy Hudson Library & Historical Society)

Sarah Edgerly, a Hudson woman—and John Brown probably knew her. She might have been the one who recommended Battels' studio in the first place.

The picture of John Brown from 1856, a sixth plate daguerreotype, mirror-view, taken in Hudson, was the one I liked the best. Jean Libby, who discovered that the daguerreotype was made in Ohio, came to Hudson in 2014 and did research that led her to believe that John Markillie was the person who produced it.[7] Most probably he was, though names of other photographers have been advanced. Markillie, a fervent abolitionist, was known as "Hudson's most prominent photographer."[8] His studio was in a business building that stood next door to his residence, with a barn behind it that housed his livery—a building constructed with David Hurn, who was both his partner and a cousin.[9] When he gave up his livery, he opened his photography shop on the second floor of the business building, and was able to reach it from his house by a covered stair.[10]

If I look at the Wooden-Farrar House downtown on the east side of North Main, a structure that's a bridal shop now, squint, then follow the street north over a parking lot and up to a flat-roofed brick building right across from old Brown Street, I can almost see the Hurn-Markillie Block—see John Brown perched on the second floor of an invisible building, floating in a chair as he poses for his Hudson daguerreotype in John Markillie's studio.[11]

Taken in 1856 after battles in Kansas, the image not only had local significance for me, but was the one I found most puzzling and disturbing. John Brown's arms are crossed, as they are in a second photograph Augustus Washington took of him in Hartford, but unlike the more formal Washington

John Brown after battles in Kansas. (Courtesy Boston Athenæum)

image, in the Hudson daguerreotype a few fingers, a prominent hand, a knob of wrist, and an inch or more of one forearm are fully exposed. The cuffs of his white shirt (always pressed and below the wrist in other photographs that show his arms) are entirely missing, and the sleeves of his jacket are too short for him.

He no longer seems conscious of the fit of his clothes (if they even are his clothes), and his eyes aren't quiet anymore. There's no hint of a smile on his narrow lips, and his face is crosshatched with lines. An unfamiliar mole crawls across his forehead. There's a tiny ball of light near each pupil, his hair is almost as crazy as Hugh Jackman's in *Wolverine* ("prairie hair," I call it), his mouth bends down like the falling needle of a barometer, and although his white collar is still crisp and high on his neck, as it was in the Hartford daguerreotype, the black silk tie he always wore and knotted at the center has disappeared. The collar, loose now, looks like covert feathers sprouting from just below his neck.

2.

As I turned my study into a little John Brown gallery, I kept thinking that he looked like someone I knew. One day Tom Vince, Western Reserve Academy archivist, mentioned that Abraham Lincoln's inaugural train stopped in Hudson in 1861, and he said a sign in town commemorated the event. John Brown took a train out of Hudson less than two years before Lincoln's arrived, he told me.

Shortly after this conversation, I found myself drawing a stovepipe hat on John Brown's head with a black marker. Next, I taped photographs of Lincoln right beside those of John Brown and stared at the two together. The images kept blending—blurring—and I wondered sometimes if my eyes had crossed.

The men weren't twins, exactly. The tall stovepipe hat of Lincoln never looked right on John Brown's head, and I knew his own crumpled fedora or wide straw hat would never suit the presidential head of Lincoln, so I didn't try to sketch them in.

Still, the two men appeared somehow related.

I wanted to ask other people if they saw resemblances, but the longer I considered my little joke, the more inappropriate it seemed. People who liked Lincoln often didn't like John Brown.

At night Lincoln and John Brown began to float above me in the bedroom, brighter in the dark than in the day. Sometimes they'd appear together, like geese flying in a V-formation, though I couldn't tell which was in the lead.

Only nine years separated them, Lincoln the younger.

The man from Hudson wasn't as tall as Lincoln (Lincoln was six foot four, the other man, five foot ten), but had a body much like his—lanky, sinewy, taut. John Brown's facial features were similar too—heavy dark hair, prominent nose and chin, sunken cheeks in later life (well, as late as life got for either man, neither reaching sixty), big-lobed ears, thick eyebrows, slightly receding hair. John Brown weighed 140 pounds; Lincoln, 180. Both dressed in black and wore white shirts with stiff collars, the fashion of the day.

Each knew Midwestern winters and commonly dressed in wool, though the fabric John Brown and his family wore often came from his own sheep. When Frederick Douglass visited John Brown in Springfield, Massachusetts, he found him "clad in plain American woolen"[12]—the product at the center of his labor as shepherd and wool merchant during his Akron and Springfield years.

They were strong, the two of them, capable of extraordinary physical feats, like Paul Bunyan or Hercules. Both could sink an ax into a tree and fell it. They could take down forests, and did. Lincoln's biographers said he could easily lift four hundred pounds, "and in one case six hundred."[13] Just twelve years old, John Brown single-handedly drove a herd of cattle from Ohio to Michigan to feed soldiers in the War of 1812,[14] something he wrote about in his autobiographical letter to Henry L. Stearns.[15]

I can't always separate life from legend when it comes to the two of them.

Even their hands were legendary. One Akron resident who had seen Lincoln and was asked about it sixty years later said his hand "was the biggest hand I ever saw."[16] The Sunday following Lincoln's nomination for President, a man named Leonard Volk made casts of Lincoln's hands in Springfield, Illinois—casts now housed in the National Portrait Gallery of the Smithsonian Institution. Volk had shaken hands with Lincoln and felt his viselike grip, calling it "a grasp never to be forgotten." He thought for a moment that his own had been crushed.[17]

The clasp of John Brown was something Frederick Douglass noticed. John Brown, he said, had a "grip peculiar to Anti-slavery men."[18]

Many of the daguerreotypes of John Brown stop just below his shoulders, but when his hands are visible in photographs, they look like creatures about to spring. Occasionally I could see his strong, thick fingers wrapped firmly around the barrel of a gun—or of his own biceps, as in the Hudson daguerreotype. The abolition banner photograph by Augustus Washington features the most visible John Brown hand I knew of[19]—broad and blurred, almost detached from his body, nearly as big as his head, a mirror image floating in the air, so ghostly that it seems to forecast everything that lay ahead.

A woman named Mrs. Russell told a story about John Brown's hands that struck me as myth in most ways, but not all. In the spring of 1859, she said he brought her daughter, little Minnie, some Ohio maple sugar and then held her "standing, on his outstretched palm." After he got her to balance, John Brown supposedly told Minnie, "Now... when you are a young lady and I am hanged, you can say that you stood on the hand of Old Brown."[20] I had great difficulty believing this, but I understood that in Mrs. Russell's mind John Brown's hands were probably twice the size they really were, and that was part of the story too.

There were physical differences besides their height. People who spent their lives studying Lincoln said he had ears so large that they formed right angles with his head. His bottom lip was thick and heavy, and his chin turned up as if to balance all that weight.

Lincoln's nineteenth-century biographers said he moved "cautiously but firmly," with arms drooped, swinging at his sides. He never led with his heel, but lifted right foot then left straight up and placed them down flat, an image that made me think of a duck.[21] One journalist said that his whole life Lincoln was as gawky as an adolescent, using "singularly awkward, almost absurd, up-and-down and sidewise movements of his body to give emphasis to his arguments."[22] When I saw Steven Spielberg's *Lincoln*, I thought Daniel Day-Lewis did a good job with the Lincoln walk, catching the oddity of it, the slight stoop forward of his narrow shoulders.

In my imagination, the other moved very differently, more lightly, like a water strider or some long-legged bird—an egret or heron—struggling to take flight. I pictured John Brown almost on tiptoe. His lips were thin, a straight twig that refused to break, though sometimes the corners drooped down like the sad mouth of a baby bird. People would have noticed his eyes first, I thought, those gray-blue orbs of light. Lincoln's were solid gray, steadier and less daunting than those gimlet eyes John Brown had that bore right into a person, even in a black-and-white photograph.

3.

I found the sign about Lincoln's railroad stop a little south of Streetsboro Street, off Maple Drive, a narrow road named Railroad Street when the depot was there. The marker isn't far from the present police station.

A silhouette of Lincoln's head is on the sign, but to me its shape seemed identical to the other man's. I felt as if I were looking at only one head and one person, not two. A strange conflation—John Brown inside Lincoln's head.

The silhouette blotted out physical differences, leaving only the interior.

Was John Brown on Lincoln's mind on February 15, 1861, the day the president-elect came to Hudson on a train? The silhouette prompted the question. We know he was thinking about his debt to Ohio when his train pulled through. Before coming to Hudson, he'd stopped in Ravenna to pick up Horace Y. Beebe. In 1860, this civic leader and passenger conductor of the Cleveland & Pittsburgh Railroad had switched his vote from Salmon P. Chase to Abraham Lincoln on the third ballot at the Republican National Convention in Chicago, giving Lincoln the extra votes he needed for the nomination.[23]

But was Lincoln thinking about John Brown too?

The two men had never met, as far as anyone knows, but John Brown was in the news, with all that recent business about Kansas and Harpers Ferry. Lincoln might have known that he was from Hudson—at least, from Ohio. He probably wouldn't have known that John Brown gave a speech in Hudson one night shortly before Harpers Ferry, or that the morning after delivering it he left town from the depot where Lincoln's train was now stopped—a

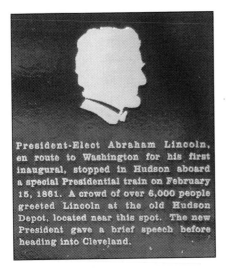

President-Elect Abraham Lincoln, en route to Washington for his first inaugural, stopped in Hudson aboard a special Presidential train on February 15, 1861. A crowd of over 6,000 people greeted Lincoln at the old Hudson Depot, located near this spot. The new President gave a brief speech before heading into Cleveland.

Sign for Lincoln railroad stop in Hudson on February 15, 1861

depot one visitor described as "a crude, cold room, having only an insignificant little stove."[24] But Lincoln surely knew that the man Virginia condemned for treason had roots in the Western Reserve.

John Brown was interviewed by leaders in the South a day after his capture, questioned by men like Henry Wise (governor of Virginia), Robert E. Lee, J. E. B. Stuart, Senator James Mason and Congressman Charles James Faulkner of Virginia, and Congressman C. L. Vallandigham of Ohio.

The interview was printed in newspapers, including the *New York Herald* and the *Baltimore American*. When asked how long he had lived in Ohio, John Brown said: "I went there in 1805. I lived in Summit County, which was then Portage County." "Have you been in Portage County lately?" was the next question. "I was there in June last."[25] I didn't think Lincoln would have missed that story or forgotten what John Brown said.

But even if he had, Lincoln surely knew something about the Connecticut Western Reserve, where John Brown was from—a region said to have had more Underground Railroad stops than any other stretch of land its size in the nation. Southerners despised it, regarding it as a separate state within Ohio. A Richmond paper called the people of the Ohio Western Reserve a "hypocritical, canting, whining, totally depraved and utterly irredeemable set of rascals."[26]

Among the places in the Western Reserve that the South hated most at the time of Harpers Ferry—certainly the places the men and troops who were

Governor Henry Wise of Virginia (tall hat, third from left) examining
wounded Harpers Ferry prisoners, sketch by Alfred Berghaus, *Leslie's
Illustrated Newspaper.* (Courtesy Boyd B. Stutler Collection of John Brown,
West Virginia State Archives)

guarding John Brown and his raiders in their Charles Town jail cells hated
most—would have been Oberlin and Ashtabula,[27] probably not Hudson, even
though Hudson was John Brown's town. Ashtabula became the home of John
Brown Jr. for years and of the Ashtabula League of Freedom, whose members
vowed to never reveal anything they knew about Harpers Ferry prior to the
raid. They watched all the roads in case federal agents approached, and threaded
black strings through the buttonholes of their jackets—leading to their being
dubbed the Black Strings.[28]

A shtabula was also the home of the *Sentinel* and its abolitionist editor,
William Cooper Howells (father of novelist William Dean Howells); of King
& Brothers in Cherry Valley Township, cabinetmakers better remembered for
stockpiling weapons for the Harpers Ferry attack than for their fine furniture;
and, in Wayne Township, of E. A. Fobes, a farmer and relative of John Brown
Jr. who stored the weapons for Harpers Ferry in his barn after the King brothers stashed them in coffins.[29] Also a resident of Ashtabula County was Congressman Joshua Giddings, the vocal and fierce abolitionist who served in the
Ohio House of Representatives from 1838–1859 and was hated by the South.[30]

Lincoln most likely read about the Oberlin-Wellington Rescue in 1858 of
John Price from Kentucky slave catchers because the story made national

news. He might have known that the Oberlin Collegiate Institute in the Western Reserve was the first co-educational college, as well as the first college to have an official policy against racial discrimination. But it's unlikely he knew that the school educated more Black students prior to the Civil War than all other colleges in America combined, or that antebellum Oberlin was twenty percent Black—a far greater portion of its population than major American cities, or of abolitionist towns like Hudson, which had only three permanent Black residents in 1850, and all of them "domestics."[31]

Lincoln at least would have been familiar with the label commonly attached to Oberlin: a "hot-bed of abolitionism."[32]

Hudson intersected with several main routes of the Railroad,[33] and is still remembered as having been a significant site in Summit County.[34] When Lincoln was young, during the days of the Ohio Black Laws and early fugitive slave laws,[35] he might have heard people talking about Joseph Keeler, an agent who was transporting two runaways from Clarksburg, Virginia, named Martin and Sam, and made the mistake of coming through Hudson from Independence on the way south. The *Cleaveland Herald* covered the story. Keeler was met by a Hudson mob, apprehended just south of town center, tried in the Cleveland Court of Common Pleas, and charged with kidnapping.[36] I assumed there were Browns in that mob—after all, the town was small, and the Browns were a leading abolitionist family, so why wouldn't there have been?

I don't think Lincoln would have been surprised to learn that several anti-slavery societies formed in Hudson shortly after prominent abolitionist and journalist William Lloyd Garrison founded the first one in New England in 1832.

The president-elect certainly would have heard about Hudson's radical abolitionists Charles Backus Storrs, Elizur Wright, and Beriah Green of Western Reserve College and about the controversy between colonizationists and abolitionists that they helped stir. This controversy not only led to Owen Brown's refusal to serve any longer at the college, but also ignited a national debate that flared in other towns.[37] Eventually it was at the center of Lincoln's national and personal crisis. Should people enslaved be freed gradually and resettled in Africa (the colonization movement), or immediately emancipated with full rights and privileges of American citizens (abolitionism)? Sparks began in Hudson that leapt far beyond the borders of the town.

I could never really know if Lincoln had made his mind up about John Brown the day he stopped in Hudson—or if he ever did.

My conclusion was that John Brown was a puzzle to Lincoln. He knew that this abolitionist had somehow led him to the presidency, but he also knew he had to keep his distance from John Brown because Democrats continued to associate any Republican candidate with the man from Harpers Ferry—even a moderate one.

Just before John Brown's execution, Lincoln spoke in Elwood, Kansas, one hundred miles north of Osawatomie, and said that John Brown's attack on Harpers Ferry was both illegal and futile. Yet, there was ambivalence in his words, a mix of rebuke and admiration. "John Brown has shown great courage, rare unselfishness, as even Gov. Wise testifies. But no man, North or South, can approve of violence or crime,"[38] he said.

A day or two after the execution, when sympathy was gathering for Old Brown (after Kansas, he was known by this name, along with "Fighting Brown" and "Osawatomie Brown"), Lincoln spoke in Kansas again, this time in Leavenworth, just forty miles from Osawatomie. He said that although John Brown's opposition to slavery was right, even a moral position like his "cannot excuse violence, bloodshed, and treason."[39]

In Lincoln's Cooper Institute speech in New York on February 27, 1860, and two days later, in New Haven, Connecticut, he encountered accusations by Democrats that all Republicans were insurrectionists like John Brown. "John Brown!! John Brown was no Republican," Lincoln told them, "and you have failed to implicate a single Republican in his Harper's Ferry enterprise."[40] Lincoln had strongly opposed Senator Stephen Douglas' argument that extending slavery into the Territories was constitutional, but at this point in his career he just as strongly opposed John Brown's active and violent resistance to slavery in states where it had long been in place. Current slaveholders need not look behind them for another Old Brown creeping up.

Lincoln knew what had to be done and said to get elected, and sometimes a comment of his on the campaign trail seemed exaggerated for the right effect, the way it is today among candidates during stump speeches and debates.

It was his colonizationist views that I found most disturbing. When I learned about Lincoln in the classrooms of Garfield High School in Akron, Ohio, or stared at his giant portrait on the wall of the A. D. Ladd Auditorium, where I sat for pep rallies or performed in school plays, I used to think that he was perfect and uniformly loved. Only after setting out with John Brown did I come to realize that Black people in Lincoln's time didn't feel that way at all about him.

Before the Civil War, Black leaders like Thomas Hamilton, editor of the *Anglo-African Magazine*, had no more confidence in Lincoln Republicans than in Democrats.[41] Black New Yorkers attacked Lincoln for tacitly supporting the Fugitive Slave Act, for failing to defend John Brown and his raid at Harpers Ferry, for thinking that slavery might end naturally on its own, and for believing for many years that Liberia was a promising solution. Black people supported Lincoln only when he declared war—and then there were new battles they fought with him. Generally, they found Republicans timid and fearful, ineffectual and unpredictable. To them, every day Republicans waited to act was another day people remained enslaved.

Lincoln was a man of contradictions. He wanted enslaved people to be free, but took too much time understanding what this meant, or what he and the country would need to do to make it possible. Still, contemporary Black historians have often come to his defense. Henry Louis Gates Jr. believed that what made Lincoln "exceptional" was that he "wrestled with his often contradictory feelings and ambivalences...and did so quite publicly and often quite eloquently."[42]

John Brown was one of Lincoln's ambivalences, if not outright contradictions. Like other problems that perplexed him, to some extent John Brown must have lived inside Lincoln's head.

I imagined John Brown hiding under Lincoln's frock coat, just waiting for the right time to step out. Even in the Leavenworth speech, when Lincoln insisted on separating himself from John Brown, there was also a hint that he had become Lincoln's weapon. If Democrats carried through with a plan to destroy the Union, he told them, they would be dealt with the same way the government of Virginia had dealt with Old Brown, and he cautioned them not to act in a way "as to render such extreme measures necessary."[43] When he needed the stern disciplinarian that he did not always feel he could be, Lincoln pulled John Brown out of his political holster.

I wondered if John Brown would have minded being used like that, and if maybe I was using him too.

Although John Brown remained unnamed in Lincoln's First Inaugural Address, I felt his presence when I read the words. Lincoln again assured Southern states that he wouldn't threaten the "property rights" of the South or test the constitutionality of the Fugitive Slave Act.[44] By denying all that John Brown represented—the right and necessity to destroy slavery—Lincoln was able to bring the issue of emancipation center stage, while tacitly making

John Brown, not Lincoln, the culprit, and separating himself from both John Brown and extreme action.

By the time Lincoln delivered his "Second Inaugural Address" on March 4, 1865, he did seem on better terms with the man and even sounded a little like him. I'd only remembered the quieter phrases from the speech, the words we had to memorize in high school—"with malice toward none, with charity for all"—but when I read it word for word in my Library of America volume, I heard the rage and anger textbooks had excluded.[45] Speaking about the bloody Civil War, Lincoln said, "Yet, if God wills that it continue, until all the wealth piled by the bond-man's two hundred and fifty years of unrequited toil shall be sunk, and until every drop of blood drawn with the lash, shall be paid by another drawn with the sword, as was said three thousand years ago, so still it must be said 'the judgments of the Lord, are true and righteous altogether.'"[46]

4.

I thought about the people crowded in nine passenger cars on the Cleveland, Zanesville and Cincinnati Railroad that had come up from Akron to see Abraham Lincoln.[47] I pictured the thousands of people who gathered near the Hudson depot on that cold windy day.

A journalist who covered the trip to Washington noticed that crowds met him at all the stopping points between Pittsburgh and Cleveland—but particularly in the Western Reserve.[48] The President-elect bowed at the Hudson stop, but didn't leave the train.

Lincoln spoke only forty-three words: "I stepped upon this platform to see you, and to give you an opportunity of seeing me, which I suppose you desire to do. You see by my voice that I am quite hoarse. You will not, therefore, expect a speech from me."[49]

Fighting a cold, the future president didn't say anything at all memorable, but Summit County was nonetheless proud of Lincoln's whistle-stop. The train chugged off to Cleveland, arriving to an artillery salute at four o'clock in the afternoon.[50]

An eleven-year-old boy from Hudson could have been standing in the crowd that day to watch Abraham Lincoln—James W. Ellsworth. He might have walked to the depot with his father, Edgar B. Ellsworth, from the family store on East Main Street where young James worked, a store that faced the Green and was just a short distance from the railroad stop, and one block from my house.

Newspaper illustration of
Lincoln's railroad stop in
Hudson. (Courtesy Hudson
Library & Historical Society)

Edgar Birge Ellsworth.
(Courtesy Hudson Library &
Historical Society)

The boy left Hudson for many decades and became a wealthy coal baron and a banker, founding Ellsworth Coal Company and the mining town of Ellsworth, Pennsylvania. Then he returned to his hometown in 1907 and used part of his fortune to modernize Hudson and invest in moribund Western Reserve Academy, which had closed its doors in 1903.

That day in 1861 young James W. Ellsworth might have been overwhelmed, even though he couldn't have known that his boyhood admiration for the man on the train might have some connection to the active role he would later play in the 1896 Republican Convention or in his own son being called Lincoln.[51]

Maybe Abraham Lincoln saw the little boy near the depot where the crowd gathered. He might have seen the town Green as his train rolled by—fenced in both to contain livestock and to keep stray animals out. And maybe, in the distance, Brewster Mansion, which became the Park Hotel after Brewster died, then a nursing home, and after that, a cluster of shops and offices.

From his train, Lincoln would have glimpsed what was then known as Ellsworth Hall on the corner of East Main and Streetsboro Street, but he wouldn't have known that John Brown's father had helped erect the building in the early 1840s as a place of worship for abolitionists in town and that it

Brewster Row and fenced-in Green, about the time of Lincoln's
visit to Hudson on his inaugural train, photo by John Markillie,
1861. (Courtesy Hudson Library & Historical Society)

was originally called the Free Congregational Church. The church was sold
to Edgar Birge Ellsworth in 1852 and by the time Lincoln passed through, it
bore the Ellsworth name and had become a community meeting place.[52]

John Brown delivered his last Hudson speech in front of it in 1859.

History was already on every corner of the town, and now Lincoln was a
part of its story too. I sometimes imagined a soothsayer standing close to the
Lincoln train, shouting up a warning that trains that passed through Hudson
took people to their deaths. Less than four years after his Hudson stop,
Lincoln was dead, and another train—a funeral train this time—brought his
corpse to Public Square in Cleveland.[53]

John Brown and Abraham Lincoln both stood on this identical spot at
nearly the same moment, and both were swept away by a train that stopped
for them on Railroad Street and hauled them off toward national history and
then to their violent deaths. How could I ever understand what a town like
this expected from me?

It was Fred Kaplan who helped me find the word for the odd sensation of
luck and obligation I felt from living in a place where stories like these could
overlap. He came to Hudson to talk about his new book on John Quincy
Adams, and I went to the library to hear him.

Loomis Observatory

"I've never been to Hudson," he said, before he began telling the audience about America's sixth president. The town seemed to hold him in a trance. Northeastern Ohio was closely associated with the abolitionists, he told the audience. He said he'd walked the streets in the afternoon before his evening lecture and sensed what he called the "seriousness" of the town. He exclaimed with wonder his discovery of the Loomis Observatory on the Academy's campus—the second oldest observatory in the United States, built in 1838.[54]

That's the word I was looking for. The "seriousness" of this place had infected me. History had infected me. Once you know the history of a place, you can't just live in it frivolously anymore. A serious place makes demands on you.

5.

The last letter John Brown wrote from his jail cell before his execution was addressed to his friend Lora Case, a man who became a leading Hudson abolitionist and was a student of John Brown's in his Sunday School class. He may not have been present the day that Lincoln's inaugural party passed through, but I know he heard the last speech John Brown gave in Hudson in 1859 and accompanied him afterwards to his train. He'd told about it in a book of reminiscences.

There was no crowd to send John Brown off the morning after he spoke, the way there had been for Lincoln. There would only be Lora Case. Eleven years younger than John Brown, Lora Case adored his Sunday School teacher, and never stopped adoring him. He wrote about him in his book, recording detail that otherwise might have been lost. The subject of the speech John Brown delivered in front of Ellsworth Hall, Lora Case said, had been the Declaration of Independence and the cost it exacted for the privilege of giving the rights it promised to everyone.

John Brown believed in the document's truth that "all men are created equal." Believed the words, I knew, in a way that Thomas Jefferson, their creator, could not, for Jefferson failed to rid himself of his belief in Black inferiority during his political and personal life, causing what one historian called a "self-imposed paralysis on the most consequential and controversial question of his time."[35]

Lora Case, Hudson friend of John Brown. (Courtesy Hudson Library & Historical Society)

Although John Brown would rewrite the Constitution in Chatham, Canada West, the Declaration of Independence was sacred to the man, and Lora Case never doubted that.[56]

When he accompanied John Brown to the depot, he continued talking where he'd left off the night before. He spoke of Pharisees and warned against them—against hypocrisy in all people—and it was clear he meant people in antebellum America every bit as much as those in the Bible. *Hypocrisy* was a favorite word of John Brown's, the straight edge he used to measure every individual by.

Lora Case described John Brown as always having his hands behind him, deep in thought.[57]

The detail merged with my own notion of John Brown as some great bird, strong bristly feathers of every length sprouting from his arms, forming wings that crossed behind him—perhaps a flightless bird like Darwin's rhea that ran at enormous speeds to evade its predators, opening its wings like sails to catch the wind and steer. I often imagined John Brown moving quickly across fields and streets, along creeks and over mountains, his neck and back bent too far forward, his head bobbing sometimes to inflect a word like *pharisee* or *hypocrisy*, his legs propelling him toward a mirage that he called *democracy*, a grand illusion produced by the refraction of light in his own eye. The world's greatest Optimist, I sometimes called him. Other times, the world's greatest Fool.

John Brown's message was as consistent as bird call, but it was getting late, and he was growing impatient. The sound coming out of his mouth that last visit to Hudson must have been shrill.

His last letter, to Lora Case of Hudson, Ohio, included his final Sunday School lesson to his former pupil: "Pure & undefiled religion befor God & the Father is as I understand it: an *active* (not a dormant) *principle*." The letter closed with the words, "Remember me to all *yours, & my dear friends*. Your Friend John Brown."[58] Minutes later, the jailer, John Avis, and the sheriff of Jefferson County, James Campbell, came for him. John Brown mounted the gallows and became a man who "stood on air."[59]

REVERIE 1
TRAINS DON'T STOP FOR PASSENGERS IN HUDSON ANYMORE

I.

Trains don't stop on Railroad Street anymore. There still are two trains that come through Hudson with passenger cars between two a.m. and three a.m. in the dark of night—one goes east to west and the other travels west to east—but their passengers board in other towns than here.

Around 1903, when Hudson's trains were elevated, the Pennsylvania Railroad built a depot on a hill close to town off Streetsboro Street.[1] It was razed in August of 2013 because it hadn't been used since 2002 and money couldn't be found to restore it. Its roof, oddly, remained intact amidst the rubble because it was infested by bees, which are so endangered now that government crews have been ordered not to destroy them or their nests.

Every ten or fifteen minutes a train passes through my town, rolling over Main Street and Streetsboro Street on trestle bridges. "NS," for Norfolk Southern, along with train graffiti, is on the side of many cars, most of them heavy with freight. The whistle and rumble of trains is the soundtrack of Hudson, always in the background of my life.

I seldom think about the trains in the daytime, but at night, when John Brown troubles me, I wait for a train—listen for it—and can't fall asleep until I hear one pass.

In 1851, the Cleveland and Pittsburgh Railroad arrived in town.[2] Hudson's wealthy—including members of the prominent David Hudson family—invested heavily in railroads. Clinton Street in downtown Hudson was named after DeWitt Clinton, the nephew of an early governor of New York who promoted the Clinton Air Line, but the venture to bring a second railroad here never went beyond a basic roadbed for the train and culverts.[3] The year 1856 brought a serious depression to the industry, and Hudson investors lost small fortunes. Business later picked up for a while. Saloons and box factories and warehouses and the Depot Restaurant built by William Bullock, a veteran of the Civil War, lined Railroad Street.[4] In 1882, the hope of living in a flourishing railroad town suffered another great setback when Western Reserve College moved to Cleveland.

I often wish I'd lived in this town when trains stopped for passengers. I wish I'd been able to accompany Lora Case the morning he walked John Brown to the depot. Wish I'd been in the crowd the day Lincoln stopped. But no one will deboard or all-aboard anytime soon on Railroad Street.

Yet, trains come through with a constant hum. *Listen*, they seem to say, *we're still here.*

And they are. One heads out of town on the trestle bridge over Main Street, a bridge painted for years with the words Freedom Is Not Free, though the town recently hired a crew to paint over them. It will then quickly cross a second bridge, over Streetsboro Street, before it roars by the ground where the Pennsylvania Railroad Station stood and curves its way out north near Cutler Lane.

The town has changed, but much remains. A whistle blows, awakes my imagination, and I'm off. That's how I sometimes travel now. At twilight I look out an upstairs window to the south and see the top of the Dissident Church, which became Ellsworth Hall, blink, and then glimpse John Brown in front of the building holding the Declaration of Independence. I look north across the street, see Town Hall, and spot him leaning on the marker that holds his vow. I look west, toward the Green, and watch him strutting like a noisy, crested bird. I walk downstairs and turn the porch light on, as if I'm waiting for a visitor.

THE CASE-BARLOW FARM AND THE UNDERGROUND RAILROAD

Case-Barlow Farm

I.

The house was built by Chauncey and Cleopatra Hayes Case, the parents of Lora Case, and it's known as the Case-Barlow Farm now. I loved the building even before I knew it was one of the first brick houses west of Pittsburgh or that Chauncey and Cleopatra Case hid fugitives in its woods or that Lora Case was John Brown's friend. It stood on 4.2 acres of land surrounded by a sixty-acre city-owned park where the community sets off fireworks on the Fourth of July.[1]

A Fall Harvest Festival is held on the grounds each year, and although I'd never gone before, one year early in my John Brown research I felt compelled to be there. I was suspicious that John Brown was behind all this.

The house was on the Ohio Historical Inventory and was named an official Underground Railroad site by the Friends of Freedom Society. John Brown himself had hidden fugitives on his property on old Chapman Road even in the 1820s, so how could I further postpone such a visit?

Soon I began to realize that not just John Brown, but something else had brought me to Barlow Road. Regret, I suppose I should call it. I found myself inviting my son, his wife, and their two small sons, Logan (seven) and Carson (three), to join me. I wanted them all to enjoy this special fall celebration with the smell of Ohio apples and smoke in the air, but what I really wanted was to make Logan like me again. I'd made a horrible mistake and hoped to repair it here.

"The people who lived in this house worked on the Underground Railroad," I proudly told Logan, almost before he stepped out of his car.

Logan Thomas Dyer, seven years old. (Photo
by Melissa McGowan Dyer)

I hoped that acquainting him in such a personal way with the history of
the Underground Railroad would help him forgive me for an indiscretion.
I'd given him a simple gift—a children's book about Mark Twain's life called
River Boy. In a hurry, I failed to read it before I wrapped it up. Logan's mother,
my daughter-in-law, reported that he'd said the gift was "inappropriate." She
laughed when she told me the story, but I knew I'd upset my grandson.

I had to check the book out of the library to find the material he'd found
offensive. Inappropriate. I wasn't about to ask him for his copy.

There it was: a picture of three startled boys looking at something floating
in the river in front of them—but the illustrator doesn't show us what it is.
Only words make it visible, but Logan was seven, and could read them: "While
exploring the island, they made a shocking discovery—the body of a runaway
slave floating in the water," the author said. Then, in a new paragraph, Sam
Clemens encountered a slave coffle on the way to a plantation in the South.[2]

Inappropriate was the word Logan used for everything that had no place
in the perfect world he thought he occupied. His parents had to explain what
a *slave* was and what a *coffle* was because Logan didn't know, and when they
did, I pictured the image of people enslaved by other people entering his head
for the first time, and for all the rest of time.

2.

I thought seeing visible proof that people fought against slavery through a network of secret routes that led fugitives to freedom in Canada would console Logan. I'd heard the story of the Underground Railroad so many times that I thought I had it right:

How people in fourteen Northern states, from Iowa all the way to Maine, helped fugitives escape. Ohio was a special state—the main artery to freedom. It was a direct route to Lake Erie. People in my town, people like the Cases ("and like you would have been, Logan," I would tell my grandson), hid fugitives in rooms of their houses, in secret cellars and disappearing attics, in brick kilns and wells, under haymows, in barns, and in woods and high weeds on their property. Other people here and in many northeastern Ohio towns transported them in covered wagons, on trains, in canal boats, on horseback, and beneath produce in carts, and, if there was no other means, townspeople walked with them toward steamboats where fugitives were hidden in holds or forecastles and then taken to Canada.

How fugitives, thousands and thousands of them, entered Ohio in darkness from different points along the Ohio River. How they were moved through Ripley in Brown County and other gateways farther east and north.[3] How people from river towns began to shuttle fugitives north, through inland towns like Hudson and Oberlin, Northampton, Northfield, and Medina County,[4] and then on to places that had harbors and ports along Lake Erie, where they boarded steamboats heading toward Canadian ports on the Detroit River and along the lakeshore east of it.[5] How they would follow a group of stars shaped like a drinking gourd to locate the North Star and be free.

I would tell Logan what the risks of the Underground were, because numbers were available, and Logan liked numbers. Fugitives were always at greatest risk because they might be returned to a master who wouldn't forget what one of his "own" had done to cut into plantation profits. Railroad conductors faced risks too, though not like those a fugitive encountered. After the Fugitive Slave Act passed, Congress mandated a fine of up to $1,000 or imprisonment up to six months for any American citizen who harbored or concealed fugitives or aided in their rescue. They also risked the threat of having to pay civil damages of $1,000 to slave owners, since the law considered the owners "the injured party."[6]

But by the time of the festival, the story of the Railroad was becoming more complicated than I'd wanted it to be. Much remained true, but a number of my assumptions were being tested.

New historians were calling many things about the Railroad "myths." When I read that, I felt as if even the ground of my own town were collapsing.[7] Research was disclosing truths about the vast role that free Blacks and fugitives played in the Railroad and about the inflation of the role of whites; about the number of fugitives who escaped (recent estimates were showing that between one thousand and five thousand people were transported to freedom each year from 1830 to 1860, a number formerly thought to have been much larger);[8] about the Railroad not always being meticulously ordered or organized, but loose in structure, and often a spontaneous thing; about the sorrowful absence of names and stories of runaways and new attempts that were being made to find out more by locating ads for fugitives in nineteenth-century newspapers.[9]

A local historian in Hudson who had studied the Railroad and the sites identified on a famous Hudson map worked on the subject as early as 1977. She used words like *legend* and *folklore* to describe the organization. "Only about 20% of all escaped slaves rode on the Underground Railroad," she said. "In folklore," she concluded, "there is always a germ of truth; in this case, how much?"[10]

Black people were among the Railroad's most prominent members, like Harriet Tubman, Louis Napoleon, Lewis Hayden, Anna Murray-Douglass, and David Ruggles. Some of the names I encountered in my reading were familiar, but many were not. The vigilance committees that formed in New

York and other places in the urban North, comprised of Black and white activists, were a vital part of the Railroad's history, yet they were new to me.[11]

One historian wrote about the need to authenticate sites, to focus on the terror each runaway experienced, to avoid seeing the Railroad as a "romantic fix" to problems of racial injustice in the present.[12] I was becoming unnerved. Why had I clung to the idea that the Railroad was run by white people who hid fugitives in fruit cellars? I'd often heard friends who bought historic houses in Hudson and other Ohio towns exclaim their pride in the certainty that a small hidden basement space in a historic house they'd just purchased had once been a safe retreat for a fugitive. I'd believed them and said similar things about an old home in town I'd lived in before moving to Church Street. But James F. Caccamo, a former archivist at the Hudson Library & Historical Society, a man who died much too soon and was a friend of mine, had debunked many of those myths decades before my research began, and I should have listened more closely to what he said when he was alive, but I didn't. By the time I knew I needed to, he was dead.

Jim wrote about the counterfeiting rings in the area that led more commonly to the building of little alcoves in houses (to print and store fake money) than hiding fugitives ever did; about the impracticality and expense of building or creating spaces within a nineteenth-century home for the few passengers that ever came through and stayed, at most, a single night; about the sheer impossibility of finding shackles in the walls, as if a passenger who was a guest in such a home would ever be bound; about how unwise it would have been for station masters to place black bands on chimneys, stone jockeys in front yards of stops—visible signals to direct fugitives (and, as well, notify authorities looking for them); about the easy availability of outdoor spaces like barns, fields, sheds, woods, so that rooms in homes and cellars were rarely even needed; about the danger a rumored encampment for runaway slaves in woods that belonged to Frederick Brown would have posed for both fugitives and the Hudson community, and the high probability that the story was untrue.[13]

There were authentic sites, of course, and my town housed staunch abolitionists. Local publications today advertise nineteen houses in Hudson that have been associated with Railroad activity (many connected with the Browns), and there is evidence for a tunnel that ran under South Main Street from the Thompson house to a property known as "Thirty Acres," where resident John B. Clark lived, a prosperous farmer who owned a thousand apple trees.[14]

Thirty Acres

Compared with the number of abolitionists who lived in Hudson, though, there really were few residents known to have engaged in Railroad activity. Residents who were outspoken members of antislavery societies and owned homes in Hudson along the route were always candidates. But James F. Caccamo studied the Railroad his whole short life and was careful to use the phrase "there is no direct evidence" if there was nothing more to it than that (as were later Hudson librarians who honored him). The Underground Railroad sign on the Hudson Green listed sixteen names of people in the "anti-slavery community," but only a handful of those were singled out by Jim in his book for having "proven" records of involvement and participation.[15]

Lora Case in his *Reminiscences* said that use of the Railroad was "a rare thing." After he married and moved to Streetsboro, he said that only three voters there "worked as section hands to keep that road in repair," that churches and ministers had opposed the Railroad (they quoted Scripture to defend their refusal), that "there was then strong prejudice in the church and throughout the state against the anti-slavery movement." He traced the route from Ravenna to Cleveland, attaching one name to each community. John Markillie, he said, ran the station in Hudson.[16]

John Markillie. (Courtesy Hudson
Library & Historical Society)

Being an abolitionist did not automatically mean that a person was going
to take the kind of risk that working on the Railroad demanded. I hadn't
thought about this very much before John Brown, but now I did. I'd greatly
preferred stories about drinking gourds and fruit cellars, but I knew I couldn't
have them anymore.

3.

Lora Case was the real thing. That's what I told Logan as we hurried toward the Case-Barlow house to get warm.

We walked into the nineteenth century when we entered. There was a woman dressed as Cleopatra Case and another working a loom. Volunteers in period clothing were caning chairs and churning butter in other rooms (the Cases were dairy farmers). Logan and my son were in the parlor looking at a display of music boxes that featured everything from singing birds to orchestral symphonies, and when we all finished exploring the first floor, we climbed a staircase and examined rugs, quilts, and old sleighs upstairs.

After a few minutes on the second floor, I saw Logan head toward the steps, so I caught up with him. "The Cases helped poor runaway slaves," I told him, pressing his shoulder close to my hip, but he seemed distracted. I saw him nod, because he's fiercely polite and would never ignore a person talking to him, but I made the mistake of thinking his gesture meant he wanted to hear more. I began to tell him the figures and names that I knew were true, but he'd stopped listening after the part about "poor runaway slaves." Logan turned around and looked up at me with his huge brown eyes, like pecans. They swelled, then cracked.

I had only one more chance before he fled the building. "A friend of a friend," I said, trying to console him. I thought that he'd remember that. It was a secret saying I'd read somewhere, and secret sayings were cool. "That was the password that let runaways know they were safe." Even as the words came out I had new suspicions that the saying wasn't true, the way that "freedom quilts" sewn by slaves and hung in windows as guideposts weren't true, or the spiritual *Steal Away* to announce the arrival of Harriet Tubman was a myth, or the story of a Southern Grand Central Station and a Railroad in the South was all made up.[17]

"I won't talk about this," Logan said as he hurried out the building. He had such an old voice when he said it.

The pride I had in the Case-Barlow house or in Hudson's abolitionist history was not big enough to solve the problem of the dead man in the book for Logan. He seemed to know that a Railroad that wasn't even a real railroad was too slow. When he traveled, Logan rode in a Jeep and sometimes on jets. He was a child of the Internet and the cellphone. If something was wrong, if it was absolutely wrong, and people were getting hurt, and it was all taking place right in front of your eyes, didn't someone have to stop it? *Why couldn't people back then have stopped it?* was what I thought was in his head.

But, of course, I was the one who put the thought there. He was upset by the words *poor runaway slaves* and the dead man in the book, that much I was sure of, but whether he questioned the efficacy of the Underground Railroad was doubtful.

I wanted to race after him and say something about what John Brown did to fight slavery. I'd told him earlier that John Brown was a friend of Lora Case, and before that I'd shown him the sign across the street from my house about the public vow John Brown took in 1837 to destroy slavery. I wanted my grandson to understand that goodness was an "an *active* (not a dormant) *principle*," as John Brown said in his last letter to Lora Case, and that courageous people really did exist, and that John Brown was an abolitionist who never stopped helping people who weren't free. Why did I hesitate to speak?

The man remained so problematic for me that I couldn't find a way to introduce him to a child. To anyone, I guess. John Brown and I were not at peace, and I knew my grandson would sense this, no matter what I said about Old Brown. Thinking about John Brown didn't always make me feel better, so why would I assume he could comfort a child? If I called John Brown a "hero," Logan would hear the waver in my voice.

Besides, Logan's heroes didn't look like John Brown or do the things that John Brown did. They were comic book heroes who wore masks and colorful spandex—mutants or people with superpowers—and no one would confuse them with a villain, the way people often did John Brown.

John Brown lived on the hard earth, and if he was a hero, it was an X-rated one.

I tried to imagine what a John Brown action figure might look like. His plastic coat and hair flying in the air, his little jointed hands with deep depressions for all his weapons and paraphernalia: Sharps rifles, pikes, swords, a Bible, the Declaration of Independence, a pen for writing letters and a Provisional Constitution. He would be dressed in blood-stained clothes, with dirt and murder under his fingernails. It was unlikely that a John Brown action figure would be manufactured anytime soon.

I wanted a John Brown who was courageous and unselfish, but non-violent and kind. Someone a little more like Mr. Rogers in *Mr. Rogers' Neighborhood*.

How could I explain to Logan that John Brown murdered and stole? That several of his sons and relatives and many of his friends died because they followed him on raids? I could talk about Harpers Ferry in the context of the Civil War, but I knew from the beginning that I'd also have to talk about Pottawatomie Creek, where John Brown and Company had hacked five civilians to pieces with broadswords and left body parts on the ground and in the water. Even sympathetic scholars often turned their backs on John Brown when he led them to the creek.

That day at Case-Barlow, much of the work required by my chance meeting with John Brown still lay ahead of me. I'd only begun to think about Pottawatomie Creek. If I spoke, all I'd be able to give my grandson were its ghastly images and the fear it evoked.

Logan already knew about Sting in *The Hobbit* and the lightsabers of the Jedi knights, but those magical weapons were very different from the brutal broadswords John Brown's party swung on the creek, and the image would frighten him. So I chose silence and watched my grandson slip away.

TWENTY-FIRST-CENTURY
OHIO NEIGHBORS

I.

Many people aren't clear about who John Brown even was. They conflate him sometimes with other historical figures, which can be good or bad for his reputation, depending on who comes to mind when they hear his name.

When I was having dinner several years ago with a friend, she asked me what I was working on, and I mentioned John Brown, though I didn't want to say too much. I asked her what she knew about him.

"Wasn't he Black?" she said.

"Oh, no," I said. "That's why he's so remarkable historically. He was the most radical white man in antebellum America."

"Didn't he have a beard?" she asked.

"Late in his life," I said, "after Bleeding Kansas."

She was quiet. Thinking.

"Oh, I know!" she said. "I'm confusing him with Frederick Douglass."

I smiled as she laughed about her mistake, but that was when the image of John Brown as a Black man entered my imagination. Only much later would I come to realize that her "mistake" had deep historical roots.

2.

He wasn't going to win a popularity contest anytime soon. The controversial nature of John Brown's life that kept Hudson trustees from approving the placement of a John Brown Memorial on the Clocktower or Bandstand Green is still alive in my town—as it is, I would guess, in towns throughout America. Opinion about him in Hudson is divided, but even people who like him choose their words carefully—cautiously—whenever he enters the conversation. Every year there's a Memorial Day parade down Main Street, but I've never seen a float in John Brown's honor.

Hudson children are usually introduced to him in school. Through the urging of the library, all third graders study the Underground Railroad and Hudson's involvement in it, and then sometimes take a field trip to the Old Hudson Township Burying Ground to see the graves of Owen and Ruth Mills Brown.

One day, as I exited the library with a book about John Brown in my hand, I saw four twelve-year-olds—all dressed in black T-shirts painted with white peace signs—gathered on the little walkway beneath the overhang of the library to avoid the rain. Two girls were spinning a glass Coke bottle on the pavement and talking a little, and two others—both boys—were pushing skateboards along the cement with their hands. They were all avoiding the eyes of a woman they preferred not to acknowledge as she waited beside them for the rain to stop.

But it kept coming down, and the youngsters couldn't flee.

"So, what do you know about John Brown?" I asked. I showed them the picture on the cover of the book I held. It was a caricature of John Brown before he grew his famous beard. Arms crossed, white collar up, thin tie loose at his neck, purple lapels of his suit coat shooting toward his shoulders like small flames at either side, sheep and a house in the background.

The bottle spinners looked up. One said "not much." The other said something about Harpers Ferry and guns. They quickly returned to the job of watching the neck of the bottle go round. One boy with a skateboard turned his head and said he thought he'd heard of him too, but he wasn't quite sure who he was anymore.

The second boy put one foot on the board and spoke from his podium. "He was an abolitionist and he fought for the slaves. We learned about him in school." And then the two skated around the brick columns of the library until the rain stopped.

Even for the children in front of me—not yet teens—John Brown took different forms. But the important thing, I thought, was that he had already entered some of their imaginations. Because they could recall him, he was there.

I'd wondered if much was made of John Brown in American high schools anymore. Friends of mine who taught American history to that age had shown me some of the textbooks they used. I assumed the students I met in the rain would soon be holding books very much like them.

Alan Brinkley in *The Unfinished Nation: A Concise History of the American People* called John Brown "a grim, fiercely committed zealot," a critic of slavery who advocated violence and was responsible for the "terrible episode" known as the Pottawatomie Massacre.[1] George Brown Tindall and David Emory Shi, in *America: A Narrative History*, provided what seemed a somewhat kinder view of John Brown, though there was clearly an attempt to remain ambiguous. The authors said he had a history of "mental instability" and was "zealous" before telling the story of Pottawatomie, but they included admiring lines from his speeches and letters, and phrases of their own about his "heartfelt commitment" and his "quixotic raid." They seemed drawn to his "penetrating gray eyes" and stepped beyond the boundaries of textbook prose when they wrote, "Brown was one of the few whites willing to live among Black people and to die for them."[2]

Libraries and classrooms are the places students learn about John Brown now. Even those young people who live in the town where he grew up find him that way.

3.

There are people I meet on the streets of town who despise him. Part of me understands it. Their lips stiffen when they say his name. They don't seem able to help themselves.

A man I know who really cares about the town feels like this. He asked one day if I was writing anything, and I told him about John Brown, and after that he stopped greeting me as warmly.

It was always small talk that we made together on street corners and in coffee shops, but his coolness bothers me now. He predictably greets me with a question about John Brown, as if he only sees him when he sees me. He's not really interested in what I have to say. The man's lips don't go as high as they used to when he smiles, and he's always in a hurry and says he has to be somewhere. "Somewhere" other than where I am. Each time I see him, his eyes seem to squint more tightly, as if he's making less and less room for me. I know he wants me to give this up.

"I wish the guy hadn't been born," he said the day I told him about John Brown. His neck swelled, and his face turned blood red. "He was a terrorist and I wish his family had never come to Hudson. He makes us look bad, and he'll make you look bad too."

I didn't entirely disagree with him, but it felt mean somehow, as if he were trying to frighten me to make me stop.

The man wants a town without John Brown in it, but John Brown is part of history and he isn't going anywhere.

4.

A side door is cut into a wall of the corner building that borders Clinton Street. The property once belonged to Owen Brown, but the land was purchased from him in 1831 by Julian Lusk, the brother of John Brown's first wife. I can't look at that corner even today without thinking of all the Browns, though much about the site has changed.

Julian Lusk built a brick house on the property—a house that also included stores and the American House Hotel—but it was radically remodeled in 1866 largely by Lucius Delong (married to a Mills), who purchased the property and added another story, store fronts that drew more attention to themselves, a mansard roof, and a $10,000 increase in tax value. It became known as the Farrar Block after Charles Farrar moved into one of the store fronts and then bought the building two years later with his brother-in-law. Ten years after that, Farrar expanded the top story into a spacious hall known as the Adelphian.

The whole corner building burned down in the famous Hudson fire of 1892. It was rebuilt, though it burned down a second time in 1911, almost as if it weren't meant to be there, or were a place meant for habitation by only ghosts.[3]

The current structure (known informally as the Saywell's Building) was erected in 1913, so I assumed the door arrived then too. In 1866 the building housed a drugstore in the south half of the bottom floor, and it remained a drugstore throughout all the fires and the rebuilding. In 1909 a man named Fred Saywell took it over from Dr. George A. Miller, and he and his family ran it as a drugstore for nearly a hundred years. Open Door Coffee Company

Saywell's corner, with awning, 1920. (Courtesy
Hudson Library & Historical Society)

and a frame shop occupy the corner building now, so there isn't a downtown
drugstore anymore, but the coffee shop feels like one sometimes. Saywell's
served coffee too, and the new shop's décor incorporates objects from old
Saywell's—a phone booth with stained-glass panels, some wooden shelves, a
marble countertop, a few old stools.

The door on Clinton Street used to be the side entrance to the Colonial
Restaurant, with wooden stairs leading up to it, but the recess was boarded
up with a piece of sheet metal for decades, first painted black and then brick
red, and the stairs removed. Recently, the opening had begun to look like a
door again. Well, not exactly like a door. It's not functional and there's no
knob or lock, but there's wood over the metal now and a man is always exiting.

He never leaves the building, though, because he's made of paint.

I read in the local paper about the decision to draw the figure of James W.
Ellsworth on the door—a trompe l'oeil painting that creates the illusion of a
three-dimensional Ellsworth perpetually exiting the building. The Hudson
Society of Artists chose Ellsworth as their historical figure, and he was painted
by Lucy Karslake and Paul Adams. The painting was later approved by the
Architectural and Historic Board of Review.[4]

It made sense. Ellsworth was a very rich man who amassed a fortune in coal,
founded the Ellsworth Mines in Pennsylvania, built the fourteen-story Ellsworth
Building in Chicago, and then returned to his hometown to save it. This man
who'd been a boy when Lincoln's inaugural train pulled into Hudson had even

Hudson clocktower

Trompe l'oeil of James W. Ellsworth
exiting false door on Clinton Street

paid for the building with the false door he would be forever exiting—the *third* building on the corner, built in 1913. Ellsworth was never the owner of the property, but he absorbed the cost of construction and architectural fees, not even requesting that it be named for him. It was one of his many gifts to the town.[5]

Honoring him was perhaps also a way of honoring his father, Edgar Birge Ellsworth, a forward-looking Hudson businessman who anticipated the arrival of the railroad in 1850 and erected a house at 154 E. Streetsboro Street for transient workers.[6] A man who taught his son how to always look ahead. In some sense, the door, and its figure, was a way to honor business in town.

James William Ellsworth is painted in his finest clothes—long-tailed black coat, rich gray waistcoat, smart tie, stiff white collar—a cane in one hand and the other hand tightened in a fist, looking down on both pedestrians and drivers as they pass. I see him levitating every time I turn the corner onto Clinton Street.

Ellsworth became the village angel when he returned to town, giving Hudson a water and sewer system, a clocktower on the Green, light and telephone wires that were buried underground, elm trees, early Prohibition, new buildings, a community club house, and Spanish tiled roofs. He was a very

Birth home of John Brown in Torrington, Connecticut. (Courtesy
Hudson Library & Historical Society)

demanding man sometimes, insisting on nine conditions before he'd agree to
even proceed, but preservationists believe that his desire to make Hudson a
"model village" was so strong that, because of it, the town remains to this day
more or less what he envisioned.[7]

Western Reserve Academy opened its doors again in 1916—thanks to
James W. Ellsworth. He even bequeathed the bell that would eventually find
its way to the Chapel belfry and ring me to morning meetings and lunch when
I joined the faculty of the school—a bell that was cast in Holland in 1611.[8]

What better candidate than he for the door?

He brought wealth to the community. He brought cleanliness and beauty.
In a very real sense, he brought me.

Yet, sometimes I couldn't help but wonder how Hudson would have been
different if someone had nominated John Brown for the door instead, or if
there had been two figures on it, not just one, and the second were John
Brown. One day in my research in the archives I found out that Ellsworth's
family and the Brown family were distantly related through the Loomis line.
Paternal ancestors of both John Brown and Edgar Birge Ellsworth had
married Loomis women from Windsor, Connecticut—thirty miles from
Torrington, where both Browns and Ellsworths had lived.[9] The detail introduced the chance of a connection. Was it possible that the town somehow
needed them both, and what did that even mean?

5.

I attended all the sesquicentennial events for Harpers Ferry in Hudson and Akron in 2009 and witnessed the controversy they stirred in Summit County residents. People in the public light were careful to choose words that had no edge to them when they discussed it. The wrong words about John Brown could set a community afire to this day. Just saying his name could be incendiary.

Hudson Library & Historical Society was incredibly circumspect, but their sponsorship of a commemorative for John Brown still caused controversy among Hudson's citizens.

On April 5, 2009, the *Hudson Hub-Times* ran a letter to the editor with the heading, "Is John Brown Tribute Appropriate?" The letter read:

> I wonder how many in town are appalled at the display honoring John Brown at the library. Religious extremism, whether in the 19th or 21st century, resulting in the taking of innocent human life, should not be acceptable in any age. Acts of terrorism should not be justified, regardless of the justice of the cause. I wonder if the town of Hudson would have a parade and display in honor of Osama bin Laden if he happened to be born or raised in this city. What has happened to simple humanity? [10]

The letters kept coming—into the *Hub-Times*, into the library—and people were upset.

I couldn't tell if people who objected knew about the specifics of John Brown's abolitionist acts. No one mentioned Pottawatomie or Bleeding Kansas, so I assumed they were protesting his attack on the United States armory and arsenal at Harpers Ferry. Some were annoyed about a scholarly panel being formed to discuss John Brown's role in history, and others by an exhibit in the foyer that focused on difficult details of his life. More than anything, I thought, people probably weren't happy that taxpayer dollars were being spent to place in the spotlight a Hudson man they still viewed as a threat.

Other residents felt that what John Brown did was justified and necessary, so they wrote rebuttals. One person countered the attack that John Brown was a terrorist this way: "Harper's Ferry was not an act of terrorism, but a matter of civil disobedience that galvanized a just cause. We would not have a country if it were not for acts of civil disobedience. Thus, I believe the writer's comparison of John Brown to Osama bin Laden is akin to comparing George Washington to Timothy McVeigh."[11]

Biographer Louis A. DeCaro Jr., who was scheduled to be a panel member at the Hudson Sesquicentennial, responded to the debate from his home in New York City: "No figure in US history is more slandered, misrepresented and misapprehended than John Brown... Hudson should be proud of John Brown, and no apology is necessary for celebrating his life, labors, and sacrifice."[12]

No encounter I'd had with John Brown had been entirely free of trouble, including Hudson's attempt to remember one of its own.

A member of the library's board of directors and the library director herself tried to ease tension in the community, sending another letter to the *Hudson Hub-Times* that read, "Our organization is neither celebrating nor condemning the raid, and we do not take a position on whether John Brown was a hero or a villain. We are simply marking an anniversary of an event which, regardless of how it is interpreted, was significant in our nation's history. Scholars throughout the United States and around the world are marking this 150th anniversary in various ways and taking the opportunity it affords to reassess the role John Brown played in the abolitionist movement."[13]

"Regardless of how it is interpreted," the letter read. The title of the Hudson Symposium—"Hero or Madman?"—reminded everyone that the controversy remained alive. Other sesquicentennial symposia across the country were titled "Famous/Infamous Abolitionist John Brown" and "Hero or Terrorist?" Two words accompanied by a question mark, so people always had a choice.

6.

On Sunday, April 28, 2013, I headed to First Congregational Church for the 10:30 a.m. service. I wasn't a member, but Gwen told me that the Men's Ensemble would be performing John Brown's favorite hymn, "Blow Ye the Trumpet," a tune he sang to his young children. A descendant of John Brown would be attending. From 1903–1966 in Hudson and Kent, the John Brown Family Association had sponsored annual reunions, but now I had to look for other opportunities—like this one—to meet descendants.

A newspaper article soon followed that advertised the event. John Brown was richly described, but with his customary epithet included—"controversial abolitionist John Brown." When was it, I asked myself, that abolitionists crossed the line and suddenly became "controversial"?

It so often came down to the matter of violence. History had come to respect nonviolent Black revolutionaries like Frederick Douglass and Martin Luther King Jr. or white abolitionists like William Lloyd Garrison.

But John Brown? He remained "controversial," and even liberal historians and biographers expressed reservations about him, just as Hudson's citizens had. It felt awkward sometimes to acknowledge the ambivalence of the town, but in many ways I shared it. I was as uncomfortable with John Brown's vicious actions as others were.

The newspaper story explained that the music was intended to be part of the worship service, "not a John Brown historical tribute."

First Congregational Church, built 1865

I knew I needed to hear the song and meet John Brown's relative—no, that I wanted to do both those things—so that cool Sunday in April I walked up the steep hill that led to a great door under a segmented stone arch.

Dedicated in 1865, the Romanesque church on Aurora Street was still John Brown's church in a way. It was the youngest descendant of the log house on the Green that had been a school but also served as a meeting place for the church. John Brown did not live to see the 1865 church, but he did see the other two. He became a member of First Congregational Church in 1816 when it stood on the Green, and he took two vows in the church on the corner of my street—a marriage vow to Dianthe Lusk and his famous vow in 1837 to destroy slavery.

Mary Buster, John Brown's great-great-grandniece, was sitting in a pew beside Tom Vince. The minister introduced the congregation's guest before the performance, and people swiveled around in their seats to look at her. I could hear the whoosh of fabric as they turned—the seasonal sound of crisp cotton and polyester.

Thirteen men sang in the ensemble. Their volume rose on the word *blow*, and soon singers' lips became metal valves and trumpet bells, sending sound back toward the farthest pew.

I hurried from my seat and down the aisle after the service ended, but no line had yet formed to receive Mary Buster. Tom Vince and I stood alone with her. She told me that she was a retired sixth-grade science teacher from Emporia, Kansas, as she welcomed me into her pew. After her Hudson visit, she said, she was going to Oberlin for another John Brown event. She was kind and easy to talk to.

The music director at the church had been quoted in the local paper: "Some have even gone so far as to say by today's standards, he would be called a terrorist... but you won't hear that from my lips." He was proud of the day, and proud of his association with the church. "To serve at the church where John Brown was is amazing," he said.

Mary Buster also had been interviewed before she arrived. John Brown, she told the reporter, was "a very non-violent man." She added, "His violence can be contained in less than three days of his entire life, but it's what people choose to remember... The more I read about him, the more proud I am of him."[14]

Her comment felt defensive when I read it, as if she thought others saw her relative with a perpetual black eye and she wanted to be the one who explained how he got it. When she spoke with me in the church about her life in Emporia, I couldn't help wondering if she thought that I, too, was demanding an explanation. Maybe I was.

7.

Even in an audience composed of members of the SUVCW (Sons of Union Veterans of the Civil War) and its sympathetic public, there were still suspicions about John Brown. Tom Vince spoke to the group at Cuyahoga Falls Library in Summit County, where several programs to commemorate the 150th anniversary of the Civil War were being sponsored. His subject was "Abraham Lincoln and John Brown."[15] I'd felt quite alone when I'd first noticed similarities between the two historical figures, but suddenly I didn't anymore.

Men dressed in Union uniforms, interspersed throughout the crowd, sometimes had medals in rows across their chests. One pin, I could see, displayed the name of the organization on the top bar, just above some brightly-colored ribbons. The present association had been the former GAR (Grand Army of the Republic), but members of that group had to prove that they were direct descendants of Union soldiers. The Sons of Union Veterans did not. The only requirement was genuine enthusiasm for all things Civil War and Union.

Sitting among men attired like those in the room unsettled me, a woman so uncomfortable with uniforms that she'd quit the Girl Scouts so she wouldn't have to wear one.

The men were calling each other "brother," and this made me feel even more like an outsider. Fraternal service organizations always seemed so strange to me when I was growing up. Once I accompanied my father-in-law to a Rotary meeting as his guest in Cannon Beach, Oregon. On the program was Miss Oregon, and the men in the room were not exactly interested in what she had to say.

Thomas L. Vince speaking at Sons of Union Veterans of the Civil War meeting. (Courtesy Nick Zaklanovich and Allyn Marzulla, videographers)

At the meeting in Cuyahoga Falls, I tried to set my biases aside. I had almost no experience with male service organizations, and certainly none with a military cast, so I knew it was important to be still and listen, even if my thoughts were rumbling.

There was a man in the room who wore a T-shirt with Abraham Lincoln in aviator sunglasses on the front, and other people with Lincoln lapel pins on sport coats or the collars of their shirts. Tom Vince himself wore a tie with portraits of Union generals.

I imagined a reversible tie with Abraham Lincoln on one side and John Brown on the other. It amused me to think about how people could decide each morning which surface of the tie to expose, depending on their mood. I almost mentioned this to Tom as I moved closer to see if there were any generals that I recognized, but I hadn't heard his remarks yet and wasn't sure he'd be amused.

We were asked to stand for the Pledge of Allegiance, which surprised me, but it shouldn't have. The SUVCW was a deeply patriotic group, and one of the principles of its mission was teaching patriotism, good citizenship, and pride in the flag.

Public patriotism, I knew, was something I needed to work on. The matter had been troubling me for years. I didn't seem as patriotic as other people in my town, though I thought I loved my country just as much as they did, and sometimes I thought I loved it more. I was young during Vietnam, and maybe I grew up a little too suspicious of the United States because of the Vietnam War and because of what happened at Kent State on May 4, 1970. I was on campus that day, a graduate student nearly as young as the undergraduates who died in gunfire. I lived, and they didn't. Memories of tanks rolling down Main Street, helicopters flying over our house at night, and dead students lying in a parking lot might have led to my reluctance to display a flag.

Or perhaps I knew I hadn't taken enough time to think the matter of patriotism through and didn't have a right to fly a flag until I did. It wasn't that there weren't examples of patriots in our family.

My father served in WWII and my uncle Paul received an award from his community of Firestone Park in Akron for flying his flag every day for fifty years. I often asked my uncle why he devoted himself to this small task, but he never answered me. He just smiled and continued to fold and unfold his flag in the natural way his fingers taught him to.

I couldn't be sure exactly what drew each man to the Sons of Union Veterans, or why some wore Union uniforms and hats and others, civilian dress. But I'd already made up my mind that at least the men in Union jackets had loved playing war and painting tin soldiers when they were boys and still enjoyed donning uniforms to add drama to ordinary life.

The brother at the podium called for a camp prayer. It began with gratitude for the men in blue. Tom Vince was then introduced and commended for his work on a PBS special called *A Trumpet at the Walls of Jericho* about Samuel Harrison—a man who'd attended Western Reserve College in Hudson in 1836 and served as chaplain in the famous Massachusetts 54th Regiment during the Civil War, the first all-Black infantry unit whose history was the subject of the film *Glory*.

Tom Vince didn't mention the physical resemblances between Lincoln and John Brown when he finally took the podium, nor did he say anything about John Brown being on Lincoln's mind when the President-elect spoke at the Hudson depot. But why would he? Those were just possibilities in my imagination.

He'd spent time turning up parallels between them of other sorts, some of them familiar, and some new.

Both were reared on the Western frontier; both were admired by William Dean Howells; both were self-educated (though Owen Brown sent his son for a short time to Morris Academy in Litchfield, Connecticut); both were Whigs for a while. Both were opposed to slavery. Both served briefly as US postmasters in the 1830s; both rose to national prominence in the 1850s. Both had wives named Mary who became financially destitute after their husbands died, but eventually received some compensation—Mary Todd awarded a pension in 1869 and Mary Ann Brown helped by Haitians, who greatly admired John Brown, and by private donors. Both Lincoln and John Brown devoted themselves to family and were loving fathers; both lost children; both died tragically.

He spoke about important political intersections between the two. Lincoln opposed the Kansas-Nebraska Act of 1854, which created the territories of Kansas and Nebraska, as well as the policy of letting settlers decide if slavery would be allowed within the new borders (the Act denounced in his famous "House Divided" speech), and John Brown fought in Kansas with his sons to help make Kansas Territory free. George L. Stearns, father of Henry and a member of the Secret Six—the group of prominent aristocrats who supported John Brown's militarism, five from Boston and one from New York— held an Emancipation Proclamation party at his house on January 1, 1863, where he unveiled a bust of John Brown sculpted by Edwin A. Brackett.[16] I later found a letter in the Hudson archives from Mary Ann Brown to Mrs. Stearns, written on January 7, 1863, containing a moving postscript: "P S God bless Abraham Lincoln and give God the glory for the day of Jubilee has come."[17]

Finally, both men traveled in their coffins on funeral trains, trips I'd already imagined had begun with their departure from the Hudson depot on Railroad Street.

That's where Mr. Vince stopped, because there was nowhere left to go.

The official in charge, one of the men in full uniform, said there was time for a question or two.

I'd sat in rooms where John Brown was the subject before, and the questions about him always felt scripted. I guessed that Tom Vince, from all his decades speaking to groups, was probably already feeling discouraged by the body language of some of the people in front of him—the tight jaws, the fingers flicking up and down on twitching thighs, the eyes half closed or beaded, as if aiming through a gun sight right at him. People who asked questions about John Brown were often adamant about something, or annoyed. They'd made up their minds before they entered the room. They weren't angry at Tom, and he knew that, but he still must have dreaded what lay ahead.

I saw him take a drink of water. He placed his free hand on the podium and held on.

The official stepped toward Tom and called on a man with a high, firm arm, fingers sewn together in a pledge, as if his bones had fused.

The man stood and spoke calmly, in a polite voice. His question was rhetorical—expressed softly, but full of hard certainty. "Do you think we make a mistake in honoring John Brown the way we do?" He didn't wait for a reply. Instead, he brought up Pottawatomie. That word was often the first one to leave people's mouths at gatherings like this. The man briefly summarized the event on the creek—the dismemberment of five proslavery men in Kansas with broadswords by John Brown's company (his sons Owen and Salmon two of the murderers), men taken from their cabins in the middle of the night. He spoke repeatedly about the swords and the deadly wounds. Then, after providing sufficient graphic detail, he reminded the group that the first casualty at Harpers Ferry, again at the hands of John Brown's men, was a free Black man—the train porter in town. He knew the trouble spots in the John Brown story and headed right toward them. "Wasn't it more than slightly ironic," he asked, "that John Brown, a man fighting for the freedom of Black people, began his raid by killing a Black man—and one who was already free?"

Poor Tom Vince. He had just a few seconds to find some brief retort that would satisfy people and also cause the man to pull back a little and sit down. "Remember to put Pottawatomie in context," he told the man. "Think of all that was going on," he said, "and remember that John Brown maintained it was retaliatory." The man was still staring at him. "It was, after all, called Bleeding Kansas for a reason," Tom said. He smiled uncomfortably and shifted his glance.

The Union officer called on someone else, but trouble stirred again.

A woman spoke this time. She stood and cleared her throat. "It's just wrong that he was so unsuccessful at business, but still goes down in history for abolition." Many biographers had touched on this common complaint, but it didn't bother me as much as the matter of violence. Tom Vince urged the woman, as he had the man, to remember the context of the nineteenth century. "There were no social safety nets," he said. "If a business failed, there were no government subsidies." John Brown, he explained, was not less successful in business than other men from Hudson. "People just assumed there would be periods in their lives when they'd be broke," he said. "They hoped they would recover, and they lived on hope."

I sat there as he spoke, thinking about John Brown and the idea of hope. In spite of disasters as great as Job's, John Brown never abandoned hope. He did eventually relinquish the idea of having property and wealth—the American dream that propelled James W. Ellsworth—but never abandoned the hope that all people could be equal. There was a price to be paid for that kind of hope, though, and not everyone agreed what it was. For John Brown, the cost was blood. His own, and that of others.

The Union officer stopped the questions and asked if he might have a final word. He was still standing near Tom Vince, but he moved a little closer to the audience now. I anticipated the worst. Some grand patriotic gesture.

But it wasn't that at all. He'd been listening while people asked questions and wanted to reply. This man in full Union regalia was a brother, speaking to other brothers, so the audience would have to pay attention to whatever he said. He could preach to them in a way Tom could not.

"Don't let the slavery issue become invisible," he said. "Slavery" was a word he knew Civil War enthusiasts often avoided.

He paused for a minute, but then talked again. "Think about the number of people who died in bondage and what was being done to them."

I could tell he was speaking to the man and the woman who had just asked questions, but he was also speaking to all his SUVCW brothers, and he was speaking to me.

"Never, never take that part out of the equation," he warned.

NINETEENTH-CENTURY OHIO NEIGHBORS

William Lloyd Garrison, ca. 1870.
(Courtesy Library of Congress)

Oswald Garrison Villard. (Courtesy
Boyd B. Stutler Collection of
John Brown, West Virginia State
Archives)

I.

I never had to ask the Man Who Avoids Me Now what he thought about John Brown, because he looked me in the eye and told me. But what had his nineteenth-century Ohio neighbors thought of him? If I read the town's old buildings for clues, shouldn't I also listen to John Brown's neighbors, if they'd spoken about him?

The Hudson Library & Historical Society held a treasure I couldn't resist— the detailed interviews of Katherine Mayo with John Brown's Ohio neighbors. It was the nineteenth-century equivalent of an audio tape. Mayo was the fearless research assistant for Oswald Garrison Villard—editor of the *New York Evening Post*, civil rights activist, a founding member of NAACP, grandson of William Lloyd Garrison. Villard's biography of John Brown, which incorporated Mayo's interviews, was published in 1910 and became the gold standard for all future John Brown research.

Villard sent Katherine Mayo to Ohio in 1908 and 1909 to sit in living rooms and find out what local people thought and knew about John Brown. His contemporaries would soon begin to vanish, but many were still alive during the years of Mayo's visits.

The interviews, along with other early sources that contained comments from his Ohio contemporaries, did not provide the whole truth about John Brown. There was gossip and rumor mixed in, but that was to be expected, and welcomed, in a way. I'd lived in small Ohio towns almost my whole life and knew what rumors sounded like. I knew there was a kind of meaning that

Henry Thompson, married to John
Brown's daughter Ruth. (Courtesy
Boyd B. Stutler Collection of
John Brown, West Virginia State
Archives)

rumors could best relay.

I also had to remember that Katherine Mayo had biases and was drawn
to sensational details about John Brown's life. Her viewpoints might have also
been influenced by Villard himself, the son of a puritanically moral mother.

I knew a degree of bias always intruded on research (or interviews), and I
began to wonder about any I might have.

Katherine Mayo was obsessed with Pottawatomie, for instance. She found
out that John Brown's daughter Ellen wouldn't agree to an interview, so she
wrote a letter to Villard and told him, "I would cheerfully have Pottawato-
mied her on the spot, with all the paternal calm & godly satisfaction." Discovering she'd be able to interview Henry Thompson, husband of John
Brown's daughter Ruth, she told Villard, "There is Mr. Thompson *a Pottawatomie participant!*"[1] It was as if she'd spotted Mephistopheles in Kansas. Katherine Mayo's disgust for what John Brown did on the creek was often on full
display, and it wasn't much different from Villard's, or, I was forced to admit,
from my own at times.

She also pressed people to confirm her own suspicion that John Brown
was an abusive spouse to Dianthe Lusk, his first wife who, like him, grew up

Banker's lamp in Hudson archives

in Hudson. Katherine Mayo wrote about the brutality of male sexuality later on (among other uncomfortable subjects), and the topic of male aggression may have already burrowed into her brain when she took on John Brown.

In spite of her shortcomings, the time she spent with John Brown's family and acquaintances as a young reporter resulted in her finest and most lasting contribution to literature. Everything else she wrote was eventually disparaged, and historians sloughed it off—often embarrassed by it.

She prowled the streets of Hudson and adjacent towns like Kent and Ravenna, sometimes staying an extra day or two if an interview spilled over or if people were struggling to retrieve memories and needed more time. She must have been a very patient woman, I thought, or just ravenous to find things out. Or was *patience* just a kinder word for greed?

The day Gwen brought the Ohio interviews out to me in the archives, I turned on the banker's lamp at the table where I sat, opened a box and then a folder inside of it, and began to read.

2.

George A. Griswald, a student at Western Reserve College in 1830, often saw John Brown at his house. Griswald told Katherine Mayo that his father, Abraham, was an Underground Railroad conductor, and that he, George, was the only student at the college who subscribed to the first issues of William Lloyd Garrison's *The Liberator*, though Professor Wright also did. George Griswald and Professor Wright were among the fifty white subscribers of the magazine's first five hundred.[2] George said this about John Brown: "We always considered him quite a nice man...I do not believe that he [John Brown] was not honest, or not kind to his wife."[3] I heard in his replies the questions Katherine Mayo asked.

Abner Caldwell, married to the daughter of Julia Lusk, Dianthe's sister, said that he admired neither John Brown's "judgment or his sanity," but he "had never heard it suggested, by any member of the family of his wife that any doubt could be cast upon John Brown's probity... [or] that John Brown failed in kindness to Dianthe."[4] Katherine Mayo was there once again.

Charles Lusk, son of Milton, the abolitionist brother of Dianthe, heard his father say that John Brown was not insane. Charles believed him. Whether or not John Brown was crazy was something people have talked about from the beginning of his "fame." After John Brown's sentencing on November 2, 1859, for what he did at Harpers Ferry, nineteen affidavits were gathered from Ohio acquaintances and family of John Brown in hopes that clemency would be extended to him if insanity could be proved.[5] It appeared that Katherine Mayo had brought up the subject of his mental health, aware there still was no consensus. Charles, a janitor in the public schools during his working years, called John Brown a "peculiar character" who had a "fiery temper," was "obstinate," but "absolutely truthful"—"as honest as the day is long." Charles kept stressing that the Lusks were abolitionists and said that Hudson's Harvey Baldwin, one of the men who signed an affidavit testifying to John Brown's insanity, "was a pro-slavery man." Katherine Mayo later interviewed Mrs. Lucy Lusk, and she said that Charles was an old Union soldier and saw John Brown "in a haze of romance."[6]

Mrs. Porter Hall, Owen Brown's stepdaughter by his third wife, remembered seeing John Brown every Sunday when he and his four sons walked two miles to church from their Hudson farm. She said that Owen Brown "was a great friend to Negroes, and used to take in every one that came along." She told Katherine Mayo about a time she visited John Brown at the Perkins farm he occupied in Akron on her way back from Oberlin. They were "living very poor," she said. She believed that John Brown "was an honest man," but that he and his brothers caused their father "financial trouble." The brothers were speculating in land in nearby Munroe Falls, as she remembered it, and Owen Brown agreed to be their undersigner. When the banks failed, he lost his farm. She felt sorry for Owen because of this, and because of his boys, but I wondered if her reactions might have been complicated by her relationship to Owen. She said that John Brown was more radical than his father and she thought the end John Brown came to "would have killed [Owen], had he lived to know it."[7]

E. O. Randall, grandson of Heman Oviatt—the first mayor of Hudson after the village was incorporated in 1837 and a man who repeatedly loaned John Brown money—recalled that even when John Brown failed to repay his grandfather Heman or disappointed him in other ways, Heman Oviatt never found moral fault with John Brown because he "thought him a visionary—a dreamer." E. O. Randall was nine years old when John Brown was hanged. He remembered that on the morning of the execution, his mother "broke out in an impassioned prayer for John Brown." This made a great impression on E. O., "for," he said, "such an act was very unusual."[8]

Ransom M. Sanford, who lived on Streetsboro Street next door to Jeremiah Root Brown—John Brown's much younger half-brother who married Abi Hinsdale—spared no criticism. He felt the affection that John Brown's children showed their father was uneven. "It used to be said that the girls liked to have him around, but that the boys—did not." He also had opinions about John Brown's marriage and was eager to answer Katherine Mayo's question about his abusiveness. "John Brown was not a model husband. Never heard that he beat his wife, but he was known to be very unkind to her. He was severe and abusive to his family… He treated Dianthe like a slave." Ransom Sanford had no difficulty going on about this. "It was not merely the austere manner of the time. It was real, abusive severity." He made sure to tell Katherine Mayo that Jeremiah opposed Harpers Ferry when John Brown talked with him about it just before the raid, implying that even his own brother thought he had come undone.[9]

John Brown was described as "not quite sane" and "very excitable" by Robert W. Thompson, who had lived in Hudson on land next to the John Brown tannery since 1835 and whose father had served as administrator of Owen Brown's and John Brown's estates. John Brown sold his tannery to his brother Oliver, who then sold it to his brother Frederick. "People spoke ill of him in connection with the Chamberlain affair," he added. "No one whatsoever approved of his course in that."[10] The Chamberlin Affair, as I'd soon understand, led to his brief sentence in the Akron jail,[11] and to his bankruptcy—possibly the event the woman at the Sons of Union Veterans meeting was alluding to when she said John Brown was "unsuccessful at business."

Christian Cackler, born nine years before John Brown, worked for Owen Brown gathering hay as a boy, and, later, for John Brown himself, building turnpike roads when they both lived in Franklin Mills (now Kent). Cackler, who moved with his family to the southeast corner of Hudson from Pennsylvania in 1804 and then to Darrow Road, finally settled in 1816 with his new wife in Franklin Township. He wanted to correct the glowing tribute to John Brown in a biography by James Redpath, so he told unflattering stories about his Hudson acquaintance in *Recollections of an Old Settler* (1874), a slim book of memories about Cackler's early years in the Western Reserve that rightly belongs with the interviews.

One of those stories concerned the way John Brown treated his stepmother Sally Root Brown. Christian Cackler said that John Brown and his brother Salmon (the second Salmon, born in 1802) tried to blow up Sally Root Brown in the outhouse with gunpowder, but the plot was discovered by a hired man named Loomis. After the failure of his Gunpowder Plot, young John Brown tried to dispose of his stepmother another way. He replaced long boards in the hayloft with short ones, and his stepmother fell through when she tried to collect some eggs, dropping fourteen feet to the barn floor, where John Brown's sister found her "lying insensible and badly hurt." Salmon and John Brown often got in trouble together. Christian Cackler suggested that this was why Owen Brown sent Salmon to Pittsburgh—to separate the two. There, Salmon became a lawyer, ending up in Louisiana—where he also edited a bilingual newspaper called the *Orleans Bee*—until his death in 1833 from yellow fever.

And what of John Brown's brand of abolitionism? Christian Cackler always found plenty to complain about, with language that matched his mood: "When he came home (from a European trip in 1849 to sell his wool) he said he didn't respect the laws of our country; neither Congress that made them, nor the President that executed them. He became a perfect outlaw, and would sacrifice home, friends, or his country to gratify his will for the nigger."[12]

The son of Christian Cackler—Christian Cackler Jr.—didn't know John Brown personally. During his interview with Katherine Mayo, he repeated the stories his father had told him, including the saga of John Brown trying to blow up Sally Root Brown. He did say that his father was a War Democrat, not believing in "a sudden liberating of the slaves" but objecting to the separation of families, and he did repeat what Marvin Kent had said to him three months before Kent died in 1908: "Your father was right in what he said of John Brown. He was a pretty slippery fellow."[13]

Mrs. Johnson Bartshe, the daughter of another of John Brown's half-brothers, was interviewed by Katherine Mayo in her home in Kent. She only could tell stories she'd heard her aunts tell, so her impressions were theirs. She'd heard only good about John Brown. Never a syllable about unkindness to Dianthe. She had strong feelings about Christian Cackler's scathing criticisms of her uncle, believing his comments were "inspired by political antagonism." "These things hurt," she said. Katherine Mayo seemed to feel sorry for Mrs. Bartshe, calling her "humbly circumstanced—perhaps not 'poor.'"[14] Mayo often made notes like this in her interviews, or sometimes added a postscript.

Amelia Hobart, the daughter of Levi Blakeslee—John Brown's adopted brother, who worked with him at the Hudson tannery John Brown built—remembered how worried John Brown was when he lived in Pennsylvania. Fearing he might be consumptive, he entered into an agreement with Levi to place his son Jason under Levi's care should John Brown die. I hadn't known he was ill in New Richmond, Pennsylvania, but he was and, in fact, arranged for every child of his to be placed with a friend or relative. Amelia recalled the story of a runaway slave coming to the house and tannery of John Brown on

Chapman Road, and of John Brown motioning him through the window to hide when they heard horses nearby. John Brown searched for him after the horses passed. "I found him behind a log," he said. "I heard his heart beat before I reached him. At that I vowed eternal enmity to slavery." Amelia Hobart said the story came from Ruth Brown, John Brown's daughter, but Amelia passed it on. I'd also read an account of it by John Jr. The story had entered John Brown lore. Her father, Levi Blakeslee, was an abolitionist, Amelia said, but Katherine Mayo added a note correcting this. He belonged to the Colonization Society. Amelia also said that Ruth Mills Brown was, in her father's opinion, a far superior woman to Sally Root Brown—"a model wife and mother, one of the best women that ever lived"—and that Sally Root had once kicked Levi while he lay on the floor with a headache, so he held her foot.[15]

Dr. Andrew Willson, the Congregational minister in Ravenna at the time Katherine Mayo interviewed him, said he could call on only what he'd heard "the best of the old settlers" say about John Brown. It was Dr. Willson's conclusion, since he knew Christian Cackler quite well, that Christian Cackler was both more honest and more enterprising than John Brown—a "sterling" gentleman, he called him.[16]

Lora Case was John Brown's disciple, in every sense. No title seemed more important to him than being the friend of John Brown, no honor greater than receiving the final letter John Brown wrote from his jail cell. In his book about old Hudson, he remembered the "mild way" John Brown expressed his opinions, as well as his strong belief "that it was more to give than to receive." The way John Brown angled his head or body—not the volume of his voice—indicated to Lora Case how passionate he was. The day John Brown prayed at the Hudson meetinghouse in 1837, vowing publicly for the first time to destroy slavery, "it was his calm, emphatic way" that Lora Case admired. He even liked knowing that he and John Brown dressed alike: "For a necktie we both wore a piece of morocco leather to hold up our shirt collar called a stock, and we both wore buckskin pants with leather suspenders."[17]

From the age of fourteen, Benjamin K. Waite lived with Milton Lusk, John Brown's brother-in-law. "John Brown was spiteful—revengeful as the devil. And conceited! But people rather liked John, around Hudson. He was looked upon as an honest man—with nothing particularly wrong with him," he said. Like Lora Case, Benjamin Waite had been a student in John Brown's

Daniel Woodruff as a young man. (Courtesy Hudson Library & Historical Society)

Sunday School class and knew details about John Brown's life. He repeated the story of John Brown trying to blow up his stepmother and added that his thrashing for the deed took place on Brown Street, near the family tannery. "John Brown," he added, "was not a hunter." He told about John Brown's jealousy of Milton, for John Brown's sons would talk to their uncle before they talked to him.[18] I tried to imagine John Brown's heart with jealousy in it, suffering from the distance his own sons both caused and needed.

C. H. Buss, son of merchant John Buss, said he heard his father call John Brown "a d—d rascal, in a business way." Heard him tell a story about John Brown refusing to pay a promissory note at the Buss Store that was overdue, unless, John Brown said, it could be paid at his "convenience." The Buss Store was Hudson's chief general store, and John Brown often purchased items there—almost always on credit. John Buss was headed to a lawyer's office after John Brown refused to pay the note within six months, but his partner at the time, Edgar Birge Ellsworth, took the note and paid it himself.[19]

Henry Myers, along with his son D. W. Myers, spoke to Katherine Mayo about the visit of John Brown in 1854 (or 1855) to the house of Colonel Daniel Woodruff, Henry's father-in-law. The two men spoke with Mayo about details John Brown had shared with the colonel concerning Harpers Ferry, and about his hope that the colonel would help train and command his troops. John Brown needed a man like Colonel Woodruff, he said, but the colonel told him he was too old. At the end of the seven-page interview, the subject changed to the Chamberlins. D. W. Myers, the son, said that he never knew anyone in Hudson "who spoke otherwise than well of John Brown save only the family of Chamberlin."[20]

What D. W. Myers said wasn't exactly true. The complaint the Chamberlins had with John Brown had been voiced by others.

3.

Attacks on John Brown for his treatment of Amos Chamberlin came mainly, though not exclusively, from neighbors who weren't especially fond of him. Still, it seemed significant that so many people Katherine Mayo interviewed mentioned the affair. In addition to comments by D. W. Myers and Robert Thompson about what came to be called the Chamberlin Affair, John Whedon, the town druggist, said John Brown "behaved very badly,"[21] Ransom Sanford said he "cared nothing for any law,"[22] and Christian Cackler said John Brown ordered one of his sons "to shoot Chamberlain, but the boy refused."[23]

People who faulted John Brown at the turn of the twentieth century for the Chamberlin incident might have felt history was on their side. Sentiment for John Brown changed once Reconstruction ended and Jim Crow stepped in. The days of John Brown being considered a martyr and hero were numbered, and biographers would soon walk onto the stage to interpret him as murderer, madman, thief—sometimes all three. But even though the shift in history might have played a role in people's reactions to the Chamberlin Affair, I wasn't convinced that the disgruntlement so many neighbors expressed was unfounded.

The episode involved the loss of Westlands, John Brown's beloved farm that straddled Hudson and the town of Twinsburg, an adjacent community north of it.

John Brown returned from Pennsylvania to Franklin Mills in 1835 to build a tannery for Zenas Kent. His wife, Dianthe, had died in New Richmond, so when he came back to Ohio and the Western Reserve, he brought with him

Mary Ann Brown (née Day), his new wife. The John Browns lived in a small rented house in Hudson when they first returned but before long moved into the Haymaker farmhouse, about eight miles away, which sat on 92.5 acres of land in Franklin Mills. He'd bought the property from Frederick Haymaker as part of a larger real estate venture, but he also owned Westlands at the time, purchased in 1838 through a loan provided by the Western Reserve Bank of Warren and secured in large part through a promissory note John Brown had signed to Heman Oviatt. He moved his family back and forth between the two properties for a few years.

Both farms became sources of financial ruin for John Brown. According to neighbors, Westlands also ruined his reputation. That interested me far more than numbers on a ledger sheet.

Westlands foreclosed and was auctioned off to Amos Chamberlin on October 12, 1840, at a sheriff's sale. What John Brown did next surely no one had predicted. He armed himself and his sons in a belligerent effort to keep the property that was legally no longer his. Along with sons Owen and John, he turned a little cabin on the farm he didn't own anymore into a "fort" and pointed rifles through holes he and his boys drilled in the logs. To say that the weapons and the "fort" caused concern among Hudson citizens would be to greatly understate the matter.

John Brown Jr. said later that they had only an old shotgun that wasn't loaded or ever pointed at anyone.[24] Other accounts recorded the incident differently, saying that John Brown and his boys aimed muskets at the new owner, Amos Chamberlin, and drove him off "their" farm each morning when Chamberlin arrived to pasture his stock.[25] John Brown sued Chamberlin for trespassing, but, of course, he was the true trespasser and rightfully ended up in the Akron jail.

The displeasure in Hudson over John Brown's handling of the Westlands affair continued. Harlan L. Trumbull, who had lived downtown just one street over from me, wrote a letter as late as 1971 about the acreage involved in the 1841 court case. The Trumbull family purchased a piece of the property on Middleton Forbush Road in 1935, nearly one hundred years after John Brown originally bought it. Harlan Trumbull said that while John Brown and his sons were in the Akron jail, Amos Chamberlin hitched his team to the "fort" and pulled it down. "The caved in cellar under said hut is all the evidence that we have to show," he wrote.

Marker to family of Amos Chamberlin,
Markillie Cemetery

He still sounded angry in the letter, pitying the "trusting souls" who were treated "unscrupulously" by John Brown. He criticized John Brown for his "consistently poor performance"—by which I assumed he meant John Brown's business practices. To Harlan L. Trumbull, the Chamberlin standoff was proof that John Brown had "a violent record even as early as 1841, that was to exact the lives of half of his offspring as well as his own."[26]

John Brown's treatment of Sally Root Brown also came to mind when I read Mr. Trumbull's words. Didn't his "violent record" extend even farther back than the 1840s? Were violence and rage inside him all along?

To be fair to my neighbor John Brown, I would have to think this through.

4.

Was there any other way to understand what John Brown did those Chamberlin days in Hudson, any way at all?

His business indiscretions even before the Chamberlin Affair were nearly impossible to enumerate.[27]

John Brown borrowed money all the time and seldom paid his debts (not even for a yoke of cattle, as Christian Cackler pointed out). According to his son John Jr., John Brown said that his tendency to do business on credit kept him "a toad under a harrow most of [his] business life,"[28] an image impossible for me to forget. Wouldn't I, too, have been happy, the way many of John Brown's Hudson neighbors were, when the sheriff arrived, found that toad, and hauled him off to the Akron jail?

He divided up the acreage of the Haymaker property into plots for a land speculation scheme. But he wasn't able to forecast the financial crisis of 1837. Nor could he predict the fate of a canal scheduled to cut through Franklin Mills—east-west, connecting Ohio and Pennsylvania—which would secure the future of the location. The Pennsylvania and Ohio Canal ended up going through Akron instead, north-south, a political shift that affected the water's course, as well as the course of John Brown's life.[29]

He tried to steady himself during the Panic of 1837 amidst a world toppling in on him. Wanting desperately to pay off creditors who kept pressuring him, he traveled to Connecticut, Boston, and New York, leaving his family behind. To make money, he grasped at any scheme or idea he could—he bred racehorses, formed a cattle company with Tertius Wadsworth and Joseph Wells of Connecticut, bought wool for George Kellogg (a New England wool agent). He spent money that new partners gave him and then found himself in even greater debt.

In April of 1840, just six months prior to the loss of Westlands, he contracted to survey land given to Oberlin College in western Virginia by Gerrit Smith, another aristocrat who became a member of the Secret Six, along with George Luther Stearns, Samuel Gridley Howe, Franklin Sanborn, Theodore Parker, and Thomas Wentworth Higginson. John Brown found a site on Big Battle Creek where he intended to relocate his own family. He submitted his reports, and on August 11 was deeded the thousand acres he had surveyed, but he didn't accept the offer until January 2, 1841. Perhaps his tardiness was due to his involvement in the Chamberlin crisis, but his delay caused the college to have a "change of heart" and retract the deed.[30]

Offer after offer was withdrawn from John Brown the "businessman," but, as far as I knew, he'd never behaved as badly when it happened as he did during the Chamberlin Affair.

The last page of the interview with Henry and D. W. Myers contained information that initially had looked like a postscript—two brief versions of a story that provided background to the high drama of the Chamberlin tale. Good business was central to the security of pioneer towns, just as it's central to a town's security now. But what I found by returning to the interview was not just about business, but something else.

Version One. John Brown's story was that he went to Amos Chamberlin for help, asking him for a loan to save Westlands from being sold or foreclosed. Chamberlin supposedly said, "No, I won't do that, but I'll go and bid the house in, if it goes at a reasonable sum, and you can give me the sum and take the house." John Brown accepted the offer eagerly, assuming that Chamberlin, his boyhood friend, would keep his word, and went to secure the money. When he returned, Chamberlin would not release the farm or admit they'd made a deal.

Version Two. Amos Chamberlin's story was that the episode John Brown described never happened. No bargain was struck.

Mr. Myers told Katherine Mayo "no one ever thought that John Brown spoke falsely," tacitly casting his vote, it seemed to me, with the interpretation John Brown had provided of the Chamberlin Affair.[31] I looked for a letter confirming that he'd made an agreement with Amos Chamberlin prior to the sale of the property, but had no luck. In Villard I did find one written by John

Brown to Chamberlin after the confrontation at the Westlands farm—composed in Hudson, Ohio, on April 27, 1841, as he tried to avert further legal action Chamberlin might take against him following the October disaster.

In his April letter, John Brown asked Chamberlin to remember their childhood friendship. He was deeply regretful of his poverty, he told Chamberlin, mainly because his creditors would not receive the payments they were owed. Without the farm, he couldn't pay them. He knew he was responsible for everything that had happened—he never claimed otherwise—yet Amos Chamberlin was not without some blame in John Brown's eyes.

That was something I wasn't ready for. How could a man so humbled by his circumstances, and so willing to confess his own fault and error, make such an assertion?

John Brown told Chamberlin that he remained "your honest, hearty friend." He claimed to be happy for his prosperity and professed to feel no envy at all for his good fortune. He asked for charity, perhaps pity, even, but in an accusatory manner that was rarely coupled in my imagination with shame or regret.

"And now I ask you why will you trample on the rights of your friend and of his numerous family? Is it because he is poor? ... Will God smile on the gains which you may acquire at the expence of suffering families deprived of their honest dues? And let me here ask Have you since you bid off that farm felt the same inward peace and conciousness of right you had before felt? I do not believe you have."[32]

He wasn't begging, exactly, but preaching. Being Hudson's Sunday School teacher still. Was he just saying what was in his heart, or trying to induce guilt in the only way he had left? Was his letter manipulative, or sincere?

It was difficult to tell.

Did Amos Chamberlin feel his conscience pricked? That was another thing I'd never know, because there was no record of a reply. The lawsuit Chamberlin was planning, and which the letter tacitly alluded to, apparently was dropped.

John Brown expected more from his friend than Chamberlin was willing to give, more from townspeople than they thought he had a right to, more from the business community than it considered "fair."

"Will God smile on the gains which you may acquire at the expence of suffering families?" The words unsettled me as I traveled back.

5.

Heman Oviatt kept losing money every time he supplied John Brown with any, but he didn't give up on him. He initially helped him buy the Westlands farm, but also paid off his $6,000 note, a tremendous sum that allowed him to keep the property a little longer. Although John Brown never repaid him and treated him badly in the whole affair, Oviatt stood by him, even while he prosecuted John Brown in court.

As impossible as it seemed, as inexplicable, after the Westlands debacle Heman Oviatt would be the one to employ John Brown in Richfield, Ohio.

Perhaps he felt sorry for him and for the suffering his family had gone through in a way that Amos Chamberlin could not. Maybe he was able to accept the hard version of friendship that John Brown demanded. For whatever reason, he refused to condemn him and gave him another chance.

Oviatt seemed to like having money and property, so his sympathy confused me. Even though he was a deacon of First Congregational Church, he refused for two years to donate land he owned down the street from his Hudson house on East Main so a new church could be built;[33] for a while he had the only general store in the sixteen townships that later became Summit County, where he traded liquor for pelts of buck, bear, beaver, and otter;[34] he formed partnerships with several men in the Kent family and kept opening new stores; he quarreled and fought with other men in town who interfered with his finances—like abolitionist William Dawes, a distinguished member of the community who was a merchant, a fellow church member, an employee of the College, and a

Captain Heman Oviatt House, East Main Street, built 1825

delegate to the World Anti-Slavery Convention in London. He drove Dawes out of town.

Heman Oviatt could occasionally be a generous man, surprising people sometimes. He endowed a professorship of sacred rhetoric at Western Reserve College, and, during the process of moving from Hudson, deeded his farm of 114 acres to the college, including his house on East Main Street—a structure that the college in turn deeded to the pastor of the Congregational Church in 1840 and that served for several years as the Hudson Young Ladies Seminary.

Perhaps John Brown was just one of those exceptions he made, one of his fortunate chosen beneficiaries. Yet there was a difference here. Unlike the college, John Brown had done little to commend himself to Heman Oviatt. What was his unexplainable appeal to Hudson's first mayor?

I tried to imagine Heman Oviatt and John Brown standing on the threshold of Oviatt's house in Richfield, a house Oviatt moved to in the late 1830s that's still there. I could hear John Brown expressing his desire to work for Oviatt now that he'd lost Westlands and all his money and had nowhere to go because the Oberlin lands had fallen through in Virginia. He would ask if he could tend Oviatt's property in Richfield and care for the sheep of Nathaniel Oviatt, Heman's relative.[35]

A materialistic man like Oviatt surely would want something from his debtor the day he called. Perhaps it was John Brown's exceptional skill that

Heman Oviatt House (built 1822), Richfield, ca. 1920. (Courtesy
Richfield Historical Society)

appealed to him. He was already known in the area for his keen knowledge
of wool. In a few years, he began speaking at wool-growers' conventions in
Ohio, writing for *Ohio Cultivator* and other farming journals, even discovering a treatment for sheep nose bot flies.[36]

John Brown's eyes graded wool with quick certainty. Just by touching an
animal he could tell its breed and origin. A friend of his told a story about a
man who tried to fool John Brown during the trip he took to England for
Perkins & Brown to sell wool. A sample of poodle hair instead of sheep wool
was handed to him for identification, and he recognized immediately that the
fibers lacked the tiny hooks which connected natural wool. "Gentlemen," he
said, "if you have any machinery that will work up dog's hair, I would advise
you to put this into it."[37]

Heman Oviatt, who had been recruited from Connecticut in 1801 by
David Hudson, would also have known that John Brown was a very good
tanner. He'd built three tanneries already, owning and operating two of them.
The third, the one he built in Franklin Mills for Zenas Kent, he never got to
run because Zenas Kent rented it to his son Marvin Kent even before the vats
were placed in the building.[38]

Or perhaps Heman Oviatt thought of himself as a visionary, the way he
had thought of John Brown, and sensed this connection between the two of
them. After Oviatt died in 1854, his family began the Oviatt Manufacturing

John Brown Tannery built for Zenas Kent. (Courtesy Hudson Library & Historical Society)

Company that later made patented inventions—Oviatt's thresher and separator, the common sense wagon, and a special sled known as an independent runner.[39] He may have been imagining the invention of technologies in the tanning business when he hired John Brown, or a new breed of sheep.

But maybe it was something else he wanted from John Brown. Something he had that Heman Oviatt couldn't name, but knew he needed. Perhaps John Brown's refusal to give up in the face of paralyzing loss? How much would that be worth, if he could have it?

Did Oviatt admire John Brown's resilience, his ability to advance and always move forward, in spite of everything?

John Brown was often sorrowful, but seldom despondent, and before long, there he was again, standing on a neighbor's doorstep asking for work. His whole life he remained hopeful, through the days of his stay in the Charles Town jail cell. It's likely that Heman Oviatt wasn't entirely sympathetic with the version of democracy John Brown was beginning to stare at off in the distance, but I do think, especially as a man growing into old age, he might have seen in John Brown the kind of hope he knew he would soon require.

No one personified hope better than John Brown did.

Heman Oviatt invited him in, agreed to his proposals, and the two began to talk about a Richfield tanning partnership and small sheep industry, which they later formalized in an agreement drafted in January of 1842. Oviatt would bring "hides and calf skins of a good quality," the contract read, and John Brown would "finish them in a neat and workmanlike manner." His labor would be applied toward the cancellation of the enormous debt he owed his employer.[40]

A debt he would never repay.

Soon John Brown moved his family to Richfield, just eleven miles west of Hudson. He built a tannery there, as he'd promised, a quarter mile north of West Streetsboro Street on what's now US Route 21. And he tended a flock of sheep, exactly as he'd said he would. But what happened during the Richfield years even a visionary couldn't have predicted.

LOSING ALMOST EVERYTHING IN RICHFIELD, OHIO

I.

Bankruptcy occurred a year before the true sorrows arrived, and John Brown and his family probably thought the worst was over the day the courts intervened.

On September 28, 1842, John Brown was officially discharged from debt by becoming a pauper and a bankrupt. Judge George B. De Peyster, the federal agent assigned to settle the estate, left John Brown and his family only the essentials they needed to survive in Richfield, where their new life was beginning. They had little when they walked into the courtroom, and less when they walked out.

The Brown family, a total of twelve when they moved to Richfield, was permitted to keep some of their possessions, but the items on the John Brown Bankruptcy Inventory were few. I thought of a family the size of John Brown's trying to survive an Ohio winter with five coats, four blankets, two candlesticks, five pair of boots, and one basket of dried apples.

I pictured John Brown and his sons as they worked to repair a house, build a tannery, run a farm, and shear sheep with just one of each tool the judge held back for them: one shovel, one pair of shears, one crow bar, one plow, one hammer, one saw, one pitchfork, one plane, one branding iron, one harrow.

They were permitted to keep eleven Bibles, volumes titled *Beauties of the Bible, Church Member's Guide, Flint's Surveying, Dick's Works* (the writings of the Reverend Thomas Dick, who died two years before John Brown was executed), thirty-six volumes of school books for the children, and Ball's nar-

rative (the account of Charles Ball, an enslaved African American from Maryland, published in 1837).[1]

In October of 1842, John Brown wrote to George Kellogg, Esq., an agent
of the New England Woolen Company—another person he owed money
to—and called himself "a bankrupt in the District Court." He signed it,
"Respectfully your unworthy friend," and mourned "the destitute condition
in which a new surrender of my effects has placed me, with my numerous
family."[2]

Bankruptcy caused John Brown great shame, though what happened to
him wasn't unique in the century, as Tom Vince had said at the meeting of Sons
of Union Veterans. Samuel Fowler Dickinson, grandfather of Emily Dickinson, became a bankrupt in 1833, a fate that strangely led him to Lane Theo-
logical Seminary in Cincinnati, Ohio, and then to the position of treasurer at
Western Reserve College in Hudson, opened by the firing of William Dawes
from the school.

It would take me time to realize that bankruptcy—losing the world in a
material sense—was a kind of metaphor in John Brown's life. Dreams of personal wealth began to fade for John Brown, allowing the wish for American
democracy to take its place, though he regretted his debt to others the rest of
his life.

Even in his jail cell he remembered his creditors and put them in his will.
He hoped to pay $50 to several people he was in debt to, like poor George
Kellogg, but he stipulated that the money would have to come "out of the final
proceeds of my Fathers Estate."[3] He had no estate of his own by the time he
died, so John Brown's will wasn't worth much more than the paper it was
written on. Even the Bibles he requested be purchased—with money from his
father's estate—were not delivered until 1864. They were taken to the family
farm in North Elba, where the Browns no longer resided.[4]

He must have thought he'd lost everything in 1842, but in 1843 John
Brown was about to lose much more.

2.

I didn't know exactly why John Brown moved his family to that third house in Richfield on West Streetsboro Road during the short span of years they resided in the town, but I had an idea why he moved from his first house to his second—the one located behind George Wilkinson's Green Valley Market on what's now Route 176.

The first house they lived in was a whitewashed log house on Route 21 near Brush Road.[5] No amount of lime on the walls, it seemed to me, could remove the stain of the horrors that visited the Browns there. Was this the reason they left? I might not have had the vitality to consider moving to a second house. Instead of packing up, I may have prayed for Death and waited to hear his scythe scrape the cabin floor.

They lost four children in twelve days. Even a stranger's heart, like mine, pumped with dangerous pressure at the thought of it.

Death was common in a nineteenth-century home, of course. John Buss, who ran the store near the Green and grew tired of giving John Brown credit,[6] kept a daily diary for over forty years, beginning in 1834, and wrote about death matter-of-factly. Death was a familiar visitor to his pages, and it wore me out to read about it all the time. The entries were usually emotionless, and always brief, and I wondered how John Buss could keep such a tally, not much different from notations in a ledger book about items he needed to restock his shelves.

There was always a funeral sermon being preached somewhere, a deadly outbreak of scarlet fever, the "last child" being buried after an epidemic. John

John Brown's third house in Richfield, photo taken 1959. (Courtesy Richfield
Historical Society)

Buss constructed single-sentence obituaries almost daily: "Mrs. Hotchkiss
buried—died in Milwaukee"; "Daniel C. Gaylord died—of a fit"; "Old Mr.
Farrar died, 75 years old"; "David O'Brien's wife died—suddenly"; "Old Mrs.
Lighton died." Page after page of it. "Four deaths in one week" in September
of 1859, a note about Benjamin Waite burying a daughter, mention of the sister
of Mrs. Harvey Baldwin "killed in a runaway," an entry that "Mrs. H. Coe
died," a cryptic line that "Mrs. J. Bishop cut her throat—still alive."

    After Harpers Ferry he said, "The history of John Brown at Harper's Ferry
fills all our papers with the history & events that are and have been transform-
ing for some time." The day John Brown was hanged on the gallows, John Buss
penned two lines: "John Brown was hung to day at 11:14 oclock... It created
a great sensation all over the whole country."[7]

    It was the nineteenth century, for heaven's sake, and people expected to
wake up dead even on sunny mornings, and in every season.

    John Brown had lost two sons and a wife in Pennsylvania, even before
coming to Richfield, and once there, four more children in a matter of days,
but I knew I couldn't prepare myself for this much death just by reading John
Buss' diary. I would drive with my husband to northwestern Pennsylvania to
find the children who had died in Crawford County, along with Dianthe—
their mother—in hopes that seeing the first graves would somehow prepare
me for those that came after.

3.

A few things remained from John Brown's Randolph Township–Crawford County days on Tract 1432, twelve miles northeast of Meadville: the foundation stones of the second tannery John Brown built and the graves he left behind.[8] The post office changed the name of John Brown's town from Randolph to New Richmond in 1935.

John Brown left Hudson in May of 1826 with his wife, Dianthe, and their sons, John Jr., Jason, and Owen, completely on his own for the first time. His new home, on 200 acres, was less than a hundred miles from Hudson. It was in this new place that he held the position of postmaster, surveyed for roads, built a free-standing schoolhouse, organized wrestling matches, served as a lay minister, became the region's librarian, and conducted political debates.[9]

Situated on a road now named for him—John Brown Drive—the foundation wall of the tannery was nearly intact, taller than I was, with holes where windows and doors once had been. The original tannery was built into the side of a hill, like a bank barn, making the foundation wall a structural event—beautiful fieldstone lifted and mortared by John Brown's hands. Eighteen tanning vats once stood inside the space where I was standing. I knew that while John Brown was clearing the land across the road for a house and a barn, and even afterwards, his children sometimes slept in the tannery. It was a place of both blood and innocent sleep, and the way these things stood so easily together surprised me.

I never would have found the graves alone. A guide named Donna who lived on the grounds led us there the Memorial Day my husband and I came to

John Brown tannery in New Richmond, destroyed by fire in 1907. (Courtesy
Hudson Library & Historical Society)

Remaining foundation stones of John Brown's tannery in New Richmond,
Pennsylvania

visit. The markers were behind the site where the John Brown house had once
stood. A wooden sign shaped like a thin arrow with the word "Cemetery" on
it was nailed into a tree at the end of a little path Donna herself had cut through
the forest. I turned the corner and saw the graves in an open field of wildflowers, weeds, and prickly grass. John Brown's son Frederick was there—his first
Frederick, who was born in New Richmond in 1827. A sickly child, Frederick
died in 1831 at the age of four—so ill during his lifetime that the Browns named
a second son born in New Richmond "Frederick" before the first was even dead.
A year after the death of their first Frederick (and two years after their second
Frederick was born), Dianthe herself died giving birth to a baby boy, who also
did not survive and went to the ground unnamed.

There were two headstones and two footstones. "In memory of Frederick,
Son of John and Dianthe Brown. He died March 31st, 1831." Beside him was

Frederick's gravestone in New
Richmond, Pennsylvania

Gravestone of Dianthe Lusk Brown,
New Richmond, Pennsylvania

Dianthe's stone. "In memory of Dianthe. Wife of John Brown. She died Aug.
10th 1832. Aged 31 years. Farewell Earth." In 1954 members of local and state
lodges of the Improved Benevolent and Protective Order of Elks of the World,
a Black organization for uplift and fellowship, laid a wreath on Dianthe's grave.[10]

Donna talked about her. "The ladies of New Richmond dressed her in
her wedding dress on her burial day. Her baby boy is in her arms. She was
strewn with lavender, and placed in an oak casket," Donna said. I imagined
sprigs of lavender spilling from their hands onto Dianthe's body and was
moved by the tribute of the New Richmond women who must have loved her.

In June of 1833, after all the deaths, John Brown married a spinner named
Mary Ann Day (just seventeen), and in May of 1835, moved back to Ohio with
his second wife and a baby girl already born to them, Sarah—as well as all the
children of Dianthe who were still alive. Mary Ann Day Brown would bear
twelve more children, and of the thirteen that would be hers, she'd watch nine
of them die.

4.

On September 14, 1842, Mary gave birth in Richfield to a son named Austin, who would join Sarah, born in New Richmond, and brothers Watson, Salmon, Charles, Oliver, and Peter, all born in Hudson or Franklin Mills. Annie would arrive next, born in December of 1843, just three months after Death's visit to the Richfield house.

The tiny two-room cabin they lived in, set in the middle of a grove of walnut trees, was named North Lodge, and even John Brown's Richfield neighbors recognized the irony of that. A single door was set in the middle of the cabin, one window to either side, and a chimney on the south end. Hardly a lodge at all.[11]

In September of 1843, four small bodies—all under the age of ten—were moved from that tiny home to a rise on a hill a half mile away, a hill not yet named Fairview Cemetery, but already waiting for the dead.

Did I really think that traveling to New Richmond to see headstones from an earlier time would help me understand this? If I did, I couldn't have been more wrong. The theme of losing a child was not one you could ever prepare yourself for. And the theme of losing several children was untranslatable.

"In the dust" is the way John Brown described the place his three young sons and daughter Sarah came to rest. In the same letter that contained these words, a letter he wrote to John Jr., who was attending school at Grand River Institute at the time, he called the disease that took his children "pestilence" and "Dysentery";[12] biographers have commonly called it *dysentery* too. Fanny

Mason Oviatt, 1809–1850. (Courtesy
Richfield Historical Society)

Fanny Abia Carter Oviatt, 1810–1886.
(Courtesy Richfield Historical Society)

Oviatt, the woman who helped nurse the Brown family through this horrifying event, supposedly called it "black diphtheria."[13] Perhaps it will be impossible to ever know what bacterium found and claimed the children, or whether
it lodged in lungs or intestines, but they were far too young to go up that hill.

According to Richfield sources, Sophie Sheldon, a neighbor known in the
community for her nursing skill, traveled to the cabin of the Browns when John
Brown came knocking. She rode toward the sick family in a buckboard beside
her father, bringing with her a bottle of thyme mixed with syrup that "had
saved many a croupy child."[14] But it couldn't save the Brown children she cared
for over the next twelve days, even when she held a tea kettle of hot water close
to their noses to help them breathe.

Charles, just five years old, died on September 11—the first death. The
family buried him in a grave of his own, probably dug with the shovel left to
them in bankruptcy—buried the boy in a coffin built by John Brown from
boards he found. If I'd been there, I would have seen what others saw that day:
a horse pulling a mud sled down the road and then up a hill to the burial spot,
a minister from the Congregational Church who stayed a safe distance and
only said a few words, and rain spilling in rills toward lower ground and dripping off trees.[15]

The Browns might have thought they were setting grief aside when they turned to walk back to North Lodge. But Death exacted a higher price. Austin celebrated his first birthday one week before he died on September 21st.

Even before they had time to prepare the baby for burial, Peter died, on the 22nd. He hadn't yet turned three.

Three children were dead before Fanny Oviatt (married to Heman Oviatt's nephew Mason) came to relieve Sophie. Sarah, nine years old, born in New Richmond, died in her care the night she arrived—September 23. A new Sarah was born three years later in Akron. There were two Sarahs, two Ellens, and two Fredericks in John Brown's life because his children kept dying, but there was not enough time for the Browns to have a third Frederick to replace the second (killed in Kansas) nor a second Watson or Oliver to replace sons who died at Harpers Ferry.

John Brown told John Jr. that the three children who died last "were all buried together in one grave." He said they rested now "in a little row together."[16] I didn't know if he dug the second grave, so ill himself, but I imagined that he did. I saw him climbing the hill, the shovel even heavier in his hands, his heels sinking in mud as he came closer to the top of the rise and the first grave he had just closed.

Fanny Oviatt supposedly took such strict precautions in her own home that none of her eleven children became ill during the epidemic, but her pity for other children who were stricken was as great as if they had been hers. She emerged a hero in Richfield lore. After sending Sophie home with orders to burn her clothes and scrub herself before going inside, she turned to Mary Ann Brown and said, "My husband Mason didn't want me to come but I said to him, 'Mason Oviatt, what would you think if it was our children sick and no one to help?'"[17]

Eunice Merton, the writer who recorded Jennie Oviatt's memories of her grandmother Fanny and of Sophie Sheldon in *The Gristmill*, wrote her account as a "dramatization" and never apologized for a certain amount of embroidery, so it was difficult to know exactly what detail was added by which narrator. It was certain, though, that Fanny Oviatt and Sophie Sheldon helped nurse the sick and dying children of John Brown when he lived in Richfield, and that was what mattered most.

5.

We went west out of Hudson on Streetsboro Street, drove for eleven miles, and arrived in Richfield to look for John Brown's dead.

We turned north on Brecksville Road and entered Fairview Cemetery. I'd read on the website that it was established in April 1845 by a gift of three-quarters of an acre made by Orson M. and Lucretia Oviatt to the trustees of the First Congregational Society. It wasn't a big cemetery, but subsequent acreage had been donated since the initial Oviatt gift.[18] When the Brown children died, the cemetery was no more than a craggy bump on the top of a hill.

I didn't have to look hard for the stone, the way I sometimes did in cemeteries. The oldest stones were on the top of the rise. They didn't shine at all in the sun, they had no glaze or color, and I knew I was going to have trouble reading them even before I left the car. A sign at the edge of the drive told visitors what was permitted here and what was not. Decorations could remain no longer than fifteen days. Containers must be unbreakable. No flowers could be picked. "Participation in any activity other than in reverence to the deceased, shall be deemed a misdemeanor."

What was the activity I was engaged in today? Was I here because the quick sequence of deaths of four children in one family was incomprehensible to me? Did I think the ground could explain something that my brain could not? Was I tempted to commit a "misdemeanor"—the act the sign warned against—perhaps stay all day and then, in twilight, summon ghosts?

Marker at entrance to Fairview Cemetery, Richfield

The gravestone was several feet high, perched on a piece of granite that it seemed to be soldered to. It listed the names of John and Mary Brown's four children, in the order that they died. Many of the other words were faded and hard to read. I was greedy to make them out.

I couldn't read "Charles," the first name at the top, but I felt the *C* and the *H* with my finger. After each name, age and date of death were listed, but barely visible. I could read "Austin" and then "Peter" and "Sarah," and a little of the line below, "Children of John & Mary Brown," but the inscription near the ground—near the rough-hewn pedestal—had disappeared long before I found this place, and little remained except a single clear *a*.[19]

The tall stone stood under a thick umbrageous tree that looked as bent and squat as an old man. Other stones near it—some covered in moss, some stark white—rested against the tree, nestled like napping children in its expansive folds. I wondered if this old tree, which showed no sign of giving up its guard on the hill, could have been alive when John Brown brought his family to Richfield.

God, of course, not trees, remained what John Brown stared at fixedly in the face of his latest tragedy. "God has seen fit to visit us with the pestilence," began his letter to his son John Jr. "This has been to us all a bitter cup indeed, and we have drunk deeply, but still the Lord reigneth and blessed be his great and holy name forever." Jason's note to his brother, written below his father's words, was a refrain of John Brown's: "The Judge of all the Earth, has done,

Gravestone of the four children
John and Mary Brown lost in
Richfield in 1843

and will do right. But let us give glory and honor and power and thanks unto him that sitteth on the throne forever and ever."[20]

What else was there to say? John Brown could have sworn, but he didn't swear, except to occasionally utter, "By the Eternal God,"[21] which probably sounded more like an oath than profanity when it blew from those hard, reed-like lips of his.

REVERIE 2
"SOME CAN BEAR MORE THAN OTHERS"

I.

Had I traveled to Richfield to discover how John Brown became stronger than Job, how he'd turned unimaginable suffering into strength? How a person could bear this kind of weight—push and pull up a hill a cart filled with so much loss, full to the brim with their own blood?

Somehow even faith didn't seem enough to explain his extraordinary capacity to recover from harm that would be fatal to the rest of us.

When Mrs. Rebecca Buffum Spring, a wealthy Quaker abolitionist and founder of utopian communities, visited John Brown in his jail cell after Harpers Ferry, he supposedly told her that he knew he was capable of enduring greater hardship than some. "There seems to be just that difference in people; some can bear more than others, and not suffer so much." He believed that it was "a constitutional difference" that allowed for this. He also mentioned that he'd been "trained to hardships," and seemed to credit the combination of these two things for any courage he had.[1]

This matter of "constitutional difference" seemed especially relevant. It had an almost contemporary feel, consistent with science that was exploring how the brain prepares our decisions before we even make them.

"Trained to hardships" sounded true as well. Expecting life to be difficult cancels out some of the disappointment people feel when turning a sharp bend and teaches them how to brace against the wind more skillfully. I've sensed that as I've grown older, but I know I'm not made of the hardened steel John

Brown was. His life had been heated to such a high temperature that he never wore out over time. Nothing, and no one, could file him down.

When some alarm goes off now, my body moves into action, and my heart grows steadier than it did when I was young, yet I worry that I'm exhaustible, that this last thing will use me up. Unlike John Brown, who remained ready— almost eager—for the next assault, I feel increased despair each time a new horror summons me, and I fear collapse. John Brown? He succumbed to great grief at times, but recovered, then moved on. Hope always prevailed in John Brown and helped him turn failure and loss into action.

He rode it out, all the way to the gallows.

MOTHERS AND SONS

Hudson Female Seminary on Baldwin Street. (Courtesy Hudson Library & Historical Society)

Emily Metcalf. (Courtesy Hudson Library & Historical Society)

I.

Another Ohio neighbor—Emily Metcalf—invited me inside the boyhood cabin of John Brown on the edge of the Hudson Green. Before I found her description, I thought Metcalf's main accomplishments were composing two historical papers for the occasion of the Centennial Anniversary of First Congregational Church and serving as principal of a Female Seminary on Baldwin Street.[1] But a detail she included—a small stroke that made Ruth Mills Brown more real for me—also secured Emily Metcalf's place as a historian of Brown family history.

I'd read so little about John Brown's mother that, initially, I almost dismissed her. John Brown is seldom associated with women, anyway. A man's man if there ever was one, I thought. Biographers frequently mentioned his mother's early death in 1808, along with Owen's remarriage within a year to Sally Root (the stepmother John Brown tried to blow up with gunpowder), and a few talked about Ruth's devout religious faith, but little more than that was ever said of her.

Yet my trips to the burial ground up the Hudson hill felt personal, somehow, and made me want to know other details about Ruth's Hudson life and, especially, her life with her son John Brown—her first son to live beyond the age of one.[2]

Ruth Mills Brown died long before John Buss began keeping his daily journal, so I found no entry about her there.

Some biographers mentioned the string of ministers and patriots who were part of her old New England ancestry and the source of her abolitionist roots. Ruth's father, Lieutenant Gideon Mills, an officer in the Revolutionary War, was the son of Rev. Gideon Mills, minister in West Simsbury, and the cousin of Rev. Samuel John Mills (born 1743), a well-known Congregational minister who was trained at Yale, preached in Torringford, Connecticut, for over sixty years, insisted Black congregants enter his church by the front door, and was known as "Father Mills" by everyone. Torrington was only a few miles away from Torringford.

Edwin W. Mills, a descendant of the Mills family, believed it was likely that the young John Brown heard Father Mills preach. Edwin Mills also said that Father Mills was thought to have been the model for Harriet Beecher Stowe's minister in *A Minister's Wooing* and was "the hub of the abolition sentiment that developed in that part of the country long before the Civil War was dreamed of." His son, Rev. Samuel John Mills Jr., though a colonization-ist, actively opposed slavery.[3]

The interior of Ruth's cabin, the detail that Emily Metcalf preserved in one of those historical papers of hers, may have reflected her ancestry, but it also was a sign of her own compassion—becoming, over time, a symbol for her heart.

It was anatomy writ in wood and candle wax.

In a letter written to a cousin from his Charles Town jail cell, John Brown remembered something he had learned very early that he felt accounted for the happiness and prosperity of his life. His cousin, a minister who lived in Windham, in Portage County, Ohio (about twenty miles west of Hudson), had tried to cheer him up, but John Brown wrote to say that he was a happy man in prison, grateful for the life he had led, and not ashamed in any way by his current circumstances or the fate that awaited him. "I have enjoyed much of life as it is: & have been remarkably prosperous; having *early learned* to regard the welfare & prosperity of others as *my own*."[4]

The cabin of Ruth Mills Brown was probably where John Brown "*early learned*" this lesson. Its structure, like its architect, literally bore the shape of the Golden Rule.

"In Mrs. Brown's cabin, which stood on the corner where Grimm's store now stands," Emily Metcalf wrote, "there was a little chamber on the wall with a bed and table and a candlestick."[5] Emily Metcalf could not have seen what she had described, born after the cabin had been torn down, but people she knew in town apparently had, and she recorded what they said.

The phrase "chamber on the wall" sent me running. Though I had no way of confirming such a structure had existed, the phrase had weight. There was a headstone, the cones from the spruce tree, and, now, perhaps, the chamber on the wall. Remnants of Ruth from her days in an Ohio town.

What was it, though?

I went online and was routed to a drawing by William Blake called *A Vision: The Inspiration of the Poet*, or *Elisha in the Chamber on the Wall*. I had seen it before—somewhere in a book or a gallery, perhaps. It was a beautiful picture in sepia tones of a deep room (almost surreal) that contained, yes, a chamber on the wall.

Why did I have to wait for John Brown before I returned to a drawing this beautiful?

It was 1819 or 1820 when William Blake drew his chamber on the wall—years the Owen Browns may still have been living in their cabin.

On the back wall of the room in the drawing a little interior house had been built—a house within a house, a sort of nesting house of decreasing size, but not importance. Of course the chamber couldn't have been as deep in the small house of the Browns as it appeared in the drawing. Blake was a symbolist, and the Browns, Connecticut realists and Ohio pioneers.

Blake's chamber had three walls. One of them, the back wall, was the actual wall of the original house (in the case of the Browns, it would have been an interior wall of their cabin); two added walls jutted out from it, creating a "chamber." There was no wall or door on the front face of the newly created space. I guessed a curtain would be hung to provide privacy, if Connecticut missionaries stopped for the night, and as Emily Metcalf explained, "were wont to turn in thither."[6] There was a little gabled roof erected on the front of the chamber (so appropriate to Western Reserve architecture, I thought), and inside the room formed by the new walls, a table, a stool, a mat that could serve as a bed, and a candlestick.[7]

Sitting at the table was Elisha.

I only knew who it was because of the title the drawing is commonly known by, but I couldn't identify the second figure—slender, gauzy—standing against a side wall. I'd heard the story of Elisha in Sunday school, but had forgotten almost all of it, so after returning to Blake, I returned to 2 Kings.

A Vision: The Inspiration of the Poet (Elisha in the Chamber on the Wall), by William Blake (© Tate, London 2018)

Elisha had been given bread by a Shunammite woman. Every time he passed her house, she offered it, and he took it. She knew this was a holy man who came to visit her and eat her bread, so she said to her husband, "Let us make a little chamber, I pray thee, on the wall; and let us set for him there a bed, and a table, and a stool, and a candlestick."[8] Emily Metcalf would have known the story, as would the Browns and other Congregationalists in town.

After the room was built, Elisha stayed in the chamber whenever he passed the house of the Shunammite woman. The woman's generous care led Elisha to ask how he could repay her. He offered to speak about her to the king or a captain, offered to elevate her position in society, but her reply was simple: "I dwell among mine own people."[9] And so he chose a different kind of reward for her, making it possible for her to bear a son. One art critic suggested that the Shunammite woman is the second figure in the drawing, and that the drawing represents the moment when Elisha announces the news to her that she'll conceive.

The son became ill and died, so Elisha was summoned to the house by the woman, and he stretched his whole body over the boy, and the boy sneezed seven times and opened his eyes. The favor had been returned, and the boy, restored.

At the center of Ruth's modest cabin was a structure exactly like the one the Shunammite woman had created—to the detail. "A bed and a table and a candlestick." Those were the objects Emily Metcalf reported. It was not random, not a coincidence of words. This was the cabin of the Calvinist Browns, and the woman who maintained it was Ruth Mills Brown. As small as the cabin must have been, strangers passed through Hudson and were always taken in.

The community cherished her. Emily Metcalf called Ruth "a woman of strong judgment and elevated Christian character."[10] Owen Brown adored her. He learned shoemaking and met Ruth Mills for the first time in Wintonbury in 1790, where he was working as a cobbler, and he loved her immediately, and loved her, it seemed, for the rest of his life. In his *Autobiography*, Owen Brown spoke sweetly about his first meeting with Ruth, calling her "the choice of my affections ever after."[11]

They married when George Washington was beginning his second term—had married that long ago—and moved from one Connecticut town to another, and then finally to Ohio, participating in the settlement of the West. In every community where he and Ruth Mills lived, they were kind to their neighbors and did them many favors. Among those neighbors were Native Americans from the Cuyahoga Valley who asked for help building a log house that would function as a fort against their enemies. Owen Brown helped them construct it, and they stayed until 1812.

Forty years and two wives later, Owen Brown had not forgotten his first wife and her tragic fate. Ruth gave birth to Sally on December 9, 1808. The infant died just hours after she was born. Ruth died just hours after that. Owen Brown remembered December 9 as the day that his "earthly prospects appeared to be blasted." He swore to his daughter Marian Brown Hand that when he thought of Ruth's death, of the days of affliction that followed it, of their poor children motherless, he found little comfort from the passing years: "this sean allmost makes my heart blead now,"[12] he wrote to her, barely literate, but not in the ways of the heart. John Brown also wrote about her loss. In the 1850s, both father and son spoke about Ruth Mills Brown as if she'd died just the day before. In a way, for them she had.

2.

John Brown was only eight when his mother died. His memories of her were probably few, but his grief bound him to her for the rest of his life. He named his first daughter Ruth.

He must have sometimes visited her up on the hill where she was buried in the cemetery behind the family cabin. Maybe he walked to her grave alone at night when he missed her most. If the dead could sense what was occurring above the ground, surely Ruth would have been both comforted and distressed by her son's wish to have her back.

A carved marker at the entranceway to the Old Hudson Township Burying Ground, where Ruth Mills Brown now rests, tells about her death. I read it every time I enter: "Ruth Mills Brown (1772–1808), wife of Owen Brown and mother of abolitionist leader John Brown (1800–1859), was the first burial here." The marker wasn't in the cemetery when John Brown was alive, because he hadn't made history yet, so for a long while Ruth Mills Brown was just like any other tenant.

But a memorial of sorts to her memory did exist even during John Brown's lifetime, and he was the one who constructed it—out of words.

In his curious third-person autobiographical letter written to young Henry L. Stearns in 1857, he called himself a "Motherless boy," as if he were standing outside his own body looking at a small child alone in a cabin or a hayloft, pitying him. Lines about his mother seemed such a curious interruption to his perpetual worry about Kansas and abolition at that time. He

Marker at entrance to Old Hudson Burying
Ground with text about Ruth Mills Brown being
the first burial there

seldom was distracted from his cause anymore.

I was almost certain that children in nineteenth-century Calvinist homes
were taught not to feel too sorry for themselves, even on nights when gloom
filled a house. But in John Brown's letter to Henry, he did feel sorry for the
small boy he once was, and the lines he wrote, born of self-pity, were irresistible because they were so rare.

Her loss also made him feel sorry for the older version of himself, almost
as if being "Motherless" had contributed in some way to later difficulty understanding women. Ruth's death, he told Henry L. Stearns in his letter, "opper-
ated very unfavourably uppon him; as he was both naturally fond of females;
& withall extremely diffident; & deprived him of a suitable conne[c]ting link
between the different sexes; the want of which might under some circumstances have proved his ruin."[13]

In the same letter, he told the story of an enslaved boy he'd met in Detroit.
I wondered if John Brown was conscious of the association he was making
when he positioned his paragraph about losing his mother right before two
paragraphs about meeting the child in the house of a United States marshal.
He was driving his father's cattle to Detroit to furnish meat to soldiers in the
War of 1812, sleeping in graveyards with the great beasts—the only enclosed
space available.[14]

True, he was just moving the narrative along—from the age of eight, when his mother died, to twelve, when he drove the cattle for the war—so the order of the paragraphs made chronological sense. But I suspected it might have been his subconscious connecting things here, as much as his reason.

At age twelve, he saw a marshal beat a Black child with "Iron Shovels." The cruelty he witnessed made him think about "the wretched, hopeless condition, of *Fatherless and Motherless* slave *children*: for such children have neither Fathers or Mothers to protect, & provide for them." I remembered the word *Motherless* from the paragraph above it about his own loss—the paragraph about the "*Motherless* boy" whose "loss was complete & permanent for not withstanding his Father again married to a sensible, inteligent, & on many accounts a very estimable woman: *yet he never adopted her in feeling*: but continued to pine after his own Mother for years."[15]

Even on the day he saw the child beaten with a shovel, he must have sensed, in his own "Motherless" heart, some slight version of the pain enslaved families might have felt when they were torn apart on the auction block, sold to different "owners" in different states during the height of domestic slavery in the United States—at least 875,000 enslaved people taken into the deep and deeper South from the Upper South and the Lower South after slave importation ended in 1808.[16] One historian I would read called these years the "half untold"—the terrifying story of "forced migration."[17]

John Brown could not possibly have known all the horror for the boy in that room, but having suffered the loss of a mother, and now seeing cruelty to a "Motherless" slave child "near his own age," he noticed a change in himself: he'd begun "to reflect."[18]

Witnessing cruelty through the senses altered the course of natural science and of history, as to some degree it altered the course of John Brown's life. Hearing a man who was enslaved scream in Brazil helped shape Darwin's belief in a common ancestor, and that belief, in turn, became the rationale of other abolitionists for equality.[19]

The nation would have to wait for Harriet Beecher Stowe to better acquaint it with the suffering of Black families split by sales at the auction block, but John Brown had already caught a glimpse of it as a boy.[20]

Ruth Mills Brown—through her life, and her death—had helped John Brown recognize what he saw at the marshal's house, and what he would never forget.

3.

I wondered sometimes if any of the homes John Brown lived in, after Ruth's, had a chamber on the wall, built in her memory. I doubted that they did, but soon I realized I was being too literal. Any structure at all that housed "the welfare & prosperity of others," the thing which John Brown told his cousin made him happiest, the lesson he'd "early learned," would be a version of the little nook in his mother's house, wouldn't it? I remembered how, in Emily Dickinson's poem "The Props assist the House," the planks and nails and carpentry of a house (or a "perfected Life") gradually disappeared, "Affirming it a Soul—."[21] That was what a gracious landlord provided.

John Brown wrote repeatedly about the joy of giving to others, and of knowing his family had done the same. In that way, I guess, he wrote about his soul and maybe also about Ruth's. To his wife and children just days before his death, he wrote, "Nothing can so tend to make life a blessing as the consciousness that you *love*: *& are beloved*: & 'love ye the stranger' *still*. It is ground of the utmost comfort to *my mind*: to know that so many of you as have had *the opportunity*; have given full proof of your fidelity to the great family of man."[22] Even his jail cell became a version of his cabin chamber, for there, to the very end, he accepted visits from proslavery Southerners who hated him—with the exception of visits from Southern clergyman, whose hypocrisy he couldn't abide. "I have very many interesting visits from proslavery persons almost daily, and I endeavor to improve them faithfully, plainly, and kindly," he told Mrs. Spring.[23]

He had different chambers as he moved through the country, yet to me they all began to look like some version of Ruth's chamber on the wall. They were sometimes hiding places for fugitives—a haymow in his Ohio barn, secret rooms in other barns, the bank of a stream near his tannery on old Chapman Road, a cave at the bottom of a massive sandstone ledge near Tinker's Creek on what's now Aurora-Hudson Road, secluded nooks of his rented Akron farmhouse, corners of his home or the home of Lyman Epps in North Elba, a dry cistern on the property of his half-brother Jeremiah, according to legend. Or the form of places in Springfield, Massachusetts, where he met with more free Black people than he'd ever known.[24] Restaurants like Massasoit House where everyone gathered; the store where John Brown ran his woolen business and where his good friend Thomas Thomas, a former fugitive from the eastern shore of Maryland, worked for him upstairs as a porter, but downstairs, in the office of Perkins & Brown, as a fellow abolitionist; his sparely furnished house at 31 Franklin Street (formerly Hastings) where he and his family hosted Frederick Douglass for a night and a day in November of 1847, and John Brown tried to explain the idea of establishing mountain strongholds from which invasions to free enslaved people in the South could be launched—and then pleaded for his help.

Later, when he became too dangerous, he was the one who required a chamber on the wall. In lodgings of friends in Kansas and New England after Pottawatomie, across the whole of Iowa during his escape with former slaves he'd taken from Missouri, in the attic room at the Kennedy Farmhouse in Maryland—the property where the raiders gathered in secret to plan their October raid on Harpers Ferry.

There would not be time to fully execute some versions he kept imagining. Caves and forts in the mountains of Virginia, with people who positioned themselves at five-mile intervals on the spine of the Appalachian Mountains and launched new invasions into the South, retreating with freed people to "an independent mountain colony" or "communities in the wilderness," biographer David S. Reynolds called them. He knew about such traditions from studying European warfare and the history of slave rebellions among the Seminoles and maroons, as well as revolutions in Haiti and the West Indies.[25]

Perhaps he could picture a mountain refuge in part because of Ruth Mills Brown. Wasn't it possible, coming from a home like hers? The places he designed were not always as safe or as comfortable as the little nook his mother

31 Franklin Street by Unknown Photographer. (Courtesy of the Springfield
Photo Collection, The Lyman & Merrie Wood Museum of Springfield History,
Springfield, MA)

provided for strangers in her Hudson cabin. The materials he used were often
raw and unfamiliar, and there were seldom gables or candlelight present. Yet
as temporary as some of the spaces were that John Brown prepared for the
shelter of others, they still reminded me of his cabin on the Hudson Green. I
always saw Ruth Mills Brown in the niches of the American landscape that
John Brown carved out.

FATHERS AND SONS

(*Left*) Owen Brown as a young man.
(Courtesy Hudson Library & Historical
Society)

(*Right*) Owen Brown in later years.
(Courtesy Hudson Library &
Historical Society)

I.

I knew from the beginning that I wouldn't be able to talk about John Brown without mentioning Fathers and Sons. How could I? The John Brown story was that story, in so many ways.

There was the story of Owen and his son John Brown, and then of John Brown and his own sons, those born to Dianthe (John Jr., Jason, Owen Jr., and Frederick) and those born to Mary (Watson, Salmon, and Oliver). There were also the stories of John Brown's sons who died before they became men: the first Frederick; the unnamed son who died in Crawford County, Pennsylvania, in 1832; Charles, Peter, and Austin, who all died in Richfield; another unnamed son who died in Akron in 1852 of measles and whooping-cough, only three weeks old.[1] Sons were everywhere—the ones he lost to disease, the ones who grew but were killed in his care, the ones who escaped him.[2]

The Seven Sons of John Brown—that's what I began to call those who survived to adulthood. It sounded almost like a fairy tale, but it wasn't that at all.

We're taught that the influence of a father on a son is great, and that a young man is inevitably shaped by him. But the shape is seldom replication, and the process can result from a complicated working out of acceptance and denial, adoration and rivalry, hatred and empathy, vengeance and self-scrutiny.

There was no formula to rely on for the story of Fathers and Sons. It was always a singular process. It began with Owen, a singular father, and John Brown, a very singular son.

It began with a question: Who was the man who fathered John Brown?

2.

The Browns weren't as wealthy as some of Hudson's other founding families. David Hudson donated $2,142 and 160 acres of his own land to help found Western Reserve College, something Owen Brown was not able to do, but the Browns were still people of considerable means, and they had status in the community.

As forceful as Owen's attitudes about abolition were, being well-liked in Hudson seemed equally important to him. His business, he wrote in his *Autobiography*, "was some what prosperious in most of our conceirns." He was proud of friendships he formed with ministers and with "business People." At times he admonished himself for his pride, pointing to the Biblical lesson in Job—"Job left us a good example loss or gain are momentary things and will look very small in Eternity,"³ but at the same time he was fond of land speculation, of buying and selling.

He bought property and was a builder (as Main Street testifies), but he also was a farmer, a shoemaker, a tanner, a civic leader, and an abolitionist. He wasn't educated, and his prose and letters are full of misspellings and grammatical errors. He had three wives, sixteen natural children, and an adopted child, Levi Blakeslee, whose daughter, Amelia Hobart, was interviewed by Katherine Mayo.

There was a story in Hudson which school historian Frederick Clayton Waite preserved about Owen Brown's wish for his cemetery plot. He had supposedly been asked what, if anything, he regretted at the end of his life, and

Original buildings of Western Reserve College, left to right, President's House, North College, the Chapel, Middle College, South College. (Courtesy Hudson Library & Historical Society)

replied, "Well you know I have had three wives and I hoped to live long enough to marry a fourth so as to have two buried each side of me."[4] Perhaps the story was just rumor, but it felt consistent with what I knew of Owen Brown. His comment didn't seem to be just about aesthetics (the symmetry of his burial ground), but acquisition—what Owen Brown always knew he had to monitor in himself.

Brown Street was eventually named for him. Property gave settlers status, just as it does today, so since the street cut through his land, sometime between 1833 and 1840 it officially became known as Brown—a narrow street just forty feet wide because no one wanted to tear down two buildings that stood on either side of it.[5] A petition to rename the street circulated in 1951. Twenty-nine residents of Brown Street had signed it and presented it to the Hudson village council, asking that the name be changed to Owen Brown Street, although an even earlier petition in the 1920s, never presented, had requested that Brown be named John Brown Street.[6]

Owen Brown was an investor by nature—both in personal property and in Hudson. He was a member of an education society that formed in Hudson in December of 1818, a collection of men whose work led to the founding of the college. A later group, designated by church elders and ministers of the presbytery as Managers of the Education Fund, met on February 15, 1825, to organize themselves as the trustees of "The Collegiate Institution in the Connecticut Western Reserve" and at that time selected three men to act "as a

board of agency to make arrangements for erecting a college building"—
Heman Oviatt, David Hudson, and Owen Brown.[7] Owen never became a
member of the Board of Trustees, as Heman Oviatt and David Hudson did,
but he still played an influential role throughout the early days of the school's
history.

Middle and South Colleges, along with the President's House, were completed by 1830, though only the President's House (now the Admissions
Office) is still standing. But by 1834, Owen Brown had stepped away from his
position because of an irresolvable issue that made it impossible for him to
stay. He was, it turned out, not quite like the other members on the board of
agency.

3.

Owen Brown had another face besides the builder and the businessman— Owen Brown the devout abolitionist.

Other individuals left Western Reserve College about the time that Owen Brown did for the same reason—the abolitionist/colonizationist controversy. Professor Elizur Wright traveled to New York to become secretary of the American Anti-Slavery Society, and Professor Beriah Green became president of a college in Whitesboro, New York. By the time Owen Brown left the school, even President Charles Backus Storrs had vanished. He died in large part due to illness that resulted from his abolitionist fervor.[8]

It might have been Elizur Wright, a mathematician, who initially stirred things up. The school and community were tightly linked then—far more so than they are today—so it wasn't unusual that the college owned one-half interest in Hudson's local paper, the *Observer and Telegraph*, or that the remaining portion was owned largely by college trustees. The abolitionist views that Elizur Wright published (using his initials "E. W.") in Hudson's paper began in July of 1832 and continued through late November. But starting in mid-August of that year, articles opposing Elizur Wright were published alongside his, often initialed "O. C." (probably Oliver Clark, a prominent Hudson businessman and colonizationist). The editor of the paper shut the column down by the end of November.[9]

And why, I wondered, had the local paper stopped running Wright's pieces and the replies, especially since the editor himself had published an editorial in 1831 urging immediate emancipation in the District of Columbia?

Elizur Wright, along with others, felt he'd been silenced at the insistence of the owners of the paper. Trustees had been attacked by national papers for the abolitionist sentiment stirring at Western Reserve College and wanted no more of it. Nearly all of them were colonizationists, and they desired abolitionism to go away and the revenue and reputation of the institution to be restored.[10] Descendants of Elizur Wright wrote a book about their ancestor, saying that "some of the conservative members of the board of trustees felt him to be a firebrand."[11]

Beriah Green, Professor of Sacred Literature, delivered four consecutive and controversial lectures beginning in mid-November of 1832 on the topic of abolitionism, so he was probably also considered a "firebrand." His lectures maintained that "a man finds a brother in every human being" and that a person who was not in favor of abolitionism did not have a conscience. They were published in January of 1833, proving even more controversial in print than they'd been as speeches.[12]

After Owen Brown left Western Reserve College, he was appointed a trustee at the Oberlin Collegiate Institute, fifty miles west—a far better political match for him. However, as a Calvinist, he gradually came to dislike the Perfectionist theology that Oberlin was strongly associated with from 1834 on, as Heman Oviatt also had, finding its "state of sinlessness" little more than what one biographer focusing on John Brown's religious life called "an enthusiastic approach to Christian piety."[13]

He left a second Hudson institution a few years after he left the first because of similar tensions between colonizationists and abolitionists. Owen Brown was a member of First Congregational Church when John Brown took his vow there in 1837 to destroy slavery, but by 1842, Owen was gone, helping to found the Free Congregational Church, the building on the other side of the street from the John Brown Memorial marker.

In the Hudson archives is a letter Owen wrote to his son-in-law Samuel Adair on September 6, 1842—a year after Adair married Owen's daughter Florella. It was filled with worry. "We are in trouble in Hudson," Owen said. "I fear for myself and I pray God to direct me so that I may not bring a reproach on the cause of Christ and I ask your prayers for me and all concerned with me." The "others" he was referring to were members from First Congregational who had made application to be dismissed. At the time the letter was written, there were twelve such people, and Owen anticipated there would be twelve more.

Beriah Green. (Courtesy Hudson Library & Historical Society)

Samuel Adair. (Courtesy Hudson Library & Historical Society)

Florella Brown Adair. (Courtesy Hudson Library & Historical Society)

Why would Owen Brown, a man far more conservative than his son turned out to be, leave the church he loved where Town Hall now stands—a place he had even helped to build?

The week before a commencement at Western Reserve College, the name of a distinguished man and abolitionist who was about to pass through Hudson, a Mr. Mahand, was given to a church official at First Congregational. Congregants who were abolitionists hoped that the official, Mr. Gravenen, would extend to the important man an invitation to preach. But he refused. His decision drove abolitionist members away. Owen Brown housed Professor Mahand and helped arrange for him to preach "five times in the Methodist House, the meetings…very full and sollam (solemn?)."[14]

Not long after this, Owen helped fund and build the Dissident Church on the corner of Streetsboro Street and East Main. It was founded on October 7, 1842, with twenty-one members listed as present at the first organizational meeting. Owen's name was on the membership roster.[15]

Itemized rules followed. On the tenth page, one item in a section labeled "Sundry Principles Rules & Duties" made me stop. It was titled Article 13, and even before I read it, I noticed that it looked different from the other points, attached with sealing wax which covered up a rule on the original document that had been lined out. I stared at it and gently touched the page until I understood what I was looking at. Article 13 was the most important item in the document—entirely about abolition and the church's position regarding it:

Whereon a great portion of the church of nearly all denominations, are withholding their testimony & influence against the Sin of Slavery & oppression & whereon we believe the continuance or Abolition of Slavery depends in a great measure upon a right procedure on the part of Christs representatives on earth, therefore we in assuming to be witnesses for Christ & Cooperators with him in the work of removing all sin from the face of all the earth, establish it as a rule in our Church to receive no one into our communion who is a slaveholder or an advocate of slavery nor will we invite a Slave holding Minister or one who advocates the system of slavery to preach or officiate in our pulpit.[16]

From 1842 to 1849, the Free Congregational Church—also known as the Dissident Church—housed Hudson's most radical citizens, and Owen Brown was among them.

4.

In one sense, Owen Brown was a model for his abolitionist son, but not in all. He was a timid and sometimes fearful man who valued material gain. It couldn't have been easy for him to want both financial security and equality for all people. He was a man who recognized his weaknesses—his acquisitive strain, his insecurity and awkwardness in social settings.

Most of his "failings," I thought, could be traced to his difficult boyhood, but strangely, in that very boyhood also resided the material of the boldest features of his heart.

I could always hear guilt and considerable self-doubt in Owen's voice, a life-long stutterer, only free of his impediment when he sang in church or prayed.[17] In a letter to his grandson Charles Storrs Adair, who was living in Osawatomie, Kansas, in the 1850s,[18] he expressed how undeserving he thought he was of God's grace: "I will acknowlege the great goodness and mercy of God in the life and health of so unworthy and sinfull creature as I am." He told the boy how to read the Book of Jonah, that he loved the boy's parents, and that eighteen inches of snow fell in Hudson the day he wrote.[19]

Even when honor came to Owen Brown, he felt inadequate, and was never susceptible to elitism or arrogance (though he *was* susceptible to wealth). Shortly after he was appointed a trustee at Oberlin Collegiate Institute, he wrote a letter to Oberlin's Father Shipherd in which he expressed his reservations about his appointment: "I trust God will make you faithful. Inform me when my seat will be wanted for a better man."

In the same letter, however, he offered suggestions for ways the institute might be improved and better run, including "planing and making handsom Gardens and Yards" and "punctual payments of the students." He also saw the need to immediately address the issue of women's equality, and told Father Shipherd that he knew of "several females students in these parts which wish to get admitted into the Institution."²⁰ His daughter Florella was among the first four women to attend and graduate. It was at Oberlin that she met her future husband, Samuel Lyle Adair, who had begun his education at Western Reserve College in 1834 but finished his ministerial training at the school west of it.

I wondered if Owen's own fatherlessness made him gentle and wise in this way—so deeply an advocate for women's education. Owen Brown was five years old when his father, who was also named John Brown, died in the Revolutionary War. Ten children were left fatherless when the news arrived, and one was born following his death. Eleven in all. When he remembered his childhood, he remembered his mother even before he talked about the difficult years when circumstances forced his large family to separate. "The care and seport of this Famely fell mostly on my Mother the labouring men were mostly in the Army. here I would say my Mother was one of the best of Mother active and sensable she did all that could be expected of a Mother yet for want of help we lost our Crops and then our Cattle and so became poor in 77 I began to live abroad my Grand Father Brown some times at home and then abroad," he wrote.²¹

Almost every year he was with a new caretaker: his brother-in-law Michel Barber, brother Frederick, brother John, Elijah Hill, Rev. Jeremiah Hallock. He intermittently returned home—in the winter of 1787, the spring and summer of 1788, the whole of 1789. He learned shoemaking and married Ruth Mills on February 13th, 1793. His sympathy for women—as well as his desire for property, for houses, for wealth—was understandable against a background like his. The stability of a home and the security of property would lure him his whole life.

Owen grew up at the mercy of others and then spent his life being merciful. It shouldn't have surprised me that he and Ruth Mills adopted Levi Blakeslee before leaving Connecticut; that Mr. Mahand was staying in Owen's house while he spoke at the Methodist Church; that he took in his widowed sister Theodosia Merrill and his son-in-law Hiram King; that in 1842 Norman Root was living with the Browns ("wandering about ever since June," Owen Brown wrote of him in a letter, "the evils that are falling on that Family are great"[22]); that Jesse Grant, father of Ulysses S. Grant, was apprenticed to Owen Brown in his tannery and stayed with the family in their Hudson house, and knew young John Brown.[23]

Ruth Mills Brown plus Owen Brown did not exactly add up to John Brown (nothing did), but it explained some things.

5.

Biographers often turn to fathers to help them understand sons who enter history books. Especially sons like John Brown, whose reputations are insecure, or who remain controversial.

Biographer Robert E. McGlone provided a strikingly nuanced discussion of what John Brown had done on Pottawatomie and offered thoughtful comments about his personality and psychological state—including material about his relationship with his father.[24] As much as I dreaded looking more closely at those bloody bodies of five civilians hacked to pieces near a Kansan stream by the swords of John Brown's men, when I encountered McGlone's interpretation, I thought that he might be on to something important that could ultimately reduce my discomfort and save me time. That someone had finally found a convincing way to explain why John Brown did what he did that horrible night in May of 1856, and I wouldn't have to think about it anymore. I could just cite McGlone—give him full credit—and move on.

McGlone first considered the theories other writers had advanced to explain the brutal night of May 24, 1856. He saw some truth in them all, but was never completely convinced by any of them. His conclusion was this: "For Brown Pottawatomie was thus an act of self-definition."

I was used to reading military interpretations of Pottawatomie, not psychoanalytical. That's what McGlone was recommending, though. And what he was saying drew me in.

He argued that John Brown "craved the admiration of his land-rich and pious father." McGlone claimed that he came to Kansas "still the pilgrim son of Squire Owen—still uncertain who he was in his own right and what his standing was with the god of 'my fathers.'" It was, in his opinion, in part John Brown's hope to surpass his father's expectations which "spurred his labors." The scholar proposed that the memory of Owen's jeremiads and John Brown's own uncertainty about his identity after his father's death on May 8, 1856— shortly before the killings—drove the son to do what he did.

For Robert McGlone, this need for self-definition required a furious break with the father. A severing as sharp as the swords John Brown and his men used to carve up settlers on Pottawatomie Creek.

John Brown was brooding, McGlone said. He had pledged to fight slavery, but was he doing enough to appease his father, the devout abolitionist who'd acted on his beliefs in Hudson? Nearly twenty years had passed since John Brown's 1837 vow in First Congregational Church, and what had he accomplished for the cause? Further, in McGlone's view, Owen's death threatened the very identity of John Brown, so he needed to perform a highly assertive and original act. Who would he be now that his father was dead? McGlone concluded, "In directing the slayings he abandoned his allegiance to his father's style of antislavery. He ceased to be Owen's disciple." Owen Brown would not have slaughtered people on the creek with a broadsword, not even proslavery settlers. It wouldn't have crossed his mind.

There's some truth in almost every interpretation, and I heard it in McGlone's. It seemed possible to me, for example, that both John Brown's early efforts at land speculation and his mild style of abolitionism in the Ohio years (the vow excepted) were attempts to explore his relationship to Owen Brown. I later found out that a Civil War historian had also focused on John Brown and the tension and resentment between his father and him, and some scholars had lightly suggested other ways John Brown's connection to his father might have played a role in the Pottawatomie massacre.[25] It was appealing, and I liked McGlone's fearless questioning and his implication that John Brown, like other people, had personal history that played a part in every act.

But the problem with interpretations—whether it was Stephen Oates talking about John Brown with guarded empathy; Malin describing him as insincere and incompetent;[26] or McGlone explaining his search for identity and his need to separate from a father whose approval he never won—was that they were all necessarily influenced not just by evidence, but by a particular brain and heart that worked to make sense of it.

I came to understand that McGlone's interpretation could not be mine, even though I admired it.

Perhaps because I was a daughter, not a son, I never sensed the kind of lasting tension between John Brown and Owen that McGlone felt was there. Most of John Brown's biographers had been men, and they might understand this matter better or differently than I could.

Maybe subtle anger buried deeply in the letters could be detected only by sons and fathers, who could read clues that I might have missed. I returned to the correspondence, looking for it, worried that I hadn't read carefully enough. It was true that John Brown wished to please his father about the issue of slavery. He wrote a letter to Owen on March 26, 1856, describing affairs in Kansas Territory, a little more sanguine about things than he soon would be. He ended with the line, "Wishing you may be continued to witness the triumph of that cause you have laboured to promote."27

But was John Brown really "the pilgrim son of Squire Owen" in 1856, as McGlone had called him? He was fifty-six years old, three years away from death. He had already entered a far more diverse world than Owen Brown would ever know in Hudson. John Brown had written his father long before 1856 about decisions and plans of his own regarding the cause they shared— written him in a very eager, confident, and independent way, it seemed to me.

From Springfield, Massachusetts, the place where I followed John Brown after Richfield and Akron, he sent his father a letter in 1849 about his future plans to work with a Black community in North Elba, New York. In 1848, he'd visited land near North Elba that Gerrit Smith, one of the Secret Six, had given to free Blacks and fugitives to farm—a sort of utopian community called Timbucto—and he'd already begun to imagine himself living there. "There are a number of good colored families on the ground; most of whom I visited. I can think of no place where I think I would sooner go; *all things considered* than to live with those poor despised Africans to try, & encourage them; & show them a little so far as I am capable how to manage. You kneed not be surprised if at some future day I should do so."28 He did what he had outlined in his letter—among many other things that his father would never have conceived of doing. Long before Kansas and Pottawatomie, he was bold. Bolder (or just more reckless, some might say) than his father ever was.

Owen Brown remained in Hudson. Remained more conventional.

Like me.

Gerrit Smith, between 1855
and 1865. (Courtesy Library of
Congress)

I sensed affection in John Brown's letters. He generally signed the ones to
Owen written from Springfield in the 1840s, "From your Affectionate but
unworthy Son." Letters written in the 1850s, from Kansas, during the time of
John Brown's rise on the national scene, he still sometimes signed that way,
but more commonly, "Your Affectionate Son." The letters were full of news
about crops and politics and weather, always respectful, deeply solicitous of
his father's health, honest, grateful for all his father's kindnesses, including
the loaning of money—a frequent request of his.[29]

Letters to his father often contained intimate details. John Brown told
Owen about removing the body of Austin, his grandson and Owen's great-
grandson, from his Missouri grave. The child, son of Jason (John Brown's
second son) and Ellen Sherbondy Brown, had died on April 30, 1855, of cholera
aboard a ship called *New Lucy* during his family's migration to Kansas.[30] John
Brown, along with his son Oliver and son-in-law Henry Thompson, found
the grave when they headed to Kansas in the fall of that year, and John Brown
dug the child up and placed him in a covered wagon, hoping to dispel a little
of Jason's grief.[31] "We came by the place where Austin was buried, & took him
up; & brought him on with us; which seems to have had a good effect on Jason,
& Ellen,"[32] he told his father after he arrived in Brownsville, Kansas Territory.

I noticed in many of his letters a peculiar candor. Children who fear their
parents—fear disapproval, competition, or any adverse response—seldom tell
the truth. Parents often discover what's going on because it's difficult to hide,

but clever children can remain hidden all their lives, even from themselves. However John Brown might have felt about his father when he was growing up, by the time he reached later adulthood, it seemed to me he'd traded any revenge he might have craved for gratitude, and any jealousy he might have harbored for the common bond between them.

John Brown wrote a graphic letter to his father about the death of his wife Dianthe, a letter he signed, "From your sorrowing son,"[33] but he also told his father about difficult matters that reflected poorly on himself—on his poverty and his failure to make any gains in the world or to support his family. From New Hartford in June of 1839, he wrote to his wife and children, telling them about the penury that most likely awaited them in spite of his recent efforts in the cattle business. "Keep this letter wholly to yourselves," he told them. "You may show this to my father, but to no one else."[34]

John Brown was willing to let Owen stare at his soul during his darkest hours.

He had discovered his own identity long before Pottawatomie, it seemed, and the motivation for his brutal deed in Kansas had little to do with any unresolved tension he might have felt toward Owen Brown. He was an affectionate son who could admit fault and had more than found his own way in the world—certainly within the cause both he and Owen were devoted to.

But I recognized that my reservations about McGlone's interpretation held danger for me. I would have to find my own way to Pottawatomie Creek, my own explanation for John Brown's brutality. That interpretation, I knew, would reveal as much about me as it would about any history I'd uncover, just as I'd felt other interpretations had. My readers would be judging me and watching me. They would know what I was made of by what I said.

I've often sensed that the heart is on display in writing. It's what has made me stop writing sometimes, and what has allowed me to continue. Pottawatomie frightened me not only because of what happened there, but because of what was going to happen inside of me as I considered it.

A WAREHOUSE AND A STOREFRONT CHURCH IN SPRINGFIELD, MASSACHUSETTS

Lyman & Merrie Wood Museum of Springfield History

I.

I followed him to Springfield, Massachusetts. After Richfield, he spent a few years in Akron raising and herding sheep as a partner with Colonel Simon Perkins, son of Brigadier General Simon Perkins, who fought in the War of 1812 and was a founder of Akron, but in March of 1846, John Brown moved Perkins & Brown to Springfield to open a wool warehouse.

I entered the Lyman & Merrie Wood Museum of Springfield History, one of the museums in the Springfield Museums complex, and walked up a graceful staircase, formed from sheets of clear plastic that were lit underneath by strings of tiny lights. I couldn't imagine John Brown climbing stairs like these, couldn't imagine anything but ground and mountains under his boots.

Tucked among displays of early bicycles and gun-making was the exhibit I came to see—*John Brown, Abraham Lincoln, & the Civil War.* It was mostly about John Brown. The wall for Lincoln featured only a series of three paintings—and just one of Lincoln himself.

Some of John Brown's possessions were in the room. The bulkiest of these was the huge desk he used for his wool business, first located in Springfield in the lofts of John L. King's old warehouse on the corner of Water and Railroad Streets, and then moved to larger accommodations on North Main Street, just north of the Agawam Bank.[1] I could almost see him leaving the warehouse at the end of a tiring day. In just the first two years of his Springfield business, he and his sons Jason and John Jr. separated and graded about three hundred tons of wool.[2] I imagined him walking across the street to the Massasoit for something to eat. When his wife and children were not with him in Massachusetts, the inn played an even larger role in his routine—"the Massasoit of Springfield" he called it in a letter.[3]

During the Springfield years, John Brown changed from wool merchant to active abolitionist. The matter of abolition grew into an obsession shaped in large part by the people and antislavery groups of the town.

I don't know if he ever laughed in Massachusetts. I couldn't hear the sound when I tried to imagine it. The only photo with a hint that his lips even curled upward was the one with his arms crossed, taken by Augustus Washington in 1847 or 1848 in Hartford,[4] so maybe an occasional smile still appeared on his face in Springfield, where he lived in at least three places—a boardinghouse in 1846 when he first arrived, the second floor of a brick home on Gray's Avenue (after his wife and children had joined him), and then the house on Franklin Street, where Frederick Douglass met with him.[5]

Several of John Brown's children became extremely ill between 1848 (when the economy dipped again) and 1849—Oliver nearly dying because he mistook a hemlock root for a carrot and ate it; Owen suffering from pain in his crippled arm that could be relieved only by treatment with a galvanic battery; Frederick, always prone to mental instability, enduring headaches and confusion; other members of the family sick with colds; Ellen, not even one year old, dying in John Brown's arms from pneumonia.[6]

The Springfield years would have done little to lighten his mood, though I tried to remember that a few rare souls, Mrs. Spring and Mrs. Russell among them, had mentioned his laugh.[7]

Other objects in the museum attracted me—some from the Springfield days, but not all. There were pieces of wood and slate taken from John Brown's fort at Harpers Ferry (every museum, it seemed, wanted a piece of him; Hudson Library & Historical Society had a stick of wood from his gallows, a swatch of John Brown's coat from his wedding, and bark from the black walnut tree on his property). There was a clay tobacco pipe and surveyor's rule that he once owned; an armless Boston rocker he gave Thomas Thomas when he left Springfield; a hobnail safe used by the firm of Perkins & Brown; and a painting of John Brown's Torrington, Connecticut, birthplace on a piece of pine clapboard that was taken from his childhood home after it burned down in 1918 from a chimney fire.

A mural of John Brown's Springfield years featured more stories about the central events in his history there, including the wool business he ran and the 1847 meeting with Frederick Douglass that Douglass himself told about in *Life and Times.*

His deep connections to Springfield's Black community were also illustrated, including his association with Black abolitionists who were active in the Underground Railroad and his formation of the League of Gileadites after the Fugitive Slave Law passed—a group of forty-four Black residents who pledged to use force to resist and fight slave catchers. I wondered if the group he formed on January 15, 1851, had been comforted or made more anxious by his "Words of Advice": "A lasso might possibly be applied to a slave-catcher for once with good effect. Hold on to your weapons, and never be persuaded to leave them, part with them, or have them far away from you. *Stand by one another and by your friends, while a drop of blood remains; and be hanged, if you must, but tell no tales out of school. Make no confession.*"[8]

No white man had ever said such things in America before. In a letter to his wife written two days after he drafted the statement, he told her, "I can only say I think I have been enabled to do something to revive their broken spirits. I want all my family to imagine themselves in the same dreadful condition." He was spending his time, often including his nights, with people in Springfield's Black community who "cannot sleep on account of either themselves or their wives and children."[9]

One detail on the mural showed a picture of a storefront church with five or six full-length windows on the first story of the building, four regular windows on the second, and a tall flat face of brick at the top, a façade that had a stepdown on either side like crenels in a castle that archers could fire arrows through. That church, the mural explained, was founded on Sanford Street in 1844. It was known as the Free Church, and John Brown worshipped there. The church was unfamiliar to me, but when I saw it I thought of Owen Brown leaving First Congregational Church to begin Free Congregational. The histories were similar.

Abolitionist members of the First Methodist Society had broken away from their church just as abolitionists in Hudson had from their "First" church. There was one difference, though. Dissidents in Springfield not only formed a new congregation of their own—called the Pynchon Street Society—but

Sketch of Eli Baptist by Unknown Artist.
(Courtesy of the Springfield Photo
Collection, The Lyman & Merrie Wood
Museum of Springfield History, Springfield,
MA)

Thomas Thomas by Unknown Photographer.
(Courtesy of the Springfield Photo Collection,
The Lyman & Merrie Wood Museum of
Springfield History, Springfield, MA)

Sanford Street Church by Unknown Photographer. (Courtesy of the Springfield Photo Collection, The Lyman & Merrie Wood Museum of Springfield History, Springfield, MA)

helped the Black community construct a church of its own and encouraged members to elect their own ministers. They named it the Free Church on Sanford Street. Frederick Douglass was a friend of this church, as was Sojourner Truth. Thomas Thomas and Eli Baptist were among its most distinguished members,[10] and John Brown was a member too. It began as a militant church and remained committed to social action.[11]

The museum archivist said the church still survived in Springfield— though with a new name and in a new building on Union Street.

It was now called St. John's Congregational Church. I wondered if the name had some link to John Brown. A history of the church said the source of inspiration for naming it St. John's wasn't clear. "There are some who feel," the history said, "that because of John Brown's close connection with St. John's, and the reverence and love the members held for him, that he shared in the name along with the beloved disciple."[12]

The museum featured a poster of a stained-glass window in the nave of the church. It was a memorial window to John Brown, and I had to see it. The archivist gave me the exact address of the church, so we punched it into our GPS and started out.

2.

The "new" church on the corner of Hancock and Union, built in 1911, was just off State Street. From a distance, I could see its corner tower of brown shingles, its Gothic windows and yellow trim.

My husband and I pulled the door, but it wouldn't budge. I walked to a building beside the church called the William N. DeBerry Educational Center, and asked if someone would be kind enough to let us in. I felt a little odd explaining that I wanted to see a window dedicated to John Brown, but the associate pastor at the door didn't seem to mind. It took a minute for him to retrieve a key from inside the center, but he soon led the two of us back toward the church.

It was a panel of glass that had brought me here, but I knew it was really John Brown who had. I wouldn't be standing in this place without him, like so many trips I'd taken in the past few years. I was about to enter an all-Black church, something I'd never done before, and the pastor, named Tim, seemed genuinely happy to have me there, and all I had to do to earn his trust was say "John Brown."

The pastor directed us to a locked glass case that held the lectern Bible John Brown had given the Free Church when he was a member. He lifted it out and rested it gently on a nearby table. "It's used only on special occasions," he said. It was bound in thick leather, and I wondered where John Brown bought it, or how he acquired it. The pastor touched the cover and then opened the book. "The John Brown Bible," someone had carefully written on

St. John's Congregational Church, on the corner of Hancock
and Union Streets, Springfield

the inside. Underneath were the words, "Property of St. John's Church," and
I spotted the publication date of 1848. John Brown probably purchased it in
Springfield during the time he was sorting wool and helping to arm Black
residents.

He was always presenting Bibles to people. He left the family Bible to his
daughter Ruth in his will: "I give to my Daughter Ruth Thompson my large
old Bible containing family record." In the will also was his wish that Bibles
be purchased for his other children (at five dollars each) and for each of his
grandchildren (at three dollars each). The money, of course, would have to
come from his father's estate, when it was settled.[13]

The pastor returned the heavy Bible to its case in the alcove and then
walked my husband and me to the center of the church. He guided us to the
back of the nave, where the loveliest panels allowed light to scatter throughout
the interior, streaming all the way to the altar at the front and to the platforms
on either side of it that were built to support musicians and choirs and vocal-
ists and ensembles and liturgical dancers.

He snapped up a black pull-down shade that covered a panel. There it was.
"We record services," the pastor told us. "The John Brown panel is right in the
sightline of the camera crew," he said, explaining the need for the shade over
the John Brown glass.

The panel featured in its top half three lilies emerging from the base of
another plant that had dagger-like leaves and resembled a pineapple. Pine-
apples were a recurring motif in art, and I'd seen them before. In colonial

John Brown Memorial Window,
St. John's Congregational Church.
(Photo by the author, appears
with the permission of St. John's
Congregational Church)

America this symbol of hospitality—of the Golden Rule, to use John Brown's
vocabulary—had been carved into bannisters, attached to tops of elegant gate
posts, stenciled onto walls and mats, turned into molds for baking, painted
on chairs and chests, and pressed into jewelry. The lily accompanied every
Easter service of my Lutheran girlhood, and a small pot of them was a standard gift to grandparents after Sunday services ended and the rock was rolled
away. The designer had intensified the emotion of the piece by placing a circle
of red glass behind the lilies, making it look like a bleeding heart whose chambers had been formed from lily stems.

The lower half of the glass was bare, except for a prominent dedication at
the bottom in a sharp white and red rectangular box that ran nearly the whole
width of the panel. No one seemed to know who had donated the John Brown
window, or exactly when, but it clearly was designed in admiration of John
Brown and seemed a costly thing.[14] "In memory of John Brown," it read.
"Hero of Harper's Ferry."

REVERIE 3
IT WAS DIFFICULT BEING ALONE
WITH THIS MAN

I.

When I returned to Hudson, I posted a picture of the John Brown window on Facebook because I thought it was beautiful. Several friends, shocked and confused, asked me why a word like *hero* was chosen to describe someone like John Brown. Some thought it was especially inappropriate for a church to dedicate a memorial window to a violent man who broke the law as egregiously as he had. A few compared him to contemporary equivalents such as Osama Bin Laden and Timothy McVeigh, a complaint I'd heard before.

Several people who usually replied to my Facebook posts ignored me, a form of passive aggression which made me despise Facebook sometimes. One good thing about John Brown, I smiled, was that he was not passive aggressive. Just the *aggressive* part applied to him. He sometimes went in disguise, but when he emerged you always knew where he stood. He said and did what he meant—in the day, and in the case of Harpers Ferry and Pottawatomie, at night.

But a few of my friends were neither angry nor silent about the post, but curious, and they tried to explain how the image had affected them. One said he was humbled by the great diversity of groups within our nation—each obviously "bearing its own bias." Another said she needed more time to think about what she'd seen. I knew the truth was that I myself was still trying to make sense of the panel, and my Facebook post was hardly innocent.

Maybe I'd posted the picture not just because the glass was so attractive and I wanted to show it to my friends and tell them where I'd gone on my last little outing, but because I knew the photo would provoke a response.

John Brown was the provocateur, not me, I'd always thought, but I began to question this. Began to be suspicious of my motive. I'd never used social media to bait people, the way I realized I just had. When I saw the stained-glass window and read the word *hero*, I, too, had been surprised, and perhaps I wanted other people to help me understand the meaning of this tribute, or, if I were really honest, wanted them to be as uncomfortable as I was. Something was happening to me, but I wasn't sure what it was. I just knew it was difficult being alone with John Brown of Hudson anymore.

I justified my post by telling myself that John Brown was everyone's project—or did I mean to say "problem"? Not just mine. People ought to help me with this, I thought, in moments when I wasn't thinking clearly at all. They ought to want to, because John Brown was America's patriotic duty— whatever I meant by that.

What I'd done, as insignificant as it was in the Facebook world, or any kind of world, for that matter, felt subversive and made me think it might be best to disappear for a while.

I deactivated my Facebook account.

THE JOHN BROWN MONUMENT
BEHIND THE AKRON ZOO

Colonel Simon Perkins Mansion, photo by Carl F. Waite, 1934. (Courtesy Library of Congress)

I.

The first time I observed the interest of Black Americans in John Brown was at a celebration in Akron for the sesquicentennial of Harpers Ferry in 2009. I'd read in the *Akron Beacon Journal* that there was a monument to John Brown behind the Akron Zoo that would be open to the public at the time of the sesquicentennial.

My aunt Ruth took her son and me to that zoo when we were kids. We'd board the city bus on the corner of Aster Avenue and Ivy Place—my aunt's street—and off we'd go for an afternoon of petting animals, and then a glazed donut at Krispy Kreme before riding the bus back home. It was heaven. When the Akron Zoo first opened, it was a children's zoo, and its simple mission was to bring nursery rhymes to life. It was a place where the only mischief in the whole world was Mary's lamb, who followed her to school one day ("which was against the rules").

The monument had been there since 1910, but no one had ever mentioned it to me. As far as I know, my family was as oblivious to its existence as I was. When I read about the tour that was planned, I tried to piece this together.

John Brown's years working with Colonel Simon Perkins in Akron, beginning in 1844 after he left Richfield, would need to be filled in. During this time, he tended a flock comprised of his sheep and the colonel's and rented a small house from the colonel across the street from his mansion—a structure that's called the John Brown House now and open to the public. The 1,300 sheep of Perkins & Brown grazed on a nearby hill known by townspeople as Mutton Hill, and the John Brown Memorial and zoo stand near it—about a mile away.

John Brown House on Diagonal Road, Akron, prior to re-siding

The monument is separated from the zoo below it by a thick border of trees and a gravel path that winds from the zoo's parking lot all the way up to the memorial.

Akron's German Alliance dedicated to John Brown a tall center sandstone column saved from the original Summit County Courthouse—which was razed in 1905, five years before the dedication. German immigrants were surprised to learn that no one in Akron had done anything permanent to remember John Brown, so they thought they should. This country was now their homeland, and a monument to John Brown was the responsibility of its citizens, they said. I thought of immigrant John Davey who wanted a statue for John Brown too.[1] Then I thought of my mother's family, the Golzes and the Haberkosts—stone masons, millers, and roofers who arrived in Akron from Germany in the 1880s—and wondered if any of them were part of the eight-thousand-person crowd gathered on the hill the day of the dedication, or if the Golz Concrete Block Company, a business my grandma's brothers owned, might have had a role in the monument's construction.

The paper provided a list of days when Akron's deputy mayor would be conducting tours, and I intended to be in line on the very first day. I couldn't wait to see what had been hidden for a hundred years, so on July 4, 2009, instead of going to a barbeque, there I was with my husband—he with a camera and me with a notebook, like tourists in a brand-new town.

2.

.

A few minutes before 9:00 a.m., Dave Lieberth, the city's deputy mayor, appeared in the parking lot with a bullhorn, waiting for people to assemble. He told the group that his office had been flooded with letters asking why so much attention was being paid to a terrorist. I'd heard it all before when I'd read the April letters about Hudson's Sesquicentennial in my local newspaper. Barely fifty people were gathered for the hike. I wondered if I should feel proud or ashamed that my husband and I were among them.

To protect the monument from vandalism, a fence had been erected in the year 2000 around the acres that surrounded it. Though a great deal of destruction had already occurred by that time, it became more difficult for vandals to get to the site, the deputy mayor said. But also, I thought, the fence—along with a high gate at the entrance to the path, topped with barbed wire—prevented ordinary people who didn't break rules from visiting.

There was talk about moving the monument, but no decision had been reached. It would cost $100,000 to relocate. Or the acres we were about to see might be used for the expansion of the zoo. "Expect giraffes!" he said.

He asked for the attention of the small crowd. "Thanks for coming," he said. He was the Chair of the Committee for the Sesquicentennial Celebration in Akron. "Thanks to the zoo, the Summit County Library, the Historical Society."

The deputy mayor knew the group would appreciate a local joke about John Brown, so he told one. "He was Akron's best-known citizen internationally before LeBron James."

Then he told the group how special we were. We would be among the first people to see the monument in decades. "Decades!" he said, almost not believing it himself, pausing for an instant as he looked into the sky. He gave a thumbnail sketch of John Brown, and then the group began the walk up a path that had recently been cleared and leveled to prevent people from stumbling. It was still narrow, though—carved into forest—and I stepped carefully.

We were in a place of wild trees, what Akron might have looked like two hundred years ago when settlers arrived, I thought. I walked to the first turn through some of the most beautiful woods I'd ever seen in the region—the ground free of weeds and rubble, the trunks of old trees cut and mulched, their wood now forming a loose border of chunky chips under my feet. This might have been the smell pioneers knew as they cleared the land.

The guide spoke like a politician as the party approached the monument, but I didn't mind. The mayor's assistant was a politician, after all, but that was only his secondary role today. He talked about the seventy million dollars the city had invested in renovating public housing in the neighborhood. About the new library branch and the new headquarters for the Urban League.

While he talked, I stared at the pillar and the exedra surrounding it. The bronze eagle originally at the top of the commemorative pillar was gone. Disappointed to find that it had been broken off, I tried to imagine how it could have been removed from its high perch, wondering if some adolescent brought a huge extension ladder and heavy hammer to knock the bird to the ground, like some old nest, or if vandals had used their bodies to construct a ladder of their own, locking legs and shoulders like Lego blocks.

Much had been cleaned and repaired by the time of the sesquicentennial. Black paint that vandals had spilled across the pedestal had mostly been removed. I saw the large letters "ME" carved on the front face of the pillar, though, and knew those were probably permanent.

I wondered if vandalism could be part of the monument's history now, even if I didn't like it. It was a new thought for me. Once I'd believed that defacing a pillar or striking an eagle down would destroy the history of a place, but my theory was being tested every day. John Brown's reputation had been tampered with a thousand times since he'd left the earth, and in a thousand ways, yet he still could be found behind the Akron Zoo.

John Brown Monument behind the Akron Zoo, Dave Lieberth at far left with megaphone. (Courtesy Summit County Historical Society)

3.

On September 25, 1938, the Negro 25 Year Club added a decorative platform and seats around the Tuscan column and dedicated the monument a
second time. A marker, which included the image of John Brown, was set into
a small section of the thirty-foot diameter bench. It read: "He died to set his
brothers free / His soul goes marching on." I held the two inscriptions in my
head: "In memory of John Brown," on the plaque from the German Alliance,
and now this one. I heard two different voices, one distant but respectful, the
second, more exuberant, reminiscent of "The Battle Hymn of the Republic."
I later learned the long history of that song, originally called "John Brown's
Song," and its importance to Black Americans.[2]

The stones around the pillar had been taken from a home that was being
demolished on East Exchange Street in Akron. It was impossible for me not
to feel at ease on this hill. Akron through and through.

I could see the tops of Akron's tallest downtown buildings through the
trees, and I'd never seen the city from such a dramatic angle. I didn't want
giraffes here. I wanted only the monument—open to the public with the gate
unlocked. There had been talk, the guide told the group, of running a little
train to the site for better accessibility.

Some people wanted John Brown in a more prominent spot than the back
of a zoo—somewhere closer to major downtown roads, the corner of Cedar
and Maple Streets and Rhodes Avenue having been suggested. The Historical
Society preferred having the monument moved to the grounds of the John

Marker with John Brown image, dedicated by
Negro 25 Year Club, 1938

Brown House, consolidating his memory. Even the sheep Perkins & Brown owned had sometimes grazed in the nearby front yard of Colonel Perkins' mansion, so I understood the society's request.

There were countless plans for the monument, Lieberth said.

But I didn't want to see it moved because it made so much sense to keep it where it was. This was the land that Col. George Tod Perkins, son of John Brown's business partner in Akron, donated to the city—76 acres of sloping ground west of Edgewood Avenue.[3] It was a beautiful natural spot. Even the arrival of light here was spectacular, the sun streaming through thick trees, weaving shadow and glare over everything—even me. How could the John Brown monument—any part of it—be ripped from this cool grove, or from the sheep so easy to imagine up on Mutton Hill?

But the conversation about the monument did not turn in the direction of my thoughts. The deputy mayor had formed a group who would decide what happened to the site. Everyone had a say, he explained, and a consensus was growing about what the city should do. On the committee were representatives from the zoo, the Historical Society, the nearby neighborhood, and Black organizations. The dominant view at the time was that the monument couldn't remain hidden any longer.

But that wasn't my view at all.

A Black woman raised her hand when the discussion about the monument's relocation became a little heated. The symbolic significance of the monument being hidden in a dense grove of trees had not been lost on her, she said. She had just called the NAACP. She seemed to be a leader in the Akron community. The CEO she spoke to told her that the NAACP had been asking about the John Brown Monument in Akron for twelve years. The woman wondered why no one from the national organization had contacted her about this, and she also wondered if the Negro Council of Women had been reached.

"Who was at the table?" she wanted to know. "National is concerned," she said. "We have a great history right here, but our history is behind the trees and nobody can get to it."

The deputy mayor assured her that the Akron Urban League had been contacted but confirmed that the NAACP had not. Dave Lieberth was an honest man, and I liked the way he let himself be moved by people. I'd come to realize over the years that I liked politicians who didn't behave like ones.

Another Black woman spoke. She had concerns about moving the monument to the business district. "This is indicative of our struggle," she said. "Will people be able to stop and take in the history?" She inflected the words "take in" so the small crowd could consider them. She wanted assurance that education would be coupled with relocation. Just moving the monument would not necessarily secure its meaning and importance in Black history any better than hiding it behind a zoo had.

"That's the only condition under which they'd move it," the deputy mayor said. It would be a place where people could pause, and there would be a building where citizens could be educated. Perhaps a parking lot for buses could be provided, he suggested. Even land for other statues—maybe Sojourner Truth, who delivered a speech in Akron at the Woman's Rights Convention of 1851.[4]

The deputy mayor knew Akron's history and wasn't afraid of it. He had moderated Bill Clinton's first town meeting on race in Akron, carried live on C-SPAN. He told the group that the conversation about race had been going on for over 140 years in Akron, starting with the Fugitive Slave Law. He talked proudly about Akron citizens who rallied behind Jim Worthington, a Black barber "arrested" by slave catchers. Residents filled a train platform, causing the man's captors to fear for their lives, and then they ran them out of town.

Yet the deputy mayor didn't shy away from talking about the Ku Klux Klan in Akron, a powerful and ugly force in the 1920s numbering 52,000, including public officials such as former mayor D. C. Rybolt and several members of the school board—a group that marched in city parades by day and routinely burned crosses at the edge of town at night.[5] I was glad the deputy mayor was the sort of man who called back history—even the difficult kind. As I listened to him, I remembered how Archwood Avenue divided people by race in my Akron neighborhood of Firestone Park, remembered the dirty jobs Black workers were given in the rubber factories where my father spent his life in lower management, remembered a story our son had written for the *Akron Beacon Journal* about the Akron Riot of 1900—the burning of the City Building and Columbia Hall, shootings, the arrival of martial law, the barriers to fair trials.

But when John Brown was executed, the deputy mayor said, all the church bells in the city rang.[6]

Now it was July 4th of the twenty-first century, and Akron leaders in the Black community were claiming John Brown, coupling his history with their own. They wanted him visible, and his association with Akron sheep didn't matter to them much at all.

I preferred the idea of a little train chugging up the path I had just taken to the monument. I had long thought of myself as a historical preservationist and wanted as little disruption as possible to historical sites. But that morning I began to realize there might be things I couldn't keep the way they were. The silence of a secluded grove perhaps was one of them.

4.

On October 16, 2009—150 years to the day after the raid at Harpers Ferry—the monument was opened a second time for a commemorative ceremony, and I attended. After that I kept watching the newspaper for further announcements about the fate of the monument but found nothing at all.

I sent Dave Lieberth an email a year after my visits in 2009, visions in my head of giraffes rubbing their backs against the pillar or of the monument being loaded onto flatbed trucks and driven to another part of town.

There were no plans right now for development or relocation, he said. No immediate plans even to re-open the John Brown Monument to the public. The Akron Zoo, he told me, was comfortable with either decision the city made: the monument could stay, or it could go. For now, the city assured its residents that the site would be well-maintained.[7]

A follow-up story appeared in the newspaper a year or so after our email exchange. The Akron Community Foundation had created an organization called the Abolitionist Movement Fund, but had raised only $14,000. Momentum died down, then out, and the reporter who did the story was left gathering pro and con arguments about the monument from two elderly Akron men who had followed the story and held strong views. One, a retired printer, wanted the monument moved. The other, a retired sales rep living in nearby Cuyahoga Falls who thought John Brown was a murderer and probably crazy, said too much glory had come to him already. "My conservative bloodstream says leave it where it is," he said. "Don't promote this guy anymore."[8]

I felt uncomfortable when I read the second quote because the man's conclusion about the monument had been my own, really, even though I thought my reasons were superior. Preserve the site as is—wouldn't that be best for history?

I wondered what would have happened if the sales rep had repeated his words in the presence of the Black woman who had voiced her opinion beside the column of the John Brown Monument (or if I had found some courage and told her what I was thinking). He had talked to a white reporter, not the Black woman at the monument, and those were two very different things. After they exchanged their first words, the man and the woman would have had to talk about John Brown, and before many seconds had passed they'd be talking about what they felt he'd contributed to their lives, and the volume would be turned up.

The last time I was at the zoo, the gate was locked, and no one was waiting to get in.

5.

Until my visit to the Akron Zoo and St. John's Congregational Church in Springfield, I hadn't considered that Black people might offer different interpretations of John Brown's story.

Works by Black writers about John Brown, as well as guidebooks to historic landmarks in Black America, began to fill my shelves, reminding me how much of the story I'd left out. There were suddenly different questions to ask, new characters to cast, and details I hadn't encountered before.

At a meeting of the Hudson History Book Club that had John Brown as its focus and was held in the upstairs of the Learnéd Owl, I knew what my selection would be. The club didn't have a common reading for its monthly meetings, like other clubs did, but just required those who attended to come prepared to summarize a book of their choice about the given topic. A woman who'd been a journalist for the *New York Times* and *Cleveland Plain Dealer* brought a thick folder of clippings about John Brown that she'd gathered over the course of her long career. Another person talked about Tony Horwitz's *Midnight Rising*. The man who organized the club and kept it going praised Truman Nelson's *The Old Man*—a book full of rich detail about Harpers Ferry.

There was no question about what book I'd bring. I selected Benjamin Quarles' *Allies for Freedom* & *Blacks on John Brown*. The double-volume set, written by a noted Black historian and scholar, had already begun to shift my perspective. They were older books—the first, a biography written by Quarles

Dangerfield Newby. (Courtesy Boyd B. Stutler
Collection of John Brown, West Virginia State
Archives)

in 1974; the second, a collection of Black responses to John Brown edited by
Quarles in 1972—reprinted together in 2001 by Da Capo Press.

Most of the gallery pictures in the Da Capo edition featured Black per-
sonalities in the John Brown story: daguerreotypes of Osborne P. Anderson,
Dangerfield Newby, John A. Copeland Jr., Shields Green, Lewis S. Leary, and
William Lambert; sketches from Frank Leslie's *Illustrated Weekly* of Shields
Green and John A. Copeland Jr. being taken by the military to their execution, and of Shields Green, John A. Copeland Jr., and white prisoner Albert
Hazlett at the Charles Town jail—the Black men sitting, the white man
standing, all dressed in dark vests and white shirts with crisp collars held high
by black-ribboned bows; a bust portrait and linocut of John Brown by Black
artist Charles White, born in Chicago; several of twenty-two prints in a series

by Black painter Jacob Lawrence called *The Life of John Brown* (exhibited at the Akron Art Museum at the time of the Harpers Ferry Sesquicentennial).[9]

The book included a full-page illustration of a magnificent painting by Horace Pippin (a Black artist from West Chester, Pennsylvania, who died in 1946) titled *John Brown Going to His Hanging*, which has features of folk art and images that are unforgettable: December trees that hold dead leaves, haunted light upon the grated windows of the jail, a John Brown bound with rope, the backs of people who stare at his gallows wagon moving by, and, most striking of all, a Black woman—supposedly Pippin's grandmother—who stands in the bottom corner of the picture (beside a man who holds a whip) and cannot bear to look at John Brown, so faces forward and looks at us instead, a deep scowl creasing her broad face.

When I read Benjamin Quarles and saw those pictures, I thought that I would have to scrap my John Brown project altogether, and start over, or maybe not start again at all, but after several days immobilized in my room, I realized that my discovery of Quarles and of Black scholarship on John Brown was part of the story I was struggling to tell, and I would need to include it as surely as I would everything else.

REVERIE 4
"READY TO RECEIVE ITS MEANING"

I.

History, I began to suspect, had a great deal to do with images. Images that people could think about over time and try to make sense of. All the details available had to be known, of course, but the image—the thing that details distilled down to—was often what remained and prompted future meditation.

I sometimes thought of John Brown as a symbol maker. He never finished what he started, but left symbols behind for other people to think about.

Glimpses of his comprehensive plan for equality were everywhere. He believed in education for Black children: "I have for years been trying to devise some way to get a school a-going here for Blacks";[1] he urged a new form of government through revisions in the Constitution (at the Chatham Convention in Canada West John Brown's new "Provisional Constitution" was approved; Osborne P. Anderson was elected to the Congress of John Brown's new government and two Black delegates were nominated to be president, though both declined);[2] he embraced the spiritual and political place of Black churches in American life (the Sanford Street Church that became St. John's); he placed military power in the hands of fugitives and free Blacks (the League of Gileadites in Springfield); he worked with Black leaders, and learned from them (Frederick Douglass and Harriet Tubman, among others).

A group of twenty-two raiders, five of them Black, couldn't possibly have composed an army even in John Brown's naïve mind. The number twenty-two is not an army, but a symbol.

The only thing he really completed was his life—and that was taken from him. In a way, he didn't finish that either.

I took *The Life of Poetry* off my shelf, a book by American poet and political activist Muriel Rukeyser that for a long time had meant so much to me, remembering she had talked at length about images—poetry's beating heart. There were the words I needed. An American poet who committed both her life and her writing to social justice, she spoke about how historical images worked to power the imagination, the way the life of a particular person sometimes "becomes an image reaching backward and forward in history," joining the past with the legacy that followed. "The gestures of the individuals are not history; but they are the images of history," she said.

She alluded in her book to John Brown's hanging and to the richness of its meaning in the minds of American thinkers. "In his country, one man who cut through to the imagination of all was John Brown," she wrote. "But that precipitating stroke, like the archaic bloody violence of the Greek plays, spoke to many lives." I thought about all the poetry written about John Brown when he died, and all the novels written since,[3] but I also thought about all the everyday people who had considered him. I thought of everyone.

Rukeyser wanted us to reclaim history by reclaiming the imagination. "Always we need the audacity to speak for more freedom, more imagination, more poetry with all its meanings."

A historical image, she said, required an imagination "ready to receive its meaning."[4]

But what made an imagination "ready to receive" the meaning of an image?

John Brown often had been seen as an American idealist or martyr by people who stared at the gallows, and that image inspired their poetry. But other people were glad he'd been hanged and found the Charles Town gallows a symbol of justice. How could this event be imagined so differently?

The imagination could be a tricky thing. What limited it, shaped it, or allowed it to grow?

Even images of John Brown's militancy had been filtered through such a wide range of imaginative lenses that I sometimes lost track of them. One man who wrote a letter to the editor of the *Hudson Hub-Times* thought Harpers Ferry was an act of civil disobedience. Several biographers have seen it as a prelude to the Civil War. Some people, like the man at the SUVCW meeting and individuals who sent other letters to the *Hub*, called John Brown an American terrorist. Michael Gold, a famous Communist writer who wrote a biography of John Brown in 1924, saw him as a "common man to the end" (a worker) and a forerunner of later historical protest movements, even placing Brown among "early American Socialists."[5] Eugene V. Debs, one of the founders of the Industrial Workers of the World, worshipped Brown, and Black power leaders like Malcolm X, H. Rap Brown, and Floyd McKissick invoked his name.[6] Scholars have stressed that to the present day there are "activists on the left and right who claim his mantle."[7]

How would I know when John Brown's story had cut through to my imagination, as the poet predicted it would? Why did it still feel as if I'd left so much out?

THE ENGINE HOUSE
AT HARPERS FERRY

I.

There were abundant images central to the John Brown saga, many of them still attached to physical remains. The monument behind the Akron Zoo, the nineteenth-century houses standing in Hudson, the town signs, the weathered gravestones in the Richfield Cemetery and the Old Hudson Township Burying Ground, Underground Railroad sites like the Case-Barlow Farm, and the chamber on the wall of Ruth Mills Brown's cabin that I still glimpsed when I looked at the Brewster block. But few images placed as many demands on me as the engine house at Harpers Ferry, where John Brown and his twenty-one men positioned themselves and fought about eight hundred militiamen, local farmers, and marines led by Colonel Robert E. Lee.

The engine house became a symbol for me of what John Brown intended to do in Virginia and what the days of the battle meant. It stirred my imagination from the first time I saw it on the street of Harpers Ferry. Gradually it became an image of much more than a single battle, further testing my notion of how to think about history.

I had to return to the story of Harpers Ferry to gather detail, because images were constructed of movement and specific gestures. Images were the true stuff of history, but they arrived later, and had no form without the content that gave them shape.

The story had been told hundreds of times, and often seemed impenetrable to me, but I tried to sort things out.

Hugh Forbes. (Courtesy
Boyd B. Stutler Collection of
John Brown, West Virginia
State Archives)

Osborne Perry Anderson.
(Courtesy Boyd B. Stutler
Collection of John Brown,
West Virginia State Archives)

Military strategists had debated the meaning of John Brown's plan since the day he failed to execute it over 150 years ago.

Some said he was bloody Old Osawatomie Brown of Kansas again when he attacked the arsenal and the Ferry, while others praised him for exerting a minimum of violence. For years John Brown had been planning for the Harpers Ferry raid, even though no one seems to know exactly when he first hatched the plot. He'd talked about parts of it with Frederick Douglass in Springfield, Massachusetts, when he proposed his Subterranean Pass Way; with Colonel Daniel Woodruff in Ohio (or so the story goes); in letters and at the Chatham Convention; and possibly with his Springfield porter and friend, Thomas Thomas.

John Brown argued about his plan with Hugh Forbes (the British soldier of fortune he'd hired to train his men in Iowa), who turned it into a timid version of itself. Disgruntled with slow payment for his services (payment was never a strength of John Brown's), Forbes eventually leaked information about the raid to three Washington senators, forcing the attack to be postponed and John Brown to return to Kansas. This, in turn, caused Osborne P. Anderson, one of the Black raiders, to characterize Hugh Forbes as Judas.[1]

John Brown was wounded and captured at Harpers Ferry, and ten of his men were killed (including two of his sons), so no further action on his part was possible. No one, in other words, would ever know exactly what he

Stereograph of Harpers Ferry and railroad bridge, 1865.
(Courtesy Library of Congress)

intended to do after he stormed the arsenal and took weapons to arm the enslaved in Virginia, sure they would swarm to his cause.

I made columns for the many accounts of his military strategy on sheets of paper. Two seemed especially prominent, but both were highly problematic. The first involved aggressive mountain warfare. After gathering arms (destroying those they couldn't carry or wouldn't need) and using hostages for any necessary negotiations with militia, they would retreat to the mountains, where they'd form a mutinous but emancipated colony. From there, they'd launch strikes on plantations, recruiting more and more enslaved persons into their ranks, until they moved into the deep South, all the way to Louisiana—a plan influenced by John Brown's knowledge of the maroons of Jamaica and Haiti, both mountain lands with enslaved populations. He'd establish a kind of mountainous Commonwealth based on the new Constitution he'd composed at Frederick Douglass' house and then taken to Chatham, Canada West, to ask thirty-four Black representatives and twelve white to ratify (their last meeting held at the First Baptist Church on King Street, a place now marked by an Ontario Provincial Plaque).[2]

The other plan, which John Brown spoke about twelve days after his capture, expressed far less confidence in the military skill of fugitives he thought would join him, and was closer to the Hugh Forbes plan. John Brown and his raiders would remain at the northern border of Virginia and Maryland

and make periodic rapid attacks on plantations, liberating anyone who was enslaved and then quickly sending them north to Canada, not recruiting them into their ranks, and not moving into the deep South. The second plan was a potentially less violent, less bloody, less "insurrectionist" plan that John Brown probably felt would earn him (and his cause) greater sympathy from the courts and from the press when he was questioned. It was closer to the plan he supposedly presented to Colonel Woodruff, though in the "Woodruff" plan he accompanied freed slaves to Canada and used Canada as his home base.[3]

It wasn't even clear how many people had died at the Ferry. Heyward Shepherd, a free Black—the porter and sometimes-ticket-seller for the Baltimore & Ohio Railroad—was without much question the first, as the man at the Sons of Union Veterans of the Civil War meeting had rightly said. At the time of the Harpers Ferry raid, Shepherd worked for his former master, Fontaine Beckham, the general agent of the railroad and the town's mayor. He was on his way to the toll-gate on the bridge over the Water Gap to see what the trouble was (John Brown's men had stopped the train before it could cross into town, and Shepherd must have heard voices and shouting). Ordered to stop, Shepherd instead reversed directions and tried to return to the depot, but one of John Brown's men shot him in the back, the bullet exiting his body through his left nipple.[4] Osborne P. Anderson, the only Black raider who escaped, wrote about this early scene in the raid, implying that the raiders who were implicated in the murder, Oliver Brown and Stewart Taylor, felt the porter threatened the success of the raid when he turned away from them and headed for his office. Anderson did not actually witness the killing, but most historians took the story he told in 1861 into account.

We're sure about others too. Benjamin Quarles said that those who lost their lives included ten of the raiders, four white people not in John Brown's party (a marine and three residents, one of them Fontaine Beckham), Heyward Shepherd, and two enslaved men, Phil and Jim.[5] Jim was a coachman for Lewis W. Washington, the great-grandnephew of George Washington who lived five miles from Harpers Ferry—one of several connections in the area to the founding father, clearly a symbol to John Brown and his men. Along with his "owner," Jim was brought to the site of the raid, proceeded to escape when the engine house was taken, reached the Shenandoah River, but drowned. Phil, the "property" of John H. Allstadt, another slave owner captured and held hostage by a raiding party, was taken to the Charles Town jail after the attack on the engine house on the charge of "sympathizing with the invaders," but he died of pneumonia within a week and his case was never pursued.[6] John Brown was indicted for treason and murder, but the involve-

Lewis W. Washington, great-grandnephew of George Washington. (Courtesy Boyd B. Stutler Collection of John Brown, West Virginia State Archives)

ment of Phil and Jim led to an additional charge: "conspiring and advising with slaves and others to rebel."[7]

The number of dead has been revised in recent years by scholars who have uncovered new documentation. Hannah Geffert wrote that "between seven and seventeen" men, in addition to those at the Kennedy Farmhouse, died with John Brown, most "local Blacks who joined Brown."[8]

So many other questions remain. Why had the raid failed? Some said it was the premature nature of the attack. Others, John Brown's hesitancy to retreat into the hills—his terrible delay. Many, his compassion for his hostages. Several said it was his naïve, inept understanding of military tactics.

Whatever he had planned to do, and however many people died during the attack, the engine house was the start of it, and the end of it, but it was also what remained for people to consider in the years that followed.

It was a very central image, in other words.

When "John Brown's Fort," as the engine house came to be called, first entered my imagination, I thought about John Brown inside with men dying around him. About the fire engines the building contained that had been shoved close to the doors by the besieged, and what they might have looked like. The engine house was an explosive place during the thirty-six hours of the battle (October 16–18, 1859), so I tried to picture guns and hear screams as I worked to reconstruct it. I'd never known war—which Harpers Ferry seemed to resemble—so I kept this picture in my head, somehow knowing I wasn't done with it, nor it with me.

It turned out that the engine house was not just a building where guns were fired and people died. It became an image of a broader American landscape, a symbol at times of the country's tendencies toward greed or neglect.

Interior of the engine house just before it was stormed, wood
engraving, 1859. (Courtesy Library of Congress)

John Brown lying wounded, beside son. (Courtesy Library of
Congress)

Most important, a symbol of the old order versus the new, with people on both
sides willing to fight to preserve what the engine house represented to them.

I certainly didn't understand this when I took my initial tour of the town.
On the first day I saw the building, with guidebook in hand, I never would
have guessed that the brick structure before me was not the solid thing it
seemed to be, was not even on the land where it had stood when John Brown
fought inside of it. Its history had only begun, not concluded, when the raid
ended that October day.

2.

John Brown's Fort at Harpers Ferry was a monument for Northern soldiers who marched by it during the Civil War, and then, for the next two decades, a sacred site for abolitionists, veterans, and, especially, Black Americans.

It was originally located near the armory and miraculously escaped destruction during the Civil War, unlike other buildings in the Ferry. Then, in 1869, it was sold to a man who wanted to industrialize the area using the region's waterpower, but his plan failed. The land, it turned out, was never paid for, so the fort and the property it was on became the government's again. By the 1880s Civil War buffs had begun to emerge, and the site, privately owned once more, became a tourist attraction. The new owner removed bricks from the building, decorated them with silver engravings of the fort, and sold them as souvenirs. He also painted the words "John Brown's Fort" on the front of the structure.

In Harpers Ferry about this time, tension in the white community was escalating, especially because of the presence of Storer College, an all-Black college that opened its doors in 1867, run by a sympathetic white administration and white trustees. Less sympathetic white people in the community began to fear that the college, along with the fort, an abolitionist symbol, would bring too many Black visitors to Harpers Ferry. Incidents erupted between the college and the Ku Klux Klan, and on several occasions a teacher at Storer was pelted with stones. The removal of the fort seemed to townspeople a very good idea.

John Brown's Fort, ca. 1885. (Courtesy
Library of Congress)

John Brown's Fort rebuilt for the 1893
Columbian Exposition in Chicago.
(Courtesy Kansas State Historical
Society)

In 1891 the structure was sold to the John Brown Fort Company, a group
founded by Iowa congressman A. J. Holmes that wanted to exhibit it at the
1893 World's Columbian Exposition in Chicago, an exposition that James W.
Ellsworth of Hudson helped to mount by serving on the board of directors
and hiring landscape architect Frederick Law Olmsted.[9] Workers disassembled the fort and shipped it by train to Chicago, where others reassembled it
on Wabash Avenue, but the process took so long to complete that the exhibit
didn't open until the final days of the exposition. The endeavor cost the
company $60,000, and the profit from gate admissions was $5.50. The
company went bankrupt and the building was abandoned.

Kate Field, the founder of the John Brown Association, rescued this piece
of John Brown history. She used her platform as a journalist (she wrote for
several major American newspapers) to raise the money that would be needed
to move the engine house back to Harpers Ferry. The B&O Railroad transported the building to five acres of donated farmland about three miles from
the fort's original location in the Lower Town. The contractor hired to rebuild
the fort was delinquent, expenses were greater than anyone had anticipated,

Cook Hall, on grounds of Storer College, founded 1867. (Courtesy Library of Congress)

and then, not long after the fort was back in Jefferson County, Kate Field died. The donor of the farmland sued Kate Field's estate and took back his property in 1901.[10]

The engine house by the turn of the century had been taken apart and rebuilt so many times, and owned by so many different parties, that I could barely keep its story straight. It was not just a building anymore, but a puzzle that could be assembled and disassembled almost endlessly, brick by brick, and year by year.

3.

The engine house wasn't destroyed, the way downtown buildings were in the Hudson fire of 1892 or Akron buildings were in the Akron Riot of 1900. Still, even if you kept putting a building back with the same materials, didn't it change a little every time you moved or rebuilt it?

The story hadn't ended yet.

The Niagara Movement, which later became the NAACP, went to the fort when the group gathered at Harpers Ferry in 1906 to commemorate John Brown's Day. It was their second meeting.[11] That morning, in gentle rain, members walked together to Alexander Murphy's farm, Buena Vista, where the engine house now stood, one man removing his shoes as if this were a pilgrimage. There were prayers and then Richard T. Greener gave remarks. The party marched around the fort singing "The Battle Hymn of the Republic" and concluded the ceremony by climbing a wooden tower inside of it to stare down at the Shenandoah Valley.

In the afternoon, the one hundred or so members of the party gathered in Anthony Hall, a building on the grounds of Storer College. It was here that the sister of Black raider Lewis Sheridan Leary spoke, as well as Lewis Douglass, the son of Frederick Douglass. W. E. B. Du Bois was one of the major speakers at the session. He rehearsed the history of Black Americans and then praised John Brown for battling injustice. "So much of life must go, not to forward right, but to beat back wrong," he said.[12]

The next morning, some of the delegates made the seven-mile trip southwest from Harpers Ferry to Charles Town to see the courthouse where John

Niagara Movement founders, middle row showing W. E. B. Du Bois second from the right and J. Max Barber third from the right, superimposed over an image of Niagara Falls, 1905. (Courtesy Library of Congress)

Brown was tried and the site of the hanging. They collected pieces of stone and branches of trees, but one person, William Monroe Trotter, brought back a fox terrier that he named John Brown. It became the mascot of the John Brown Jubilee, held in Boston three years after John Brown's Day. The travelers got back to Anthony Hall in time to hear the reading and approval of "An Address to the Country," a manifesto written largely by W. E. B. Du Bois that listed strongly worded steps that the country needed to take to rid America of discrimination.

John Brown was present in his remarks.

In one breath, Du Bois spoke of deploring violence. In the next, he embraced its results. "We do not believe in violence, neither in the despised violence of the raid nor the lauded violence of the soldier, nor the barbarous violence of the mob, but we do believe in John Brown, in that incarnate spirit of justice, that hatred of a lie, that willingness to sacrifice money, reputation, and life itself on the altar of right. And here on the scene of John Brown's martyrdom we reconsecrate ourselves, our honor, our property to the final emancipation of the race which John Brown died to make free."[13]

Lewis Sheridan Leary. (Courtesy
Boyd B. Stutler Collection of
John Brown, West Virginia State
Archives)

Jefferson County Courthouse,
Charles Town, West Virginia

I read the biography of John Brown that Du Bois was under contract to
write at the time he traveled to Harpers Ferry. David Roediger and Henry
Louis Gates, scholars of Du Bois, seemed quite certain that John Brown
changed W. E. B. Du Bois forever. Du Bois published his biography in 1909
(just months before Villard's biography appeared), and lived another fifty-four
years, but Roediger said that Du Bois "remembered the years during which he
wrote *John Brown* as a period of deep personal transformation."[14] Henry Louis
Gates said the experience of writing the biography paved the way for Du Bois'
shift "from professional academic to full-time activist," and that, for Du Bois,
John Brown "would remain the emblem" of the Civil Rights Movement.[15]

Du Bois had wanted to write about Frederick Douglass or Nat Turner for
the American Crisis Biographies Series when its editors contacted him. Douglass, however, had already been assigned to Booker T. Washington and Nat
Turner was too controversial to be approved by editors of the series, so Du Bois
ended up telling the story of a white man.

John Brown had a way of refusing to leave.

4.

The history of the engine house didn't stop with the mile-long walk of the Niagara Movement in 1906, or the Du Bois manifesto. The structure kept its political edge.

Trustees of Storer wanted the fort near the college and voted in 1909 to buy it for $900, and so it was disassembled again and rebuilt in 1910 on college grounds near Lincoln Hall. Alumni placed a plaque on the building in 1918, which is now secured behind a protective panel bolted to the brick:

> That this nation might have a new birth of freedom, that slavery should be removed forever from American soil, John Brown and his twenty-one men gave their lives. To commemorate their heroism this tablet is placed on this building which has since been known as, John Brown's Fort.

The school closed in 1955, but the fort remained where it was several more years. Then in 1968 the National Park Service moved it again. Its original site in the Lower Town was under fourteen feet of fill, and on railroad property now, so the building was moved to the arsenal yard, but still on Potomac Street. A scholar of the fort—and every fiber of John Brown left on earth seems to have its very own scholar—said that even though the fort had been moved so many times, "What has not changed significantly is the way a large portion of the African-American community has embraced the John Brown Fort (as one of the few Civil War monuments that can be claimed as its own)."[16]

At first what he said sounded odd. Harpers Ferry predated the war.

But sometimes monuments (like time itself) were fluid things. It almost seemed that they were living—organic. The date on a cornerstone of a building could be misleading, for every generation left impressions on a site. John Brown and his raiders fought in the engine house and then the struggle continued as people took it apart repeatedly (sometimes only in their minds), attached inscriptions to it, and chose new ground for it to rest on. Was Harpers Ferry over yet, I began to wonder, or would it ever be?

5.

Some of the battles for the engine house have been over words. People have fought for permission to write its story on stones and plaques from the time the building stood on the grounds of Storer College to the twenty-first century.

Words about what happened at Harpers Ferry have been contested, refused, crated up for decades, negotiated, applauded, arbitrated. Who would have the authority to say what the building—the image—finally meant?

President Henry T. McDonald of Storer College supported the enthusiasm of his students for John Brown and his raiders (five of whom were Black), even though McDonald was white. But on Saturday, May 21, 1932, when busloads of delegates from the NAACP arrived in Harpers Ferry to present a bronze commemorative tablet for installation on the fort—a tablet President McDonald had originally agreed to accept—he refused it. He had decided that the inscription was too inflammatory. Trustees had wanted this: "John Brown—His Soul Goes Marching On," anticipating words the Negro 25 Year Club would choose for the John Brown Monument in Akron. They hadn't objected to warm praise for John Brown (more tolerant than the rest of the community), but they'd been troubled by a direct attack on the South in the inscription, wanting no more fires there.

These were the words W. E. B. Du Bois wrote and the school refused:

Here
John Brown
Aimed at Human Slavery

A Blow
That woke a guilty nation.
With him fought
Seven slaves and sons of slaves.
Over his crucified corpse
Marched 200,000 black soldiers
And 4,000,000 freedmen
Singing
"John Brown's body lies a-mouldering
in the grave
But his Soul goes marching on!"[17]

The dedication ceremony proceeded, but the tablet, supposedly key to the celebration, lay on a chair and was never mentioned. It just rested there, like an uninvited guest who had wandered onto the podium.

The objection to the Du Bois plaque was caused in part by the pressure Storer trustees were receiving from the United Daughters of the Confederacy, a group committed to funding patriotic memorials almost from the day of its founding.[18] On October 10, 1931, six months before the arrival of buses from the NAACP, the UDC, along with the Sons of the Confederate Veterans, dedicated a plaque attached to a boulder near the original site of the fort in honor of Heyward Shepherd, a plaque they had spent ten years getting approved. They didn't want any other version of John Brown's battle to be on display.

Originally, the words on the UDC plaque and its intended location were found objectionable by President McDonald, who also served as town recorder and would become mayor of Harpers Ferry after that. Slowly, the most offensive words and sentences were removed from the inscription, a new mayor was elected in 1930, and a local druggist gave the memorial committee permission to install the boulder on his property, approximately where the UDC wanted it to begin with.[19]

Two major addresses were delivered at its dedication, praising the old order and the devotion of Black mammies.[20] Although the inscription on the stone had been revised, it still offended members of the college and the NAACP and soon became known as the Faithful Slave Memorial. It bore these words:

On the night of October 16, 1859, Heyward Shepherd, an industrious and respected colored freeman, was mortally wounded by John Brown's raiders. In pursuance of his duties as an employee of the Baltimore and Ohio Railroad Company, he became the first victim of this attempted insurrection.

This boulder is erected by the United Daughters of the Confederacy and the Sons of Confederate Veterans as a memorial to Heyward Shepherd, exemplifying the character and faithfulness of thousands of Negroes who, under many temptations throughout subsequent years of war, so conducted themselves that no stain was left upon a record which is the peculiar heritage of the American people, and an everlasting tribute to the best in both races.[21]

The fort and Heyward Shepherd had both become symbols to the local chapter of the United Daughters of the Confederacy, but its members read those symbols differently from the way Du Bois and the NAACP had. For the committee of the UDC, Harpers Ferry symbolized the end of a free Black man's life, but it also symbolized the end of the old order at the center of their own.

6.

When the fort was moved in 1968 to its current site in the Lower Town, about 150 feet east of its original location, people might have thought it was finally at rest.

But the story continued. I read about the renovation of the buildings in Harpers Ferry in the 1970s and found out that the United Daughters of the Confederacy monument had been placed in storage. It was returned to its site in 1981, but quickly covered because of criticism and the threat of vandalism or destruction. The park superintendent finally decided to crate it once again.[22]

On June 9, 1995, the boulder was uncovered because the NAACP and the UDC had struck a deal. The monument could stand if a wayside marker were placed beside it, both exhibits in the Lower Town on the southwest side of Potomac Street.[23]

When I visited Harpers Ferry early in my John Brown travels, I'd seen the wayside marker, but read it quickly. I hadn't connected it carefully enough to the boulder close by or to history. I examined the words on the marker more carefully later, when I needed them, finding them on a site called Stone Sentinels.

Two columns were displayed. On the left, under the caption "Heyward Shepherd," was a little biography of Shepherd, as well as details about his murder and the dedication of the boulder by the United Daughters of the Confederacy. On the right, under a second caption, "Another Perspective,"

John Brown's Fort, located on Shenandoah St. and Potomac St.,
Harpers Ferry

was information about W. E. B. Du Bois, including the words he had scripted
which the college had rejected.[24]

Boulders standing firm, then boxed up only to one day be uncovered again
with an addendum off to the side—what was history except that?

In July of 2006, NAACP Chair Julian Bond, social activist born in 1940,
brought attention to the fort again when he led a pilgrimage patterned on
W. E. B. Du Bois' failed trip in 1932—complete with an eight-car train ride from
Baltimore to Harpers Ferry (not buses this time, but the idea was identical)—
to lay a replica plaque of Du Bois' original on the grounds of former Storer
College, now the National Park Service's Mather Training Center. The words
had been inscribed on the wayside marker installed in the 1990s, but the
NAACP wanted a replica of the bronze tablet to be unequivocally accepted
where it had formerly been refused.

"No other white person, including President Lincoln, has been so widely
admired by Black Americans as John Brown," Bond said during the ceremony.
"Slavery to Brown was the sum of all evil... It denied millions their right and
their dignity."[25] He talked about the violence associated with John Brown at
Harpers Ferry. "Most condemned the violence but celebrated the impulse,
and I think that that's generally true today... They're not celebrating the vio-

Julian Bond. (Courtesy Library of
Congress)

lence that he perpetuated. They're celebrating his commitment to racial justice, and we think it's fitting to continue that celebration."[26]

As much as I would have liked to believe it was possible to separate the violence of John Brown from his "impulse" for social justice, the way Black leaders like W. E. B. Du Bois and Julian Bond had tried to, and the way Lincoln had, I knew that it wasn't. Without the violence, John Brown would have been just another white abolitionist.

FREDERICK DOUGLASS
AND JOHN BROWN

Head-and-shoulders portrait of Frederick
Douglass, photo by J. W. Hurn, 1862. (Courtesy
Library of Congress)

Harriet Tubman, portrait by Benjamin F.
Powelson, 1868 or 1869. (Courtesy Library of
Congress)

I.

"Including President Lincoln," Julian Bond had said. John Brown was the best white person ever in the estimate of Black Americans, he meant. Not even Abraham Lincoln was a contender. Distinguished Black scholar Lerone Bennett went even farther than Bond in his defense of John Brown. He was openly critical of Lincoln in his biography *Forced into Glory: Abraham Lincoln's White Dream* (2000), as Julian Bond had tacitly been, and so radical in his praise of John Brown that he found him superior in some ways to established Black icons. "More than Frederick Douglass, more than any other Negro leader, John Brown suffered with the slave," he said in an essay.[1]

Prominent nineteenth-century Black figures had also praised John Brown, including abolitionist and former fugitive William Wells Brown. Ezra Greenspan, biographer of William Wells Brown, said that John Brown was "a living, looming presence in his life for years."[2] Wells Brown led anniversary celebrations at Harpers Ferry after the Civil War, met Mary Ann Brown, and in his writing credited John Brown with playing a major role in protecting fugitives in Springfield from the Fugitive Slave Act.[3] It was William Wells Brown, a man who once worked on the waterfronts of Cleveland, Ohio,[4] who first published John Brown's "Words of Advice" and "Agreement," the documents that explained the principles and methods of the League of Gileadites.[5]

Frederick Douglass himself—a person school children probably learn about much more frequently than John Brown—found John Brown's courage greater than his own. He may have been hurt by Bennett's comparison, had he been alive to hear it, but I'm not sure he would have disagreed. When Douglass compared himself to John Brown in an address at Storer College in 1881, he found he didn't fare too well. "His zeal in the cause of my race was far greater than mine—it was as the burning sun to my taper of light—mine was bounded by time, his stretched away to the boundless shores of eternity. I could live for the slave, but he could die for him,"[6] he said.

His respect for John Brown even leached into letters he composed in praise of Black leaders. Great leaders. Douglass wrote to Harriet Tubman from Rochester on August 29, 1868, and his words made me uncomfortable. "The midnight sky and the silent stars have been the witnesses of your devotion to freedom and of your heroism. Excepting John Brown—of sacred memory—I know of no one who has willingly encountered more perils and hardships to serve our enslaved people than you have," he wrote.[7] I wondered how Tubman felt when she read these words—if she was insulted by Douglass' comparison, or perhaps agreed.

In 1848 Douglass had written in his newspaper, *The North Star*, that Brown, "though a white gentleman, is in sympathy a Black man, and is as deeply interested in our cause, as though his own soul had been pierced with the iron of slavery."[8]

Bennett said of him, "John Brown *was* a Negro." In another breath, he spoke of him as colorless. "He was of no color, John Brown, of no race or age. He was pure passion, pure transcendence. He was an elemental force, like the wind, rain and fire."[9]

I began to wonder if this was the same man I was spending my days with. Sometimes I didn't think I knew John Brown very well at all.

2.

Lerone Bennett and even Frederick Douglass himself, it seemed to me, were too hard on Douglass, both sometimes viewing him as John Brown's inferior. John Brown took great risks and was zealous—there was no denying that. He ordered the rifles, shot them; saw that the blades were sharpened on Pottawatomie Creek and put them in his own sons' hands. He died for his cause, after all. His actions drew national attention and perhaps changed the course of history, or at least moved it along.

I'd certainly never thought of Douglass as John Brown's "inferior" until Douglass and Bennett invited me to, though recently a contemporary Black writer raised the issue again. James McBride, whose novel *The Good Lord Bird* won the National Book Award in 2013, scolded Douglass and with humor made a little fun of him. His book was fiction, and I of course had to remember that.[10]

His novel followed John Brown from Kansas to his Charles Town jail cell. The narrator, Henry Shackleford, nicknamed "Onion," was the son of a man who was enslaved by Dutch Henry, one of the real-life "Shermans" who were central to the Pottawatomie story in Kansas. The fictional Onion, pretending to be a girl until the end of the book, traveled with John Brown and his party after his father was killed at Dutch Henry's proslavery store.

McBride portrayed Onion as weak-willed and confused about almost everything. I loved Onion (he made me laugh), and I loved the book, but clearly the character McBride intended me to admire most was John Brown.

Abolitionists, by Milan Kecman, from his series
Head2Head. (Courtesy Milan Kecman)

Mcbride's John Brown had faults, but they seemed small ones. Young
Onion called John Brown a religious fanatic, a lunatic, and the most long-
winded man imaginable, but the boy ended up strong because of him. Ended
up loving him, too.

The book featured many of the Black characters in the real story of John
Brown and gave Frederick Douglass a major role. The novelist scripted a new
part for history's Heyward Shepherd, calling him "the Rail Man," making him
no longer a simple porter employed by the railroad company, but a "Hiver" who
worked in secret and rebellious ways to recruit Black people to the cause.

McBride, clearly, was aware of the vital role Black people played in their
own freedom. Although a writer of fiction, he would join in spirit national and
regional scholars who were recording the nearly century-long involvement of
Black individuals in emancipation ("not so much a proclamation as a movement," one scholar called it[11])—some focusing on the activism of free Blacks
or the resistance of fugitives;[12] others concentrating on Black community and

Ritner Boarding House, Chambersburg, Pennsylvania

Black activism in Harpers Ferry long before John Brown arrived;[13] another documenting the role of Canadian Blacks in the raid;[14] a few locating records of activity after the raid that confirmed Virginia would never be the same again—the fires, the mass selling off of enslaved people, the great loss of money for slave owners.[15]

The Life and Times of Frederick Douglass must have been on a shelf of McBride's study, because the Chambersburg scene in his novel in many ways resembled Douglass' account. John Brown, who was staying at the Ritner Boarding House in Chambersburg during the summer of 1859, met Douglass at a quarry the weekend of August 19 to August 21, in the company of John Kagi and Shields Green, a site preserved by a historical marker which erupts incongruously by Loudon Street Bridge—near Southgate Mall, some rock outcroppings, a grove of trees, a CVS, a Firestone Store, and a Rent-A-Center.[16]

In both meetings at the quarry—*Life and Times* and McBride—Douglass told John Brown that he was walking into a "steel-trap," that the government would immediately retaliate, and that his plan was little more than suicide. John Brown, in both versions, told Douglass that he needed him to hive the bees (a metaphor he used to describe the uprising of enslaved people he was sure would occur when he attacked Harpers Ferry) and that he would protect him with his life. Most important of all, in both the autobiography and the novel Douglass refused to accompany John Brown to Harpers Ferry.

In *Life and Times* Douglass analyzed his own motive for saying "no" to John Brown. He wasn't sure, he said, if his decision was based on "my discretion or my cowardice."[17] Much earlier, in a letter he wrote from Canada West on October 31, 1859, shortly after John Brown was captured and Douglass fled the country, he admitted that he was "most miserably deficient in courage," but said he had never promised anyone he would go with John Brown and, therefore, had disappointed no one.[18] Not everyone close to John Brown, however, agreed that he'd made no prior commitment.[19]

In McBride's novel young Onion (who was present at the scene in the novel along with the four men from history) was quite sure what caused Douglass to refuse. "He was a man of parlor talk, of silk shirts and fine hats, linen suits and ties…a speeching parlor man."[20]

David Blight would speak with great care and nuance about Douglass' complicated relationship with John Brown. "His problem with the Old Man was strategic," he believed, "not ethical, although Douglass continually struggled to square killing with reason."[21]

Most people who study Frederick Douglass and John Brown are hesitant to blame Douglass for choosing life over certain death. John Brown's biographer Louis A. DeCaro Jr. said, "Frederick Douglass clearly preferred to live for the slave as an orator, activist, and politically respected leader. We should be grateful that he chose to do so."[22]

David Blight saw Douglass as a man who had a plan to live; John Brown, a plan to die.[23]

W. E. B. Du Bois, in his John Brown biography, raised the question, "Why did not Douglass join John Brown?" First, he said, they were of entirely different temperaments—which reminded me of John Brown's words about "constitutional difference." Second, he said, Douglass knew "as only a Negro slave can know, the tremendous might and organization of the slave power," and believed "only national force could dislodge national slavery." Du Bois imagined how fugitives who reached Canada might have replied to a summons to arm. "What more did they owe the world? Did not the world owe them an unpayable amount?"[24]

Warren Lyons, a painter in New York City I learned about from a descendant of Ellen Sherbondy Brown (Jason Brown's Akron wife),[25] had finished a portrait of Frederick Douglass, along with other antebellum figures such as Harriet Tubman and Sojourner Truth. He was now struggling to complete a portrait of John Brown that he'd worked on for several years—a task, I realized, that in some ways resembled my own.

We began to correspond about John Brown, but in the process he also made me think about Douglass, the man he had had to learn to understand in order to paint.

Warren Lyons talked once about the "pain and emptiness" that Douglass must have known, and said these things had to be viewed "with compassion, rather than accusation, if the species is to survive."[26] He said it was the common thread between John Brown and Frederick Douglass that mattered more than their differences. Both faced the reality of their time, rejecting the sleepy response of the masses, and "shouldered it."[27]

Yes, I thought, both men were activists in America's fight against injustice, though their makeup was not the same. John Brown's fight was brief and intense; Douglass' long and intellectual.

In an interview, McBride said he hoped people wouldn't take his portrayal of Frederick Douglass' faults "personally." He liked the man, he said—called him a "great leader" and "gifted writer." Besides, he said, "It's just an illumination." But his depiction of Frederick Douglass nevertheless did, in some way, elevate John Brown. "I wanted to communicate the overwhelming moral power and courage and drive of John Brown to release Blacks from slavery whether they wanted to be released or not,"[28] he said.

Still, I wasn't willing to cozy up to John Brown the way McBride had. As much as I loved McBride's book, when he added comedy to the massacre on Pottawatomie Creek, for instance—when everyone was quaking like chickens or howling like coyotes or bellowing like broken calves, and people were scrambling to get away—well, such a raucous scene was terrific fun to read, but it didn't calm me down one bit when I thought about what actually happened there.

Even when the appeal of McBride and his book increased for me by a visit the author made to Hudson, I resisted liking John Brown as much as I thought the author wanted me to, and kept my distance. In her role as archivist, Gwen arranged for McBride to speak at the Hudson Library, so he came—for her, and for the town that had raised his hero.

He talked about the days when he was in a band, before he did a lot of writing. He told a story about flying to Montreal to open for Rosemary Clooney when he was a young saxophonist. On one particular flight, he defended a Hasidic boy who was being made fun of. He was proud of himself for what he'd done. People sometimes have to get in arguments, he said, because only by standing up does "the collective good inch forward that much more."

He'd brought a band along. He read and then they all played and sang, traditional spirituals, mainly—*Since I Laid My Burdens Down*; *He Walks with Me and He Talks with Me*; *It's Me, Oh, Lord, Standing in the Need of Prayer*; *Oh, Sinnerman, Where You Gonna Run to on Judgment Day?* His presentation and his songs brought alive every sensation in the book.

But McBride's book, I had to remember, was just a version of John Brown, as mine would be. Plenty of people throughout history had questioned some of John Brown's decisions, and Frederick Douglass was one of them.

I found myself siding with the man of greater moderation.

REVERIE 5
"CHIAROSCURO"

"Eclipse," by Warren Lyons. (Courtesy Warren Lyons)

I.

The methods Warren Lyons used for his portrait of John Brown helped me think about my own work. He told me he applied paint only with his fingers, trying to dissolve what he felt were the arbitrary boundaries between himself and John Brown that brushes imposed. He never turned his eye away from the complex task of seeing the man whole, so his portrait became three dimensional. John Brown was taking longer than any of his other abolitionist portraits had—ten years now. He exhibited his John Brown, which he titled "Eclipse," at the Staten Island Museum in 2017, but even then wrote on the gallery label that the portrait was "a work in progress," and started work on it again after the exhibit ended.[1]

Throughout history, John Brown himself had been a "Work in Progress," I sometimes thought, so how could a book or a portrait about him ever be finished?

Warren Lyons saw a divided image of John Brown in photographs he studied and knew he had to find a way to hold both visions on the canvas at once. He saw contrast in the vertical hemispheres of the pictures he held up to the light. "If you were to cover the right side of the head with a straight edge," he told me, "the left side of the face evidences tracings of a stern, severe, and unyielding, vindictive visage, reminiscent of accounts of an enraged, severe and unyielding avenging 'angel.'" But the right side? There he found "an almost heart-rending sadness, tenderness and compassion such as that seen in depictions of Christ while in the presence of children or, better, of Christ in the garden of Gethsemane."[2]

His portrait of John Brown would pose complex problems for him of balancing shadow and light. The beatific and the tormented. The "chiaroscuro," he called it, "the dance of light and dark." He saw John Brown, finally, as a human being struggling to live in balance (which also included, for the painter, the "universal process of living and dying and resurrecting"), and he felt that painting John Brown was not just a matter of art and craft, but of spiritual will on the part of the artist—"the will to see without judgment or contempt of the self or others."[4]

When he described the difficult problem of balancing the contrasts in John Brown, I knew it was my problem too. *Contrast* was a word close to *ambivalence*. I liked abolitionists, and therefore liked John Brown, but the way he went about his work continued to make me uneasy, and I did find myself judging him sometimes.

There was startling violence in some of his deeds, without any question. Yet, the word "terrorist," which was often used to describe him (and sometimes I considered using too), never felt quite right and threw the balance off.

Paul Finkelman talked about the way domestic terrorism in recent decades had heightened the debate about whether or not John Brown was "America's first terrorist," and I understood how that could happen.[5] But was it really a "debate" that people wanted to engage in when they used the word? It always felt dismissive. There would be no further conversation, that single word declared, though I wish I'd had the courage to force it. Instead, I retreated to the page.

I'd sit in my chair and try to find a way to make light and shadow resolve. Chiaroscuro.

NORTH ELBA AND TIMBUCTO

I.

He moved his family to North Elba, New York, in May of 1849, but lingering obligations to Perkins & Brown quickly called him back, so there wasn't time to build a house. For two years the Browns occupied a farm owned by a Mr. Flanders, a little place on the road from Keene to Lake Placid. John Brown brought his Devon cattle, a hardy breed with rich mahogany hide, so the family at least had milk and meat, though little else.

He was more a visitor to North Elba than a resident. The instability of the wool industry, caused by manufacturers not placing orders (seeing if they could drive the price down) and then growers crying for payment that wasn't there, kept him constantly attending to the difficulties of his business and his partnership with Colonel Perkins. In August of 1849, he left for Europe to see if his luck selling wool would improve, but ended up, instead, with a loss of $40,000. For several years after that, he traveled throughout the northeast trying to resolve grave matters of litigation and debt for Perkins & Brown, living mainly in Springfield and Ohio, occasionally making side trips to New York. By March of 1851, it was clear he wouldn't be able to settle with his family in the Adirondacks for some time, so he moved everyone back to Akron, where Perkins wanted him to be.[1]

He didn't return his family to North Elba until the spring of 1855, to an unplastered four-room house built by Henry Thompson, the husband of John Brown's daughter Ruth. Visitors can tour the structure today, owned since

North Elba farmhouse. (Courtesy Hudson Library & Historical Society)

1896 by New York State, though the home has been remodeled and restored since Henry Thompson built it.

By the middle of August 1855, John Brown was absent from North Elba once more, heading with Henry Thompson to Chicago, where they met Oliver and bought a horse for their wagon and began the slow journey toward Osawatomie, Kansas—which they reached on October 6.[2] (This was the trip when they dug up John Brown's grandson Austin.) After fighting commenced in Kansas, North Elba for John Brown would be little more than an address on an envelope.

It wasn't good land that had drawn John Brown to North Elba, so he seldom seemed disappointed in his farm and its location, the way that others did. In his letters addressed to North Elba, he cautioned his sons to "feed out" potatoes very carefully, to not waste hay, to protect the shed from breaking in the heavy snow of the Northern latitudes.[3] But what he mainly offered was advice, not complaint.

It wasn't just the prospect of a thriving farm that brought him to the Adirondacks.

John Brown had visited North Elba in 1848, the location of the 120,000 acres that Gerrit Smith, one of the Secret Six, had given to free Blacks and fugitives, and after that visit he hoped to make the community, at first named Timbucto (it also came to be known as a Freed Slave Utopian Experiment), a central part of his life. He planned to help its Black residents learn how to farm and, after the Fugitive Slave Law passed, how to fight and resist.

Very little went right for the "Negro colonists" in what one biographer termed "a dreary and an inaccessible place."[4] The original white settlers who were there didn't like the arrival of their new Black neighbors and often over-charged them for supplies and materials; the summer season was too short for fields to be productive; ice and rocks were unfamiliar to people from the South; free Blacks who came to live there were tradesmen by experience, not farmers.

But John Brown persisted in thinking that every problem could be solved, even in "the high Northern Lattitude."[5]

North Elba—hard, resistant ground—was John Brown's kind of place. I couldn't help thinking that it somehow resembled him. It had begun to turn into an image in my brain even before I set out to find it.

2.

Thomas Wentworth Higginson, friend of Emily Dickinson and member of the Secret Six, compared the mountains familiar to him in Vermont and Massachusetts with John Brown's Adirondacks when he traveled to North Elba to fetch Mary Ann Brown, hoping she could help persuade her husband to be rescued from his Charles Town jail cell.[6] "Coming from the soft marble country of Vermont, and from the pale granite of Massachusetts, there seems something weird and forbidding in this utter blackness," he wrote. "Black and bare as iron" was how he described the Adirondacks.[7]

But those were his words, not mine. I'd have to travel to this place and find my own. Feel the pressure of its high air on my Midwestern lungs and try to understand John Brown's attraction to such desolate ground.

I loaded the car and we headed for North Elba to visit his home above the ground, as well as the one below, since John Brown had chosen to spend eternity there.

Lake Placid, a village within the town of North Elba, didn't have the Olympic Center and a resort hovering around its edges when John Brown was a resident. Nor did it have the Ford Ironman Triathlon—the event that was going on the day my husband and I arrived, an all-day competition comprising a 2.4-mile swim, a 112-mile bike ride, and a 26.2-mile run. I hadn't known about the race. In some ways, our timing couldn't have been worse.

Signs about an Ironman competition greeted us on the roads around Keene, where state troopers and official-looking people in orange ponchos began slowing cars and directing them to a single lane marked off by matching orange cones. Just north of Keene, their heads and arms hunched over handlebars, cyclists began to spill down Route 73 like an insect horde. They wore little beetle helmets and goggles that made their eyes big and yellow. Their muscles were as firm and defined as the bars and pedals of the bikes that propelled them into town or to the next station where people were standing with arms extended, holding between their fingertips bananas and Gatorade ready to be plucked in flight.

The rain that had begun that morning would not let up. The already dangerous course through the Adirondack Mountains was treacherous now— slippery roads full of winter potholes overflowing with water. We drove slowly past Mt. Van Hovenberg and Whispering Pines Campground. Bikers to our left were struggling up hills, standing to gain speed and changing gears to find a way to make mountain inclines a little friendlier to human calves and thighs. The land was rising higher, then higher still, and I wondered at the number of people who had come here, and why. Some, perhaps, hoped to win. Most, I thought, were here for other reasons—to get fit, accomplish something remarkable, lose weight, outwit mortality.

It was exciting to watch—all that movement, all that color, all that health and energy spinning up the mountainside. I cracked the window just a little to hear the sound of the world arriving on the wheels of people whizzing by.

We crossed the Ausable River.

Few cars appeared. Only tourists, like us, were on the road today.

3.

John Brown Road had been blocked off for the race. A police officer approached us on foot as we slowed and asked us where we were headed. He seemed surprised when I said the North Elba farm, but he removed the traffic cones, permitting us to pass.

We soon came to a circular drive with a walkway and a monument and some lilies at the center. Nearby was a mailbox with an address: 115 John Brown Farm. We had no trouble finding a place to park.

The gravesite and the house looked familiar because I'd seen pictures of this place. A famous sketch by an artist for the *New York Illustrated News,* printed on December 24, 1859, showed the house and the rock behind the grave, a few horses and wagons that had brought the mourners, the mourners themselves huddled close together, and four men leaning over a hole—holding ropes that supported the coffin of John Brown and helped ease it into the ground.

We went directly to the graves, since the sky was becoming even darker and I wanted to make sure I saw the burial site.

In front of the gate that now surrounded the graves were large wayside markers with historical information about the Browns, not unlike those at Harpers Ferry. Under our umbrella, I scanned stories about Mary Ann Day Brown, the Brown children, Harpers Ferry, the raiders, the headstone. Watson and Oliver had separate graves next to their father's—two green swatches of rectangular land with metal markers at the head of each. Watson was alone, just as most of us are in our burial plots.

Mailbox on site of North Elba farm

Sketch of burial of John Brown at North
Elba, *New York Illustrated News.* (Courtesy
Boyd B. Stutler Collection of John Brown,
West Virginia State Archives)

But Oliver was not. Along with his bones, the marker said, were those of
the other raiders killed at Harpers Ferry. Watson and Oliver arrived at North
Elba for burial long after John Brown did, even though they both died at the
Ferry in October of 1859. They were brought to North Elba in different years—
even in different decades—but I learned their strange stories after our trip.

Only John Brown had a headstone, and it was housed in glass, though its
protective casing seemed fairly new.[8] John Brown had wanted that particular
stone over him. He had it brought to North Elba sometime around 1858 from
Canton, Connecticut, where it had served as a cenotaph for his grandfather,
the Captain John Brown of the Connecticut 18th Regiment who had died
from dysentery during the Revolutionary War somewhere near New York
City.[9] John Brown had leaned the commemorative stone against the house or
barn until it was needed, with these words exposed: "In Memory of Capt.
John Brown Who Died At New York Sept. Ye 3 1776 in the 48 year of his age."

Sometime between the arrival of the stone and John Brown's execution, he
arranged to have an inscription for his son Frederick carved on the back. Frederick's body remained in Kansas, but John Brown wanted his memory preserved at the North Elba farm. "In memory of FREDERICK son of John &

John Brown headstone, North Elba farm, photo by
S. R. Stoddard, 1888. (Courtesy Boyd B. Stutler
Collection of John Brown, West Virginia State
Archives)

Dianthe Brown Born Dec. 21, 1830, and murdered at Osawatomie Kansas, Aug.
30, 1856 for his adherence to the cause of freedom."[10] John Brown turned his
son's epitaph into a statement about his cause, a justification, perhaps, for his
boy's dying so young (shot by the Reverend Martin White), or, maybe, for his
own role in bringing it about.

In bitter January of 1860, a local stone carver named B. A. Barrett arrived
at the farm to finish the work in the kitchen of the family's farmhouse.[11] In a
last-minute letter to Mary Ann Brown the morning of his execution, John
Brown wrote quick instructions about how to complete the inscription on the
old family stone, assuming his sons would be returned to North Elba along
with him (instead of thirty or forty years later): "Oliver Brown born   1839
was killed at Harpers ferry Va Nov 17th 1859; Watson Brown, born   1835
was wounded at Harpers ferry Nov 17th and died Nov 19th 1859; John Brown
born May 9th 1800 was executed at Charlestown, Va, December 2d 1859."[12]
John Brown had confused the month of the raid (it was October, not November), and had forgotten the months and days when his two boys had been born.
A life like his left little time to remember family celebrations.

John Brown's grave and the "Big Rock," North Elba, photo by S. R. Stoddard, ca. 1896. (Courtesy Library of Congress)

The original headstone now had five names inscribed on it.

It kept raining, harder even than it had. I could barely see the outline of the Adirondacks that surrounded the farmland of North Elba, a great amphitheater of mountains when it's clear, Mount Marcy and Whiteface Mountain and the Keene Valley all visible. Could barely see the Olympic ski lift in the distance, though I knew it was there.

The labradorite in front of the house was the one thing I could make out. Glaciers had dumped a huge rock in John Brown's front yard—a giant stool where he would sit sometimes, read his Bible, and pray. Only the word "John" was legible on the face of the stone itself now, but at the turn of the century his full name and the year of his execution had been carved into its surface, like chatter marks.

I moved toward a plaque bolted into the rock. It held a summary of the story of John Brown, beginning with his emigration to Kansas in 1855 and ending with his execution at Charles Town. There were lists. "Here Lie Buried with Him Twelve of his followers," one began. A correction had been made on the wayside marker: Jeremiah Anderson, one of the "twelve," was not buried here. His body had been used for "anatomical study," and his final burial site was "not known." The other raiders killed in battle had been hurriedly thrown into a store box, which was then tossed into a shallow hole until years later, when it was dug up.

Gravesite, North Elba, showing the rock with plaques installed
(background) and three grave plots (foreground)

Two of the nine raiders in Oliver's grave had been captured, then hanged,
on March 16, 1860—Albert Hazlett and Aaron Stevens. They arrived at
North Elba by a different route than the other men, because Rebecca Buffum
Spring had arranged to bury them on her property at Eagleswood Mansion
in New Jersey but agreed to give them up for reburial with Oliver.

On the bottom left of the plaque attached to the great rock were the names
of those hanged on December 16, 1859—John E. Cook, Edwin Coppoc, Shields
Green, John A. Copeland. They weren't buried with Oliver, so I'd have to look
for them the way I would for Jeremiah Anderson.

On the bottom right were the names of the men who tried to escape and
did: Owen Brown, Francis Jackson Merriam, Charles Plummer Tidd, Barclay
Coppoc, Osborne P. Anderson.[13]

A second bronze plaque on the large stone, installed in 1946 by the John
Brown Memorial Association, commemorated the women in John Brown's
family. On it were the names of John Brown's two wives, of his fatherless
daughters, of his daughters-in-law who had lost their husbands at Harpers
Ferry, and of Mary B. Thompson, who lost both her husband, William, and
her brother-in-law, Dauphin.

It seemed so quiet with the rain falling and everything underground now,
but the names on those plaques were anything but still.

4.

The site manager, who lived in a small blue house nearby, saw my husband and me moving from the gravesite toward the John Brown home and came dressed in rain gear to let us in.

"It's the wettest summer since I've been up here," he said, unlocking the door.

"We're from Hudson, Ohio," my husband said.

The ranger looked a little differently at the two of us after that.

In the parlor the guide told the story of Gerrit Smith and Timbucto and the construction of the John Brown house. He showed us a writing desk, built by Henry Thompson, along with a bookcase and some chairs Thompson also made. "They wagon-trained to California, and these pieces probably just stayed," he said about the Browns, who left North Elba a few years after John Brown sank into the ground.

He talked about slavery, the funeral trip, Harpers Ferry, and then Pottawatomie, as if he knew the subject would come up eventually, so he might as well address it.

"Brown is considered the poster-boy for violence in Kansas. However, there was plenty of violence in Kansas before he showed up. He was threatened, so he pulled the ringleaders out of their homes and had them killed. It probably saved the situation, but it was the worst thing he could have done for his reputation. From then on he was known as the Bad Man of Kansas. He was the bogey man to the proslavery people. That was part of his effectiveness

North Elba farmhouse

too. If you're proslavery and considering acts of violence, you're a lot less likely
to do them if you know that one night John Brown might knock on your door
and be there."

It didn't surprise me that a man in his position would try to defend John
Brown as best he could. Who could talk about John Brown every day of the
year and take care of his property and tend his grave—who could do these
tedious custodial tasks—if he thought the man he was representing was a
deranged murderer?

*And who could write about John Brown every day for years and visit family
graves, if she believed her subject were a vengeful killer?* Sometimes my thoughts
alarmed me.

He talked about what a hard place this was—especially when John Brown
was absent. "It was tough going," he said. "The women wore home-spun
dresses. They made their own soap and candles. They had rope beds and tightened them. That's where we get the expression 'Sleep Tight.' Imagine the
whole area stacked floor to ceiling with firewood. That's how much you would
need to fuel the stove for a year."

We exited the house, opening our umbrellas when we stepped out.

"How many people come here a year?" I asked.

"Maybe sixty thousand, but not everyone who comes to the grounds
wants to see the house."

Annual pilgrimage to John Brown gravesite by John Brown Memorial Association, May 9, 1930. (Courtesy Boyd B. Stutler Collection of John Brown, West Virginia State Archives)

"And the huge trees on the property?" I said. "What are they?" "Maple," he said.

I wondered if this sometimes–symbol maker I was following across the country would have recognized the continuity of his life in the symbol of this tree—his roots in maples that flourished throughout Ohio, especially in the cool climates and acidic soil of the northeastern part of the state. He adored its sweet substance—its syrup and its sugar—and took some to little Minnie Russell when he stayed with her family in the East. Or was continuity something he ever thought about? Maybe only other people agonized over such things. A life that came full circle may never have been of any importance to him.

His life was all about trajectory.

Before the ranger left, he mentioned the statue at the entrance to the property. It was dedicated on John Brown's birthday in 1935 by the John Brown Memorial Association, the same association that furnished a plaque honoring the women who had made sacrifices for John Brown, and that had undertaken annual pilgrimages to the gravesite beginning in 1922 to lay wreaths and deliver speeches. Lake Placid schools closed in honor of the day. When members came on pilgrimages, the ranger said, they stayed in private homes because lodging was only available to white people.

On May 9, 1935, J. Max Barber, whose dream had been to have a statue of John Brown on the grounds, delivered the dedication address to over two

Joseph Pollia statue of John Brown

thousand people. The speech included a comparison between John Brown and Lincoln that brought back the image of the Hudson silhouette, as such comparisons always did for me. "Pushing up beside Lincoln must always appear the name of John Brown. He was the voice crying in the wilderness. He it was who kindled the beacon fires of freedom on a thousand hills. He was the grim, grey herald of that awful conflict which robed the nation in fire and blood...After John Brown there could be no peace with slavery in the land."[14]

The day I was at North Elba, no one was present except my husband and me. We approached the statue alone, following the sidewalk we'd earlier come down, a path that cut a circle of grass in half, like an equator.

John Brown was standing with a Black child, a boy. On a large block of granite supporting the figures, a simple inscription read, "John Brown," and then, "1800–1859." A narrow bronze base under their feet contained a few familiar words: "His soul goes marching on."

I stared up at it. Sculpted by Joseph Pollia, the statue stood over eleven feet from the base to the top of John Brown's head, though his body was only eight feet high. The same height as the rock. The boy beside him, shoeless, with his

Lyman Epps Sr. (Courtesy Boyd B. Stutler
Collection of John Brown, West Virginia State
Archives)

shirt slipping down one arm, didn't quite reach his companion's shoulder. The
theme of the monument was "Inspiration."

I liked best the human detail on the bronze. The arms and bodies and feet
of both figures, where not covered in cloth, looked as if they had life in them,
perhaps because bronze sculptures often begin with clay molds that hold
texture in an uncanny way. Six tons of bronze, yet I could feel the warmth of
the sculpture, which had first been caught in the grain of the earth.

I wasn't entirely smitten, though. I made a note about how the paternalis-
tic pairing bothered me, but after returning home, I put parentheses around
what I'd written. I realized that my response had been too quick.

Why had I focused on this when there was so much else to consider—the
pleas and passion of J. Max Barber; the donors who scraped money together for
twelve years; the two thousand people who attended the dedication; the aged
hands of Lyman Epps' son unveiling the statue—a person who'd sat on John
Brown's knee as a child and sung at his funeral as a young boy;[15] the thousands
of visitors who came to North Elba every year to look at the statue and the
graves; the ranger who lived in the blue house and dressed in rain gear so that
my husband and I could take a tour in bad weather; the John Brown Memorial
Association that struggled to pay respect?[16] I'd forgotten the many hardships
that brought the bronze figure to this place. Not just the financial sacrifices
people made, but all the obstacles Jim Crow had placed in their way. The statue
of John Brown at North Elba was more theirs than Joseph Pollia's, and certainly
more theirs than mine.

5.

Citizens of Hudson thought John Brown would be buried in their town. On December 4, two days after his execution (he dangled from a rope for thirty-five minutes before he was cut down), town fathers held a meeting to talk about who would deliver his eulogy. It made sense to people that John Brown would come home.

Hudson was his home in so many ways—the place he'd lived longer than anywhere else and returned to his whole life. The family plot of the Browns was firmly established in the Old Hudson Township Burying Ground by the time of his death, and his mother and father were there. So were other relatives: stepmother Sally Root Brown; brother Salmon Brown (marker), half-brothers Watson Hugh Brown and Lucien Brown, and half-sister Martha Brown; aunt Theodosia Brown Merrills.

John Brown had outgrown any conventional idea of a hometown long before he stepped onto the gallows, but I still wondered if particular reservations he'd voiced about Hudson had in any way influenced his decision. When he lived in New Richmond, Pennsylvania, in the 1820s and 1830s (formerly Randolph), he wrote a letter to his brother Frederick about hoping to one day start a school for Black children, believing completely that education "would most assuredly operate on slavery like firing powder confined in rock, and all slaveholders know it well." Randolph, he said, might be a good place to do this, for in that location "there would be no powerful opposition influence against such a thing."

John Brown riding on his coffin to his execution, *Frank Leslie's Illustrated Newspaper*. (Courtesy Library of Congress)

He went on to mention why Hudson was not his first choice for such a school. "I think that a place which might be in some measure settled with a view to such an object would be much more favorable to such an undertaking than would any such place as Hudson, with all its conflicting interests and feelings; and I do think such advantages ought to be afforded the young blacks, whether they are all to be immediately set free or not."[17]

Hudson archivist Gwen Mayer once told me that antebellum Hudson was one-third abolitionist, one-third colonizationist, and one third undecided. Hudson has in its archives a Copperheads Voters List of 1863, a list of men who were also known as Peace Democrats, or Butternuts, citizens who thought it would be best to make peace with the South and let the region keep people enslaved. On that list are forty-six names of prominent Hudson men, as well as nine other men who refused to vote in the 1863 election and were probably Copperheads too, men who believed deeply that Lincoln had turned into a tyrant—threatening the union by removing constitutional rights from the people and by placing too much importance on the matter of slavery.[18]

John Brown knew that the "conflicting interests and feelings" present in his former town would not be ideal for his school, and perhaps this realization informed his later decisions too.

The citizens gathered in Hudson that day to talk about John Brown's eulogy—Doctor Ashman, John Markillie, John Buss, Frederick Baldwin, Mr. Messon, W. Pettingill, Professor Hanford, Mr. Fairchild, Mr. Darling,

Sheriff James Campbell, who hanged John Brown.
(Courtesy Boyd B. Stutler Collection of John Brown,
West Virginia State Archives)

William M. Beebee.[19] They didn't know that Mary Ann Brown and John
Brown had made different plans: after his execution John Brown's body would
be taken to North Elba on a funeral trek so arduous that I could barely
imagine it. I could imagine the idea of it, and I could retrieve some of the
details about it from my reading, but was it possible to ever know all the physical hardships in the mid–nineteenth century of moving a coffin from Charles
Town to that high hill in the Adirondacks—530 miles by today's roads?

John Brown had proposed another twist to his funeral that his Hudson
neighbors never would have guessed. He was a practical man, and it was probably when he thought about the struggle ahead for Mary that he decided to
remove the weight of his lifeless body from her new list of burdens. In his last
interview with her, according to his jailer, he directed Mary to "place us all
together on a wood pile, and set fire to the wood, burn the flesh, then collect
our bones and put them in a large box, then have the box carried to our farm
in Essex County and there bury us." It would cost so much less in every way to
burn the bodies of John Brown, his two sons, and the two Thompson boys, he
told her. But Mary Ann Brown was repulsed by the idea (as Christian Cackler
had been when he found out, calling it "heathenish") and refused. "I really
cannot consent to do this," she supposedly said.[20]

Instead, she would find ways to move the coffin by rail and wagon and
boat, across mountains and lakes, through forests on nearly impassable roads
to the North Elba farm she had failed to tame, and place her husband, according to his wishes, "in the shadow of a great rock," the labradorite I now had
seen.[21]

Place him where he knew he belonged, in land as remote and difficult as
his life had been—as he had been. Place him in the hard, stubborn soil of
America, where he'd remain for the rest of time, "a-mouldering in the grave."

6.

It began with boxes.[22] He was placed in a pine coffin, and then, about 4:00 p.m. on the day of his execution, with a military escort, the box was placed on a train that traveled seven miles from Charles Town to Harpers Ferry. There, Col. Shutt of the Baltimore and Ohio Railroad protected the body until the next leg of John Brown's final adventure. Mary Ann Brown, who was staying in the Wager House Hotel in Harpers Ferry during the hanging, saw her husband dead for the first time.

The funeral party gathered at the Harpers Ferry railroad station on the morning of Saturday, December 3. In the party were Mary, the coffin, Hector Tyndale (a lawyer making a name for himself in Philadelphia, soon to become a Union general), and J. Miller McKim, a Philadelphia abolitionist. At the urging of Henry C. Wright—an abolitionist who supported nonviolence but had encouraged slave insurrections in his famous Natick Resolution speech—Boston orator and abolitionist Wendell Phillips joined the group in New York City, where he tried to convince Mary to give the body over to him for burial at Mount Auburn (founded in 1831) in Cambridge, Massachusetts. He did not succeed.

At 12:45 p.m., the entourage arrived at the Philadelphia railroad station, where a mob of mostly sympathizers greeted the body. But not all were friends. The day of John Brown's execution, there had been a vigil held at the First Congregational Unitarian Church in Philadelphia at National Hall on Market Street, and extra police had already been called out for that. White hecklers had attended it, along with friends of John Brown, many of them members of Philadelphia's Black population, and newspapers had reported both applause

Charles Town street
scene, showing back of
courthouse. (Courtesy
Library of Congress)

and hisses at this volatile gathering. Other services and vigils took place in
Black churches throughout the town that day. John Brown had arrived to a
place of high emotion, in other words.

Everyone struggled to see the box. It soon became clear that John Brown's
body would not make a visit to the undertaker in this town, as had been originally
planned. The mayor, afraid of violence, loaded a decoy coffin (a long toolbox
wrapped in deerskin) onto a wagon whose destination, people were told, was the
antislavery office where the body would lie in state.[23] John Brown couldn't avoid
disguises, even in death. While the wagon with the toolbox moved across town,
a furniture car pulled the real coffin to the Camden depot, where it was loaded
into the baggage compartment and then shipped to New York City.

Rev. Joshua Young, the minister who spoke at John Brown's funeral and
wrote about the funeral trip, described "the increased excitement" the coffin
was causing and "the divided state of public opinion."[24] The funeral party
became secretive, quietly moving the casket to the rooms of undertakers
McGraw & Taylor on the Bowery. There, it was prepared by Dr. J. M.
Hopper—kept on ice ($8.00), washed and laid out ($3.00), switched to a 5 x
10 walnut coffin ($16.00; the Southern coffin John Brown arrived in was con-
sidered unacceptable and corrupt, since it had been manufactured in a slave
state, just as John Brown had found his grandson's being buried in Missouri
ground unacceptable, so he dug him up), slid into a coffin case ($4.00), deco-
rated with a lawn cravat collar ($3.00), removed to the railroad ($3.00), and
attended by people who assisted Dr. Hopper ($5.00).[25] The press found out
the location of the body and insisted on a public display, which they were
granted. Rev. Young recorded one paper as having written, after the viewing,
"Henceforth let no one say the Vampyre is a fiction."[26]

At 2:00 p.m. on Monday, the party reached Troy and stopped at the American Hotel, a temperance hotel that had been one of John Brown's favorite spots. Late in the afternoon they arrived at Rutland, Vermont, spent the night there, and pushed on at five the next morning. By Tuesday at 10:00 a.m., they were at Vergennes, Vermont. The body was moved to the shore of Lake Champlain, where a boat was ready to change its course to deliver its cargo near the town of Westport.

Rev. Joshua Young was at the time the minister of the Unitarian Church in Burlington, Vermont. When a parishioner told him that the body would cross the lake at Vergennes and asked if he would accompany the procession to the funeral, he agreed. This decision led to his being ridiculed and ostracized by the public and his congregation when he returned to Vermont—even caricatured by the press—but also led to his being remembered by history. Those things were often coupled. A risky act that made people outliers in society during their own lifetime, and had great personal cost, might one day be recognized as a deed that moved human history in a better direction.

The parishioner and Rev. Young were too late to accompany John Brown on the boat that bore him across the lake, but they found a ferry crossing. The ferryman hesitated to help, partly because of a storm, but also because he thought John Brown deserved to be hanged. "He has crossed this ferry with me a hundred times," the ferryman said. "We all like him but he had no business meddling with other peoples' niggers."[27] We don't know, of course, if people in Burlington all shared the ferryman's hateful viewpoint, but we do know that Rev. Young received a no-confidence vote from his congregation in 1862 and resigned. He'd become too closely aligned to John Brown—an association Rev. Young's congregants could not forgive him for.

The weather changed, the ferryman's mood improved, and he agreed to transport the minister and his parishioner. Once safely on shore, they proceeded to Elizabethtown, Essex County's county seat ten miles away. The day before, the John Brown party had made a similar journey of twenty-five miles from Westport to Elizabethtown, starting out by sleigh, but finishing by carriage when the rain began and turned the snow to slush. The body had rested in the courthouse, guards patrolling it all night.

Rev. Joshua Young and his parishioner entered the valley of Keene, which Rev. Young called "a region of the grandest and most majestic scenery to be found any where in the Adirondack country."[28] Nothing but a narrow road for carts intruded on this wild land—land made of cliffs two hundred feet

Arrival of John Brown's body at the North Elba farm, sketch by Thomas Nast, *New York Illustrated News*. (Courtesy Boyd B. Stutler Collection of John Brown, West Virginia State Archives)

Final viewing of John Brown's body, sketch by Thomas Nast, *New York Illustrated News*. (Courtesy Boyd B. Stutler Collection of John Brown, West Virginia State Archives)

high, a steep gorge walled in by black perpendicular stone, and thick trees claiming the slopes that lay beyond. When Rev. Young arrived in North Elba, Wendell Phillips greeted him and asked him to officiate, and he did.

A simple funeral took place on December 8. At 1:00 p.m., the family of John Brown's neighbor Lyman Epps sang John Brown's favorite hymn, "Blow Ye the Trumpet, Blow!" The song was followed by spontaneous prayers and eulogies by J. M. McKim and Wendell Phillips.[29] Then another hymn. The body lay on a table just outside the door of John Brown's small frame house, his head uncovered for all to view. Rev. Young reported that half the people in attendance were Black.

A short procession began from cabin to gravesite, men lifting the coffin, residents from the community following behind, and then the long string of widows that Harpers Ferry had produced. As the body was lowered into the ground, Rev. Young recited from Paul: "I have fought a good fight, I have finished my course, I have kept the faith."[30]

It was 3:00 p.m.

THE UNBURIED

Little Roundtop, watercolor painting by Sarah Brown, ca. 1889. (From the private collection of F. G. Brown)

Jeremiah Goldsmith Anderson. (Courtesy Boyd B. Stutler Collection of John Brown, West Virginia State Archives)

I.

The unburied are part of history too, but it took me longer to find them than it did John Brown, or to acknowledge how much they mattered to the story. The movement of the engine house to multiple locations was an exhumation of sorts, but the actual moving of bones—not just brick and mortar—was an even more disturbing illustration of the way history worked. The interaction of the living with the dead. Wasn't that what I kept witnessing?

There had never been such a rattling of bones in America as there was in the years following the Harpers Ferry raid. A veritable Halloween season began in October of 1859, when the raid occurred. Even recently, people have campaigned to dig up John Brown's son Owen Brown in California for reburial in North Elba.[1]

Although the unburied had been on my mind for a while, I hadn't planned to follow them. I'd made a note about the detail I found on the wayside marker at North Elba—the body of Jeremiah Anderson being used for "anatomical study," and never found. Earlier, I'd casually placed a check mark by a long paragraph in Villard about Oliver's body being buried at the edge of the Shenandoah River, along with other raiders who had died, and Watson's body having been taken to Winchester Medical College as an "anatomical specimen."[2]

"Anatomical study"? "Anatomical specimen"? The macabre phrases stuck.

We were on a trip to Staunton, Virginia, to see some Shakespeare plays at Blackfriars Playhouse and, if truth be told, to get away from John Brown for a

Blackfriars Playhouse in Staunton, Virginia

couple of days. He was a demanding fellow, but even before we reached Staunton, I knew he'd sneaked into the car somehow. When we shot south to pick up Route 81, I saw a sign that read "Winchester." We rolled right by it, arriving in Staunton in time for an evening performance of *The Two Noble Kinsmen*, but I couldn't stop thinking of Winchester.

In a coffee shop in Staunton the next morning, while my husband read, I googled the town of Winchester, located southwest of the Ferry about thirty miles. The sites I found claimed that the cadavers of Watson Brown, John Copeland, and Shields Green had been brought to Winchester Medical College, and federal troops burned the college down because of it. Was that true?

On the way home, we found ourselves driving into downtown Winchester and parking in front of Handley Regional Library on Piccadilly Street, an arresting Beaux-Arts structure with a copper dome and a three-story rotunda. We climbed the stone stairs to the reference desk, where I asked a librarian for directions to the archives. While my husband remained on the first floor, I made my descent to the basement.

I explained to the archivists that I was trying to find out what happened to the raiders who'd been brought to Winchester Medical College after being killed at Harpers Ferry or (in the case of Copeland and Green) hanged in Charles Town. I thought when I started out that perhaps their bodies had been

Watson Brown. (Courtesy Boyd B. Stutler Collection of John Brown, West Virginia State Archives)

donated to the college, but as the archivist brought out more and more information, and I read it, I realized that innocence had limited my understanding.

A doctor who'd been a teenager in Winchester at the time of Harpers Ferry wrote a retrospective editorial in the *Virginia Medical Monthly* explaining how Winchester had come to acquire the corpse of Watson Brown. He saw it when it arrived, "shot directly in the umbilieus [sic]." He said that the body—which had originally been mistaken as the corpse of Owen Brown, and which the writer continued to misidentify—was found by students from the medical college close to Hall's Rifle Works at the upper end of Harpers Ferry, lying in tall weeds by the banks of the Shenandoah. They'd ridden in on the train when they found out a battle was going on, grabbed the corpse, put it in a store box, and shipped it to the school.

The writer of the editorial added, "A dried preparation was made of the body and it was afterward used for teaching purposes." He explained that the college, which functioned as a hospital after the Civil War began, was burned by order of a General Banks, but before the fire "this body [Watson's] was sent north."³

Another physician, Abner H. Cook, wrote an article about the college that concurred with the report in the editorial, saying he believed the raid "gave impetus to sectionalism." He said, "In 1862, while the City of Winchester was occupied by General Banks, the College building was burned by his order... because the body of a son of John Brown, who had been killed in the Harper's Ferry raid, had been dissected there. The building, equipment and all records of the College were destroyed and 'finis' was written above the ashes."[4] An archivist at Handley Regional Library who published a book about the town during the Civil War wrote that "the college paid a terrible price for these students' ingenuity when the Union army occupied the town in March 1862," and that the burning of the college was the only act of purposeful arson recorded in Winchester during the entire Civil War.[5]

Watson, it occurred to me, had participated in the Civil War, even though he was dead.

One essay by A. Bentley Kinney had a title like a thriller—"A Skeleton's Revenge: The Burning of the Winchester Medical College." Here I encountered the rumor that John Brown's son was tanned in the tanning yard beside the medical school, an image that stayed in my head.[6]

When I returned home, I hurried to the Hudson archives to see if I could find out more about Winchester in the collection of Clarence S. Gee.

2.

In January of 1863, Horatio N. Rust, John Brown's friend who communicated with blacksmith Charles Blair about ordering pikes for Harpers Ferry, sent Mary Ann Brown word about the fate of her son. Nurses at the temporary hospital set up at the school during the Civil War told Rust they had been working at Winchester Medical College and saw members of the 10th Main Regiment bury Watson's body.[7] This must have brought some comfort to Mary, but the rumor turned out to be untrue, and thinking that it was for so long probably made truth more difficult to bear when it did arrive.

Watson's body did not rest for twenty more years. It remained above the ground, though no longer in Winchester. Another rumor circulated that Dr. Hunter McGuire had taken it, but it was actually removed by Dr. Jarvis J. Johnson, a surgeon in the 27th Regiment, Indiana Volunteers. Dr. Johnson wrote the editor of the *Chicago Tribune* explaining that after Union troops took Winchester, he found the body of Watson Brown ("elegantly prepared, with all the muscles, blood vessels; veins, etc., intact, one of the most beautiful specimens I ever saw") and General Banks gave him permission to have it before the building was burned.[8]

He kept Watson's remains with him in the Midwest until the day he heard that Mary Ann Brown was in Chicago participating in a celebration to honor John Brown.[9] When he discovered she was alive, he offered to give her the "specimen" that was her son. It was ghoulish, but Mary was used to ghouls. When she found out that the long-dead and unburied body of Watson was

Oliver Brown. (Courtesy Boyd B.
Horatio N. Rust. (Courtesy Boyd B.   Stutler Collection of John Brown,
Stutler Collection of John Brown,   West Virginia State Archives)
West Virginia State Archives)

about to be delivered, she proceeded to "buckle up," just as John Brown said
to do in a storm—and life with John Brown was a veritable nor'easter. He
knew all about buckling up and how to "be prepared for the tempest," and so
did the women and children who lived with him. "I have sailed over a somewhat stormy sea for nearly half a century" was the way stoic John Brown put
it—a sizeable understatement, in my opinion.[10] Most of his days had been
lived in hardship, his terrifying training ground.

Dr. Johnson returned what was left of the body in 1882. John Brown Jr.
went to Martinsville, Indiana, where Dr. Johnson had the peculiar corpse,
and identified it. Watson was then shipped to Put-in-Bay, the island in Lake
Erie where John Jr. lived out his life and other Browns stayed for long periods
of time. Mary Ann Brown joined her family there for what must have been
both the most joyful and horrifying reunion of her life, and then visited communities from her past in Ohio and Pennsylvania before she met John Jr. at
Meadville, where the two of them would begin their trip to North Elba with
"the remains" so that Watson, at long last, could be buried.[11]

Mary wouldn't be alive in 1899 for the reburial of her second son killed
in the raid, Oliver, if *reburial* is even the right word, given what happened to
him and other raiders shortly after they died on the grounds of the Ferry. They

Marker at grave of Watson Brown in North Elba

weren't exactly among the "unburied," the way Watson was, but being tossed into a cardboard store box and dropped into a quickly-prepared grave close to the Shenandoah hardly seemed to qualify as a burial, even though a local man named James Mansfield was paid five dollars to do the job.

No one bothered the raiders on the bank of the river until July 29, 1899, when three men, led by James Mansfield, located the unmarked grave— Thomas Featherstonhaugh, Captain E. P. Hall, and Professor O. G. Libby— and one of them wrote about it in detail.[12]

Dr. Libby took the larger bones that had not yet deteriorated to North Elba in an ordinary traveling trunk that aroused no suspicion. Before the raid, friends of John Brown and his party had sent blanket shawls to the Kennedy Farmhouse to keep the men warm, and they had worn them in battle instead of overcoats (there were no uniforms), so when the men were dug up in 1899, wool was everywhere.[13]

Miss Katharine E. McClellan arranged for the 1899 North Elba funeral— a real one this time. Rev. Joshua Young, who had buried John Brown, now buried the bones of all the men who had been returned, including Hazlett and Stevens. Fifteen hundred visitors and neighbors came to the funeral.[14] Mary Leary Langston, the grandmother of Langston Hughes, and the former wife of raider Lewis Sheridan Leary, wrote a letter to Rev. Young on the occasion expressing her gratitude.[15]

Burial of Oliver Brown and his fellow raiders at North Elba in 1899, Rev. Joshua Young
standing far left and Col. Richard Hinton next to him. (Courtesy Boyd B. Stutler
Collection of John Brown, West Virginia State Archives)

The town purchased a single casket for the bones. It had silver handles
and nameplate, and on August 30, 1899—the anniversary of the Battle of
Osawatomie—was wrapped in an American flag and then lowered into
ground beside the graves of John Brown and Watson Brown.[16] Three wooden
boxes now rested side by side.

It was the end of the nineteenth century, and not even the bones from the
raid on Harpers Ferry had settled yet, much less its history.

3.

New horrors emerged with the stories of Shields Green and John A. Copeland Jr., the two Black raiders hanged on December 16, 1859 (along with white raiders John Cook and Edwin Coppoc, later that day). Both were buried not far from the gallows in hurried graves that everyone understood would be defiled. Within an hour, medical students dug them up for dissection.[17] A contingency of students from Winchester attended the hanging, and, one scholar said, people seemed to know that they'd come for the cadavers—well, those that were Black.[18] The young man at the college who had seen Watson arrive also had witnessed the arrival of the "two negro men, Shields and Copeland"— brought to the college with the rope that had killed them still dangling from their necks.[19]

George Stearns, after the disappointment that the body of John Brown would not be brought to Cambridge, got in touch with J. Miller McKim to see if he could at least claim the bodies of John Copeland Jr. and Shields Green. He wanted to bury them temporarily in Pennsylvania and then erect an elaborate monument in Mount Auburn, where he planned to have them reinterred. The inscription would identify them as John Brown's raiders. Stearns knew the importance of paying special attention to Black raiders in the party, since only they could have fully known what the fight at Harpers Ferry meant.

Stearns was not aware that antislavery men from Philadelphia had made similar requests of Governor Wise for the bodies of the Black raiders.[20]

Shields Green, hanged December
16, 1859. (Courtesy Boyd B. Stutler
Collection of John Brown, West
Virginia State Archives)

John Anthony Copeland Jr., hanged
December 16, 1859. (Courtesy Boyd
B. Stutler Collection of John Brown,
West Virginia State Archives)

Two days before the men were hanged, seven white people from Orange,
New Jersey, including Lucy Stone, a suffragist, and her husband, Henry B.
Blackwell, a reformer, sent a letter to Governor Wise asking for the bodies,
but the letter arrived five days after the execution. Mrs. Rebecca Buffum
Spring of Perth Amboy, who visited John Brown in his jail cell and provided
his funeral attire, also made a failed attempt to recover the bodies of the executed men.[21]

Black groups tried to get the bodies too. Groups from New Bedford (Massachusetts), New York, and Philadelphia wanted them. The group in New
Bedford corresponded with jailer John Avis about the matter. A group in
Philadelphia struggled over the language they would use in a letter to Governor Wise, and many of its members were extremely disappointed with the
final wording—a description of Shields Green and John Copeland as "poor,
miserably misguided men" who had "recklessly torn themselves from home
and friends."[22] It was language meant to earn the governor's sympathy, but
people knew it compromised what they believed to be true.

John Copeland Sr. of Oberlin, Ohio, sent a letter to Governor Wise
asking for the body of his son. The governor wired a response, agreeing to the

John Avis, John Brown's jailer.
(Courtesy Boyd B. Stutler Collection
of John Brown, West Virginia State
Archives)

James Monroe, 1850s, who traveled
to Winchester, Virginia, to claim the
body of John Copeland Jr. (Courtesy
Oberlin College Archives)

request, but stipulated that he would only turn the corpse over to a white man. "Yes to your order to some white citizen. You cannot come to this state,"[23] he said. Two days after receiving this message, John Copeland Sr. wired the governor to request that the body of his son be delivered to a K. H. Stevens. Since Stevens was not able to travel to Charles Town, he asked the sheriff of the town to send the body to the mayor of Oberlin. The request wasn't honored, since the governor apparently had no intention of shipping the body home, even though the bodies of Cook and Coppoc, the two white men who also were hanged on December 16, were carried by Adams Express from Harpers Ferry to relatives in Williamsburg, New York, and Springfield, Ohio, eventually to be buried in their respective home states.[24]

The day after the execution, the mayor of Oberlin wired the governor asking him to send the bodies of Green and Copeland express and collect. There would be no expense for anyone. But the governor didn't reply. At this point, the parents of John Copeland Jr. almost lost hope that they'd ever see their son again.

The family of John Copeland heard rumors about the removal of their son's body to Winchester Medical College and contacted James Monroe, a close friend of the Copelands from Oberlin, Ohio—a professor at the college whose house is now a museum. Monroe agreed to go to Winchester, Virginia, to claim the body of John Copeland Jr. on behalf of his family.

He anticipated that the name of his hometown would arouse suspicion in the South, so at his hotel in Winchester, he said he was from Russia. Oberlin was in Russia Township.

The faculty of the school seemed agreeable to Monroe's request to have the body, even though on December 12 the medical director of the college had written to the governor about being in desperate need of skeletons for their museum.

Monroe was so certain of cooperation after meetings with faculty that he directed the undertaker in the town to prepare the body of John Copeland Jr. for transport. Students strongly objected to the faculty's compliance and came to Monroe's hotel, Taylor House, to argue their case. They spoke of the body as if it belonged to them—they'd worked for it, earned it.

In a Thursday lecture at Oberlin delivered nearly forty years after his visit to Winchester, Monroe recalled something of the sentiment and language of their leader, a tall red-haired young man. "Sah, this nigger that you are trying to get don't belong to the Faculty. He isn't theirs to give away. They had no right to promise him to you. He belongs to us students, sah. Me and my chums nearly had to fight to get him ... I stood over the grave with a revolver in my hands while my chums dug him up. Now, sah, after risking our lives in this way, for the Faculty to attempt to take him from us is mo' 'an we can b'ar."[25]

Monroe left the medical school without the body of John Copeland Jr., not because the students had overridden the permission that faculty had granted James Monroe, but because in the middle of the night they had stolen into the dissecting room, taken the body (for a second time), and hidden it.

Waiting for a carriage to take him to Martinsburg and the train that would roll into Wheeling, Monroe was permitted a quick glance at the unclad body of Shields Green as he lay in a garret, frozen and bloody. When I read his account of that moment, it startled me because I wondered what my response would have been. Monroe was preoccupied with the life and story of John Copeland Jr. at the time—with his own interests, in other words—but suddenly there was Shields Green, "lying on his back—the unclosed, wistful eyes staring wildly upward, as if seeking, in a better world, for some solution of the dark problems of horror and oppression so hard to be explained in this."

Monroe "banished the thought of him," though Shields Green had been executed too, but later realized his error. "Who was I," he asked himself, "that I should be spared a view of what my fellow-creatures had to suffer?"[26]

Was it possible to neglect other people who suffered along with John Brown if my pursuit of him was too narrow? Had he become so large in my mind that his shadow blotted others out?

It's been presumed that the bodies of Green and Copeland were destroyed in the blaze the Union army set during the Civil War.[27] I could only assume, as others had, that Jeremiah Goldsmith Anderson was lost then too, unless his skeleton had been stolen, in this story of so much theft.

The day before Christmas, James Monroe returned to Oberlin without the body of Oberlin resident and college student John Copeland Jr. On Christmas day, Professor Henry E. Peck preached a funeral sermon for the lost raiders at First Church in Oberlin. Over three thousand people attended the service,[28] and $175.00 was collected in the offering plate.[29] Some of it went to pay James Monroe for his trip to Virginia, and the rest was committed to the erection of a white marble cenotaph.

4.

In 1860, the cenotaph was dedicated to the three Black raiders who were thought to be from Oberlin—John Copeland, Lewis Leary, and Shields Green. Someone on the planning committee for the monument had made an error, since Shields Green had never set foot in Oberlin. It was Lewis Sheridan Leary, originally from Fayetteville, and John Copeland Jr. who were residents and had been recruited for Harpers Ferry in Oberlin by John Brown Jr., but the name of Shields Green remained on the monument because people thought he was brave.[30]

After I learned about the cenotaph, I drove fifty miles to see it. Straight west down Streetsboro Street, through Peninsula and Richfield—the approximate route Owen Brown would have taken when he traveled from Hudson in the nineteenth century to fulfill his duties as trustee of Oberlin Collegiate Institute.

I accompanied a docent through what had been the former home of Professor James Monroe (later turned state congressman), walked Oberlin's sidewalks, visited Westwood Cemetery and the Wright Park Soldiers Monument, and then angled in on a tall piece of marble.

Crossing Main Street to East Vine from the Soldiers Monument, I soon reached Martin Luther King Memorial Park, which featured markers and pieces of sculpture commemorating Oberlin's Black heritage. A professor of art emeritus at Oberlin had created one piece with Martin Luther King's face

Marble marker in Martin Luther King Jr. Park, Oberlin,
commemorating Oberlin-Wellington rescue, with image of
rescuers in front of Cleveland jail

abstractly embossed on it. King had spoken at Oberlin several times and delivered the Commencement address in 1965, three years before his assassination.

A brick and black marble monument in honor of the 1858 Oberlin-Wellington Rescue depicted twenty Oberlin citizens, Black and white, all about to be jailed in Cleveland for safely rescuing John Price from slave catchers.

But it was the cenotaph that drew me, like some Lake Erie beacon, more public now than it had ever been in remote Westwood Cemetery—its original location. Its greater prominence caused me to consider again whether moving the memorial behind the Akron Zoo might be advisable.

A part of me wished the bones had lain beneath the stone, though I loved the old Greek word *cenotaph* that meant empty tomb. It felt as if a resurrection were possible, and resurrections, somehow, were closer to the truth of history than burials.

Only a few words were still legible, those cut most deeply into the column: "These Colored Citizens of Oberlin," "John Brown," and "The Slave." A more recent marker—bronze—lay flat on the ground, close to the cenotaph, and it preserved the fading words, making the task of deciphering the monument easier for people like me who ambled through the park on a sunny day.[31]

I knew the bones of Black raider Lewis Sheridan Leary, killed at Harpers Ferry, were in the ground of North Elba, with Oliver Brown, but those of John

Cenotaph in Martin Luther King Jr. Park, Oberlin, in memory of John Copeland Jr., Lewis Leary, and Shields Green

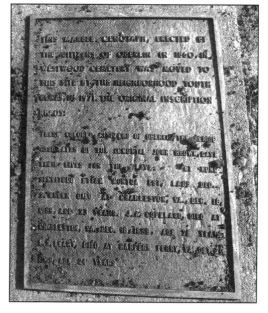

Bronze ground marker displaying full text of the cenotaph, Oberlin

Copeland Jr. and Shields Green were not buried anywhere (nor were those of Jeremiah Anderson). They were the lost raiders, and they were nowhere and everywhere all at once.

5.

Other things I found in my search for the unburied I hid in notebooks because they didn't feel safe anywhere else. Why did I keep returning to them, though? Why did I need to look at them again?

For a while I didn't talk about the autobiography I'd found in Handley Regional Library of a medical student from the mid-1850s, though I'd taken notes on it. The student wrote about the practice of "resurrecting" bodies from graves for use in the medical school, and I suddenly remembered that the word *resurrection* could be used this way, as well as to describe a spiritual state.

He answered some questions about the practice of digging up corpses ("a shovel, two-inch auger, rope and pole") but raised others that were even more troubling.

I knew a few things about the "resurrectionist" tradition. Victor Franken-stein acquired his corpses from "vaults and charnel-houses," I'd learned from Mary Shelley.[32] Mark Twain included a scene in his original draft of *Huckleberry Finn* in which Jim was sent into a "dissectin' room" of a "doctor college" by Mars. William to "git [a corpse] soft so he can cut him up," and when I read the segment I thought about America's medical schools being legendary for body snatching.[33] A scholar said the theft of British corpses had occasioned the revision of anatomy laws, the invention of the Patent Coffin (marketed as an "anti-resurrectionist device"), and debates about what class of people could be dissected (paupers and those who died in workhouses were prime candidates).[34]

But the beliefs behind Winchester's "resurrectionists" were especially troubling, perhaps because they were so essentially "American." Every institutional practice in America in the nineteenth century, it was beginning to seem, had been badly tainted by racism, including this one.

The medical student talked about the potential danger of such thefts, as well as the excitement they brought students. He spent considerable time describing the advantages of choosing "specimens" of the "ebon variety"—"no white skin to excite the curiosity of the late casual night walker!" Almost all specimens were Black—not only easier to steal at night, but few, if any, repercussions for the thieves, should they be caught. Who would care? Who would have the power to object? It should not have surprised me that it was medical students from Winchester who knew where the fresh graves were of the two Black raiders hanged on December 16—of Shields Green and John Copeland Jr.

The memoirist detailed the "mortal dread" that "darkies" had of student doctors because of their belief that they couldn't be resurrected unless their bodies remained whole. He laughed at their inability to understand what medical students so clearly did: it made no difference to a person's salvation if their skull happened to be used "as a candle-stick, with a candle in the foreamen magnum occipitis."

The only exception students made came in the form of a request by a white "owner" that his slave not be dug up. "We duly respected the claims of those whose slaves had died, if they requested us not to disturb their bodies," the medical student wrote.

The author grew nostalgic as he remembered his time at Winchester. "We passed through the session studying, reciting, dissecting and operating on cadavers, with great advantage to ourselves. The old college building is gone. The war broke up the school, and the building was burned, but there are many pleasant remembrances left."[35]

The thought crossed my mind that stealing a dead body, preferably one with Black skin, was not much different from owning a living one. I felt ill as I walked up the stairs of the library and stepped into daylight.

It would take time before I'd recognize how badly I'd needed to be in the basement of Handley Regional Library on Piccadilly Street, just as it had taken time for James Monroe to know what had happened to him. Before this ended, I would recognize that sometimes it was necessary to sit in a dark crypt with the dead.

NATIONAL GREAT BLACKS
IN WAX MUSEUM

I.

I drove with my husband into Baltimore, looking for the National Great Blacks in Wax Museum to find John Brown. A friend had told me he was a figure there, which I found surprising. I'd seen him sculpted in wax in a museum at Harpers Ferry, which was odd enough, but why was he commemorated here, in Baltimore, in a museum dedicated to famous Black men and women?

The museum included a whole block of East North Avenue, though not all of it was being used. The founders of the museum, Elmer and Joanne Martin, started their collection on Saratoga Street in 1983 with just four wax figures, but the museum now occupied a part of the block on North that totaled thirty thousand square feet and included a few apartments and an old fire station on a corner whose doors eerily reminded me of those on the Harpers Ferry engine house. The Martins had been invited to move to the Inner Harbor, but they chose to stay where they were, and Joanne Martin, a widow now, is currently directing an expansion of 120,000 additional feet.

We parked on Broadway and began following an arrow that pointed toward the museum.

For a few minutes we stood in the broad, comfortable lobby of the building and looked at a huge exhibit of Hannibal riding an elephant and another of W. E. B. Du Bois. A set of lobby doors led to an area called the Horror of Captivity, and inside a middle-aged man, a Mr. Wilson, invited my husband and me to listen to a presentation he was going to give to school children.

The group that arrived were mainly teens, with chaperones right behind them—probably middle schoolers, my husband said, a veteran teacher of that age. The man began by asking them about their knowledge of the Middle Passage and the triangular Atlantic trade. Most of the young people were shy at first, but then hands went up. Some talked about the trip's length, and some about its deadliness for Africans.

Mr. Wilson gave them details about the crucial role of Africans in the economy and how the triangle worked—about the use of manufactured goods from Europe to buy Africans, the trading of them for agricultural products from the Americas (produced by other Africans), and then the return of those goods to European markets.

"Turn around," he told the group, "and look at a bale of cotton that weighed five hundred pounds—what an enslaved man was expected to pick each day." Solomon Northup often failed to pick that amount and then was beaten for it, the guide said. Some knew Northup's story—a free-born musician captured in New York, drugged and shipped to a slave market in New Orleans, sentenced to slavery on plantations in central Louisiana for twelve years—a story that would be released to the public in just a few months when *Twelve Years a Slave* came out in theaters.[1] The guide told them that fifteen million enslaved people were brought to America, and three million died. There were probably many more deaths, he said, since the numbers available were only the ones confirmed by insurance policies and claims (enslaved people were insurable, since they were considered "property").

He talked about sharks and abductions and kidnappings, but before everyone was invited to disperse and explore the museum, Mr. Wilson issued a few warnings. The exhibits in the basement were difficult to look at, he said. Located down two separate staircases were the Slave Ship (the "belowdecks," where the human cargo was kept) and the lynching exhibit. School counselors were asked to determine who might not be ready for what was below and keep them from descending.

One man from the school carried two boxes of Kleenex in his hands the entire time the group was there to minister to the children when he saw eyes cloud up.

Mr. Wilson wanted to talk just a minute more about the exhibits in the room where we all were standing, even though I was sure he could see how restless the children were becoming.

His subject turned to "Seasoning," the process of breaking a slave's will. He showed the children a mask that people newly enslaved were made to wear. This mask was attached to a wall, and people were permitted no food or drink during the time they wore it. Weights were strung across their bodies, and then they were lifted slightly off the ground, internal organs caving in on them and lungs shutting down. Then he showed everyone in the room the iron collar placed around necks of enslaved people who spoke out or hinted at rebellion, with studs on the inside and a metal rod at the back, lined up with the spine and running all the way to the knees (so a person couldn't bend) and traveling a foot above the head where tiers of metal bells were attached to horizontal bars to frighten other laborers in the fields. The sound of those light bells must have carried far into the air.

An exhibit in the corner showed a young enslaved man being force-fed some repugnant gruel through a foot-long blue funnel. I couldn't see the form without feeling again my own repugnance when doctors told me that my mother, in her tenth sorry year of Alzheimer's, had forgotten how to swallow and would die unless food was administered by drilling a hole in her stomach and inserting a tube. I said "no," and within two weeks, she was dead.

The scene before me was more horrifying still. There was no daughter (or mother) to consult, no option offered less brutal than a funnel tube rammed down a person's throat—not even death. There was no understandable reason at all to force-feed. Alzheimer's was an inexplicable horror, but I understood the science. I knew what had happened to my mother's brain, and I had words like *tangles and plaques* and *hippocampus* to attach to it. There were no words for what was behind me.

The man leaning back with a funnel tube in his mouth was so young—half of enslaved people prior to the Civil War were under sixteen. He was wax, but it didn't seem that way when I looked at him. Nothing would have been wrong with his brain. He was in perfect health, but he'd already lost all desire for his life, and for the nutrition that supported it.

2.

I thought I'd tour the basement areas first and get that over. The hard part would be done.

The walkway of the Slave Ship was right behind Mr. Wilson, so I went up a ramp and then down a steep flight of stairs with a rope railing. A soundtrack began—the rush of water on the seas, people coughing, screaming, moaning. The sounds of the Middle Passage and the belowdecks. Bodies of wax men were chained together and pressed too close, chest to back, filling every inch of space given to them, only their sides visible, black wax alternating with brown.

"Men's Quarters," it was labeled, this place of shirtless men whose arms were shackled to the ship and necks imprisoned by iron collars. It was the centerpiece of the room, though small scenes were crushed into its crevices and cracks—as they were throughout the museum. Here, in the belowdecks, a beheading and a rape staged in a glass case were set off to the side, but, clearly, connected to the brutality of the main exhibit.

When I got home I read a book called *The Slave Ship: A Human History*, and it gave numbers even more gruesome than those the guide had provided in the museum, but the concentration of the book was on terror—what the author called "the defining feature of the slave ship's hell."[2]

I squeezed my arms for comfort in the belowdecks of the museum, becoming aware that the men on the ship were denied even this small pleasure.

I read other books after my trip, including Charles Johnson's *Middle Passage,* published in 1990, a National Book Award winner that I'd missed when it first came out. The cruelties aboard a vessel named *Republic* had caused the young narrator's hair to go white. His log entries told about the "scummy darkness foul with defecation, slithering with water snakes," about Guinea worms, amputations, the deadening of exposed dental nerves with arsenic, cases of distemper, the Black Vomit.[3]

When I left the belowdecks, I grasped the rail rope in my hands, dizzy, the soundtrack of fathomless water and human pain still rushing in my head.

3.

A second guide met me at the top of the ramp, and we walked together up a few steps to a room full of politicians. We stood in front of the figure of Barack Obama for a while, and then moved toward an exhibit that included Robert Smalls, a man who escaped from slavery during the Civil War by commandeering a Confederate ship and who later became a member of the US House of Representatives in South Carolina.

In the alcove with Smalls were figures of two white men—the only other white figures I knew about in the museum.

Charles Sumner was one. A hand with a cane came through the wall, aimed at Sumner's turned head, blood dripping down it. Sumner nearly lost his life when that gold-headed cane, in the hand of South Carolina Congressman Preston Brooks, struck him repeatedly in the Senate chamber on May 22, 1856, just prior to Pottawatomie (John Brown knew about the episode). Sumner was an abolitionist and thought the Kansas-Nebraska Act was an obscenity, and said so, offending Brooks, whose kinsman had co-authored it.

Thaddeus Stevens was the second white figure, a Radical Republican who was frustrated by Lincoln's early reluctance to oppose slavery vigorously enough; who battled moderates during Reconstruction and, after Lincoln's assassination, battled Andrew Johnson; who wanted land confiscated from planters and distributed to the newly freed, an idea that William Tecumseh Sherman, Edwin Stanton, and Black religious leaders from Savannah would shape into a plan familiarly known as "Forty Acres and a Mule," which would not survive any longer than Lincoln did.

Reparations, it was called. Soon after my visit to the wax museum, I started to notice the particular matter of Black reparations in the news. Ta-Nehisi Coates used it in the title of an essay he wrote for the *Atlantic*, which won the George Polk Award.[4] He spoke at the Cleveland City Club and in other towns about what he'd said, and then a few years later wrote about reparations again, saying that white supremacy was the foundation of American history and that "plunder" and "robbery spanning generations" were its tactics. Something so deeply rooted in the fiber of the nation required "not simply an outlay of money but also a deep reconsideration of America's own autobiography," he said.[5]

Even before I read Coates, the wax figures in the room began to pose hard questions for me about America's story.

The guide in the museum must have noticed my particular interest in this room of politicians. He told me that the figures often went on tour, and that the technology was much better today than it had been when the museum first opened. It took $40,000 to make a wax figure now, he said, and he asked me if I might have someone in mind. He said Barack Obama had no Michelle and smiled in my direction.

I needed to make a second descent, so I thanked the man for his help and exited the room.

4.

We found the staircase to the lynching exhibit. On the floor plan given to us at the start of the tour, the location was marked with the words "Parental Discretion Is Advised." Normally that warning seemed irrelevant to a person my age, but not today.

Greeting me at the foot of the stairs was the figure of Ida B. Wells-Barnett, someone I knew a little about, and this was initially comforting. She was born during the Civil War and became a newspaper editor and a Black leader in the Women's Suffrage Movement. Here, in the basement of the building, the display emphasized something else—her tireless effort as an anti-lynching crusader.

Just around the corner from her was the first major exhibit in this portion of the museum. The Mary and Hayes Turner exhibit depicted the horrific lynching of them both. In Jean Toomer's novel *Cane* (published in 1923, just five years after the lynching), a character tells the story of the Turner lynching, using the name Mame Lamkins for Mary Turner, tells it while women in the background at a neighboring church shout and scream.[6] The lynching in the book came to life for me when I looked through the glass of the museum case.

Everything that had been done to the couple was molded in wax. Mary had protested her husband's lynching and, for that, her legs had been cut off and she was set on fire and shot several times. Her baby, near term, was cut from her womb and crushed on the ground. The audio guide said that her executioners took two cats that were eating the intestines of her husband and stuffed them inside Mary's empty womb, sewed it up, and then placed bets on which cat would claw its way out first.[7]

In glass jars on a shelf—glass jars housed in glass cases—were wax specimens of body parts, including wax penises and wax eyes, barbarously removed during and after lynchings and commonly hawked as souvenirs. Hayes Turner was castrated and his ears and nose were sliced off. It was unbearable to look at him, and it's unbearable to write about.

The teenagers from the group couldn't help staring, but they quickly turned away. They couldn't figure out what the baby on the ground had to do with the cats until they started to read or listen to the audio. Necks swiveled quickly from the cases and adolescent voices cracked. They tried to talk about it, but there was nothing anyone could say, not even the counselors, so a few children hurried upstairs. Others gathered in groups and wound their arms around each other. Some looked for the Kleenex Man.

I almost passed by the second major exhibit in the lynching room. Some of the teens who were most upset and had fled upstairs had missed it altogether. It stood, as did the first exhibit, amidst a myriad of clippings and pieces of history. It was called "Boulevard of Broken Dreams." Drug users and addicts tipped and tilted through a nightmarish landscape of urban rubble and waste. A caption read, "Now We Lynch Ourselves." I turned and took the steps.

5.

When I emerged from the lynching exhibit, I gathered my composure and realized I'd forgotten John Brown. But this often happened. Something that at first seemed unconnected to John Brown distracted me but soon became part of his story too, since he existed in the rest of history.

The next section I passed through helped me to relax. A statue of Martin Luther King met me, and then, exhibits of literary figures whose work I knew: Zora Neale Hurston, Langston Hughes, Phillis Wheatley, James Baldwin, James Wendell Johnson, Richard Wright, Alexander Pushkin. I loved the exhibit of musicians Billie Holiday, Eubie Blake, Paul Robeson, and Howard Rollins. Booker T. Washington walking through a life-size page of his auto-biography, *Up from Slavery*, right toward museum-goers, was wonderful.

And then I found John Brown. There he was in a little scene with trees painted on the backdrop behind him. But he wasn't alone, which seemed odd to me because I'd so often thought of him that way. The renegade, the rebel. The exhibit had formerly been called *Rebellion*, but now the banner read *Slave Revolts*. With John Brown were Toussaint L'Ouverture and Nat Turner. Their little booth was positioned next to the Underground Railroad exhibit, in a sequence of increasingly more violent antebellum acts.

There was a framed plaque that attempted to articulate the multiple "methods" used to aid the enslaved. The focus—except for John Brown—was on Black leaders. Harriet Tubman, the plaque said, "sought to help slaves escape bondage," and the Underground Railroad was her vehicle. Frederick Douglass and Sojourner Truth (they appeared together in an exhibit in another wing of the building, Douglass as a huge mask on a wall and Truth standing at a podium) were not grouped with Black abolitionists, but with people of language, with those who "assailed slavery with words as mighty as the sword."

The most militant personalities were identified on another plaque: "Toussaint L'Ouverture of Haiti, Cudjoe and Queen Mother Nanny of Jamaica, and Gabriel Prosser, Denmark Vesey, Nat Turner, and John Brown of America ring loudly as leaders who believed that slavery could not end without the shedding of blood."

Denmark Vesey, who planned a potential slave revolt in Charleston in 1822—a plot that was uncovered—did not appear in the tableau, but I'd soon see his name in the news as if he'd never left the earth. Nine Black congregants would be shot in Emanuel AME Church in Charleston by a white man, and Vesey had once been a leader in that very church.[8] Barack Obama delivered a eulogy for members who'd been murdered and led the congregation in singing "Amazing Grace."

Toussaint L'Ouverture, whose nickname was the Black Napoleon— dressed in knee-high socks and pantaloons, a grey velvet jacket, ruffled shirt, and bicorne reminiscent of Napoleon Bonaparte's—was standing in the middle of the tableau. On the eve of John Brown's birth, L'Ouverture, identified on a museum sign as the "Architect of Haitian Independence," had freed the enslaved of Santo Domingo, an act that led to the rise of other leaders, most especially Jean-Jacques Dessalines, and to the sovereignty of Haiti in 1804 as the first Black republic. He tilted forward slightly as he stood on a narrow bridge with rails behind and in front of him.

Nat Turner, the second militant, sat to the right of Toussaint L'Ouverture. He was called a "Slave Revolutionary" in the biography framed below him and was dressed and positioned differently from L'Ouverture—seated in a tired, prayerful posture, his eyes focused on the ground, wearing a flannel shirt and a flannel hat. In August of 1831, in Southampton County, Virginia, he slaughtered at least fifty-five white people, the sign said, with the help of forty enslaved—four of them his close accomplices. He was hanged on November 11, 1831, which, ironically, would become America's Armistice Day (now Veterans Day). Nat Turner had always been for me a footnote in American history, but he wasn't here. "After Turner's rebellion," I read, "slaveholders could no longer pretend that slaves were happy-go-lucky lot who were totally satisfied with their condition."

And then, on the left, was the man I'd come to see.

Close-up of John Brown
in *Slave Revolts.* (Photo by
the author, appears with the
permission of National Great
Blacks in Wax Museum)

Portrait of John Brown reproduced
from a photo by daughter Sarah
Brown, ca. 1900, black crayon with
charcoal and white pastel. (Courtesy
Saratoga Historical Foundation and
Saratoga History Museum)

The sign about John Brown talked about Harpers Ferry almost exclusively. It mentioned the "five Black men" who helped stage the raid, and "seized possession of the US Arsenal in the hope of arming the slaves."

If John Brown had stood alone, or if there had been no sign to identify him, I wouldn't have known who he was. The Sharps rifle in one hand and the Bible in the other probably would have given him away eventually, but his body and appearance were all wrong. His hands were raised high in the air, his face didn't have the ferocity I was looking for, and by the time of Harpers Ferry he wouldn't have had the long beard I was staring at.[9] He didn't look angry at all, but placid, almost as if he were about to sing in a church choir. The label the museum had chosen for him was this: "God's Angriest White Man," but in the wax image, I couldn't find that anger anywhere, not even in the open mouth that showed his perfect teeth.

Even if he'd had a beard at Harpers Ferry, it would have been curly, the way it was in the last daguerreotype taken of him in 1858—not straight, as in the tableau.[10] The smooth skin and boyish features the wax figure depicts were long gone by the time of the raid. The daguerreotype showed deep bags under his eyes, rows of crow's feet, a long, thin nose, amazing hair. That Old Osawatomie was not the man in front of me.

Maybe wax was just not the right medium for John Brown, I thought. He was real and one-of-a-kind and not subject to mimicry. Nothing—not even wax—could catch him.

6.

"What color is John Brown's skin?" I asked my husband, nonchalantly, as if the matter were really of little concern to me. He'd said nothing about the *Slave Revolts* tableau, always calmly standing back and watching when I'm in research mode, offering comments only when asked, or when my note-book's closed.

"I wondered how long it was going to take you to notice that," he said.

I had noticed from the beginning, but I had no idea what to say about it. It was easier to talk about his hair and clothes than my strange uncertainty about the color of the wax. The complexion of the figure was as dark as his taupe boots, his skin tone only a little lighter than Nat Turner's or Toussaint L'Ouverture's. Black writers and artists had sometimes imagined John Brown as Black, so I wondered if his dark tint had been deliberately chosen.

It's always difficult to talk about the color of someone's skin, even when it's wax.

When I got home, I sent an email to Joanne Martin, the cofounder of the museum, to ask about the shade. I'd written to her once before my visit after discovering on the museum's web page that there was no Lincoln in the col-lection.

She'd explained that the museum had owned a Lincoln, but he was one of the older figures and the wax dissolved and they hadn't replaced him yet, but they intended to. In passing, she added that the museum had continually been asked if their Lincoln was Black.[11] The second time I contacted her, she said the figure of John Brown was the same vintage as the former Lincoln, a very early figure acquired around 1980, and both had been manufactured by a company called Dorfman Museum Figures. She didn't think the dark complexion of either man was deliberate, but the result of methods and materials that were available at the time.[12]

In spite of the flawed process perhaps responsible for the John Brown figure having darker skin than he really did, I couldn't dislodge the image from my head.

7.

We exited Baltimore on Franklin Street. Since the expressway was closed for construction, we were routed in this direction. The miserable condition of the row houses was quickly visible. Structures were being torn down, and big demolition vehicles were in position to strike. I'd read before we traveled here that Baltimore was refurbishing old property for public works. Five thin figures holding candles were painted on the side of one building, a version of a famous Maya Angelou quotation printed at the top—*And still we rise.*

Soon the neighborhood of Sandtown-Winchester—a short distance away—would wake up to walls covered with hand-painted murals of Barack Obama and Ta-Nehisi Coates (who'd grown up in Baltimore), along with Billie Holiday and Freddie Gray. Shortly after I visited the museum, Freddie Gray died at the hands of police in Sandtown-Winchester, as other young Black men were doing in neighborhoods across the country.[13]

In 2015, Coates published *Between the World and Me*—a prose letter written to his teenage son that spoke of all the dangers to Black bodies in America and won the National Book Award for Nonfiction. "To be Black in the Baltimore of my youth was to be naked before the elements of the world, before all the guns, fists, knives, crack, rape, and disease. The nakedness is not an error, nor pathology. The nakedness is the correct and intended result of policy, the predictable upshot of people forced for centuries to live under fear," he wrote. For him, white people had the authority "to destroy your body."

The policy was not born of race, he said, but of racism. "Race is the child of racism, not the father."[14]

The day we drove down Franklin Street and exited the city, I wasn't thinking yet the way Coates would urge me to. If I had been, I might have heard the name of Freddie Gray already in the air.

REVERIE 6
"CONFLICT OF EMOTION IN MY HEART"

I.

No matter how much I admired John Brown's steadfast commitment to the Golden Rule and his passion for equality and justice ("I pity the poor in bondage that have none to help them"[1]), his courage to act, and his willingness to give his life for the cause of defeating slavery, there remained the matter of John Brown's murderous hands (and weren't murderous hands necessarily attached to murderous hearts?).

It wouldn't leave me.

I kept adding names to my list of people who throughout history had tried to separate John Brown's message from his methods. Abraham Lincoln, W. E. B. Du Bois, Julian Bond all had done it to varying degrees.

Some Black leaders had chosen even more dramatic ways to distance themselves from John Brown's violence. Booker T. Washington, the heir of Frederick Douglass, wouldn't attend a John Brown celebration for Black Americans on May 9, 1909. He sent his regrets.[2] One historian, in his discussion of John Brown's legacy, said that Martin Luther King Jr. "rarely, if ever, mentioned John Brown in his civic discourse."[3] And Barack Obama, the son of Ann Dunham, a Kansan native born in Wichita, stood at a lectern on the stage of Osawatomie High School in 2011 and didn't allude a single time to John Brown—Old Osawatomie Brown—who waged a battle in this town between Free-State and proslavery men on August 30, 1856.[4]

John Brown was perhaps too radical for Washington, too dangerous for the nonviolent agenda of King, too threatening to the reputation of America's

Statue of James A. Garfield on grounds of
Hiram College

first Black president. They all probably feared that his image evoked only violence for most people, if people remembered him at all, and that associating
with him would undercut all their attempts to unite people—for both altru-
istic and political ends.

At Hiram College, where I taught, I sat in my office in Bonney Castle, a
former nineteenth-century inn, thinking about all the people who had struggled on the page, or in public, with the problem of chiaroscuro in John Brown's
life—the light and the dark of him. As I looked out the window at the west wing
of the Garfield-Zimmerman House, I thought about President James A. Garfield—yet another person who'd tried to account for the whole of John Brown.

It was impossible to imagine Hiram College without also imagining Garfield. He attended Western Reserve Eclectic Institute (which became Hiram
College) for a while, left, and then returned to accept a position as both professor of ancient language and literature and the school's president until the Civil
War began. The day John Brown was hanged, Garfield wouldn't have been in
the house I was staring at, but because he'd returned to the school by that time,
he might have been sitting at a desk somewhere in town.[5]

Garfield and his wife, Lucretia ("Crete"), bought the house beside Bonney Castle in 1863 (adding, shortly afterward, the wing I could see from my office) and, after the death of their first daughter, Eliza Arabella "Trot" Garfield (1860–1863), attended a séance in the inn John Bonney built.[6] It took place downstairs in a room below my office.

Five days before the Harpers Ferry raid, Garfield was elected to the Ohio State Senate, and began to serve one month after John Brown was hanged. James A. Garfield was Ohio's state senator right before John Brown left the earth, so I doubt they ever met. He might have heard of Garfield toward the end of his life, but I don't think he would have sought him out.

In a letter to Frederick Douglass in 1854, written from Akron, John Brown railed against all the "malignant spirits—such fiends clothed in human form" who undermined democracy, and his list included editors of proslavery newspapers, as well as "a majority in our national Legislature, and in most of our State Legislatures... the offices of judge, justices, commissioners, &c., who follow that which is altogether unjust... marshals, sheriffs, constables and policemen— brave cat paws of the last named, ever prompt to execute their decisions."[7]

John Brown would not have regarded Garfield as one of the foul fiends of government, though—just as he didn't Ohio's Republican Congressman Joshua Giddings, with whom he'd even corresponded,[8] or Charles Sumner, whom, according to James Redpath, he'd visited with Redpath after the Massachusetts senator was beaten by Preston Brooks, supposedly even asking to see his bloody coat.[9] In a pocket diary the day of John Brown's death, Garfield had written the Latin inscription *servitium esto damnatum* (slavery be damned).

He'd written a longer entry about the day in his regular diary, and I sat with a copy opened on my desk.

"A dark day for our country. John Brown is to be hung," he wrote. "I have no language to express the conflict of emotion in my heart. I do not justify his acts. By no means. But I do accord to him, and I think every man must, honesty of purpose and sincerity of heart... it seems as though God's warning angel would sound through that infatuated assembly the words of a patriot of other and better days, the words 'I tremble for my country when I reflect that God is just, and his Justice will not always slumber.' Brave man, Old Hero, Farewell. Your death shall be the dawn of a better day."[10] Garfield hated violence but knew it had arrived.

As I stared at the open diary and then out the window, I felt the wonder of having lived my life as a neighbor of both John Brown and James A. Garfield, two Western Reserve celebrities who seemed present in the room with me. It was as if a second séance were being conducted, and I was the medium who'd summoned ghosts. But my delight in the image was short-lived, since I quickly recognized how presumptuous I'd been by casting myself as the medium. I recognized that a medium brings a message from the dead as they speak through her, but my resistance to John Brown prevented me from being a satisfactory conduit. "The conflict of emotion in my heart" were words that Garfield might have written to describe the whole world's struggle with John Brown, not just his own, and sometimes they felt like the very thing that prevented me from receiving news from the dead.

2.

Even some of my most political friends who'd been activists since Civil Rights confessed they'd grown disenchanted with John Brown when they learned about his unsavory methods. When they were children, some of them told me, their liberal parents thought John Brown was a saint. Their educated mothers, especially, had taught them the myth of John Brown—a story of hero and martyr, not blood and mutilation.

I'd considered protecting my grandson from all that blood by focusing solely on John Brown's martyrdom, but I was already too familiar with the man to fool myself—much less fool Logan Thomas Dyer. My friends had grown up resenting their parents for what they'd omitted from the story, and perhaps resenting John Brown because they'd been fooled. Scholars and biographers, communities and friends—all were puzzled by John Brown's bold contradictions and leery of his extremes, especially of Pottawatomie Creek. One scholar said John Brown's mixed legacy "contradicted basic American values."[11] There was a case to be made for that, I supposed.

His key biographer, the grandson of William Lloyd Garrison, said that because of Pottawatomie, "All this great moral superiority was flung away." Of this he was certain: "If he deserves to live in history, it is not because of his cruel, gruesome, reprehensible acts on the Pottawatomie, but despite them."[12]

I kept returning to the problem John Brown posed. Without the threats and violence, he wouldn't have been John Brown or "sparked the Civil War," as many scholars claimed he had. He wouldn't have been John Brown without the trouble he caused.

I decided to ask a somewhat different question than I had before. What did I think I'd gain by allowing "the conflict of emotion in my heart" to continue? By constantly carrying around a chalice of blood?

DANGER FOR THE SECRET SIX

GEORGE L. STEARNS

GERRIT SMITH

FRANK B. SANBORN

T. W. HIGGINSON

THEODORE PARKER

SAMUEL G. HOWE

The Secret Six. (Courtesy Boyd B. Stutler Collection of John Brown, West Virginia State Archives)

I.

People who accompanied John Brown were always in danger. Men who fought with him at Harpers Ferry were killed, but even people far from Virginia that October day suffered. Blame fell on anyone with connections to the man.

Oberlin was especially susceptible. Federal authorities wanted to question several Oberlin residents, including the Plumbs. Along with Charles H. Langston (abolitionist and grandfather of Langston Hughes) and many others, Ralph Plumb was one of the leaders in the Oberlin-Wellington Rescue of John Price. After the Harpers Ferry raiders were sentenced, people in missionary outposts across the nation were jailed for even having letters stamped from Oberlin.[1]

Frederick Douglass fled to Canada on October 19, 1859, after learning that two agents from Virginia were headed to Rochester to question him. He set sail for England in November, where he stayed until summertime.

The infamous Secret Six who helped fund John Brown's attacks—Smith, Stearns, Howe, Sanborn, Parker, and Higginson—were suspected of the worst. Letters from many of them were found at the Kennedy Farmhouse after Harpers Ferry. They feared for their lives, and most of them ran.

Some of the letters—including those from Gerrit Smith to John Brown— were published in the *New York Times* and the *New York Herald*. The *Herald*, a proslavery paper, named Smith and Frederick Douglass "accessories before the fact."[2] When Gerrit Smith read this, he felt Harpers Ferry had been his fault

State Hospital, Utica, New York, ca. 1905 (formerly State Lunatic Asylum). (Courtesy Library of Congress)

and that his life was in imminent danger. He was afraid he'd be hunted and prosecuted or killed for his offense, yet part of him wanted to go to Charles Town and stay with John Brown in his jail cell. Fear coupled with desire felt familiar, similar to the "conflict" James A. Garfield had described, and, I imagined, to what I was feeling on sleepless nights. John Brown often split people in half.

Fear and longing pulled on the ends of Smith's nerves until he came unraveled. Gerrit Smith was committed to the New York State Asylum for the Insane in Utica on November 7, 1859, convinced to go only when people told him he was being taken to Charles Town to see his friend John Brown.[3] His illness also conveniently kept him from testifying at the Mason Committee, a commission established to investigate Harpers Ferry after John Brown's execution. It lasted six months, from January to June of 1860.[4]

Franklin Sanborn hurried to Quebec, burning his correspondence with John Brown before he departed. Samuel Gridley Howe and George Stearns went by train to Montreal on October 26 and stayed there until after John Brown's execution. These three denied any association with Harpers Ferry. Howe wrote a letter in Canada insisting that he had no prior knowledge of John Brown's plans, and it was published in the *New York Tribune*. Later, in testimony before the Senate hearing on Harpers Ferry in February of 1860, he claimed great lapses in memory.[5]

Theodore Parker was in Rome, dying of tuberculosis.

Even John Brown's raiders who were captured tried to distance themselves from him while they were in prison. A book about John E. Cook focuses on his "tragic confession," which includes the naming not only of Frederick Douglass, but of raiders who had escaped. This confession allowed Governor Wise to offer rewards for the wanted men: Barclay Coppoc, Charles Tidd, Francis Merriam, and Owen Brown—with a physical description of Owen that "could have served to hang him." But Cook's biographer explained that other raiders who'd been captured also "broke ranks with Brown at some point." Stevens, he said, gave Virginia authorities names, Edwin Coppoc and Green complained about John Brown misleading them, and Copeland supplied Ohio federal marshals with names of men from his hometown of Oberlin who had paid for his trip to Harpers Ferry. Hazlett was the silent one, but only because he denied any association with John Brown, so what would there be to say?[6]

Governor Salmon Chase, of Ohio, denounced citizen John Brown immediately after Harpers Ferry. This shouldn't have surprised me. Chase was a politician seeking the Republican nomination for president, and John Brown was dangerous to political ambition, as I'd noticed many times before.[7]

Courage is always hard to find. For the most part, people protect themselves when danger gets too close. Human legs, I thought, were jointed for a reason—made to run, not stand fast, the way a tree would. When I see courage in any form, I can only stare at it. So I looked at Thomas Wentworth Higginson, the last member of the Secret Six, with incredulity.

Higginson, who later served as colonel of the First South Carolina Volunteers, a federally authorized Black regiment, remained in Boston and refused to deny his association with Harpers Ferry or with the man who'd brought it about. He accused his collaborators of cowardice and dishonor. He didn't run or destroy evidence in his possession, choosing, instead, to help plan the rescue from the Charles Town jail not only of John Brown, but, a little later, of raiders Aaron Stevens and Albert Hazlett—rescues that would all fail. The government knew Higginson would turn an appearance before a committee into a "cause célèbre," so they never called him to testify.[8]

He wrote from Worcester about the danger in a note to a friend, but he remained calm and incomprehensibly sensible. "Of course we are all deep in

Thomas Wentworth Higginson, photo by
William Notman. (Courtesy Library of
Congress)

Browns," he said, "and you can imagine how stirred up is Worcester generally,
especially since the rumored arrests of people in Boston as witnesses—I mean
proposed arrests; but I don't think it will come to anything."⁹

In a way, he was right. Two members of the Secret Six who had fled the
country returned after John Brown's execution, and one who had to flee twice
required help from the townspeople of Concord to resist capture. Gerrit
Smith remained in the New York State Asylum for the Insane until late
December. Eventually, though, people came home and went on living their
lives.

But none of the Secret Six had the surname "Brown."

DANGER FOR JOHN BROWN'S FAMILY

SALMON BROWN

JOHN BROWN, JR.

JASON BROWN

OWEN BROWN

Four sons of John Brown. (Courtesy Boyd B. Stutler Collection of John Brown, West Virginia State Archives)

I.

John Brown's frequent absence caused terrible consequences for his family, even before he was dead. The North Elba farm had to run without him when he was away. There was always debt, there were always stern demands. John Brown was in Springfield when his one-year-old daughter Amelia was scalded to death in Ohio in a kitchen accident caused by his oldest daughter, Ruth.

He was absent for other deaths and burials. Absent for births. Absent for birthdays and weddings and anniversaries. He just wasn't there most of the time, especially after he took up his cause.

His final absence, his disappearance on the gallows, resulted in what I've decided to call the Brown Family Migration. People would leave familiar places and scatter. John Brown knew what was ahead for them. "You *cannot imagine* how much *you* may *soon need* the consolations of the Christian religion," he wrote his wife and family in one of his last letters from his jail cell, and he was right. He knew that the best he could do in the face of such overwhelming "need" was entrust those he loved to the care of God. "And now dearly beloved *Farewell* To God & the word of his grace I comme[n]d you all,"[1] he ended the letter.

From his jail cell, he called on God many times to be the father or the husband he no longer could be (and perhaps never was). To his sisters Mary and Martha, he wrote, "May the God of peace bring us all again from the dead."[2] To his younger children in North Elba, "Trust in the Lord and do good, so shalt thou dwell in the land; and verily thou shalt be fed. I have enjoyed life much;

why should I complain on leaving it?"[3] To his older children living in Ohio, "The God of my fathers take you for his children."[4] Letter after letter ended with similar good wishes, pleas, and hope.

Still, daughters Annie and Ruth would develop severe nervous problems that one biographer claimed "stemmed from their ties to Harpers Ferry—and for Ruth, from Henry's actions in Kansas."[5]

I often imagined his family reading those final letters of his. *Yes, father, husband,* they might have thought, *but what am I to do if God forgets us? Where can I call home? Who am I without your plan for me? Where can grace be found when men are hunting us and we're afraid to say your name, we're afraid to say our name, and there are prices on our heads, like items in a general store?*

Whence cometh our help, and please, don't say God again, the children of John Brown who didn't believe in God anymore might have thought.

People in the family looked for new homes, because John Brown had never really provided one. In those last letters, he urged them to repair what he had left them, but North Elba was too shattered to fix. "Try to *build again*: your broken walls : & to make *the utmost* of every *stone* that is left,"[6] he wrote, but he surely must have meant his words to be read metaphorically, for what was it he wanted them to build with when there was only rubble in his wake?

Was it just a coincidence that after the events of 1859 the Browns found islands and caves and mountaintops to occupy? Just chance that so many of them traveled practically to the antipodes to get away, or broke entirely from the mainland where John Brown had left tracks so large and so deep that they feared they might fall in?

His son Salmon Brown talked about the stress of being in his family. "Despised bitterly by all who sympathized with slavery and considered as the victims of a righteous wrath by many of the North, our family was long buffeted from pillar to post. Efforts to forget were fruitless. The passing years did not heal the horrible wounds made by the country,"[7] he said, as late as 1913. Salmon shot himself in the head six years later, perhaps due in part to the lingering despair he talked about, but also to sheep epidemics that devastated his flocks, paralyzing accidents and illness that confined him to bed, and other sorrows it's not our right to know. [8]

In 1934, Hudson's Clarence S. Gee delivered the eulogy for Lucy Brown Clark, daughter of Jeremiah Root Brown, and said that for years after the Civil War "there was much hard and harsh criticism of the deeds of John

Ruth Brown Thompson. (Courtesy
Hudson Library & Historical
Society)

Salmon Brown. (Courtesy Hudson
Library & Historical Society)

Brown." Gee admired Lucy Clark because attacks on her family "left no trace of bitterness."[9]

One biographer of the women in John Brown's family said that "Brown children's poverty was paraded before curious Americans in the press" and "some of the Brown siblings' descendants were taught not to acknowledge their link to him—or not even told of it at all!"[10]

Even while they were in Kansas, a heavy fee was exacted from the Browns. John Brown Jr. suffered mental collapse after Pottawatomie, though he'd refused to participate in the murders. He was mistakenly arrested after the massacre, as his brother Jason was, and driven with rope around his wrists and upper arms from Paola to Osawatomie, over difficult land and through water. The yellow flint of Bull Creek tore through his boots and left painful cuts on his feet. A correspondent for the *New York Times* in 1856 talked about the tight trace-chain and padlocks used to link the ankles of John Jr. to another prisoner as they were made to walk sixty-five miles as a gang to their trial—twenty-five on two of the days.[11]

The Brown family believed that after Kansas John Jr. was never normal again (whatever "normal" was for a Brown). Even though at first he'd said he'd go to Harpers Ferry, he ended up assuming a secretarial role: preparing the Sharps rifles and shipping them, recruiting men for the attack, waiting on his farm in Ohio to hear results the day his father entered the history books. Kansas had in some way damaged all of the sons who had gone there, not just John Jr. It had killed one of them—Frederick. When the sons who survived the battles of Kansas Territory came home, they told Mary, mother or step-mother to them all, that not a single one of them would follow their father down a violent path again. Some stuck to their vow, and some did not.

2.

There was a $25,000 reward for Owen Brown, now a fugitive. He told his story to reporters many times after Harpers Ferry, and when I read the accounts, I thought it was miraculous that anyone in his party survived. Even if half the stories Owen told about his escape were true, I knew he must have been his father's son—lean and spry, in perfect health (except for his crippled arm), at home in the wilderness. He understood the mountains, a veritable mountain lion himself. Ralph Keeler, an Ohio-born journalist, talked about "the woodsman in him," saying his sense of direction and knowledge of trees were phenomenal.[12]

What an escape it was, according to the account Owen Brown gave Keeler. Owen climbed to the top of a tower to check the lay of the land; spread blankets taken from the Kennedy Farmhouse in a briar patch and then cut more briars to cover his company; clipped off Meriam's beard and mended his coat to disguise him before he boarded a train; climbed a ravine and crossed Baltimore pike to avoid the gap, which was guarded by dogs and "a hundred fires in view, flaring out of the darkness,—alarm fires . . . of those who were watching for us"; one night "crossed two valleys and a mountain and got into the woods of another mountain before day"; wrung chickens' necks and put them in a provision sack; evaded packs of hounds in the middle of a fox hunt; located a shanty that he knew had been built for the purpose of peeling hemlock bark from the trees in the area; knew and used the properties of laurel—the darkness they supplied and the way they could be cut and stuck into the ground for protection because they wouldn't wilt; carried fifty pounds of provisions on his back up steep mountainsides and ferried weary men across rivers and streams the same way.[13]

One man in Owen's party, Cook, was captured, and three others gradually departed on different paths, leaving Owen alone. He stayed at Townville, Pennsylvania, for several weeks until his presence aroused suspicion. Then, he told the journalist, "began a series of flights from one place to another, for myself and brothers John and Jason … I went to Oil Creek, thence to Elk Creek, and finally to Ashtabula County, Ohio, for none of us for months dared stay very long in one place."[14] During this tense time, the editor of the *Ashtabula Sentinel*, the father of William Dean Howells, helped protect John Brown's raiders in his newspaper office.

When the Civil War began, the nation turned its attention to other matters than John Brown or his descendants. But for nineteen months from Harpers Ferry to the firing on Fort Sumter, the Browns were on the run, looking for a place to hide. Even after that, many continued their search for remote locations.

Owen lived for many years in a shanty on Put-in-Bay, the island where John Jr. had a vineyard. In the winter months he lived an even more secluded life as caretaker for a mansion on the adjacent island of Gibraltar, a property owned by Jay Cooke, the financier largely responsible for paying for the Union effort in the Civil War. Lydia Ryall, a journalist who interviewed Owen Brown on the islands, talked about the "intense animosity … engendered against the Brown family and their allies in proslavery circles" after Harpers Ferry,[15] which she believed drove Owen Brown to this place.

Owen left the Lake Erie islands in 1884 and moved to a mountainside north of Pasadena, California, a location accessible only by a trail. His brother Jason accompanied him, leaving his wife (Ellen Sherbondy Brown) in Akron.[16] A Pasadena paper that carried Owen Brown's obituary said the brothers originally homesteaded a bench of mountain land at a location called Las Casitas, but they sold it quickly to move even higher up the mountain, where they cleared and worked a few acres, and according to the article, "lied there—two feeble old men, alone."[17]

Jason, John Jr., and Owen at mountain cabin near Pasadena, California. (Courtesy Hudson Library & Historical Society)

3.

The Lake Erie islands appealed to many of the Browns. Ruth Brown
Thompson and her husband, Henry, visited John Brown Jr. and ended up
staying on Put-in-Bay for ten years, their last child born there in 1871—Mary
Evangeline Thompson. But like Owen, they eventually moved—first buying
a farm near Necedah in Wisconsin, and later locating to Pasadena, where
Ruth is buried.

But John Brown Jr. stayed on the island, and I wanted to find out what
kept him there. I like architecture, houses, landscape, bodies of water, cemeteries, authors' homes, and local maps. Place can be anything from backdrop
to destiny for an individual, from a permanent haven to a temporary stop,
from a portrait to just a sketch. It can leave an impression on a person, or a
person can leave an impression on it.

I needed to visit the place where John Jr. chose to spend his remaining
days.

While I was on Miller Ferry heading to the south shore of Put-in-Bay, I
read an interview John Jr. gave to Nora Marks in 1889. She kept comparing
the son to the father and made me think of the story of Fathers and Sons
again. Was it that story, I wondered, that explained John Jr.'s permanent
retreat to this spot of land? Was the vast mainland of America John Brown's
terrain, but not his son's? I tried to imagine the appeal the island held for him,
and what he hoped to accomplish there.

John Brown Jr. (Courtesy
Hudson Library & Historical
Society)

Wealthy Hotchkiss Brown.
(Courtesy Hudson Library &
Historical Society)

The scars from Kansas hadn't disappeared. John Jr. was an agent of emigration for the British North American Provinces (1860–1861) and a captain in a Kansan brigade during the Civil War, but his sciatica from earlier years returned and brought an end to all of that. In 1862 he bought a ten-acre vineyard on Put-in-Bay from Joseph de Rivera St. Jurgo, a Spaniard who lived in New York City. There were nearly five hundred permanent residents on the island in the early 1860s, largely because grapes were found to flourish there.[18]

John Brown Jr. grew fruit for wine until 1882, when he resolved to sell his grapes only for "table use." In a letter to Frank B. Sanborn about his change in practice and politics, he asked, "What are our principles worth if we are unwilling to make sacrifices for them?"[19] I couldn't help but notice his selection of words like *principles* and *sacrifices* for so seemingly slight a thing as managing a vineyard—just decades after he'd recruited raiders for his father's cause.

John Brown had called himself a "teetotaler" by 1830,[20] so, had he lived, he may have been proud of John Jr. for thinking about the implications of selling wine, and proud, too, of Owen and Jason for being inducted into the Woman's Christian Temperance Union (WCTU) in Pasadena, along with their sister Ruth.[21] Still, it's difficult to know if he would have been sympathetic toward his son's version of sacrifice.

Nora Marks strained to find John Brown in the room the day she interviewed his namesake, and said John Jr. belonged to "a race of Spartans." I wondered, though, if that was really what she saw. John Jr. had talked to her about
his torture and imprisonment after Pottawatomie and about Harpers Ferry in
a room where the portrait of his father and other relics were displayed, but he
was deeply an island man by the time of the interview. He told the journalist
to come back someday—next summer, perhaps—to look at his geological specimens (he kept these, including some from the Black Hills, in a cabinet near
his father's portrait and his daughter's piano[22]) and to "talk of peaceful days
and eat grapes," but she probably didn't, since the John Brown Jr. of Put-in-Bay
would have been of little interest to her.

The most powerful detail in the interview for me was John Jr.'s nod to his
only son, John Brown III, who happened to be in the room. Nora Marks
described the thirty-seven-year-old as "a big, harmless man, who looked at us
in uncomprehending good nature." This was a character in the saga of the
Browns I'd not met before, except through genealogies. I couldn't stop thinking about his son while on the ferry or on the island, and even though I'd come
to find John Jr., I suddenly wanted to find his boy, too. I'd made the mistake of
assuming that this island story of Fathers and Sons was about John Brown and
John Jr., but there was a second father and a second son of importance here—
John Jr. and his own son, John III.

Genealogies I'd read had said little about John III, except that he was
"mentally retarded." The journalist, who seemed to concur, traced his disabil-
ity to the Kansas years, calling him "an intellect wrecked through the suffer-
ings of his parents."[23] I knew that John III had been in Kansas during the tur-
bulent 1850s, so I didn't discount the analysis of Nora Marks, but I also guessed
that the situation was more complex, and that John III was probably born into
the world with a congenital condition.

No matter what the source of John III's difficulty, the care he required
became important to me. Could John Jr. have embraced this place of stone as
much for his son as for himself? Had he sought the privacy of an island for his
child—a simple place whose roads and houses spanned only six hundred acres
(2.5 square miles), a place his son could navigate and where he'd never be lost?

John Jr. was not a complete recluse once he brought himself and his family
to the island and began growing grapes, but he only stayed away for short
periods and always enjoyed returning home.[24]

Crown Hill Cemetery, Put-in-Bay

He knew he would die on the island and planned for it. In 1886, serving as oarsman and surveyor for geologist Edward Orton ("Johnny," his son, accompanying him), he found its highest elevation—fifty-seven feet—and chose it for his family's burial plot.[25]

I found him the second day of our trip at the top of Crown Hill Cemetery, on the corner of Catawba and Niagara Avenues. Always happiest as a family man, he assumed that guise even in his final resting place. All the people he cared most about were assembled in two neat rows at the crest of the hill, as if seated at a long rectangular table waiting for some magnificent dinner to arrive. John Jr., his wife, Wealthy, their son, John III, were on one side; Edith, their daughter, and T. B. Alexander, her husband (the mayor of Put-in-Bay), on the other.

The priest-in-charge at St. Paul's Episcopal Church, which the Browns attended, told me later that day that the only job John III ever had during his life on the island was ringing the bell of St. Paul's.[26] He was presented with a gold watch to commemorate his retirement as bell ringer, and according to local lore the island's archivist shared with me, he dropped the watch the moment it was handed to him, and it shattered on the ground.

In this ancient place that had been carved by a glacier ten thousand years ago, John Brown Jr., an amateur geologist, could collect stones, hang a portrait of his father on a wall, build a house for Wealthy and his son (and in just four years, a daughter who would play the piano), grow his grapes, visit neighbors, teach the island's children about geology (his legacy), measure the elevation of his own cemetery plot. Even have a cave named after him.

St. Paul's Episcopal Church,
Put-in-Bay

Perhaps most of all, he could keep John Brown III safe in a way that his own father could not keep him.

Old Brown had never provided safety for John Jr., and if John Jr. could give this to his own son by living on an island, well, he would. Could this have been a conscious thought? Did he ever think that perhaps choosing a safe place like this for his son in some way made him a better father than his own? Perhaps it had.

Neighbors on Put-in-Bay helped keep the family safe, chasing summer guests away if they got too close.

It's a role that neighbors there still seem to play.

On the days of my visit, as hard as I tried I failed to find anyone willing to disclose the location of John Brown Jr.'s house, though I knew it still stood, and several people told me that.

On the island, rules for privacy remained, and no one broke them. "You are close to John Brown Jr.'s house!" they said, but when I asked for directions, I was only told that the owner was "private and sensitive." There was no further conversation.

I felt in that silence that John Brown Jr. and his son were still being guarded by their fellow islanders after all this time. I wasn't an intruder, exactly. I was a guest on Put-in-Bay, and always made to feel welcome. But there are secrets on an island, and islanders protect them. Sometimes, I realized, the best thing for a stranger to do is board a ferry and head for home.

4.

The story of the Brown Migration had to include mention of Mary Ann Brown.

The North Elba farm, so difficult to work, posed new dangers for a forty-three-year-old woman without a husband anymore. Just a little over a year after John Brown was hanged, Mary wrote to her friend Samuel E. Sewall "to know if I could get two hundred dollars from some sourse to help me get through the winter and to so fix things on the farm that we can have something at home."[27] Shortly after she decided to leave New York, she told her son Owen, "I very much regret that I ever spent a cent on that farm in North Elba but I did not know what I do now."[28]

She moved in the fall of 1863. Salmon and Henry Thompson already had plans to leave the Adirondacks, and on August 4, 1863, Mary told Mrs. George L. Stearns that she did too: "I have thought that perhaps I had better as it would give Annie and Sarah a chance to do something for themselves in a new country that they cannot have here."[29] She herself might have wanted to profit from the move as well. One scholar felt her departure might have had something to do with the need to escape the terrible dependency "that had plagued Mary for decades."[30]

I wondered sometimes if she left North Elba not just for her young daughters and possible financial gain, but because it had become a place where life itself couldn't be sustained anymore. John Brown's tombstone was in the front yard. In January of 1860 the stone carver arrived from his business in Wadham's Mills, thirty-five miles away, and stayed a week to enter the names and dates of her

Mary Ann Brown with
daughters Annie (left) and
Sarah (right). (Courtesy
Library of Congress)

husband and sons Watson and Oliver onto its surfaces. She must have felt the
farm had become the residence of the dead.[31]

Family members continued to die after Mary became a widow, and the
ground beneath her feet swelled with the dead even before her sons and the
raiders arrived. The same month the stone carver visited, Salmon and Abbie
Brown lost an infant daughter. That child joined an infant brother who
already lay in North Elba soil.

And then it was February. Martha Evelyn Brewster Brown, the young
wife of Oliver, delivered a daughter who, like Abbie's child, died in infancy,
living just a few days.[32] She was named Olive.[33]

Martha suffered four hard weeks of illness and then died in early March.
Mary took care of her and told McKim that Martha "was willing to go; said
she wanted to go where Oliver & her baby was." Mary confessed in her letter
that she was "most wore out."[34]

In August of 1863, Freddy, a favored grandchild—the young son of Isabella
M. Thompson Brown and Watson Brown, born in 1859—contracted diphtheria in North Elba and died. I couldn't help but think that the loss of that young
child sealed Mary's fate.[35] The death of Freddy—"our dear little Freddy" she
called him—seemed to tip things for her. "It is a bitter cup indeed to us all but
the good Lord knows best," she wrote to J. Miller McKim. I heard the "but,"
the conjunction so typical of Brown prose at times of loss. The fulcrum. It was
the sort of line that Mary usually ended with, for there was no more to say after
God restored balance to the world. But in the case of Freddy, she continued. "I
am afraid we all thought to much of him,"[36] she said.

The farm was unsold when Mary moved away, but I think she would have
burned it down if she hadn't gone when she did.

Ella Thompson Brown scrapbook, "Mrs. Belle Thompson Brown—wife of Watson Brown and their son Frederick."(Courtesy Brown Family Collection, The Huntington Library, San Marino, California)

They left New York, heading first to Cleveland so they could stop at Put-in-Bay to see family. Lyman Epps, their friend and neighbor, drove Mary, little Ellen (now nine), Sarah, and Salmon and his family twenty mountainous miles east to the railroad station in Keene, New York, where their trip began. Sarah decided to stay on the island for a while, but the others took a train to the Midwest. They originally intended to head to California, but along the way they found Decorah, Iowa, such a beautiful place that they bought a farm there, not expecting the winter of 1863–64 to be as hard as it was—no better than winter had been in New York.[37]

Both Sarah and Annie eventually joined the family in Iowa, Sarah from the island and Annie from Norfolk, Virginia, a Union-occupied town where she was teaching Black children and adults.[38] Shortly after their father was hanged, the girls attended F. B. Sanborn's School in Concord—boarding at the home of Bronson Alcott[39]—and, following that, Fort Edward Institute in New York, not far from North Elba, where Sarah studied art with Mary Artemisia Lathbury, who later helped develop Chautauqua Institute just a few miles from Jamestown, New York.[40]

Sarah arrived in Decorah quite ill. Scarlet fever was racing through the community, but the Browns didn't wait for the Red Death to call.[41] If they kept moving, Mary must have thought by then, maybe Death wouldn't catch Sarah, or any of them, the way it had when they stood still.

In the spring of 1864, the Browns began a two-thousand-mile trek to California in covered wagons pulled by oxen. It took six months.

5.

I saw a film unfold in my mind whenever I read about the episode, resembling an old movie about the American West. I first saw three wagons, each led by an ox. In one were Mary and her three daughters; in a second, Salmon and his family; in the last, two young men the Browns had hired to guard their supplies and the animals in the wagon, including the merino sheep Salmon had brought to begin a flock. They waited a long while to cross the Missouri River by ferry at Council Bluffs, but they did cross, and then they were in Omaha, Nebraska.

They joined a wagon train on its way to Denver, the captain of the train a Union man. It would be another year before the Civil War ended, but the Browns thought they were safe with a Union captain, even though many people in the train were Southerners, and not at all sympathetic when the captain flew the American flag instead of the flag of the Confederacy.

At Fort Kearney the Browns left the train and began to follow the Oregon Trail along the northern side of the Platte.

Everyone was a little worried about being in "Indian country," so they joined a second wagon train from Indiana that had in it several Black families. That train merged with an even larger group of wagons, in hopes of greater security. As people feared, they were met by a large party of Sioux along the way that bothered them, but never attacked. They rode beside the wagons until they tired of the company and turned away. The larger group the Browns had joined, though, included deserters from the Confederate army, and when they learned the Browns were among them, they hatched a vicious plot against them.

Four of the six merino sheep Salmon had brought were poisoned at Sublette's Cut-off. Then, a rumor spread that the Browns were about to be murdered themselves. Southerners from Tennessee and Missouri planned to take revenge for what John Brown had done at Harpers Ferry, so the Browns slipped away, saying they were just going to camp for the night over a rise. They disappeared and didn't come back, but were followed by an angry posse comprised of Confederates.

Headlines from the *New York Tribune* and the *Commonwealth* claimed that the Browns were dead.

But they'd escaped. In the way and tradition of their husband and father, they disappeared, crossed Wyoming and rode into Idaho to Soda Springs, the location of a Union outpost at Camp Connor. Confederates from the wagon train were still after them but now posed less threat.

A military escort assembled to protect the Browns, a lieutenant and six soldiers traveling with them now, bouncing on horses at either side of the wagon train for two hundred miles until the party was safe. From the Nevada desert to California they slowly advanced—reaching Red Bluff, their first home in their new state, on September 30, 1864.[42]

6.

I don't think Mary ever planned to live in a California cabin that sat on 160 acres of land high up a mountainside, but that's where she ended up, just as Owen and Jason did. What she was running from soon became more complicated, and less visible, than the Confederate deserters, the Sioux, and the vicious men who had pursued her party over mountain and plain.

Mary lived three places during her years in California—four counting her stay in San Francisco at the end of her life with her daughter Sarah, who became an adjuster in the Coiners Department of the US Mint serving under the presidency of James A. Garfield.[43] Sarah helped Mary battle what was called a "liver ailment" but would probably be diagnosed as liver cancer today.

She stayed first in the town of Red Bluff, then Rohnerville, near the coast of Humboldt County, and finally, on a mountainside in Saratoga in Santa Clara County. Her locations became increasingly remote. When she arrived in Saratoga, her final community—with an elevation of 480 feet—she chose not to live in the village proper. Her house, three miles from town and up a winding road that was almost impassable, stood 1,900 feet above sea level.[44]

I wasn't the first person to propose that Mary's move up a mountainside might symbolize something. American critic George Hamlin Fitch already had. He included a description of Mary Ann Brown's house and property in an essay he wrote for a collection edited by naturalist John Muir, a location Fitch had found by traveling down "a winding way, made dark even at midday by madrones and redwoods." Standing on the site of her mountain home, he thought there was no lonelier spot in the world than here—no roads, no

Sarah Brown. (Courtesy Hudson Library & Historical Society)

Two-story house incorporated into Mary Ann Brown's original cabin home in Saratoga, California. (Courtesy Boyd B. Stutler Collection of John Brown, West Virginia State Archives)

sounds, nothing but giant trees. This, for him, was one reason Mary chose it. The view was another: the ground on this high peak fell dramatically in one place, a sudden drop into the Santa Clara Valley that the critic felt could not help but soften the dire memories of her tragic losses.[45]

"I like the mountain air, the grand view and even the isolation," Mary Brown told a reporter from the *San Francisco Chronicle* who'd come up the mountain on his mustang to speak with her.[46]

It wasn't the unfriendliness of California's towns that drove Mary up that mountainside, though life wasn't quite as perfect for the Browns in California as they probably hoped it would be.

Red Bluff was good to them, for the most part. The *Red Bluff Independent*, a pro-Union publication, campaigned to raise money so that Mary could have clear title to the property the town had bought for her—four city lots on Main Street—and to construct a house on the land. The effort was called the "John Brown Cottage Fund."[47] There too, she found out that her North Elba farm had sold, and she saw her daughter Annie fall in love with a blacksmith and marry him—moving to a house just up the street from her own.

Salmon's sheep herd in the nearby city of Corning prospered.

But in 1870, Mary Ann Brown said she wanted to move, this time to Rohnerville. But why? One scholar suggested that perhaps she just desired a change.[48] But she'd been in Red Bluff only six years, and his reasoning seemed questionable to me. Why would she desire to move so soon, and at a prosperous season in her life? A second historian mentioned that her health was poor and she wanted to be nearer the ocean.[49] I wondered about that explanation as well. In 1873 Mary Brown wrote to her brother-in-law Jeremiah Root Brown advising him not to relocate to Rohnerville because it was much too foggy and would not improve the physical ailments he'd been experiencing, for already she knew of two local consumptives who were looking to leave.[50] Another historian pointed to the attacks in newspapers that were debated within the Red Bluff community—criticism of Reconstruction, of Radical Republicans, and of John Brown himself.[51]

For whatever reason, they left, and once they arrived in Rohnerville, there was more good news. Ellen married a schoolteacher, James Beatty Fablinger, and Salmon's flock, which had begun with the two sheep that survived the poisoning on the Oregon Trail, had grown to 14,000 head, and his pasture— now in Bridgeville—had expanded to three thousand acres. Mary had a house in town again, and an acre of land, purchased for $125, and Salmon and his family moved next door.[52]

But she was restless, and ten years after the move to Rohnerville, she moved again. Not everyone went with her to Saratoga, though. Salmon stayed where he was. Annie stayed too. They must have wondered what was wrong with Mary.

Historians had no more luck explaining this move than the one before. One new theory was that Salmon and Annie were doing better financially than Mary, who wanted more opportunity. But competing with her children didn't seem like something Mary ever cared to do. Even something that would cross her mind. In 1879 James Townsley had published a first-hand account about the Pottawatomie massacre that soon produced new hostility toward the Browns, and perhaps this influenced Mary's most recent departure.[53] A local historian even proposed that a mineral springs in the region might have lured Mary to relocate.[54]

Whatever the cause, the widow of John Brown left Rohnerville in 1881 and traveled south three hundred miles with Sarah, who never married, and with Ellen and her family.

Sensational journalism led to the mounting of yet one more relief fund for Mary Brown in Saratoga, but, oddly, stories about her children Salmon and Sarah this time were at the heart of it. Mary Brown's poverty (or what the community interpreted as her poverty) had been linked to Salmon's inattentiveness to his mother's financial needs. Sarah defended her brother. The uproar against them in newspapers and the sympathy it provoked for Mary

Jeremiah Root Brown. (Courtesy Hudson
Library & Historical Society)

made it possible for her to acquire a deed to a cabin on a mountainside.

In the summer of 1882, she came down the mountain to make one last
trip East—a trip that included claiming the body of poor Watson and burying
him, "at long last," in North Elba on October 13. Special ceremonies were held
in her honor at Chicago's Farwell Hall, and in Boston, Springfield, and
Topeka.[55] It was a long, tiring trip, and shortly after she returned in December,
she sold her cabin and moved off the mountain for good, dying in 1884 at the
age of sixty-seven.

Reasons people had provided for her peripatetic behavior always seemed
unconvincing to me. Slightly incomplete. What was it that she struggled with in
the middle of the night in towns she couldn't sleep in anymore?

Place hadn't always meant the same thing to John Brown and to his wife
Mary. The postscript John Brown attached to a letter he sent to his "Wife and
Children, Every One" just weeks before his execution spoke of place as something that provided little comfort or permanence to those who, after he was
hanged, would be tossed so turbulently by the events of his life and his cause.
"But, beloved ones, do remember that this is not your rest,—that in this world
you have no abiding place or continuing city."[56]

Maybe Mary was tired of hearing that kind of thing, and wanted to find
that "abiding place," that "continuing city" that John Brown denied her.
Wasn't there a chance that she could, if she searched hard enough? Wasn't
there hope that the great John Brown was wrong, and that it was possible to
find a place to rest in this world?

Yet, maybe in California she gradually came to understand that what
John Brown said just weeks before he died was true for her as well. Maybe she

had fled his words and tried to prove them wrong, but all the homes she established failed to bring her peace. Had she discovered for herself something that
John Brown had learned on his travels for his cause? Had she found that there
was for her "no abiding place"—not even California? That a democracy was
a process, not just a region on a map? That America was "not your rest," but a
country that demanded action and movement—embodied in Mary's perpetual restlessness?

REVERIE 7
"FOR THEE AND FOR MYSELF,
NO QUIET FIND"

I.

Why did I feel in danger too, with no shared lineage to John Brown and two centuries between us? How could a dead man have this kind of hold on me?

I'd been reading a book about hawks and falconry, and at first it helped me consider my relationship with John Brown in a more positive way. There was risk involved in falconry, but there might be advantages too. Holding something as fierce as a hawk on your wrist and observing it carefully might teach your ego how to become more hawk-like, more *accipitral*. The author, Helen Macdonald, bereaved by her father's death, said, "I was in ruins. Some deep part of me was trying to rebuild itself, and its model was right there on my fist."[1] Maybe the act of calling John Brown onto my hand might...

Might what? I wasn't at all clear how something so fierce could heal or "rebuild" a person. A falconry bird is tethered on a block for a reason. It perches safely only on a gloved hand, wears a hood to keep it calm, has bells and bands and jesses on its legs. The longer I looked at the bird, the more I saw the restlessness and danger of the hawk, not the redemptive trait that Macdonald had promised.

And, yet, I couldn't dismiss the image the bird began to evoke of something that would force a change if I kept it on my fist long enough.

Throughout the night, I spun narratives to explain John Brown's incendiary behavior, each version unraveling by morning with some new complication, its fragile threads broken by noon, nothing left of my imagination by the end of a day. But the bird remained perched on my hand, insisting I keep it there.

It grew no lighter.

I didn't know if I feared the man or loved him, or what name to use for what lay between. Nothing would resolve. The only thing I found to match my mood were lines from a Shakespeare sonnet, so I taped them to the frame of my computer screen.

"Lo, thus by day my limbs, by night my mind, / For thee, and for myself, no quiet find."²

ACROSS ALL OF IOWA

I.

I was tired of the battle. Even God, I sometimes thought, thinking about the early questions Gwen Mayer had posed to me in the archives, might not know what to say about John Brown. Wasn't it possible? Would God let him in heaven's gate, or shut him out? I thought of the questions William Blake asked. How could God create both the Innocence of the Lamb and the Experience of Blake's fierce Tyger?[1]

One morning, I had the idea of going back in time and interviewing all the dead who had either welcomed John Brown or turned him away when he rode across the state of Iowa with formerly enslaved people he'd taken off Missouri farms. Following the route of John Brown's trip would allow me to listen to what Iowa neighbors said when he knocked on their doors with new blood on his hands. I could watch other people grapple with the dilemma of John Brown and maybe feel less alone—even if my companions were only ghosts.

West to east he rode in horse-drawn wagons from Civil Bend to Davenport, with several of his men and eleven fugitives that he'd liberated (twelve, counting a baby who was born shortly after the liberation took place). If I documented all the reactions there were to him, and to what he did (which involved blood), it would be like a scan of the country in 1859, wouldn't it? If I charted those responses on a graph, certainly I would have a better notion where to stand.

John Brown was an outlaw when he fled across Iowa. He'd recently returned to Kansas, crossed the border into Missouri with his men, and freed enslaved people from several farms, though the Kansas he returned to in 1858 was far more moderate than the one he left.[2] In the course of his raid, his band stole horses and killed a white man. There was a bounty on his head again.

Black artist Jacob Lawrence has a painting of John Brown liberating people in Missouri. Only the leg and coat of John Brown are visible, his trunk and face far off the canvas on the right. He's leaning forward into his next long stride. Mainly exposed on paper are blue footprints pressed into white snow, a suggestion of red blood winding right beside his prints. The caption reads, "In spite of a price on his head, John Brown, in 1859, liberated 12 Negroes from a Missouri plantation."[3] I would later discover two errors in the caption, but they wouldn't alter the effect the print had on me.

I'd follow those footprints of John Brown as he crossed the state on his way toward a train that took members of his party to Chicago and Detroit, travel that broad expanse of land with him, wake people from their graves, ask them what happened in their towns when John Brown rode through. I'd watch and listen carefully, and maybe find just the model I was looking for.

2.

He was "Shubel Morgan" when he returned to Kansas in 1858 and then crossed the Missouri border. I loved the names he chose when he went in disguise. He was "Brown," most of the time, but also "Hawkins," "Morgan," "Smith." Common names. Nothing fancy for John Brown, even when he played a role.[4]

He surely knew that the Shubael in the Bible was a direct descendant of Moses, and John Brown was arrogant enough to compare himself to the prophet—to imagine himself saying to Pharaoh, "Let my people go."[5]

It didn't surprise me that after Harpers Ferry many of the men who were trying to escape with Owen Brown, as well as Owen Brown himself, took names other than their own whenever they left the mountains: Owen Brown was Edward Clark, once Owen Smith; Charles Plummer Tidd was Charles Plummer; Barclay Coppoc was George Barclay. The men in Owen Brown's party invented stories about being woodchoppers when they approached farms in search of food. Another raider, John Henry Kagi, named by John Brown as his Secretary of War, took the name J. Henrie as he gathered weapons for the Harpers Ferry attack, and John Brown Jr. called himself John Thomas when he recruited men in Oberlin, Ohio.[6]

Isaac Smith was John Brown's alias during the Harpers Ferry episode. Just prior to the assault, he identified himself as a cattle dealer and rented the Kennedy Farmhouse (about seven miles from Harpers Ferry on the Maryland side of the Potomac River) for $35 in gold from July to October of 1859. It was

John Henry Kagi. (Courtesy
Boyd B. Stutler Collection of
John Brown, West Virginia
State Archives)

Kennedy farmhouse, where raiders gathered
before Harpers Ferry

the hideout for the raiders, part of the ruse, and I'd traveled to look at it when
I visited Harpers Ferry—a remote spot with a house at least a hundred yards
off the road, lifted high on a stone foundation. It had been purchased in 1949
by the Improved Benevolent and Protective Order of Elks of the World—the
same organization that would lay a wreath at the grave of Dianthe Brown in
New Richmond—and turned into a national shrine for Black youth, then
sold to a Black physician, purchased by a real estate firm, declared a National
Historic Landmark in 1974 and restored by the Maryland Historical Trust
at Annapolis. It would later be converted into a heritage tourism destination—a living history center called the John Brown Raid Headquarters.[7]

When John Brown met Shields Green and Frederick Douglass at a stone
quarry in Chambersburg, Pennsylvania, in August of 1859, he was dressed as
a simple fisherman—even wearing a fisherman's hat.

But before he played the role of Isaac Smith at Chambersburg and
Harpers Ferry, he was Shubel Morgan in Kansas, and he had a beard. He'd
begun to grow it in the fall of 1857, perhaps as part of a disguise, or, some
people think, to hide a bout with Bell's Palsy that may have left a facial nerve
partially paralyzed.

This was the beard of his final daguerreotype, as well as the wild beard
depicted by John Steuart Curry in his controversial mural about Bleeding

John Steuart Curry standing on a ladder by the *Tragic Prelude* mural in the Kansas State Capitol. (Courtesy Kansas State Historical Society)

Kansas on the walls of the Kansas State Capitol—*Tragic Prelude.* The mural led to such public outcry that the Kansas legislature made it impossible for Curry to finish his work of depicting the state's history.[8] He left the state for Wisconsin and never signed his completed panels, but the painting is still on people's minds. Poet Kevin Young alluded to it in his volume *Brown*, calling John Brown's eyes in the mural "wild-wide" and his beard "afire."[9] It's not a painting that's easy to forget.

3.

Many biographers include just a page or two about the Missouri invasion or don't mention it at all. Kansas and Harpers Ferry and the hanging generally attract far more attention. But Villard's biography was comprehensive in scope, so when "Iowa" caught my interest, I knew his book would be my starting point.

Villard called the escape—which took place on December 20, 1858, not 1859, as Jacob Lawrence thought it had—"one of the most picturesque incidents in John Brown's life, without which its warfare against slavery would hardly have seemed complete." Coupling the word *picturesque* with the liberation of enslaved people off Southern farms, an event that involved a killing and a lot of risk for everybody, seemed an odd word choice.[10] "Certainly, nothing could have wound up his final visit to Kansas in a more dramatic way,"[11] Villard said.

John Brown went into Missouri to free people on farms because of an enslaved man named Jim Daniels, who had crossed the Missouri line with permission of his "owner," supposedly to sell brooms. He proceeded to southeast Kansas, where he told a man named George Gill his story, and Gill, who would accompany the John Brown party across Iowa, immediately went to find John Brown. Jim Daniels, along with his wife and two children, were about to be sold in an "administrator's sale," along with several of their friends. He had come into Kansas to seek help, not really to sell brooms at all, and he

George B. Gill. (Courtesy Boyd B. Stutler Collection of John Brown, West Virginia State Archives)

James Buchanan, 15th President of the United States (1857–1861). (Courtesy Library of Congress)

couldn't have been more fortunate, I suppose, than to have landed in John Brown's backyard. John Brown quickly organized two separate parties for a raid into Missouri. The first, consisting of ten men led by John Brown (including George Gill, Jeremiah Anderson, and John Kagi), would remove the Daniels family from the home of Harvey G. Hicklan. The second, eight men led by Aaron Stevens (and including Charles Plummer Tidd and Albert E. Hazlett), was to raid other plantations and liberate anyone enslaved, though they weren't supposed to kill a white man in the process.

The raids, which featured theft and the murder of David Cruise, caused enough chaos in Missouri to eventually shake national ground. After it was over, President Buchanan offered a reward of $250 for the arrest of Brown, and the governor of Missouri offered $3,000 for his capture. John Brown fled Missouri across the Kansan border, pulling the fugitives in a wagon drawn by a team of oxen. For six weeks after that, he sometimes separated from the caravan (for many days the fugitives stayed without him in a cabin south of Osawatomie that belonged to a Vermont man named Charles Severns). He fended off a posse from Missouri and arranged to hold a "war council" with William Hutchinson present—the chief Kansan reporter for the *New York Times*—making sure the details of his raid stayed national news for the next two months.[12]

John Brown supporters, including Jacob Willetts, standing on far left.
(Courtesy Kansas State Historical Society)

On January 20, shortly after a new baby was born to the Danielses at the
home of Dr. James G. Blount, twenty-five miles from Osawatomie[13]—bringing the party to twelve—the group left for Lawrence, where they traded their
wagon and oxen for horses and smaller wagons. Five days later they approached
Topeka, where they were welcomed into antislavery homes, and the next day,
helped to cross the Kansas River.

Something happened just before the crossing that both amused and surprised me, and I wanted to remember it.

A man named Jacob Willetts, who was chaperoning John Brown's
company to the crossing, saw John Brown shivering and his legs shaking as
he descended to the river. Willetts had already gathered pairs of old shoes and
some money from the Topeka neighborhood to give to the fugitives, but now
his attention turned to John Brown. Riding beside him, he reached down and,
according to his own account, "felt of his pantaloons, and found they were of
cotton, thin and suited to summer, not to the cold weather we had then." He
looked at him and said, "Mr. Brown, have you no drawers?"

John Brown admitted that he was not wearing undergarments.

"Well," Willetts said, matter-of-factly, "there is no time to go to the store
now; but I have on a pair that were new today, and if you will take them you

can have them and welcome." They exchanged a few more words, which Jacob Willetts did not record, and then he wrote a final line. "We got down beside the wagons on the boat; I took the drawers off, and he put them on."[14]

I felt embarrassed—not for Jacob Willetts or for John Brown, but for myself. As someone with autoimmune disease, I'd had to think about my body nearly my whole adult life, yet I'd forgotten to think about John Brown's. I knew some of the lyrics to "John Brown's Song," the tune that became the "Battle Hymn of the Republic," words about his body "a-mouldering in the grave." But he remained for me, too often, an idea on a page. I needed to be more vigilant, to bring back the John Brown who lived in a body. The John Brown who was exposed to all the elements, like the rest of us.

4.

They proceeded twenty-eight miles to Holton, but John Brown felt that the community wasn't as friendly to his cause as it once had been and traveled six more miles to stay in the empty cabins of Dr. Albert Fuller on Straight Creek. They reached Fuller's property on January 29 in a fierce prairie snowstorm, but the unusually mild weather which preceded the storm caused more trouble than the storm itself, for the creek was overflowing and the roads were deep dishes of mud. All they could do was wait.

In Lawrence, Samuel F. Tappan had loaned John Brown a two-horse wagon and a driver, so while they watched the water recede, John Brown sent Tappan's man back to Topeka to collect two members of his party who had remained to gather provisions. Meanwhile, a tracking party was discovered near Holton, and word was sent to Topeka through a quick-riding messenger—an antislavery farmer named Wasson—that reinforcements were needed. Sixteen men assembled in Topeka (a Congregational Church service stopped to make the call for help), and soon both the recruits and a wagon filled with provisions were in the Holton area.

Groups of vigilantes had formed, the largest led by John P. Wood, an impromptu deputy. But they failed to contain John Brown and his party. At first they misidentified them, unaware that the oxen and original wagon had been traded for horses and smaller wagons. And, like so many others, they were terrified of John Brown and his strategy of having his men stand in

Augustus Wattles. (Courtesy Kansas State Historical Society)

Stone house built by Augustus Wattles in Linn County, where John Brown wrote "Parallels" (or, possibly, in a log cabin on this site before this structure was built). (Courtesy Kansas State Historical Society)

double file as they advanced toward the enemy—this time moving toward the fording point of the stream.

The skirmish came to be known as the Battle of the Spurs, named, perhaps, for the amusing and awkward appearance of Wood's men when they ran, untying their horses so quickly from bushes and trees, in such a state of confusion that two men often tried to mount the same horse at once. Those who succeeded spurred their horses furiously in retreat, while those who failed to mount held tight to the tails of the animals and sailed in the air like twisting ribbons. Some of Brown's men chased the vigilantes, eventually capturing five horses and five prisoners—all released the next day.

On February 1, an Underground Railroad man named William Graham accompanied Brown's party over the border into Nebraska, hoping to help them cross the difficult Nemaha River. Then fifty more miles toward Nebraska City, and on February 4, 1859, the crossing of the Missouri River and entry into Iowa, escaping another posse of fifty just before they came into a new state.[15]

He'd met with anger and hostility for his raid from Missourians and others in the Territory, but even some of his friends had begun to pull away from him. Augustus Wattles—who gave shelter to John Brown and his party in Kansas after the Missouri raid, as well as on earlier trips—censured his friend when he learned a man had been killed. John Brown wrote a document now known as "Old Brown's Parallels" to defend what he'd done—a letter that appeared in the *New York Daily Tribune* (January 22, 1859) and was composed earlier in the house of his friend.[16] But for Augustus Wattles, Free-State Democrat George A. Crawford, and others in Kansas Territory, John Brown had, in more than one sense, crossed the line.

5.

The knocking on Iowa doors began.

I liked to think I'd have been an abolitionist if I'd lived when John Brown did, raised on the soil of the Connecticut Western Reserve, the way I was. Most of the people whose doors he knocked on during his trip across Iowa were abolitionists, many of them migrants with deep roots in the Western Reserve, and a great many of them Quakers.

But would being a white abolitionist necessarily have determined how I'd have behaved? One third of Hudson's population were abolitionists in those years, Gwen had told me, but few of them chose to risk working on the Underground Railroad.

Historian Ira Berlin wrote about the complicated issue of some free Blacks, especially in the South, not automatically becoming abolitionists for fear they would "stir the slaveholders' wrath." According to Berlin, no one knew "the sting of the master's lash" better than they did. Alliances with those enslaved held immense risk for free Blacks, so they sometimes found it advantageous to their survival and well-being to distance themselves from the enslaved, even, at times, becoming slave owners. It was free Blacks in the North who were "the leading edge of the movement against slavery." They didn't have the burden of the South and were able to see the connection between their own freedom and the absolute necessity of freeing others.

The lack of that kind of connection compromised white abolitionism, Berlin said, comparing the two. The extreme material differences between white and Black abolitionists and the capacity of white abolitionists to know only the idea of slavery, not the suffering it caused, led them to often be patronizing or aloof. They might sign a petition in church, I thought, but wouldn't necessarily work on the Underground Railroad. Berlin claimed that it was part of human nature to be "risk-averse."[17]

Of all the white abolitionists nationally who said they supported John Brown, only a few, most especially the Secret Six, consistently raised funds for his maneuvers. After Harpers Ferry, most of the Six ran.

So, how many varieties did abolitionists come in, and which would I have been?

6.

On March 18, 1859, the *New-York Daily Tribune* ran a story about the fugitives in John Brown's party finally reaching Windsor, Canada. It told mainly about all the attempts to arrest John Brown and capture the fugitives, as well as the route of the journey and its extent—"1,100 miles, 600 miles of which was made in wagons, the remainder by railroad." There were a few personal details as well. The fugitives were from four families. A man, his wife, and their three children; a widowed mother and her children; a young man; and a woman whose husband (the son of the widowed woman) was not home when the raid occurred. "One of the women had had six masters," the article said, "and four have had sixteen masters in all."[18] I thought about the correspondent for the *Tribune* gathering that information, asking about the number of masters each woman had had, because he knew that number in part defined her. Five women had endured twenty-two masters, he reported. I lost my breath.

The "younger child" the newspaper article referred to when the matter of the children in the party was discussed was the baby born just before the party crossed over into Iowa. He'd been christened "John Brown Daniels." I was touched by the name, by the faith the infant's parents seemed to have in the angry man who had come for them.

So often in accounts of John Brown's surprise attack in Missouri only the high adventure found a place on the page, but Lowell Soike published details I'd found nowhere else. He provided names (further filling in what I read in

Sam and Jane Harper (1894),
former enslaved people
from Missouri farms who
were liberated by the parties
of John Brown and Aaron
Stevens in 1858. (Courtesy
Kansas State Historical
Society)

the *Tribune*): Sam Harper, Jim and Narcissa Daniels, along with two of their
children, joined John Brown from the Hicklin (or Hicklan) farm. From the
farm of John LaRue, John Brown took five more people—George and David
were two of their names. And the Stevens' party found the enslaved woman
Jane at the house of David Cruise, the wealthy settler who didn't survive their
visit. Jane's release had specifically been requested by Jim Daniels.[19]

Soike had included a portrait of Sam and Jane Harper from 1894. They
were married by a justice of the peace in Springdale, Iowa, but I didn't know
when they fell in love. There apparently was constant disagreement between
John Brown and Jane Harper on the trip across Iowa because she was a wonderful cook, but John Brown always prided himself on his cooking and "insisted
on being the cook for the whole company of his men and fugitives from slavery
that he assisted...from Missouri to Canada."[20]

The story of John Brown's raid to free enslaved people that began in Missouri and ended in Canada featured both a wedding and a birth. And the
death of David Cruise.

Mural showing John Brown with fugitives from Missouri in the Torrington, Connecticut, post office

In November of 1859, when John Brown was calling his Charles Town jail cell "home," a Canadian correspondent reported more news about the Iowa party. Seven of the twelve fugitives in the caravan were still living in Windsor, Ontario, just across the Detroit River, and the others, in the country about nine miles away. Those in Windsor were working at various jobs, including sawing and general labor. Two of the women rented an acre of land and were planting corn and potatoes, and both owned houses with small gardens. They'd been able to purchase three hogs. The five in the country were sharecroppers. "They have about sixteen acres of corn, potatoes, &c., part of which are theirs; and they are all anticipating the day when they can get a piece of land of their own," the correspondent said.[21] Richard Hinton, writing in 1894, was sure to mention that John Brown Daniels still lived in Windsor at that time, apparently having "never set foot in the United States." He added, "the Missouri freed people are nearly all living, doing well, and having large families about them."[22]

Most of the time John Brown took up all the space on a page. He was a rogue, an outlaw, a rebel. He was the picturesque hero of his own story who raced across the prairie as free and wild as a dust storm. But as I followed John Brown across Iowa, I began to realize that he rode in the company of people who had names and stories and whose wagons sat outside every door where John Brown knocked.

7.

We'd driven on I-80 to Des Moines many times because my in-laws had lived in that town, and we'd also traveled to Iowa City, where my brother-in-law taught before he moved to Boston. But that was all I really knew about the state.

The only Iowan I felt I could contact for advice before I left Ohio was Mary Swander, a friend I worked with at Lake Forest College near Chicago in the late 70s. The Iowa Quakers were important to John Brown, she said, and recommended that I visit the website of the State Historical Society of Iowa.

The society had researched Underground Railroad activity through the Iowa Freedom Trail Project and posted a map online called the John Brown Freedom Trail of 1859 that traced John Brown's route with a line that loosely followed I-80, sometimes veering off a few miles north or south, and included dots that marked each stop: there was information, and there were pictures, for every site—Civil Bend, Tabor, Malvern Vicinity, Lewis Vicinity, Grove City Townsite, Dalmanutha Townsite, Redfield Vicinity, West Des Moines, Yellow Banks Park Vicinity, Grinnell I-80 Rest Stop Vicinity, Grinnell, Marengo Vicinity, Iowa City, Springdale, West Liberty, Davenport. Along the trail there apparently were wayside markers that featured brief biographies about the people who'd lived there and transcriptions of actual letters important to the story of John Brown's trip. Mailboxes from the past.[23]

Lydia Maria Child. (Courtesy
Library of Congress)

I read the words "Congregational" and "Quaker" repeatedly as I scanned
the entries. This matter of Quakers, I wanted to believe, would be simple. I
knew about the role Quakers played in convincing Parliament to abolish the
slave trade in Britain in 1807, and the effect of that on American slave importation (though both countries found ways to break the laws for a long time
and heavy fines on ships had to be imposed). The Religious Society of Friends,
along with Evangelical Protestants like William Wilberforce, led the campaign.[24] A kind, old Quaker man in a long coat and broad-brimmed hat found
William Wells Brown (formerly "Sandford Higgins") sick on a road and
helped him escape. The fugitive, in gratitude, took the Quaker's name.[25]

That's what I wanted to believe it meant to be a Quaker.

But I'd also read Ralph Keeler's account of Owen Brown's escape from the
Kennedy Farmhouse, and things had become a little murky. Quakers, like
every other group, didn't always agree about the methods abolitionists should
use. A man named Benjamin Wakefield, in Pennsylvania, directed the Owen
Brown party to a Quaker cousin of his. They found the man, and he was willing
to let them board in his house after Harpers Ferry, but three Quaker women
who also lived there—a mother and two daughters—leaned out windows in
their night caps and told the men they couldn't come in because although the

women opposed slavery, "they were also not in favor of putting it down by force."[26] They finally consented when the raiders promised to give up their guns, but they refused to join them, not even coming down for breakfast.

Quaker Augustus Wattles drew the line at the murder of David Cruise.

John Brown's violence repelled American abolitionist and women's rights activist Lydia Maria Child—a Quaker too. She said so to John Brown in a letter, even as she asked to visit him in prison.[27] Perth Amboy's Mrs. Spring, though, the woman who helped assemble John Brown's funeral clothes and buried two of his raiders on her property, was not the same kind of Quaker that Child was. She wanted to make sure that John Brown's violence was not born of revenge, but seemed otherwise quite happy—even pleased—that he'd acted while others stood still. Even the few famous Quakers I'd read about, in other words, were not of a single mind regarding the use of force.

As I crossed the state, I reminded myself that the Quaker reputation for quietism was probably not the whole of it.

8.

We sped across Illinois, and then the northern part of Iowa all the way to the western boundary, where John Brown began his trip. Near the Nebraska border, we turned the car around, pointed it toward Davenport—hundreds of miles east of where we sat—and started out.

We were sitting in the middle of a cornfield trying to find Blanchard Cemetery and the gravestone of Dr. Ira D. Blanchard. The town Ira Blanchard lived in, Civil Bend (sarcastically named by hard-drinking river men), no longer existed, but the Historical Society of Iowa said the cemetery did—named by Ira Blanchard in honor of his wife, who died in 1864. I thought of Owen Brown burying his wife in David Hudson's former apple orchard and of John Markillie burying his mother under an elm tree on land he owned—of sorrowful pioneers who relinquished people they loved to the ground that had lured them West.[28]

We wouldn't have found the cemetery without my husband's GPS and his Find A Grave app. I flipped the pages of a notebook that held old maps of Civil Bend while my husband stopped the car to consult the app—did something that actually might get us there. The two of us had navigated these trips so often—for his work, for mine—that we quickly fell into our roles.

In a way, when I said I depended on his apps, I really meant I depended on him. He stayed close by until a problem was solved—even when he didn't have the technology—sharing the driving with me and being tirelessly patient when my health made it necessary to pause. Nothing I wanted to find out ever

seemed trivial to him. He didn't think it was at all laughable to be in a cornfield looking for a man named Ira D. Blanchard who was buried in a cemetery
no one visited anymore in a town that had disappeared. I couldn't imagine
making long trips without him.

At first, I thought John Brown had given me energy for the trip—just
holding tight to his coattails let me fly. Who wouldn't be inspired by a person
who found the courage to race across state lines, drive cattle and lead oxen,
cross rivers to outwit an enemy, travel in disguise, clear the land or survive in
the wild—as he'd taught his sons?

I'd been able to do so much in the last few years. How could I not conclude that it had been John Brown who had given me this newfound strength?
When he was visiting Harriet Tubman in St. Catharines, Canada West, in
early April of 1858 with J. W. Loguen, John Brown was amazed that she
"hooked on his whole team at once," and described her as "the most of a man,
naturally, that I ever met with"—using masculine pronouns when he spoke
of her.[29]

I knew I lacked the moral courage of Harriet Tubman, but I hoped that
John Brown might at least have admired the energy I displayed since I met
him, the way he had hers. Hadn't he, in large part, been responsible for what
I'd accomplished?

But when I heard myself whisper *without him* in the cornfield, I knew it
wasn't John Brown who was sustaining me. My physical strength was limited.
It was true that John Brown often did inspire me to try new things, but my
health was always on the line, sometimes coming in great spurts, other times,
gasps.

I'd kept my husband small in my book. John Brown took up all the space.

But it wasn't John Brown, really, who got me where I needed to go. He
never drove, he only rode along. He accompanied me to Blanchard Cemetery,
it's true, but he wasn't the one who took me there.

Daniel was.

9.

The GPS said to exit at Percival, a town that was close to the spot where Civil Bend once stood.

The historical map I'd brought along—begun by Fremont County resident Samuel P. Ricketts and his daughter Grace, and finished by Jean Ricketts Schobert—showed Copeland's landing and the original 1850s shore line of the Missouri River.[10] Names and property lines of some of Civil Bend's old residents were on it, including the land owned by Dr. Ira D. Blanchard, which abutted the farms of Lester W. Platt and George B. Gaston. The map showed the fist of land between the Missouri River and Percival, the area originally known as Civil Bend—as did a second map I later was provided drawn by Rev. John Todd in 1854 that marked sawmills and gristmills in the area.

I loved the old Ricketts map. Its lessons were still relevant. Just by looking at it, I could feel the proximity of the community to the river and the importance of this crucial bend in the lives of fugitives who secretly passed through. They came to Civil Bend to flee what one historian called "a prison house," and in the process exposed what he labeled the "lie" of "the idea of the 'united' states."[11]

Some of the farmhouses were inside a federal levee now. The area on the map was underwater the summer of 2012. Flooding of the river in this rich bottomland was what originally led some of its settlers, including George Gaston and John Tabor, to leave Civil Bend in 1852 and found Tabor on higher ground. It was what, I assumed, had caused a levee to be built in the first place.

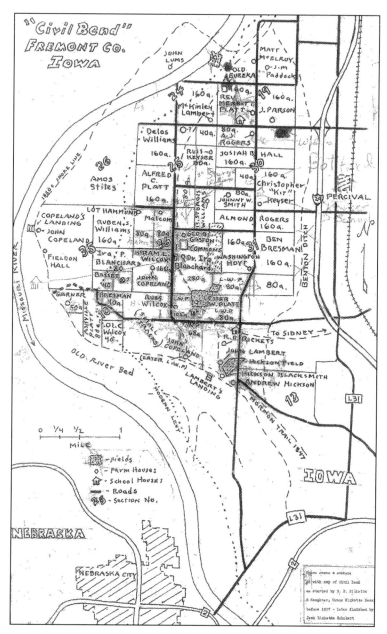

Civil Bend map drawn by Ricketts family. (Courtesy Tabor Historical Society)

Jesse James dead in his coffin.
(Courtesy Library of Congress)

My husband's phone app led us to 175th Street. It was such a big-numbered street for a land of cornfields and bumpy roads and forgotten cemeteries—so peculiar, so incongruous, as if we were in New York City. The older map seemed more true, somehow, with words and symbols that approximated the stark simplicity of the place. There was To Sidney, with an arrow pointing east, an area marked Benton Ditch, and the words Small Tracks in parentheses. Little houses were drawn to show where schools had been.

At a school in Civil Bend, Jesse James and his gang fought with a posse on June 5, 1871, two days after the gang robbed a bank in Corydon, Iowa. The gang fled to the stable of the schoolhouse and refused to surrender, mounting their horses and heading south. The horse of one member was killed. After the fight, these items were found near the stable: a linen coat, a pair of gloves, several revolver holsters, one actual revolver with "W and W" carved into the butt.[32] A Louis DeCaro blog mentioned that Jesse James and John Brown were sometimes compared, except that Jesse James was generally regarded more sympathetically. Yes, I thought, that probably was true. History liked outlaws sometimes. Billy the Kid. Butch Cassidy. But John Brown? Not so much.

The Eastern press romanticized both John Brown and Jesse James, but it was curious that a native Missourian who left his state to fight as a Confederate guerilla in the Civil War retained a romantic hue. He was part of Quantrill's Raiders in Kansas, a merciless group responsible for the Lawrence Massacre of 1863. Jesse James claimed that his life of outlawry had been forced on him by the persecution his family endured in the war. John Brown, a militant abolitionist, couldn't compete with Jesse Woodson James. For some reason he still felt like a threat.

From the moment we exited at Percival, the road grew more narrow. Asphalt soon disappeared, replaced by gravel and dirt. Soon even that surface ended and we were riding on original prairie soil. Dirt filled with seeds had spilled out of the cornfields onto the roadbed, and as we drove it coated the fender of our car and blew through open windows. A deer walked beside us, shot in front, and then vanished in a field. The road grew bumpier after that, and we slowed down, crossed a small bridge, and soon saw gravestones on the right.

Roosters were crowing on the property that stood next to the cemetery, loud enough to wake the dead. Maybe that was why they crowed each dawn, I thought: they had a lot of work to do, and it would never end. I wondered if the last sound on earth, after everyone was gone, would be a rooster's crow.

Just inside the swinging gate to the cemetery, and just before the first row of gravestones, was a wayside marker about the John Brown Freedom Trail— the first of many I'd see on this trip. In the right-hand corner of the sign was a circle that would become familiar: the upper body of John Brown imposed on a solid beige map of Iowa, with a thin white line that marked the route through the state racing across his chest, the words "John Brown Freedom Trail" bending around the upper edge, and the inclusive dates of his journey (beginning with the Missouri raid) following the curve of the lower (December 20, 1858–March 12, 1859).

Civil Bend was founded by Blanchards and Platts and Gastons—by people who were either former missionaries to Pawnee and Delaware tribes or Congregational ministers from Ohio. The small town soon became an abolitionist stronghold, a shelter for fugitives and Kansas-bound Free Staters.

Dr. Ira D. Blanchard stayed in Civil Bend after the flood, and John Brown lodged in his home several times. The Platts also stayed, and it was at the house of Elvira Gaston Platt that John Brown and his company spent their first night after crossing over from Nebraska City on February 4, 1859. She had talked to local journalists about the Underground Railroad in Civil Bend shortly before John Brown and his party arrived, saying she was proud that it "ran through our yard." Forty years later, while a resident of Oberlin, she

Blanchard Cemetery in old Civil Bend

wrote a letter to William E. Connelley of Topeka, Kansas, that included a sentence the wayside marker at the edge of the cemetery had immortalized: "He slept at my house when he made his last trip from Missouri, but greatly to my regret I was with Tabor friends at that time."

I wondered if I would ever feel regret like that about John Brown—great regret for having missed him during so many of my Hudson years, and all the years before that when I'd lived in Akron and Kent (his towns, too). I knew I hadn't yet felt for him the kind of deep longing and affection that Elvira Platt had.

I found the stones of neighbors I'd come to see. Ira D. Blanchard, who had the tallest monument, was in the very front row. Mary W., his wife's name, was engraved on a second face of his stone. Mary's own stone, a smaller one, stood nearby, where she'd been buried by her husband eight years before he died. Later I learned that the words on her stone came from an 1830 hymn called "The Dead in Christ" that people in Civil Bend must have sung with regularity: "High in heaven's own light she dwelleth, / Full the song of triumph swelleth; / Free from earth and earthly failing, / Lift for her no voice of wailing."[33]

Gravestone of Ira D. Blanchard,
Blanchard Cemetery, old Civil Bend

Corn and wheat triumphed here now, lining the visible edge of every horizon. Corn would have been in this spot even when John Brown rode through, pioneers growing it on former grasslands and in wooded clearings since their arrival. Maria C. Gaston, of nearby Tabor, Iowa, talked in 1856 about a cannon that was covered in corn to elude enemies.

I was standing on prairie soil that I'd soon learn Iowa poet Paul Engle had called "fat dirt"[34] and reached down for some before I stepped into the car again. I smelled it, then closed my eyes and saw horses and wagons coming toward me. I heard a new baby cry. The Blanchards weren't in the cemetery yet when John Brown came through, so their stones disappeared. I saw a cabin with a yard that connected to Iowa's James Lane Trail in the distance—an escape route for fugitives—and I waited for a signal. But all I heard was the hum of a distant tractor on a summer day.

10.

John Brown passed through Iowa more than once between 1856 and 1859. The state was important strategically for him and his cause. Springdale, Iowa, in the eastern part of the state, was where his men trained for Harpers Ferry in the winter of 1858, believing that would be the year of the raid. And Tabor, near the western border of Iowa not many miles northeast of Civil Bend, was a place where he and his men often recuperated after fighting in Kansas and where he sometimes stored arms.

I planned to look in Tabor for the home of abolitionist Rev. John Todd, supposedly the only structure that survived in the town from the John Brown days.

As we approached, I saw houses with wagon wheels in the front yards, resting against trees and porches. We turned onto US 275 and I made a note about Tabor's stores—the Tabor Market, 2nd Time Around, First State Bank, and a Casey's.

We drove down Orange Street two blocks. A swath of green now known to residents as the "park," but called Public Square in the 1850s when Tabor was platted, stood at the center of town. It was an area nearly twice as wide as the Hudson Green and big enough to accommodate a multi-purpose sports field, picnic tables, and swings. In the 1860s, buildings would appear just north of the Square—a church and a college that the founding fathers envisioned, the athletic fields of the college spilling onto the Square. I imagined Kansan settlers camped on the ground—their wagons and livestock every-

Entering Tabor, Iowa

where—ready to train for the battles that awaited them when they crossed
the Missouri River, but I had to squint out solar panels on posts to keep the
image from fading.

A sign about historical Tabor labeled "Fighting Slavery—Aiding Runaways" featured in large letters what Thomas Wentworth Higginson had said
about the town in the *New York Tribune*: "The citizens of Tabor are entitled to
everlasting gratitude for their unwearied kindness to our emigrants. The sick
have been cared for, clothing has been made, and every house, stable, and melon-
patch, has been common property. Let the Eastern States hold this thriving
little village in grateful remembrance."

His words were written in 1856, but John Brown came through with his
fugitives in 1859. The sign mentioned how townspeople did not respond well
to John Brown during his trip across Iowa—his image soiled by murder and
theft.

Accounts I'd read from proslavery newspapers said that in addition to five
enslaved people, raiders took from the Lawrence estate and from the property
of Harvey Hicklan (who was serving as tenant and temporary master for the
estate) "two good horses, a yoke of oxen, a good wagon, harness, saddles, a
considerable quantity of provisions, bacon, flour, meal, coffee, sugar, etc., all
of the bedding and clothing of the negroes... Hicklin's shotgun, over-coat,
boots, and many other articles belonging to the whites." And from Larue, in
addition to five more people, "six head of horses, harness, a wagon, a lot of
bedding and clothing, provisions, and, in short, all the 'loot' available and
portable."[35]

Tabor plat map, 1858. (Courtesy Tabor Historical Society)

Aaron Stevens and his party took Jim Daniels' friend Jane but killed her "owner," David Cruise, who seemed to be reaching for a weapon—a perfectly understandable maneuver, since strangers had entered his house. The Cruise family accused the party not only of murder, but of "wholesale looting of the house, the taking of two yoke of oxen, a wagon-load of provisions, eleven mules and two horses," along with "a valuable mule...taken from another neighbor, Hugh Martin."[36] Rufus Cruise, the young son who fled from the house barefoot and in nightclothes before his father was shot, later learned that Jane had watched John Brown's men through a window as they sat at the Cruise fireplace warming their hands, and laughed. Then, supposedly, she "went back to the kitchen and began to pack up," taking all of her bedding, all of her clothes, and $60 in cash—money, Rufus reported, that was "part hers and part my mother's."[37]

Aaron Dwight Stevens. (Courtesy Boyd B. Stutler
Collection of John Brown, West Virginia State
Archives)

John Brown argued that the property belonged to the people they'd liberated, and it was needed by them (the word "reparations" entered my mind, as
did the image of Thaddeus Stevens and the meeting in Savannah), but he
admitted to not distinguishing at the time of the raid between the property of
the enslaved and the property of Mr. Hicklan. He said in "Parallels" that when
they found this out, they "promptly returned to him *all we had taken.*"[38]

The town of Tabor was not pleased with John Brown's behavior in Missouri, nor was it convinced of his innocence. "Brown quickly noticed the displeasure of the townspeople over his actions," the sign read. Some interpretation by the historical society followed: "Assisting freedom seekers escaping
slavery was one thing, actively freeing the enslaved from their masters and
killing people in the process was entirely another." The sign said that John
Brown was "dismayed by this cool reception," and because of it left sooner
than he'd planned. I couldn't read about the disgust John Brown felt for
Taborites without thinking of his earlier response to Amos Chamberlin's lack
of charity. He tolerated neither very well and felt no inclination to understand
the other side.

There had apparently been less sympathy for John Brown in the larger
community of Tabor than in Civil Bend.

The house of Rev. John Todd, the first minister of Tabor's Congregational
Church and one of the town's founders, a man educated at Oberlin College,
was just opposite the Square, with a large sign labeled Todd House in the front
yard. It told about the use of native trees to build the home and about its adobe
foundation, but the most significant information on the sign was that the

House of Rev. John Todd, Tabor

house was not only a station on the Underground Railroad, but served as an arsenal and hospital during "The Kansas Free State Fight." Hidden in the basement were two hundred Sharps rifles that arrived in Dr. Root's wagon, and in the barn, Dr. Root's brass cannon. There was no indication on the sign of any reluctance to help the cause. There was every indication of militancy.

The weapons of Rev. John Todd, who served loosely as the model for the narrator's grandfather in Marilynne Robinson's *Gilead*, as Tabor served as the model for her fictional town,[39] at first seemed to mix naturally with the tools of his rural life—as necessary to the work of fighting slavery as plows and scythes were to the preparation of soil. Both sets of implements appeared to be central to his religion. In 1857, the Freedom Trail sign read, he sent the rifles East, many to be used later at Harpers Ferry. So, I thought, surely this man would receive John Brown without reservation, even if others in town did not.

With Villard in hand, along with my map, I sat on a bench in the middle of old Tabor Public Square to try to sort this out.

II.

The day after the company arrived, and after the fugitives were situated in the Tabor schoolhouse, John Brown handed Rev. Todd a note, asking that it be read to the congregation, but the minister refused. Rev. Todd, it turned out, was, after all, a part of the cool reception John Brown received in Tabor.

John Brown requested the church to "offer public thanksgiving to Almighty God" for the freeing of the fugitives, but Rev. Dr. H. D. King, who was sharing the pulpit that day with Rev. Todd, advised him to refrain. Rev. Todd agreed to withhold the blessing.

A meeting with the church community to compose a resolution about the matter was scheduled the next day. But a slave owner happened to enter the church just as John Brown was beginning to explain himself, and he refused to proceed with the man present. His intolerance for the slave owner incited the community. After hours of discussion about John Brown's escapade in Missouri (John Brown having quietly withdrawn from the meeting), town citizens drafted a document: "Resolved, That while we sympathize with the oppressed, & will do all that we conscientiously can to help them in their efforts for freedom, nevertheless, we have no Sympathy with those who go to Slave States, to entice away Slaves, & take property or life when necessary to attain that end."[40] The community voted, and the resolution passed.

Taborites supported violence in Kansas to keep slavery out of the Territory. Rifles and cannons were not designed to wound, but to kill, so I could only assume that citizens of the town and Rev. Todd himself fully understood the implications of the weapons they stored.

But the rules were different regarding Southern states where slavery was established. Tabor was an abolitionist town, and most residents deeply believed that it was a good thing to assist fugitives who made independent decisions to run away, but they did not believe it was a good thing for abolitionists to go into "Slave States" and "entice away Slaves, & take property or life"—even if taking those things was necessary to make people free.

I recognized that the phrase "entice away" might have had a somewhat different connotation for abolitionists than for slave owners, and I tried to account for that. The community was established by Congregational missionaries, had a strong commitment to the Underground Railroad, and was more familiar with the history of fugitives than most other towns. Tabor might have sincerely worried about serious consequences for enslaved people taken off farms and plantations. Long before the Fugitive Slave Act of 1850 was passed, the Fugitive Slave Act of 1793 posed great dangers for any fugitive fleeing the South.

Even abolitionist Harriet Tubman (John Brown called her "General Tubman") made sure that enslaved people felt ready to accompany her before she led them away. On all the trips she made to the Eastern Shore of Maryland to help fugitives escape (parties often included her family members), she sought people's consent, though once they agreed, she pulled her pistol out if they changed their minds when things became difficult on the trip North. She refused to let them return to be slaves.

As much sympathy as I tried to bring to the resolution of Taborites, though, I ended up agreeing with the people who wrote the sign on the Square. Tabor's white abolitionists generally thought it was wrong to go into the South and "actively free" enslaved people at gunpoint. I wondered sometimes if their knowing that Jim Daniels had crossed the border of Missouri to ask for help because he and his family and friends were about to be sold on the auction block would have made any difference at all in the wording of the resolution.

I returned to what Ira Berlin said: white abolitionists had the capacity to hold the idea of slavery in their heads and in their hearts, but not the suffering that it caused. Even in a fervently abolitionist town like Tabor, it seemed easier for citizens to imagine the anguish that theft of property, or loss of life, caused a slave owner than the despair that loss of freedom caused a slave.

There were boundaries Taborites and other white abolitionists drew, and I could see them in the document.

I, too, had drawn my own lines around John Brown.

But John Brown crossed them all and would not be contained. His cause was quite simple to him—to make people "free." In his "Parallels," he used the words "liberate" and "freed" many times, perhaps naively, to defend his decision to go into Missouri, and he implied that David Cruise was killed because he "fought against the liberation."[41] John Brown left a trail of words and deeds that would force people to examine his impulses, and then confront their own.

12.

So many stops between Tabor and Grinnell, Iowa, but I made them all.

I found the approximate site of the former cabin in Malvern Vicinity where John Brown stayed with Charles W. and Sylvia Cast Tolles, even though the picture I snapped there showed nothing but good bottomland near a bluff, a bridge, and a river. I visited some of the places associated with his Iowa cousin, Oliver Mills, a man born in Trumbull County, Ohio, who lived just south of Lewis, and with his antislavery friend Rev. George B. Hitchcock, who lived a mile west of Mills and whose brown sandstone house we toured.

I located a tiny historic marker for Grove City, a twenty-four-block town where John Brown stayed at Grove City House, run by David A. Barnett, an Underground Railroad man. Like Civil Bend, the town was gone. Several miles away, at the Dalmanutha Townsite, I found the ghostly remains of a hamlet originally on the main stage line, and in Dalmanutha Cemetery, the even more ghostly remains of John Porter, whose hotel John Brown's party stayed at on February 15, 1859.

I arrived at Redfield, on the Middle Raccoon River, and drove a mile east, where Jonathan M. Murray had lived, though he'd taken up residence in Redfield Cemetery now. In West Des Moines, I located the home of wealthy James C. Jordan, as well as his resting place in Jordan Cemetery, and thought about his transformation from slave catcher to abolitionist and his willing eagerness to hide John Brown and his company in timber on his land. I paused in Des

Rev. George B. Hitchcock house near   James C. Jordan House, West Des
Lewis, Iowa   Moines, where John Brown's party was
                                           hidden in timber

Moines, where John Brown had Kagi summon John Teasdale—the editor of
the *Des Moines Citizen* (which would shortly acquire the new name *Iowa State
Register*) who was a friend from Akron and had attended the same church
John Brown had—and Teasdale met John Brown at a bridge that crossed the
Des Moines River,[42] and then, as George Gill told Richard Hinton, "paid our
ferriage across."[43]

I followed Vandalia Road to reach Yellow Banks Park, where I found a
campsite with a mailbox shaped like a fish at its entrance, ball fields, areas for
canoeing and biking and camping (trailer and tent). I thought about John
Brown's friend Brian Hawley, a sawmill owner and carpenter from New York
who kept the party there overnight on February 18, 1859.

At the Grinnell I-80 rest stop (more of a museum than a rest stop), I found
the approximate location of a farm where the party stayed the next night. Corn-
wall Dickinson, a fervent abolitionist who grew up on the restless ground of
Ashtabula County in northeastern Ohio, owned this land.[44]

It began to seem remarkable how often the Western Reserve left its mark
on ground that had no European settlers until 1833, when the Blackhawk Purchase brought them to Iowa Territory.[45]

13.

    I followed John Brown to his next stop in Iowa—Grinnell. Just three or four miles from the I-80 rest stop, the town was founded in 1854 on the divide between the Iowa and the Skunk Rivers. In 1859 it had ninety houses, five hundred citizens, and the reputation of being a safe place for both travelers and fugitives to stop.[46]

    It was an abolitionist town, like Tabor, and it even bore physical resemblances. There was a pleasant park at its center, for instance. On the edge of the park was a sign for a Farmer's Market, with a picture of corn. A white metal table with benches soldered to it said "Grinnell, Jewel of the Prairie" on the top in black and green letters, narrow green leaves sprouting from the city's name with a yellow streak of color bursting between them—it could have been corn, it could have been sun. An obelisk by the gazebo read "Let peace be in our homes and communities."

    A large stone in memory of Josiah Bushnell Grinnell sat next to a wayside marker that told the story of John Brown's stop in 1859.

    The marker explained that Iowa had not always embraced its role in the Underground Railroad. "For Iowa residents this involvement in Underground Railroad efforts was dangerous and illegal business. Not only did most at the time want to keep Black settlement out of the state, they saw abolitionists as fanatics agitating the slavery issue they wanted to avoid." But, the sign said, "Gradually... ever more persons in Iowa saw the state becoming a western beacon of anti-slavery hope," and Grinnell acquired its reputation as "a safe harbor for runaways."

    I supposed that Grinnell greeted John Brown in much the same way that Tabor had. I made the mistake of assuming that abolitionist towns held a single point of view, but such reasoning was no more true of towns than it was of individuals.

Commemorative
stone in Grinnell city
park opposite site of
homestead of Josiah
B. Grinnell

I had concluded that Tabor, a larger town than Civil Bend, used its insti-
tutions—primarily the church—to argue for a conservative abolitionist stance
toward slavery, a stance that favored freeing the enslaved (of course), but also
favored methods that were legal—"Christian"—and less aggressive than
enticement and, certainly, theft and murder.

The sign in the park, after all, mentioned that "dissent" in the "antislavery
majority" existed over how much freedom to allow and the methods for attain-
ing it, so didn't this imply Grinnell was much like Tabor?

Yet Grinnell looked upon John Brown with greater favor than Tabor had.

John Brown stayed in Grinnell from February 20 to February 22. There
was no resolution in Grinnell's church to condemn what he'd done.

Josiah B. Grinnell and Amos Bixby—perhaps the two most vocal anti-
slavery abolitionists in the town, along with Leonard F. Parker and Samuel F.
Cooper, from Oberlin—welcomed John Brown in a different way. I don't
know if some in the community tried to urge Grinnell's leaders to use caution,
but no sign of timidity on their part was recorded. There would be consequences for not writing a resolution in church and not banishing John Brown
and his party of fugitives, but Grinnell's leaders, unlike those in Tabor, didn't
seem to care.

Josiah Bushnell Grinnell, between 1855 and 1865. (Courtesy Library of Congress)

A letter composed by Amos Bixby to his brother, a lawyer from Maine, the day John Brown left Grinnell suggested that the town's residents listened to the more radical members of the community. "I may as well say that last Saturday old Capt. John Brown of Kansas arrived here with 12 slaves on the way to Canada," Amos Bixby wrote. "The old hero & his company created quite an excitement in our little town. They stayed over Sunday. We gave them $25 & provisions enough to last them several days. I mean we the people of Grinnell gave it."[47]

Newspapers attacked the town's Congregational minister Josiah Grinnell as a "Negro stealer" and a person who glorified a man who committed "murder and theft,"[48] and his political opponents (he was elected in 1862 to represent Iowa's 4th district in the US House) dubbed him "John Brown Grinnell."[49] Grinnell was born in 1821, and hadn't even met John Brown until he passed through the town in 1859, but that brief encounter was enough to allow his enemies to condemn him.

There were probably whispers behind church doors, but unlike Rev. Joshua Young of the Unitarian Church in Burlington, Vermont, Josiah Bushnell Grinnell was not delivered a no-confidence vote by his congregation.

John Brown had always been a hard test for people, something I was growing to understand.

14.

Next stop: Springdale, Iowa, fifty miles west of the Mississippi River. Land of the Quakers. The fugitives arrived in John Brown's wagons on February 25, 1859, and stayed two weeks.

John Brown knew the town was friendly from his earlier visit. He'd come here in December of 1857 with ten men, planning to use the nearby farm of William Maxson, who had Quaker roots, as training ground for Harpers Ferry. Hugh Forbes, who later betrayed John Brown, led drills on Maxson's property. In the evening people from several miles away assembled for debates in Maxson's farmhouse.[50]

On that 1857–1858 visit, John Brown left Springdale before his men did, heading East to raise money for Harpers Ferry and to write his new Constitution ("Provisional Constitution and Ordinances for the People of the United States") at the home of Frederick Douglass, an impractical but highly symbolic act. Its Preamble changed the Constitution's original wording from "We the People of the United States" to "we, citizens of the United States, and the oppressed... together with all other people degraded by the laws thereof," and condemned the "utter disregard and violation of those eternal and self-evident truths set forth in our Declaration of Independence," and then, in Article 1 of forty-eight articles that followed, promised that the government would protect all people—"whether proscribed, oppressed, and enslaved citizens."[51]

I explored the three city blocks that now composed the town of Springdale. Flowers grew everywhere, even in sidewalk cracks. Little rock gardens decorated front yards, and vegetable gardens peeked from the back. I found a marble marker as shiny as a new cemetery stone near the road: "Former Site of Springdale School, First Accredited School in Iowa." It was hot, and no one was outside.

William Maxson House, photo by C. C. Woodburn, 1934. (Courtesy Library of Congress)

We drove to the site of William Maxson's house, because the story of the fugitives stopping in Springdale in 1859 was connected to the story of the visit a year before. John Brown was moving quickly now and depended on former connections.

I knew where the Maxson marker was from a travel piece in Louis DeCaro's blog, text and pictures provided by H. Scott Wolfe. A farm machinery shed now sat on the site of the house, but a marker from 1924 was in front of it, close to the street. Wolfe had said that the stone and plaque were overgrown, nearly hidden, but a metal post with the fire number "1779" would help people locate it.[52]

If not for Wolfe's directions to look for a metal post, I might never have found the marker, since the stone was surrounded by deep grass and draped by a huge sycamore tree. I looked for snakes, saw none, and waded in. I wondered if anyone came here anymore, and then laughed because I realized that I was here, and my husband was right beside me. John Brown's troops had been here once, marching left and right across the fields where grain elevators, an old windmill, and storage sheds now stood. Cornfields would soon rise up so broad and vast from the low sprouts in front of me that they would hush this spot by late July, barely leaving room for birdsong.

After pulling out handfuls of grass, I could finally read the Maxson marker. "Here was the home of William Maxon, a station on the Under-

Author near marker for farm of William Maxson

ground Railroad where John Brown of Ossawatomie recruited and trained 11
men for the attack on Harper's Ferry."

After that were lines from "Brown of Osawatomie" by John Greenleaf
Whittier, a nineteenth-century poet who was both an abolitionist and a
Quaker, and had an important connection to Hudson as well.[53] "Let some
poor slave-mother whom I have striven to free, / With her children, from the
gallows-stair, put up a prayer for me." The story of John Brown kissing a Black
child held up to him by his mother as he exited the Charles Town prison was
the subject of Whittier's sentimental lines, although that encounter never
took place. Another story, I thought sometimes, made up to soften John
Brown a little.[54]

The owner's name was misspelled, as was the name of the Kansan town
responsible for John Brown's epithet, but what mattered more was the simple
rock that brought us to this place.

Sessions of a mock legislature held by John Brown's men in the Maxson
farmhouse—nothing more than a phantom house now—sometimes grew into
loud quarrels between young men who were too sure of themselves or felt
trapped by an Iowa winter. But, as one biographer said, for the most part the
Springdale community of Quakers had "sheltered and protected the boys," even
though at times they were censured for misusing the privilege granted them of

courting Quaker girls.[55] Benjamin F. Gue, who served as Lieutenant Governor
of Iowa after the Civil War and wrote the history of his state, said that John
Brown "won the enduring friendship of William Maxson, Dr. H. G. [sic] Gill,
Griffith Lewis, Moses Varney and other good citizens of Springdale and vicinity, that winter."[56]

It was no surprise that John Brown returned to Springdale in 1859.

15.

It was rumored in the Quaker town that the Buchanan-appointed postmaster, Samuel Workman, was assembling a posse in Iowa City to capture John Brown and recapture the fugitives.

They were more than rumors.

John Brown and John Kagi had secretly gone to Iowa City one night to arrange for a train car to transport the entire party out of the state and up to Chicago, then Detroit, where the fugitives would board a ferry for Canada. While they were hiding in the back of a restaurant, two men came to the front door with rope in their hands and demanded the release of the "damned nigger-thief of Kansas."[37] Jesse Bowen hid John Brown and Kagi in his house overnight and early the next morning Col. S. C. Trowbridge guided them to Springdale by back roads.

Mrs. E. S. Butler, who lived in Springdale at the time, said later that when rumors began about a posse, the fugitives gathered in the local schoolhouse and were given arms to protect themselves. She said that Springdale Quakers were armed too: "Outside were stationed the most heroic young men of the neighborhood, well-armed and ready for conflict should it be necessary."[38]

I didn't know what to make of that.

Did it really happen that way? Or was Mrs. E. S. Butler not remembering things rightly, or embellishing them years later for the sake of a more exciting story? Or was it a moment in Springdale history, maybe, when the idea of believing in emancipation was suddenly so real that every religious principle was tested, and some dismissed or set aside? A time when the relationship of peace to violence was unclear—when the conflict became not only a moral debate, but a physical fact?

Would Springdale residents let the fugitives be taken because Quakers had sworn an oath of nonviolence, or would they sacrifice their most heartfelt principle to defend the fugitives with force? Had some Quaker men begun to believe, as John Brown certainly had long before he arrived in their town, that taking up arms would be necessary to bring about emancipation? American history had posed a difficult problem for the Quakers before John Brown arrived. In the eighteenth century, General Nathanael Green, son of devout Quakers, relinquished Quaker practice by 1773, serving George Washington as a major general in the Continental army.[59]

What would have been the consequence of not fighting that night in Springdale, in the shadow of an invasion by Iowa City men? Which would have been more difficult to live with—the eternal wrath of a God Quakers believed wished them to remain pacific, or the anguish of twelve free people returned to captivity?

Typically, members of the Quaker community who had anything to do with arms were "disowned." Unchurched.

John Painter was one of them. He wasn't punished for housing John Brown's militia before they moved to the Maxson house, but for his direct involvement with the guns John Brown was storing. In 1858, when John Brown left his party in Springdale to head East, he asked John Painter to carry fifteen boxes of Sharps rifles and two hundred pistols to the train depot in West Liberty. They were marked "carpenter's tools" to account for their weight and then shipped to John Brown Jr. at Conneaut in Ashtabula County, Ohio, who moved them several times until he eventually shipped them as hardware from the canal at Hartstown, Pennsylvania, to Chambersburg in the summer of 1859.[60] Painter was "unchurched" at the Friends' Yearly Meeting.[61]

Two raiders who were born to Quaker parents in Salem, Ohio, but were living in Springdale when they first met John Brown—Edwin Coppoc and his younger brother Barclay[62]—were also disowned by the Springdale Friends, Edwin for refusing to stop dancing,[63] and Barclay, who escaped after Harpers Ferry, for bearing arms when he returned to Springdale after the raid.[64] Not long after that, Barclay Coppoc died as a Union soldier in the Civil War when his train derailed over the Platte River.

Edwin Coppoc. (Courtesy
Boyd B. Stutler Collection of
John Brown, West Virginia
State Archives)

Barclay Coppoc. (Courtesy
Boyd B. Stutler Collection of
John Brown, West Virginia
State Archives)

For the most part, the response of the Springdale Quakers to guns and
violence was simple: disown people who chose to bear arms. Yet no group
better demonstrated the sharp tension between principle and method than
the Quakers did.

Many people struggled to understand the conflict John Brown brought
into the Springdale community whenever he entered it, causing its members
to tacitly—sometimes overtly—support militant behavior. There were defenses
of Springdale Quakers mounted to counter accusations of their complicity in
Harpers Ferry. After all, they had let John Brown and his men train for the
attack on Springdale ground.[65] Benjamin F. Gue, raised a Quaker, illustrated
the community's ambivalence. Made aware of the Harpers Ferry plan during
John Brown's 1859 stay in Springdale, and worried about the lives of Quaker
recruits (and John Brown), he helped write an anonymous letter to the secretary of war to warn the government about the impending raid, though it wasn't
taken seriously.[66] Still, in spite of his whistleblowing, he understood the affection Springdale Quakers felt for John Brown's men and his cause, and not only
shared it but came to applaud the result of the October attack—what he had
once called John Brown's "desperate enterprise." Speaking about the military
maneuvers of 1858 in Springdale, he said, "While the Quakers were by tradition and principle opposed to war, so warm were their sympathies for the

oppressed that they found a way to hold in the highest esteem and admiration these fearless young men who had risked their lives and struck sturdy blows for freedom in Kansas."[67]

That expression—"they found a way"—was the very one I had struggled to understand almost from the beginning, then across the whole state of Iowa.

16.

While John Brown and Kagi visited Iowa City, Josiah Grinnell and Iowa City Republican and lawyer William Penn Clarke made arrangements behind the scenes for a train. A boxcar arrived in West Liberty at 11:00 a.m., on March 10, as innocent as morning dew.

West Liberty was celebrating its 175th anniversary when I visited, but I ignored the banners and, instead, thought about the boxcar rolling in.

From Iowa City, the first morning train of the Chicago and Rock Island Railroad arrived. It dropped off the car for the John Brown party near Keith's Steam Mill, where everyone was staying, and then pulled away. The doors of the boxcar quietly opened, and John Brown's company entered, townspeople watching them board. George Gill would not travel any farther with the party, his "inflammatory rheumatism"[68] having flared up after the two-month ordeal he'd just gone through, and he would not be well enough to fight at Harpers Ferry. Kagi rode in the passenger car to keep his eye on a man who looked suspicious.[69]

The engineer tucked the boxcar between the engine and the express car, and it rolled away through the little bit of Iowa that was left, crossed the Mississippi River at Davenport, and then headed north toward Chicago, where the famous detective Allan Pinkerton helped house the fugitives. Later the next day, they were routed to Detroit. Kagi accompanied them on one train,

Downtown West Liberty, displaying 1838–2013 anniversary banners

while John Brown followed on a second—his train heading toward a meeting with Frederick Douglass.

I was amazed when I thought about this small piece of history, this story of the escape of twelve fugitives across Iowa that I'd never heard before and was still largely hidden from public view. How many moments like it, I wondered, had been lost?

The Mississippi bridge we crossed from Davenport into Illinois was not the same bridge John Brown's train had traveled over. That first bridge lay 1,500 feet upstream. It was completed in 1856, though its completion was opposed by Jefferson Davis, secretary of War under Franklin Pierce. Davis knew that finishing it would result in the Transcontinental Railroad going through the North, an obvious disadvantage for Southerners. Abraham Lincoln ended up being the attorney who defended the bridge after a steamboat collided with it—an accident that's been seen as a symbol for the clash of railroad and steamboat cultures. Even a bridge, several years before the Civil War, was a hotly contested political issue and seemed to be a kind of rehearsal for the War itself—as had Harpers Ferry and so many of the conflicts John Brown participated in, or, more precisely, began.[70]

Railroad bridge opened in 1856 across the Mississippi from Davenport to Rock Island.
(Courtesy Putnam Museum and Science Center, Davenport, Iowa)

We were on our way home. It had been a long trip, I was tired, and my
husband was driving now. I closed my eyes and leaned my head on the window
glass. Even as I tried to rest, I knew the dead I'd met here and the words I'd
heard them say would come whirling back, dust storms formed from the "fat
dirt" of Iowa.

REVERIE 8
"THEY FOUND A WAY"

I.

My trip to Iowa introduced me to many people who had "found a way" to be friends with John Brown. There was Jacob Willetts, Elvira Gaston Platt, James C. Jordan, Josiah Grinnell and Amos Bixby, James Townsend, and some of the Springdale Quakers (apparently). I liked all of them more than the people who rejected John Brown and began to wonder if I were negotiating my friendship with him too stingily.

Shortly after he arrived in Springdale on February 25, 1859, John Brown took notes about his earlier reception in Grinnell and sent them to George Gaston at Tabor.

I reviewed his list carefully. In addition to supplying John Brown's party with free lodging, food for their trip ("Bread, Meat, Cake, Pies"), "sundry articles of clothing for the fugitives," and a contribution of $26.50, the people of Grinnell gathered for both a "Public thanksgiving" and two nights of meetings in which three Congregational ministers "took part in justifying our course"—without any dissent.[1]

He ended the letter with a postscript that implied that the Springdale reception had been just as cordial. Clearly, he wanted Taborites to know where they had fallen short. To know what real friendship looked like.

2.

I wanted to be his friend. I wanted to set everything aside that prevented it. I was tired of arguing with John Brown.

But I was not Elvira Gaston Platt. I was a woman of the twenty-first century, and John Brown had been dead over 150 years.

My husband, I'm sure, was tired of listening to me, though he never showed any irritation and tolerated my complaints. I drowned out the sound of the spring peepers we used to hear on our quiet walks across the Hudson Green before Robert Sullivan arrived.

Underneath the annoyance in my voice, my husband sensed my growing affection for John Brown, which I couldn't disguise, and he seemed to welcome the change in me, though I wondered why. Sometimes I'd watch his eyes grow wide or see him nod his head when I told a John Brown story in a certain way, and he even wrote a birthday poem for me shortly after our Iowa trip that spoke directly to my guarded admiration. "He *is* your friend, you know? (A friend— / or, 'neighbor,' as you're calling him.) / Despite the struggle he has caused. / What is a friend but someone so / complex that he demands a heart / to comprehend? A *heart*, not mind." My husband understood something about John Brown's friendship that I'd missed, though I was the one studying the man.

A "*heart*," I thought? Could a heart really decode the complexity of John Brown? I wished my heart were a compass I could calibrate with a half-quarter turn of a thin dime, but it was not.

And a "*friend*"? I knew there was a difference between a friend and a neighbor, but I hadn't thought this through. There was a deep connection I had with friends that was absent with neighbors. I liked them all, but friends knew how to steady each other in a manner neighbors generally didn't pretend to. I navigated toward my friends the way insects used moonlight to help them maintain a steady course.

A neighbor, I thought, was porch light, but a friend, the light of the moon.

I found a passage that spoke further to this matter of friendship in a book called *Here and Now*, an exchange of letters between Paul Auster and J. M. Coetzee. Auster wrote about the way admiration of another person "enhances him in your eyes, ennobles him, elevates him to a status you believe is above your own." But if that person admires you also, their admiration "enhances you, ennobles you, elevates you to a status he believes is above his own."

I read on. "You are both giving more than you receive, both receiving more than you give, and in the reciprocity of this exchange, friendship blooms." At that moment, he believed, "you are in a position of absolute equality."

If my heart was telling me to come a little closer to John Brown and find a way to be his friend, not just his neighbor anymore, my next step would be to figure out if I could admire him the way Auster said friendship required—"for what he does, for what he is, for how he negotiates his path through the world."[2] I would later have to consider whether it would be possible for him to admire me, for friendship depended on a reciprocal exchange, but I didn't want to think about that until I'd made my mind up about him. I'd test the first part of the equation. That was difficult enough.

BREAKING THE GOLDEN RULE

I.

Since it seemed to be his profound and essential goodness that I admired, I tested that first. When Southern leaders and officials interviewed John Brown the day after his capture at Harpers Ferry, he told a bystander why he'd done everything he had.

"Upon what principle do you justify your acts?" the bystander said. "Upon the Golden Rule," was his reply.[1]

"Therefore all things whatsover ye would that men should do to you, do ye even so to them." That was the rule he professed to live by.

But did John Brown always practice the Golden Rule—the principle he was so often praised for, and which would allow me to ennoble him? Was his commitment to equality and justice so irresistible that it permitted people to overlook his unsavory acts?

But what if his principle was tainted? What kind of friend could he be to me if that were true? Perhaps finding fissures in his practice of the Golden Rule would allow me to set friendship aside without having to think about the murky matter of his methods again.

It would be easier that way.

I'd already suspected imperfections. The most obvious and well-known example was his failure to protect his sons and his eagerness to recruit them to his cause.

Russell Banks, in *Cloudsplitter*, had Owen Brown narrate the destructive consequences for the Brown family of living with a zealous father like John Brown.[2] Should I, too, blame him for his severity?

John Brown probably would have said that the love he had for his sons, and wanted them to have for others, had little to do with being safe. Being good people, John Brown believed, involved risk and action. And he meant it.

Besides, although he was a forceful father, certainly, the pressure he placed on his sons sometimes eased. He didn't demand that they fight at Harpers Ferry and arranged for his son Owen to stay at the Kennedy Farmhouse instead of accompanying the other raiders, which ended up leading to his escape. He wrote to Rebecca Buffum Spring in his jail cell asking her to help his son Jason, a man "bashful and retiring" and "too tender of people's feelings," but clearly an "ingenious" person he adored—"a most tender, loving, and steadfast friend, and on the right side of things in general."[3]

He grudgingly accepted his children if their religious views were different from those he'd so sternly raised them on, though this matter was always painful to John Brown. He wrote about his ambivalence with both a degree of understanding and the conviction that he was right. "My affections are too deep-rooted to be alienated from them," he said, "but 'my gray hairs must go down in sorrow to the grave' unless the true God forgive their denial and rejection of him, and open their eyes."[4] Just before his death, he called his son Jason "a practical Samaritan (if not Christian)"—using language that measured Jason on his own terms, not John Brown's anymore.[5]

When it came to the matter of whether John Brown loved his boys, or loved them the right way, there was room for debate. Given who he was, and how he lived his life, he probably did the best he could.

But were those long absences of his a kind of silent crime, I wondered?

He was not just absent, but gone. Children needed more than a letter now and then. They needed someone to teach them how to grow sturdy in this world and prepare for what was coming next, needed time to develop the layers of trust that would armor their delicate hearts against terrible onslaughts of unkindness and betrayal, needed a place where there was something that resembled happiness so they could remember what it looked like, needed someone to remove them from terror—not cause it, not place guns in their hands, not take sleep away. They needed more than his concern, which was always genuine.

After learning that his daughter Amelia had been scalded to death, John Brown told his family not "to cast an unreasonable blame on my dear Ruth on account of the dreadful trial we are called [to] suffer." I wanted to believe that this was John Brown at his best, begging his family not to judge his seventeen-year-old daughter for causing a kitchen accident that killed his one-year-old daughter—Ruth's half-sister. (I sometimes wondered how Mary Ann Brown would have read that line in his letter, John Brown seeming to favor the daughter of Dianthe over the dead daughter Mary had borne him and Ruth had inadvertently burned to death.)

But I didn't think it was merely sympathy for Ruth that caused him to write what he did. I heard defensiveness in his voice. If Ruth was neglectful, certainly John Brown was far more so. Where was he when the accident had occurred? Had he been home, might he have prevented it? He was in Springfield, Massachusetts. Even after receiving word of Amelia's death from his son Owen and Mr. Perkins, he wasn't able to assure his family that he'd be home anytime soon. If they couldn't forgive Ruth, how could they forgive him?

How could he forgive himself? "If I had a right sence of my habitual neglect of my familys Eternal interests; I should probably go crazy," he told them in a confessional line. He had a conscience, and guilt could warm his cheeks, in spite of the great ego that kept them cool almost all the time.

Soon his composure returned. He began to extract meaning from the tragedy and said he hoped that this event would teach them all the importance of the "doing of things seemingly of trifling account," of "the saying of one little word."[6] A few days later he wrote another letter, this time one that contained a highly reflective remark. "In immagination I seem to be present with you; to share with you the sorrows, or joys you experience,"[7] he said. For John Brown, house and family were his imaginary life; his cause, the real one. He knew this.

Even his critics never accused him of being less than deeply loving toward his family. He was attentive, constantly inquiring about them in correspondence and displaying special affection for his young children when he was home. He offered advice (though it often took the form of letters) and tried to get money and supplies for his family when he couldn't provide them himself.

Even in jail, he wrote letters to ask others to assist with the welfare of his poor family. He turned to his Quaker friends: "I always loved my Quaker friends, and I commend to their kind regard my poor bereaved widowed wife and my daughters and daughters-in-law, whose husbands fell at my side … They, as well as my own sorrow-stricken daughters, are left very poor, and have much greater need of sympathy than I."[8] He pleaded for favors from Quaker Lydia Maria Child for both the adults and children in his family and in his letter to Rebecca Buffum Spring asked if she might help Jason and his family relocate to her neighborhood near Perth Amboy, New Jersey, a Utopian community where people might encourage his son when John Brown couldn't anymore.

He asked Jeremiah, his half-brother, to help as well. The money that would come from his father's estate, he told Jeremiah, he wanted "paid to them"—his sons, his wife, his daughters—without the encumbrance of "legal formalities to consume it all."[9]

He kept his family "forever" in mind. He might have been thinking of them even as the rope was hung around his neck on the gallows.

But John Brown's true love was his cause, and his true children were the children of that cause—perhaps more real to him sometimes than his own daughters and sons. His very last words, in a note to a prison guard, predicted the Civil War and were entirely focused on his cause, not the Brown family he was about to leave behind.

He had twenty biological children, but there were nearly four million people enslaved. He could not have lived the life that his son chose on Put-in-Bay, a life devoted to one son, one daughter, one wife, and an abundance of grapes. His heart was committed to nearly thirteen percent of the nation's population.[10] As I began to understand that, John Brown again escaped my wrath.

2.

There was one indiscretion toward his family—his treatment of his wife Mary Ann—that I thought might be inexcusable. It wasn't just a general lack of warmth toward her I was talking about, but a specific and egregious act that violated the Golden Rule he repeatedly said his life was founded on.

That isn't to deny that warmth wasn't a problem for John Brown, because it was. Now and then an insensitive remark left his pen and headed right toward Mary, and right toward history, where all those letters people didn't lose were gathered up.

In his jail cell, John Brown continually wrote letters, and some of them were to his wife telling her how reluctant he was to have her visit him, and, in his "most decided judgment," how much more good, for him and for her, would come from "quietly and submissively staying at home." It would require the use of "all the scanty means" they had to get Mary to Charles Town, and she would become a "gazing-stock" to people and newspapers along the way. Besides, he said, such a visit at best could bring only "little comfort" in the face of the final separation just ahead of them. He'd found the excitement produced in the town by visits of "one or two female friends" something that was "very annoying," and, he said, "they cannot possibly do me any good."[11] He refused to yield to her request until November 26, 1859, and they finally met only the day before he was hanged, even though her grief was great throughout the period of his imprisonment.[12]

Charles Town jail, where John Brown stayed, razed in 1930. (Courtesy Boyd
B. Stutler Collection of John Brown, West Virginia State Archives)

The words he chose to finally summon her, it seemed to me, were not the
ones Mary would have wanted to hear. After a warning not "to make yourself
& children any more burdensome to friends than you are really compelled to
do," he wrote: "I will close this by saying that if you *now feel* that you are *equal*
to the undertaking do *exactly as you* FEEL *disposed to do* about coming to see
me before I suffer. *I am entirely willing.*"[13]

Willing? It was Mary's custom to snip off the salutations of her husband's
letters that were addressed just to her and save them, yet this was the best he
could do for her?[14]

According to his daughter Anne, John Brown was "strong for women's
rights and women's suffrage," and he traveled to hear Lucretia Mott and Abby
Kelley Foster "even though it cost him considerable effort to reach the place
where they spoke,"[15] but sometimes John Brown chose language and behavior
that were inconsistent with what I think was being said in the rooms where
those women stood.

But it was not his occasional tendency to be tactless that was troubling
me most.

There are stronger words that might be used for someone who deliberately
tries to keep a person from getting well, who doesn't believe that person when
they say that something is very wrong with them. *Abusive? Selfish?*

Mary Ann Brown arriving in Charles Town to visit her husband, December 1, 1859, sketch by Alfred Berghaus, *Leslie's Illustrated Newspaper*. (Courtesy Boyd B. Stutler Collection of John Brown, West Virginia State Archives)

Mary was ill, but John Brown refused to support her attempt to recover. Though Rebecca Buffum Spring was hard on Mary Brown, calling her a "coarse sort of woman,"[16] Mary was a deeply devoted and admiring wife. I can't imagine how any woman could have endured the demands of John Brown as well as Mary did. She asked for little in return for giving her life and labor to her abolitionist husband and to the children she bore him—as well as to all the children Dianthe had borne—and to the cause she cared for as if it were her child too.

She was a genuine abolitionist in her own right. She responded to the carnage of the Civil War with both grief and acceptance, much as her husband might have, writing in a letter, "Oh what a dreadful war this is when will this nation be willing to do right to love mercy Justice and truth. I feel that we deserve all this punishment from the hands of God but when I read of so much suffering I feel to cry out how long Oh Lord how long shall this people continue in their sins and the innocent have to suffer with the guilty. God is just and will do all things right."[17]

The Last Supper, John and Mary Ann Brown in the parlor of jailer John Avis the
evening before his execution, sketch by David C. Hitchcock, *New York Illustrated News*.
(Courtesy Boyd B. Stutler Collection of John Brown, West Virginia State Archives)

But even stalwart Mary lost strength at times, and her body failed her.
Why had her husband thought that she could bear all the weight of her own
life, of her children's lives, and of his? Why did he grow angry, and balk when
she needed care?

Why did alertness to suffering—a trait he professed was central to his life
and to his country's life—not extend to Mary Ann Day Brown?

3.

This is the story of how John Brown neglected his second wife.

Mary Ann Brown traveled in August of 1849, without her husband's knowledge or permission, first to Springfield and then to Florence, Massachusetts, for a "Water Cure" at a center established by Black abolitionist David Ruggles.[18] Her health had been poor even the spring when the family arrived in North Elba, but it worsened during the months that followed.[19] John Brown had set sail for Europe the day before her arrival in Massachusetts, hoping to sell wool at a higher cost than Springfield manufacturers would pay. John Jr. and his wife, Wealthy, lived in Springfield with John Brown at the time and were surprised to see Mary arrive, since it was irregular for her to travel alone.

John Jr. wrote to his father about Mary's water cure, and she was relieved she didn't have to write herself. "I'm glad you told him," Mary wrote to her son. "He has never believed there was any disease about me."[20]

Biographer Louis DeCaro thought John Brown also might have opposed Mary's decision because he saw Ruggles' institution "as a Garrisonian fad." He would have objected to her associating with "high-profile abolitionists," individuals known for their pacifism.[21]

Ruggles, a self-trained doctor of hydrotherapy, was a free-born Black known for his grocery business, his founding of the first Black printing press and magazine (*Mirror of Liberty*), his Underground Railroad activities, his role as agent for Garrison's *Liberator*, his antislavery writings and speeches,

Portrait of Mary Ann Day Brown, by daughter
Sarah Brown (1846–1916), black crayon with
charcoal and white pastel highlights (enlarged
reproduction of a photo). (Courtesy Saratoga
Historical Foundation and Saratoga History
Museum)

and his formation in New York City in 1835 of the Committee of Vigilance
for the Protection of the People of Color (a biracial committee that actively
thwarted efforts of slave catchers).[22] His dangerous experience in the city contributed to his ill health and near blindness (he always wore thick glasses and
at one point had to be led from place to place) and caused him to explore
hydrotherapy as a means of recovery.[23] Though New York had outlawed slavery
in 1827, Northerners frequently broke the law. They knew that their economic
wealth depended on preserving the slave South—the cotton South.[24]

Ruggles opened his own center of hydrotherapy on Mill River, in Florence, Massachusetts, in a three-story building with baths and water treat-
ments. Rooms in a community boardinghouse for guests rented for $5.00 to
$8.00 a week, and it was here that Mary stayed until November, residing with
Lucy Stone and Sojourner Truth. I loved to imagine her in their company.

He diagnosed Mary as having "neuralgia" and, according to John Brown
Jr., a "Scrofulous humour" of her glands. She was most likely prescribed a Gra-
hamite diet that required the avoidance of "alcohol; rich, salty, highly spiced, or
high-temperature foods; sugars; red meat; and tobacco," long walks and the
"wet-sheet" or "sack" regimen, and periods of quiet conversation and reflection.[25]

When John Brown returned from Europe, he visited Mary and his friend
Thomas Thomas from the Sanford Street Church. "He may have expected his
wife to pack her bags and return with him, but she did not," DeCaro wrote.
He left for North Elba without her, and after he arrived he wrote a letter to
John Jr. asking him to send a message to Mary about his safe return. DeCaro

Excerpt from *The Disappointed Abolitionists*, cartoon of Isaac T. Hopper, David Ruggles, and Barney Corse, drawn by American cartoonist Edward W. Clay, the only contemporary image of Ruggles known to exist. (Courtesy Periodyssey)

thought he wrote to John Jr. instead of Mary because he was so irritated with her—"too perturbed to write for himself."[26] Or, I wondered, could he have grown a little fearful of this woman who had taken it upon herself to seek a water cure, and try to heal herself?

By mid-December, John Brown was in Springfield, and Mary was back home. The two were apart once more.

John Brown had benefited greatly from the care of other people. When he returned to Kansas in 1858, he was ill. Suffering from fevers and weakness (probably malaria) most of the summer and fall before the Missouri raid, he was cared for by the Adairs, Kagi, and, especially, the Wattleses, whom he praised in a letter for ministering to him.[27] A little later Jacob Willetts paid attention to John Brown's shaking legs and gave him warm clothes.

Physical suffering touched John Brown's skin repeatedly, perhaps beginning with his fear in New Richmond, Pennsylvania, that consumption would take his life.

What was his excuse for not looking more tenderly into Mary's eyes? Toward the end of her life, she needed medical care once more, this time in California, and without hesitation her daughter Sarah arranged to move with her into the home of physician "Mrs. Dr. Moore," where Mary was provided with treatment comparable to her earlier water cure with David Ruggles— "hygienic physical and electric baths."[28]

John Brown either missed the cues or ignored them.

If he'd looked at her more closely, he might have seen not only a woman who was ill, but also the mother of his children, and in that glance remembered the

Florence water cure establishment of David Ruggles near Northampton, pictured shortly after his death, when Charles Munde became the new proprietor. (Courtesy David Ruggles Center)

"complete & permanent" loss he experienced from his own mother's death when he was eight years old. When Mary went to Massachusetts, she had several teenagers, as well as a son who was ten, a daughter who was six, and another girl who was three. What if they should lose her?

Perhaps his own mother's early death was ironically what had prevented a better response from John Brown to Mary. In his letter to Henry L. Stearns, he'd said he feared that losing his mother could possibly have impaired his ability to form connections with women—"deprived him of a suitable conne[c]ting link between the different sexes."²⁹ His mother, perhaps, had not lived long enough to show him what intimacy between men and women could look like, and maybe that helped explain his obtuseness to a degree, so I extended some sympathy to him once more and subtracted a little of my ire.

Were there other issues at work in him that might explain his anger? Did he wonder how he could proceed to repair the deadly divisions in the nation if his own home had come undone? Was this new friction, like so much else in his life, really about his cause?

I began to suspect one more thing that softened the punishment I'd set out to wield. A personal bias was getting in my way. I found John Brown's lack of sympathy especially painful because I'd conflated my own struggle for health with Mary's, and was annoyed with John Brown. I wished he'd behaved better than he did, but annoyance was not a reason to dismiss a person like John Brown. This was something Mary knew when she took her health into her own hands.

4.

John Doy seemed my best chance. I thought I finally had John Brown where I wanted him.

What he did to John Doy was surely his greatest breach of the Golden Rule.

I found the story of John Doy mentioned in Villard, and only briefly alluded to in one other biography. A scholar who wrote about Iowa and the antislavery movement west of the Mississippi had spent time telling his story too.[10] Both Villard and the Iowa scholar assumed that everything in John Doy's narrative was true.

Villard's account led me to *The Narrative of John Doy, of Lawrence, Kansas*, written by John Doy himself. Advertised as "A Plain, Unvarnished Tale," with a picture of the author in the front, seated, holding a Sharps rifle. It was "Printed for the Author" by Thomas Holman and notarized as being "true" by Charles Nettleton in New York City on February 7, 1860—the notice printed in the front of the book, right after the Preface.

Public documents, letters, and articles in the *Lawrence Republican* confirm the main lines of the Doy narrative.[11] It was a tale full of adventure and great woe.

John Doy, an abolitionist from Rochester, New York, who came to Kansas as a Free-State settler, agreed to lead a caravan of Black men and women who lived in the Lawrence area to a safe location. Although they were all technically "free"—they were all free-born or had free papers—the Fugitive Slave Act placed all Black people in danger of being kidnapped and sold by slave hunters. In the party were three women, two children, and eight men—including

Wilson Hays (from Cincinnati, Ohio) and Charles Smith (from Brownsville, Pennsylvania), cooks both employed at the Eldridge House in Lawrence.[32]

Within hours of Doy's departure on January 25, 1859, his entire party was captured twelve miles from Lawrence. Some twenty men, "armed and mounted,"[33] Doy wrote, including the notorious kidnapper Jake Hurd, were hiding behind a bluff at the bottom of a hill and attacked members of Doy's party when they emerged. The kidnappers drove the wagons hard into Missouri, where John Doy was tried and eventually removed to a jail in St. Joseph until ten Lawrence men rescued him in July of 1859.

Except for a man named William Riley, who escaped by burning the frame of the window in his jail cell so that the bars could be removed, the captives were all sold into slavery, just as free-born Solomon Northup had been. Even Riley was soon captured again on his way to Nebraska.[34]

To John Doy's credit, although he focused on his own grim experiences in jails—one cell 8 x 8 and seven feet high, made of iron, without a single window—he sometimes recorded images and sounds of fugitives brought into the jails where he stayed, and even included drawings of the implements devised to torture them. Doy showed concern for what this capture meant for the people who'd been in his care.

Although Doy rarely mentioned John Brown in the story, he included him in a backstory after the narrative of the capture ended. In Appendix C, Doy called John Brown's behavior regarding the Doy party into question, perhaps hoping to avoid being accused "of rashness in undertaking such an expedition." John Doy told a secret in Appendix C about the role John Brown had played.

According to Doy, he originally consented to transport the party from his community only because there had been a prior agreement to travel with John Brown's Missouri fugitives (Doy referred to him as "the old hero"), an arrangement he thought would assure "a guard of ten men," and thereby be better able to protect both groups. On the evening of January 24, Doy wrote, John Brown changed his mind. Doy couldn't get him to budge even with "earnest remonstrances," so he had only two choices, neither one attractive: he could abandon the attempt to move the party, or travel without much protection twenty miles to "Oscaloosa," where Doy could possibly assemble a guard.

Elsewhere in his document, John Doy had admired John Brown. In Appendix H he called him "that kind-hearted old hero" and included strangely visionary words he'd spoken the night of their conference. But in Appendix C he held him accountable and even included a footnote to further support his claim:

Artificially created photograph of John Brown with John Doy. (Courtesy Boyd B. Stutler Collection of John Brown, West Virginia State Archives)

"After our capture [John Brown] frequently expressed to those who were with him his regret that he had not yielded to my arguments."[35]

I realized as I thought harder about the *Narrative* that I had a choice to make too. I could dismiss Appendix C, and John Doy's complaint about the Old Hero, or choose to act as if it were true. As far as I knew, there was no other record of this secret meeting, and surely Doy was suffering from abundant guilt when he wrote Appendix C and his footnote. People in Doy's care had been sold into slavery and their families had been divided on the auction block. And John Brown was dead by the time Doy's book was published, so he could neither confirm nor refute the blame John Doy had cast on him.

Or, even though the story possibly wasn't true, I could choose to act as if it were.

And that's exactly what I did.

It horrified me to think that John Brown could have refused to join his wagons with those of John Doy or failed to extend his help. I wanted to rewind the clock to let John Brown make a better choice. I could think of no excuse for his behavior.

There were reasons proposed for John Brown's decision, but I found none of them convincing.

"Circumstances," Villard said, had changed. He said that John Brown's escort party had shrunk, causing him to hesitate to take others in. He had "besides Archibald, only Gill and possibly one other."[36]

When had having too few men for any kind of battle ever dissuaded John Brown from a fight?

Doy recorded John Brown's own excuse for not keeping his promise, though Doy didn't seem convinced by it. John Brown supposedly had said that his party was made up entirely of enslaved people, and he felt they were therefore in much greater danger than Doy's free people, who "were not supposed to be sought for."[37]

But John Brown understood that the Fugitive Slave Act was ruthless—and slave hunters never confined their search to runaways, so I found John Brown's purported explanation no more persuasive than Villard's. How could John Brown have said such a thing?

As I continued to think about John Brown's culpability, I began to recognize how eager I was to cast blame. Why had I so quickly believed the story? And so readily dismissed explanations in his defense? Why did I find comfort in the memory that George Gill and Rebecca Buffum Spring had accused John Brown of this sort of arrogance on other occasions?[38]

What was I expecting of John Brown? Was I looking for a hero, when perhaps history had none to supply? Couldn't he have had fears or plans for his own group, or his own life, that remained uncommunicated and whose details would never be known? Wasn't he always needing to make calculations regarding the progress and success of his cause—some of which would be regrettable, the way the calculations of other people who have tried to improve the nation invariably have been?

Other great leaders in the abolitionist movement had to choose and select all the time, but I wasn't willing to permit John Brown this privilege. In 1860 Harriet Tubman made a trip to Maryland to liberate Rachel, her last sibling, but Rachel had died. Tubman brought members of the Ennals family North instead, but life for conductors was becoming too dangerous, so she decided this would be her last trip into the South to escort enslaved people to freedom.

John Brown, too, left things undone. How could it have been otherwise with a problem as profound and extensive as slavery?

Why did my need to blame run so deep regarding John Brown? I remembered what Louis DeCaro had written in the *Hudson Hub-Times*: "No figure in US history is more slandered, misrepresented and misapprehended than John Brown."[39]

Was I guilty of this too?

It crossed my mind that maybe my willingness—no, eagerness—to blame John Brown was not unlike John Doy's. Was there some failure inside of me that I refused to name—preferring, like Doy, to call it "John Brown"?

TERROR ON POTTAWATOMIE CREEK

I.

I'd been too hard on John Brown regarding the Golden Rule. If I placed all of his indiscretions on one of the weighing pans of a balance scale (a block for Amelia, Mary Ann Brown, John Doy, and his raiders and sons), and all the acts of kindness toward his family and the human family on the other (with weights marked "Compassion," "Social Justice," and "the Enslaved"), the fulcrum would tilt toward the second basin—for it had greater weight.

I thought that finding out the worst about John Brown's failures of principle would allow me to banish him, but oddly, his failings made him more approachable, since there was a little less distance between us now. John Brown, apparently, was like the rest of us—a person capable of hurting people that he loved and not immune to the irresistible pull of selfishness or to moments of self-interest. Maybe, even, occasional moments of self-doubt.

I'd have no choice except to return to the matter of his methods, especially that terrible streak of violence in him. Focusing on the practices he chose to get what he wanted would surely tip the balance scale against him. Yet as I looked at his wild deeds and the people he harmed, I had difficulty faulting him for most of what he'd done.

I couldn't side with Amos Chamberlin, for example, no matter how despicable I found John Brown's business practices, his fiery temper, or his antics at the Westlands fort, because John Brown's moral argument for compassion to the poor outweighed other things, even if that argument did seem strategically timed to his advantage. And the murder of David Cruise? Could I say

John Wilkes Booth with the
Richmond Grays at the hanging of
John Brown, left of Caskie (man
at center with goatee), photo by
Lewis Graham Dinkle. (Courtesy
Library of Congress)

that I'd turn back the clock, if possible, and let the liberation of twelve fugitives not have occurred to save this man?

Harpers Ferry began to seem like a necessary prelude to the Civil War, a
point many biographers had convinced me of. David S. Reynolds called it
"almost the Civil War in microcosm"[1] and subtitled his biography "The Man
Who Killed Slavery, Sparked the Civil War, and Seeded Civil Rights." I was
beginning to think of Harpers Ferry as the first event in the Civil War.

It was more than a little ironic that Colonel Robert E. Lee was respon-
sible for John Brown's capture at Harpers Ferry, that J. E. B. Stuart (who
would become a major general and cavalry commander for the Confederate
States) forced John Brown's surrender in the engine house, that Thomas
Jackson (soon to be "Stonewall") was an officer at the hanging, and that John
Wilkes Booth had convinced members of the Richmond Grays, a militia
company, to give him parts of their uniforms so that he could help guard
Charles Town at the time of John Brown's execution.[2] John Wilkes Booth
reappeared at the final speech Lincoln delivered on April 11, 1865, two days
after Lee surrendered to Grant. When Booth heard that Lincoln proposed
limited Black suffrage, he said, "That is the last speech he will make."[3] Later,

of course, Booth killed the President, one of the goals of his elaborate conspiracy plan.[4]

How could I deny the historical weight of that, and view Harpers Ferry as unconnected to the Civil War? A "spark," a "prelude," a "rehearsal"—the words sounded true to me.

Pottawatomie Creek was John Brown's one act that seemed so fanatical it evaded reason. It returned me to my former self, to the person who knew the difference between necessary violence and unforgivable brutality, between right and wrong. To the person whose heart would not allow her to admire what John Brown did on the creek, and therefore, could never truly embrace him as a friend.

I thought again of Helen Macdonald and hawks. She said that the bird not only had the capacity to symbolize courage and redemption, but evil and malevolence.

It was the destructive hawk I now imagined when I thought of John Brown on the creek, the bird Macdonald said Hermann Göring delighted in—hawks as "living paragons of power and blood and violence that preyed guiltlessly on things weaker than themselves."[5]

I hated John Brown for Pottawatomie. I didn't want to feel any sympathy at all for the butchery that occurred on the creek, but at times I still did.

To keep hold of my fury and stay strong, I quickly recalled the names of people I respected who found Pottawatomie unpardonable.

Horace Greeley, editor of the antislavery paper the *New-York Tribune* and a staunch abolitionist, said that Kansas had driven John Brown mad, which he thought Harpers Ferry demonstrated. It was the Pottawatomie killings he was alluding to, though, when he said John Brown was a person "born of rapine, and cruelty, and murder."[6]

Oswald Garrison Villard could find no way to forgive John Brown for Pottawatomie in his biography. "It must ever remain a complete indictment of his judgment and wisdom; a dark blot upon his memory; a proof that, however self-controlled, he had neither true respect for the laws nor for human life, nor a knowledge that two wrongs never make a right," he wrote, genuinely aggrieved and angry with John Brown for sullying the reputation and character of Northern abolitionists, for whom Villard thought John Brown stood.[7]

Some prominent people who had supported John Brown through Harpers Ferry and his execution turned their backs on him once they read

Villard and learned what happened on Pottawatomie Creek. The incident had faded from view for decades, even though shortly after it occurred it was reviewed by the Special Committee Appointed to Investigate the Troubles in Kansas, and on July 23, 1856, twenty thousand copies of the committee's full report (subtitled "With the Views of the Minority of Said Committee") were ordered to be printed for members of the US House of Representatives.[8]

After John Brown was hanged, William Dean Howells wrote a rapturous poem, praising him in "Old Brown" as a captive Lion, a "hero of the noblest plan" over whose gallows "Shall climb the vine of Liberty, / With ripened fruit and fragrant flower."[9] Years later, he read Villard's description of what happened on the creek, and found the murders abhorrent. Howells was forced to question his former "unqualified reverence and affection": "The deed haunts the story of his whole life thereafter and his life theretofore; it throws its malign gleam forward upon the hero of the scaffold at Charlestown and backward on the father in his simple Ohio home bidding his sons kneel around him and share his oath never to cease warring upon slavery."[10]

I decided to finally get the brutal story out, instead of keeping it in my head and losing sleep. Why was I worried about condemning him for it? Many great people from history had.

Why was I losing confidence in my own moral stance?

He'd ordered swords to be sharpened and had his men slaughter five civilians, after all, many of them brutally dismembered, their body parts found floating in the stream the morning after the assault.

If I told what really happened, my brain and heart could rest. Even my imagination, the thing that always lingered last, would have no more work to do.

I was sure of it.

2.

First, there were the weapons.

Those cutlasses. Who would have guessed that they came from Akron, Ohio? My hometown. My backyard. General Lucius V. Bierce—whose name adorns the library of the University of Akron and who was the uncle of writer Ambrose Bierce—spoke in John Brown's honor in Empire Hall in Akron after his execution. Earlier, he'd presented several cutlasses of unusual shape to John Brown, who took them to Kansas, where they were driven into the flesh of five proslavery men on Pottawatomie Creek. John Jr. and Jason sharpened them before the men in the Pottawatomie party headed out, and a boy, Bain Fuller, turned the grindstone.[11]

They were a gift from General Bierce, who'd been a member of a secret filibustering society in Ohio called the Grand Eagles, a company of men who had fantasized about freeing Canada from England.[12] The weapons had originally been artillery broadswords, but were sold to the society as surplus. Each had an eagle etched on its blade, and the beaks and talons of those eagles tore through arms and heads and fingers on Pottawatomie Creek.[13]

In the speech that Lucius V. Bierce delivered in Akron on the day of John Brown's execution, he said he was "as noble as Leonidas, as brave as Caesar, as pious as Cromwell," talked with pride about the arms he had lent him, and praised John Brown for both waking the sleeping lion in Kansas and for not being charged with any crime. He managed to avoid the word "Pottawatomie" altogether.[14]

But I knew what the creek looked like the morning after the cutlasses were returned to their scabbards.

3.

Five men—two quite young, just twenty and twenty-two, but never a day older after that—lay on the ground. Although they were all proslavery men, none of them owned slaves. Some of them had served warrants for Judge Cato, who ran a bogus proslavery court at a store on Dutch Henry's Crossing set up by the German man the crossing was named for ("Dutch Henry" Sherman) to help Missouri Border Ruffians start new lives in Kansas; one was a proslavery constable; many of them threatened to kill Theodore Weiner, who had a Free-State store for emigrants close to Dutch Henry's, if he didn't vacate his store right away; another was a prosecuting attorney for Judge Cato's court and served on the proslavery legislature. James Doyle and his older sons, from Tennessee, were employed on plantation patrols when they lived in the South, and Doyle fed information about his Free-State neighbors to the proslavery Buford camp.[15] They all, supposedly, threatened to kill Free Staters, and were especially determined to harm the family of John Brown.

The John Brown party met Col. J. Blood on the road about sundown on May 23. According to a letter that Col. Blood wrote to G. W. Brown in 1879, John Brown asked him not to mention their meeting and told him "they were on a secret expedition."[16]

They camped that night between two deep ravines a mile north of Dutch Henry's Crossing and set out about 10:00 p.m. the next day, May 24, 1856. They followed California Road and crossed Mosquito Creek, heading for the settlement on Pottawatomie Creek. With them were the double-edged swords from Lucius V. Bierce.

Owen and Salmon Brown were the first to kill, slaughtering Mr. Doyle and his two older sons, William and Drury. Of John Brown's sons with him that night, Frederick and Oliver did not kill, but Owen and Salmon did. Mahala Doyle, the wife of Mr. Doyle, found the body of her husband and of William the next morning in the road about two hundred yards from their house.

John Doyle, who was only sixteen and had been spared by the murderous party because of his age, located the body of his brother Drury because his mother was too upset to proceed. He was the one who provided testimony. "I saw my other brother lying dead on the ground, about one hundred and fifty yards from the house, in the grass, near a ravine; his fingers were cut off, and his arms were cut off; his head was cut open; there was a hole in his breast." He described the wounds of his other family members: "William's head was cut open, and a hole was in his jaw, as though it was made by a knife, and a hole was also in his side. My father was shot in the forehead and stabbed in the breast."[17]

Townsley, the participant who published his account of Pottawatomie in 1879, said no "intentional mutilation" occurred, that all the wounds were given exclusively in the process of cutting the victims down.[18] The only wound John Brown inflicted was the gunshot to Doyle's head, which occurred after the man was dead. Clearly, different stories were being constructed (concocted?), but no matter what words people used to cast or deflect blame, the deed was brutal.

People who try to grapple with Pottawatomie often return to the bodies. How much—if any—of the mutilation was intentional? How vicious, really, was this crime?

What about the victim named Wilkinson? Depending on the account, he was said to have been killed by a Brown, or by Henry Thompson and Theodore Weiner. According to Mrs. Wilkinson: "Next morning Mr. Wilkinson was found about one hundred and fifty yards from the house in some dead brush. A lady who saw my husband's body, said that there was a gash in his head and in his side; others said that he was cut in the throat twice."[19]

Finally, the murder of William Sherman ("Dutch Bill"), the brother of Dutch Henry Sherman, who was probably not killed by the Brown boys but by Thompson or Weiner. James Harris, who owned the house William Sherman was unfortunate enough to have been visiting the night of the massacre (along with two other men), described the wounds of Sherman in an affidavit: "That morning about ten o'clock I found William Sherman dead in the creek near my house... I took Mr. William Sherman out of the creek and examined him. Mr. Whiteman was with me. Sherman's skull was split open in two places and some of his brains was washed out by the water. A large hole was cut in his breast, and his left hand was cut off except a little piece of skin on one side. We buried him."[20] The Brown party had been looking for Dutch Henry, but he was away from the creek searching for cattle he'd lost, so Dutch Bill was slaughtered instead.

Maybe if the group had used pistols and given their victims time to pray, or there had been a duel or the men they slaughtered had been allowed to fight or run or if they'd all met on a street and argued and then killed one another or gotten little bands of men together and had a shootout by a river or ravine the way settlers were supposed to murder one another on the frontier—maybe then the killings wouldn't have seemed so bad.

I very much disliked Andrew Johnson—a Democratic senator from Tennessee who would become Lincoln's vice president his second term and then the 17th President of the United States after Lincoln's assassination—but when I scanned the bloody canvas of the creek, something Andrew Johnson said about Pottawatomie in a speech he delivered to the Senate just a few days after John Brown was hanged almost sounded fair. He proposed that Providence had intervened at Harpers Ferry, punishing John Brown and his two sons for their earlier murders of James P. Doyle and his two sons.

Harpers Ferry, Johnson said, was a "rebuke."[21]

4.

Even after all the bloody details were in front of me, I couldn't sustain my anger. What was wrong with me?

I found myself inching away from Villard, Howells, the man at the meeting in Cuyahoga Falls, and, perhaps it goes without saying, from Andrew Johnson. I couldn't help hearing in their reprimands something ugly and tedious—flat—the way a vinyl record sounds when the needle leaves its grooves.

My ambivalence hadn't disappeared because I wrote down the graphic detail of Pottawatomie, as I had hoped, but only intensified.

It was exhausting me—day and night. At one point, when a surge of sympathy for John Brown became too strong, I decided to confront the horror of Pottawatomie directly. To go to the creek and stare into its dark waters to try to get my conscience back.

I threw my little terrorist "friend" in the back seat of the car and set out with him (and with my husband) for Kansas and Pottawatomie Creek, a drive of 925 miles.

Just before I left, it crossed my mind that I'd like to drown John Brown there, and wondered if I could.

I would take Villard with me—make John Brown carry Villard's book in his lap so he'd remember the weight of the sin his biographer accused him of. At rest stops and in motel rooms, I opened the huge volume and read again the gory details of the scene until they took better hold of me, and then I read them out loud in the car when my husband drove, hoping John Brown was not asleep in the back.

5.

When we arrived, I discovered that the area of the massacre wasn't marked well and not roped off—not the way Black Jack and Osawatomie were. The Battle of Black Jack occurred on June 2, 1856, a few days after Pottawatomie, and was directly connected to it. Henry C. Pate and his company burned Free-State cabins and other property in their search for John Brown, but John Brown pursued him until he forced Pate's surrender.

The Battle of Osawatomie took place on August 30, 1856—a lopsided battle in which John Brown and his men tried to defend the town.

Both battle sites were carefully marked and tended, with brochures and literature in plastic protectors, with maps and paths and well-mown grass.

But Pottawatomie wasn't a "battle," exactly. It was a massacre, an act of terror, and how would you commemorate that? No one seemed interested in calling much attention to it. It was a little like placing a marker at the site of the worst thing a person had ever done in their life.

I did find one obscure sign about Pottawatomie in a small community called Lane. It was located on Kansas Avenue and Fifth near Pottawatomie Creek in a park with playground equipment.

Lane was such a small place that I had trouble deciding what it even was. A town? A crossroads? Technically it was classified as a *city*—with a population of 225. Originally called Shermanville when it was laid out in 1855 (for the brothers of German origin who settled there—Dutch Henry, Dutch Bill, Dutch Peter), its present name was given in 1863 to honor Senator James H. Lane, a Free-State man.

Soldiers Monument at Osawatomie, commemorating the five men killed, including Frederick Brown

John Brown Drive, on the way to Lane, Kansas

We reached Lane by going due west on John Brown Highway, turning left after seven miles onto Vermont, then off Vermont onto John Brown Drive. John Brown's name was everywhere in this part of Kansas, as common as the wildflowers along the road. Towns seemed almost friendly to him here, but I wasn't used to this. Hudson, where he'd grown up, chose not to name Brown Street "John Brown Street" or to install a John Brown Memorial on the center Green. How had Kansas, or Franklin County, found the nerve to name both a highway and a drive that led straight toward Pottawatomie Creek after a man who had caused such horror there?

I noticed that a post office was still operating in Lane, but most of the downtown buildings were empty and there was no hint that they'd be occupied anytime soon. We drove down a few side streets, spotting a Methodist Church on the corner of one of them, but little else. Across from the park were stalls and booths, and an announcement that the Lane Fair was coming in August. It appeared that in the intervening time the town would be still.

We returned to the park where the marker was, and read it:

On the night of May 24–25, 1856, a small band of abolitionists led by John Brown murdered five proslavery men just north of here along Pottawatomie Creek. This massacre in "Bleeding Kansas" was one of the most famous

events leading up to the American Civil War. Brown was later captured, tried
and hanged for his unsuccessful raid on Harpers Ferry, (West) Virginia in
1859. Franklin County Historical Society.

The black paint of the metal sign was chipping badly, and no one seemed
to tend it anymore. Weeds hid some of the words and crawled over the face of
others. In front of the marker, off to the right and a little closer to the road,
was a bell suspended on three feet of concrete and hung from steel, erected by
the Lane Bicentennial Committee. "Happy Birthday America," it read.

The sign called what happened on the creek a "massacre," and the crime
committed there, "murder." But the inscription also suggested that Pottawatomie was connected to the Civil War, which somehow elevated it. I began to
wonder if it was possible to see the event this way.

As I stood on the small piece of land in Lane, Kansas, that held the sign,
I saw other boundary lines collapsing. A sign about a massacre stood next to
a bell wishing America a happy birthday—a happy bicentennial. Blue teeter-
totters and a yellow slide and a basketball net rose behind the bell and the sign.
How could a sign about a massacre share ground with a patriotic bell and
playground equipment for children?

We crossed a concrete bridge over Pottawatomie Creek and left our car
on the side of the road. I walked the banks of the stream, having no idea how
close I was to the slaughter, but knowing I was south of it, according to the
sign in the park. A fisherman sat on gravel that rose steeply from the creek to
the bridge, but his face was turned away from me. Uprooted trees lay along
the banks on either side, many leaning into the rapidly moving water.

I held a copy of a picture of Dutch Henry's cabin site that I found in the
Kansas State Historical Society collection, photographed between 1890 and
1910. Old settlers surrounded it, perhaps men who'd known Henry Sherman.
It wasn't clear why they'd gathered there (or been gathered), but there they
were. No structure remained, only tall grass and weeds that rose nearly to the
chests of the men. It must have been a windy day, since one man's duster was
blowing, and he braced his hat with his hand.

The trees and foliage along the creek were thick and dense now, and I could
see no break on the bank that led to a grassy spot like the one the picture
showed, a place for old settlers to stand and remember Lane when it was Shermanville and Dutch Henry and Dutch Bill and Dutch Pete were its proprietors.

Dutch Henry's cabin site in Franklin County, showing old settlers standing nearby. (Courtesy Kansas State Historical Society)

I heard doors slamming, swords whistling as they made their way toward human flesh, the bull dogs of the Doyles growling at the threshold of the Doyle house when intruders arrived.

There were no answers here, only my imagination.

Why had I expected to find them when I packed up and headed out? No fingers floated on the surface anymore, the houses were gone, and even the land was hidden from view. No hawk full of bloodlust perched on the bank. There were no easy metaphors—just a marker, a creek, and the picture in my hand.

What I'd found here were questions, not answers—only more bewilderment, moving as rapidly as the creek. I'd quoted James Baldwin on the matter of questions and answers for my students many times, but never really understood before Pottawatomie how difficult the task was that I'd assigned them. In an essay called "The Creative Process," Baldwin insisted it was necessary for artists (for everyone, it began to seem to me) to "drive to the heart of every answer and expose the question the answer hides," to conduct an "unflinching assessment" of not only our own interiors but also "the darker forces in our history," to "correct the delusions to which we fall prey."[22] I believed what he said, but I also knew that uncertainty could lead to madness. Or was certainty always the greater risk?

I needed to scavenge for questions that lurked beneath the fallen trees that lined the shore, even though the method was unsafe. I had more work to do.

6.

I wanted to see the rest, since I'd come so far, and since the job of thinking about Kansas was not over yet.

We drove a few miles to John Brown Memorial Park, which featured a museum that housed in its interior the cabin of Samuel and Florella Brown Adair (John Brown's brother-in-law and half-sister), a structure that had been moved to the site.

Nearby, several hundred Border Ruffians, led by John W. Reid and Rev. Martin White (the man who murdered John Brown's son Frederick), fought forty or so Free-State men commanded by John Brown. The Battle of Osawatomie, as it became known, was fierce but ended in the retreat of John Brown and his party across the Marais des Cygnes River. Outnumbered, their only choice was to float away, up to their waists in water, and leave the marauders to loot Osawatomie and burn it down.

I asked the site administrator what he thought about the massacre on Pottawatomie Creek. Living in the middle of all this Kansan history, he'd surely have an opinion, I thought.

He used words like "complex" and said, "no one is all good or all evil." But then he tried to justify John Brown's brutal night to make it more palatable to visitors. It was H. H. Williams who had given John Brown the list of men his party had killed, the guide said, and they had never intended to mutilate them. I'd heard such things before but hadn't been convinced.

John Brown Museum and Adair Cabin, John Brown Memorial
Park

The guide explained that the Browns and their accomplices killed "selectively." They "interviewed" people about their positions on slavery before they decided to murder them. Those who displayed no proslavery sentiment were saved, as were women and the very young.

I knew this was true and had read that John Brown and his party felt they were on a military mission. When the men stepped into the houses of their victims, they announced "they belonged to the northern army."[23] In December of 1855, Free-State leader Charles Robinson appointed John Brown as captain in the "First Brigade of Kansas Volunteers" and placed him in command of the Liberty Guards, a group of Free Staters that included John Brown's sons and fifteen other men.[24] The group was soon disbanded, but John Brown continued to be known as "Captain John Brown" for the rest of his life. I thought again about the sign in Lane with its suggestion that the Civil War had already begun in Kansas. Even from the decades of my own life, I knew that wars seldom started in a neat way or at a precise moment. There were often a hundred preliminary skirmishes.

Welcome to Osawatomie sign

John Brown Statue, John Brown
Memorial Park

Later, I found a welcome sign to Osawatomie, which identified the town as the "Cradle of the Civil War."

But Pottawatomie was so extreme that it still seemed to me more of an impulse than a plan, and the argument that it was a military venture was difficult to make. The guide claimed that the murders were an effective deterrent. Several Free Staters and neighbors of John Brown initially called Pottawatomie an "inexcusable outrage," but later felt it was "a justifiable act."[25]

Kansas became bloodier for a while, so I wasn't sure even about Pottawatomie's being a deterrent. I did know that proslavery families on the creek moved out after John Brown paid a visit and I did know that proslavery parties were afraid of abolitionists in a new way after the massacre. The whole deep South, in fact, was afraid, now believing that the North was stocked full of militant abolitionists who were ready to come for them, just like John Brown.

7.

What did his family, his friends, his neighbors say? What did the people who were with him that night say? And did John Brown himself ever speak of it?

New questions began to form as we drove back home.

I wondered sometimes if Transcendentalists who wrote floridly about John Brown's sainthood knew about Pottawatomie and just chose to ignore it. Biographer David S. Reynolds believed that people like Thoreau and Emerson knew what he'd done and "embraced him anyway."[26] He cited a line from Thoreau that suggested (for Reynolds, at least) that he had knowledge about the massacre. In "A Plea for Captain John Brown," Thoreau asked people to honor John Brown "even though he were of late the vilest murderer, who has settled that matter with himself."[27]

Some of John Brown's party didn't talk about the slaughter for years, if they ever did.

James Townsley, whose written account in 1879 caused a new wave of wrath against the Browns, claimed that he wanted to go home but John Brown refused to let him, that John Brown killed with intention and purpose, that although he didn't approve of the killings, he came to conclude they'd "resulted in good."[28]

John Brown's son-in-law Henry Thompson, one of the executioners, said as even an old man of eighty-six that the massacre was "a necessary and righteous act," though he worried privately about going to hell for what he'd done.[29]

Jason Brown (sitting, left), grandson Gerald Herbert (standing),
son Charles P. (sitting, right), great-grandson Edward, ca. 1911.
(Courtesy Hudson Library & Historical Society)

His children? Both those who were on the creek and those who stayed
back? Jason Brown, who wouldn't participate, reported that John Brown
denied having committed the murders, but his father then added, "I approved
of it." Purportedly after that, Jason told him, "I think it was an uncalled for,
wicked act," and John Brown replied: "God is my judge. It was absolutely necessary as a measure of self-defence, and for the defence of others."[30]

The brochure printed for the Akron Sesquicentennial said that Jason Brown
attended the dedication of the monument behind the Akron Zoo and had been
overcome, calling it "the crowning event of my life." He then said, "I can die happy
now. I have seen my father honored."[31] I wondered how he found peace over his
lifetime with an episode he once viewed as an appalling act of pure evil.

John Brown Jr. defended his father by explaining that he'd provided justification before the attack, having resolved with a private council at his camp that it "should be likely to cause a restraining fear."

Salmon Brown testified, "The general purport of our intentions—some radical retaliatory measure—some killing—was well understood by the whole camp."[32] In a narrative written just before his death, he refused to implicate himself in the murders: "Owen Brown cut down one of them and another of the Browns cut down the old man and the other."[33]

What about John Brown himself?

In public, he avoided the word "Pottawatomie" when he spoke about his Kansan adventures. The detailed notes he used throughout his unsuccessful fund-raising speeches in New England in the spring of 1857, exhaustively rehearsing Kansan battles and confrontations and losses, conveniently sidestepped Pottawatomie. He made much of being called out to defend Lawrence on May 20 and 21 (immediately before Pottawatomie), an antislavery town whose printing presses and newspaper offices had been destroyed, its hotel burned down, its buildings plundered. Then he skipped to May 30, 1856, when, John Brown said, Jason and John Jr. were imprisoned without having committed any crime—a statement he must have known was a half-truth. He even used props, rattling the chains that bound John Jr. Next, he recounted the wounding of his son-in-law at Black Jack on June 2.[34]

"I killed no man except in fair fight," he said in his interview with authorities a day after his capture at Harpers Ferry. "I fought at Black Jack Point and at Osawatomie; and if I killed anybody, it was at one of these places."[35] He had ordered the killing on the creek, not done it himself. Technically, he was telling the truth, but in every other sense his statement was a lie.

He did mention several times that he thought proslavery marauders were planning to kill Free-State settlers on the creek, once supposedly telling Colonel Edward Anderson in a statement that the men he murdered were intending to "wipe out the Free Soil settlers."[36] His few words directly on the matter, as David S. Reynolds said, ranged from "self-indictment" to "self-righteousness."[37]

In June of 1856, the month after the slaughter, John Brown wrote to his wife and children about Kansas and its battles, using the word *Pottawatomie*. He said only one ambiguous thing about it after mentioning his futile trip to save Lawrence and his overnight stay with John Jr. and his company of riflemen: "We were immediately after this accused of murdering five men at Pottawatomie, and great efforts have since been made by the Missourians and their ruffian allies to capture us." F. B. Sanborn, who first collected this letter, made a notation that there had been an erasure at this point on the original, and that a note had been appended that read, "There are but very few who wish real facts about these matters to go out." John Brown continued with the story of their pursuit by Henry Pate, including the Battle of Black Jack on June 2, 1856—providing no more detail about the Pottawatomie incident.

Yet a stray remark toward the end of the long letter seemed to imply that Pottawatomie was on his mind: "We feel assured that He who sees not as men see, does not lay the guilt of innocent blood to our charge."[38] I thought again of Gwen's early question in the archives. "What would God say about John Brown?" she asked. Apparently, John Brown had a suggestion for Him.

8.

I kept going over justifications for Pottawatomie that the thoughtful curator of the cabin had named or that John Brown's contemporaries had advanced or historians and biographers I'd read had found some meaning in.

Self-Definition. McGlone had seen Pottawatomie as a fierce act of self-definition by John Brown, both confirmation of Owen Brown's code and defiance of his father's pacifism.

The Retaliation Theory. Stephen Oates (and Salmon Brown) took that position, though it seemed Oates found the topic of the massacre as painful as I did. "I have accepted the 'retaliatory blow' thesis (but only after lengthy deliberation) because it seems to fit the logic of events and the behavior of Brown in all the frustration and hysteria that surrounded the sacking of Lawrence," he said. But he also said, "the exact reasons may never be known," and listed other possibilities.[39] I could imagine Oates writing his opinion, then rewriting it—what I'd been doing too. Samuel Adair, John Brown's brother-in-law and Kansan neighbor, expressed a similar view to the one Oates held, even admitting his great uncertainty.[40]

Michael Gold, the Communist writer of the 1930s who wrote a short biography of John Brown, included harrowing tales about actions of the Border Ruffians that Gold said preceded the Pottawatomie attack, and he was much more comfortable with Old Brown's retaliation on Pottawatomie Creek than Oates or Samuel Adair had been. In Gold's exaggerated account, an old settler was hanged and then let down, only to be threatened with an axe; a woman was horribly attacked in childbirth by the Ruffians; Dutch Bill, drunk, arrived at a settler's house and threatened to drink the "heart's blood" of the settler's young daughter. Gold criticized Oswald Garrison Villard for his "timorous" assessment of Pottawatomie. "When a thug assails one with a gun, or threatens one's wife and children, is one to practice non-resistance on him?...even a Villard would refuse to yield up his life to a thug," he wrote. Gold was very uncritical of John Brown. "He had no vices," he said.[41]

Even George MacDonald Fraser, a historical novelist so serious about his work that he sometimes alluded to specific biographers of John Brown, considered the merits of the retaliation theory. He had a character named Crixus in his picaresque novel about Harry Flashman's adventure with John Brown who believed the murders on the creek were justified by the destruction of Lawrence and the attack on Charles Sumner in Congress. But not entirely content with this interpretation, Fraser also had "Flashy," in an aside, tell the graphic truth about the manner of the Pottawatomie killings and say about John Brown, "even his worshippers have never been able to explain it away; most of 'em just ignore it."[42]

The Preemptive Strike Theory. Louis A. DeCaro Jr. said, "Brown intended the Pottawatomie strike to be done quickly and in stealth in order to remove the major figures of proslavery aggression in the vicinity, and to eradicate their imminent assault upon Osawatomie, especially as it targeted the militant egalitarian Brown family."[43] In his book about John Brown's religious life, DeCaro carefully and meticulously reconstructed the aggressive threat that proslavery forces posed, a group increasingly emboldened by a fraudulent government and the license it gave them. In another account, he described Pottawatomie as, at best, "a precise counter-terrorist strike."[44] He urged people to frame the killings with "a fundamentally different question"—one that focused on the "circumstances" that led to such a desperate act.[45]

I'd read in the narrative of Salmon Brown, and elsewhere, the story of John Brown using his surveying skills to investigate the danger his family was in. He ran a surveying line directly into the camp of the proslavery faction a little southwest of Pottawatomie Crossing, taking people with him, including Jason, to carry his surveying tools—flags and chains and other implements probably left to him by Judge De Peyster years before. Surveyors were appointed by the Pierce administration, so they were generally Southern sympathizers. As John Brown moved in the guise of a surveyor, men emerged from their houses to talk to him about property lines. They said, according to Salmon, "that they had come to Kansas to help themselves first and the South next. And there was one thing they would do—they would annihilate every one of 'those damned Browns' and would stand by Judge Cato 'until every damned abolitionist was in hell.'"[46]

Another scholar, talking about Harpers Ferry, said "by contemporary definition, John Brown was undoubtedly a terrorist to his core," but felt his "obsessive target" of American slavery "absolved him from the cold label of terrorist."[47] A prominent legal historian said John Brown's actions on the creek were "clearly violent," but did not "comport with what we know about modern terrorism." To him, Bleeding Kansas was "in the midst of a civil war," and Pottawatomie might be better seen as "guerilla warfare"—an act that is "brutal and bloody, but it is not terrorism." John Brown, he thought, was better viewed as a "revolutionary" than a "terrorist," for he lived in a place where a bogus proslavery government closed off political options, making free speech and the opposition to slavery crimes.[48]

Insanity. People had made this argument from the beginning. Reynolds even thought that Emily Dickinson's poem "Much Madness is divinest Sense" might have been inspired by the debate over John Brown's sanity, a debate that spanned his career.[49] The "insanity" plea during John Brown's trial was mainly a trumped-up charge by John Brown's lawyers (and close friends) to keep him from the gallows. On October 21, 1859, when John Brown certainly was not at his best (or healthiest) and when Governor Wise of Virginia had more than slight cause for irritation with him, the governor said that John Brown was "a bundle of the best nerves I ever saw cut and thrust and bleeding and in bonds...a man of clear head, of courage, fortitude and simple ingenuousness...cool, collected and indomitable."[50] He found him immensely sane. Yet the argument about John Brown's sanity persists.

When the Hudson Library & Historical Society brought James McBride to town to talk about *The Good Lord Bird,* I sat close to a woman who had just come back from visiting the John Brown House in Akron, a place John Brown and his family rented and lived in on and off from the mid-1840s to 1854—a house of such historical importance that the state of Ohio would award a $250,000 grant to help replace its tulip poplar siding with quarter-sawn cedar, have its trim and roof restored, and later, remodel its interior.[51] The woman had made a day of John Brown. I'd been to the John Brown

House a few times myself, usually after I visited the zoo, so I couldn't resist listening.

"I think he was nuts. Really off," I heard her say. She'd just purchased a copy of McBride's novel at the entrance to the meeting room and the receipt was sticking out.

A friend of mine in town, a lover of art and nature, had been educated in Kansas and told me matter-of-factly that she'd been taught in school that John Brown had inhaled too many fumes from the chemicals in Ohio tanneries and that's what had damaged his brain. As mad as a hatter.

The list of interpretations continued to grow, often dividing into sub-categories of their larger selves, forming intricate webs, increasing the number of possibilities and blurring everything. *Pre-emptive Strike. Retaliation. Deterrent. Conspiracy. Complicity. Madness. Terrorism. Counter-terrorism. Prelude to the Civil War. Restraining fear. Self-definition. Self-defense and defense of others.*

I kept going over the justifications, looking for the right one for me, just as I had with the tally sheet I'd prepared from my trip through Iowa. But no explanation completed the puzzle, even if I combined them all.

What could account for those sharp swords and the bodies of five men carved up like meat?

REVERIE 9
THE HAWK COMES FOR ME

I.

The hawk had come for me.

It must have seen me lying on the shore, exhausted by the futile labor of returning to this place again.

The bird picked me up and carried me off.

It wasn't the hawk that had given Helen Macdonald courage when her father died, nor the one that sanctioned Hermann Goring's blood lust. It was a bird, this time, that hovered high in flight with an unbroken view. A creature that saw panoramically, even beyond the boundaries of Kansas Territory.

The cone cells of a bird's eye expand the spectrum and let in ultraviolet light and colors human beings can't detect. Can't even imagine. Their wider pupils and larger lenses fill the whole eye from lid to lid.

To have eyes like a hawk is something we say for a reason.

So quick to notice details other creatures miss, so adept at measuring distances from the air. So skilled at circling and circling and knowing when to strike.

It would take a hawk's eyes to see beyond that shameful creek incarnadine.

2.

We witnessed the massacre from the sky.

Blood fell in the stream, then gushed across the bank of the creek on the other side and poured through crevices in the land until the fringes of Kansas dissolved and all the ground of slavery had been marked.

It pushed across the country, through border states, then through the upper South, the lower South.

It poured over fields of small farms and large plantations, cut rivulets through cotton, tobacco, rice, tinted the waterways of Alabama, Arkansas, Delaware, Kentucky, Louisiana, Maryland, Mississippi, Missouri, North Carolina, South Carolina, Tennessee, Texas, Virginia, soiled the white cuffs on the pants of plantation owners, as well as people who didn't own slaves but profited from slavery's fact. Blood surged North to find them all.

The tears of four million people caused runnels to form; rills of new blood, struck from their bodies in a thousand brutal ways, hurried the streams along.

Channels of blood rolled toward new ground, and toward another time, where 10,500 battles were fought and over 750,000 soldiers died.[1] Bull Run, Shiloh, Antietam, Fredericksburg, Vicksburg, Gettysburg, Chickamauga, Cold Harbor, Nashville[2]—all fed the stream and changed the nation's topography.

We suddenly were back, staring down into the creek again.

If I could just see into the heart of John Brown, I told the bird…

But it was the one place even the hawk couldn't take me.

I'd found out so much about John Brown during our time together, but a person is a veritable kaleidoscope of motives, and some of them remain hidden even to the people who perform the act.

What if slavery, that cause of his that seldom left his mind—the whole of it, I mean—was tightly tangled with his fury on the creek? The fact that John Brown interviewed people in their cabins about their proslavery sentiment before deciding to kill them certainly suggested that it played a central role.

Slavery's expansion was the thing people came to Kansas to stop or seek.

He was dealing with specific threats in Kansas, but was it a battle over even broader ground that led him to this ghastly deed?

Wouldn't it be better if I saw the way the hawk had seen?

Of the hundred explanations I read, none struck me as more convincing than the words John Jr. had used—his father had wanted to cause a "restraining fear." For too long I thought this referred only to the troubles in Kansas: the need to restrain Border Ruffians, Dutch Henry Sherman in his store at the Crossing, the bogus legislature, settlers who were plotting the demise of the Browns, and, most of all, the possible expansion of slavery into the Territory.

But wasn't the worry about slavery moving farther West—a grave worry the Kansas-Nebraska Act of 1854 had introduced—deeply coupled in John Brown's mind with the sickening fact that it already thrived in fifteen states? What if all the enslaved in antebellum America had been on his mind when he stepped onto the creek, as well as those a proslavery vote in Kansas might bring? What if he decided there was nothing to do in the face of such evil except what he did?

This was, after all, his first major military strike. It had been nearly twenty years since he'd taken his vow in Hudson to destroy slavery—right across the street from me. But slavery wasn't ending, nothing was getting better, and it had to stop.

I remembered the words of the Sons of Union Veterans officer who'd lectured the audience of Civil War buffs in Cuyahoga Falls. Reprimanded them. "Never, never take the word *slavery* out of the equation," he said after a man disparaged John Brown because of Pottawatomie. "Think about the number of people who died in bondage and what was being done to them."

And so I put the word back.

What if he thought his attack on the creek could somehow restrain slavery—not just in Kansas, but everywhere?

John Brown was a great naïve. That much I could document. Frederick Douglass, Du Bois had said, understood that "only national force could dislodge national slavery."[3] But for a long time, John Brown believed otherwise. He really thought he could end it "without verry much bloodshed"—and perhaps Pottawatomie was part of that plan. In a final note he handed to a prison guard just before his execution, he admitted he'd underestimated what emancipation would cost, and in that utterance predicted the Civil War. "I John Brown am now quite *certain* that the crimes of this *guilty, land: will* never be purged *away*; but with Blood. I had *as I now think: vainly* flattered myself that without *verry much* bloodshed; it might be done."[4]

And the swords, those glittering swords? Could they have been another part of an equation that had *slavery* in it? I might have found a way to be content with some of the justifications people posed for John Brown's murders on the creek if it hadn't been for those swords. This was, after all, Bleeding Kansas, as Tom Vince and other historians reminded people, and horrible fights between proslavery and antislavery settlers occurred all the time. One historian believed that most of the 200 killings in Kansas between 1855 and 1860 "were politically motivated and tied to slavery and Bleeding Kansas."[5] Words like *deterrent* or *retaliation* or *preemptive strike* would have sufficed, but none of them explained the brutality of Lucius V. Bierce's double-edged swords. Had they really only been chosen, as James Townsley and Salmon Brown proposed, to avoid the noise of guns?[6]

David S. Reynolds had said something I'd been thinking about, but hadn't had the courage to address. He talked about "a racial element in the murders," calling them "sword murders." What he said had alarmed me, but I couldn't forget it. The murders, Reynolds said, were committed in "the spirit of the retaliatory savagery" of Nat Turner or Native Americans who went on "scalping raids." "John Brown," he said, "not only wanted to kill proslavery people, he wanted to do it in a way that insurrectionary slaves or embittered Native Americans would have done it."[7]

What if this were true?

What if Pottawatomie were, as Frederick Douglass would propose in *Life and Times*, written long after the event occurred, "a terrible remedy for a terrible malady"?[8]

I thought about the tableau of John Brown with Nat Turner and Toussaint L'Ouverture in the National Great Blacks in Wax Museum in Baltimore, and of the Black writers in nineteenth-century America who so often had connected John Brown with Nat Turner—the enslaved man who'd led a revolt in Virginia with swords, hatchets, knives.[9] John Brown had studied both men—Nat Turner and Toussaint L'Ouverture. Did he know that when Nat Turner was captured from a hole he'd dug under a fallen tree, a sword was still in his hand?[10]

Were the swords a deliberate part of his plan? A brutal warning that slavery had to end? A white man who would turn on other white men with insurrectionist fury and weaponry was perhaps in John Brown's eyes a glimpse—or a symbol—of all that slaveowners now had to fear.

I'd read the sign in Osawatomie. "Cradle of the Civil War." If Osawatomie was the "cradle," I thought, maybe Pottawatomie was the bloody birthing room.

I realized, though, that I could never prove what was on John Brown's mind that day. All I could prove was the effect my long trip to the creek had had on me. I was conscious, perhaps for the first time, of "the darker forces in our history" that James Baldwin urged people to confront. Conscious of what Ira Berlin meant when he said that "undoing the violence of enslavement required just as much brutality as the creation of chattel bondage, if not more."[11]

I'd thought John Brown was the danger, but there had been a far greater danger in the world he occupied.

Muriel Rukeyser had written about the importance of John Brown's gallows to the American imagination, but it now seemed that the image of Pottawatomie might be of equal importance. That ugly, bloody wound on the American landscape left us no choice except to unflinchingly reconsider America's past.

I did not condone Pottawatomie. How could I? I certainly didn't admire it any more than I ever had. But I knew now that it had to be reckoned with. That the "darker forces" in the story of America all had to be reckoned with and imagined again.

James Baldwin thought that a "constricted white imagination" was among the most dangerous and destructive forces in America.[12]

Why did the words feel so personal to me?

John Brown equated imagination with compassion. "I want all my family to imagine themselves in the same dreadful condition,"[13] he said in a letter home, speaking of the dangers in lives of fugitives in Springfield after the Fugitive Slave Act passed.

In so many ways, my imagination had been jarred awake by the arrival of
John Brown in the Learnéd Owl Book Shop in Hudson, Ohio, and the time
we spent together after that.

Every object that he showed me, each letter I read of his, all the books I
opened, every event he led me to, all the people who guided me through
churches and museums and libraries and houses where he'd left his mark, each
person from the past that he brought to life, the myriad pictures he placed in
front of me, the countless markers and gravestones he forced me to find, all
the years he took from me, every symbol he demanded I consider, each trip I
made with my husband across America to find him, the lost stories he required
me to tell, the many sleepless nights I spent on the bloody banks of Pottawatomie Creek—all of it gave my conscience a chance to be reborn, and was a gift
from my friend John Brown.

Afterword

In their published exchange of letters, Auster and Coetzee said that friendship was a reciprocal process. I was so worried most of the time about whether I could be John Brown's friend that I seldom thought about whether he'd want to be mine. He'd given me a different imagination and a better conscience, and I feared that I'd given him nothing. Nothing that would let him view me as a friend, at least.

All I really had was my book. So I'd give him that.

I sometimes liked to imagine John Brown as a man of letters, writing in his jail cell from dawn until dark. For approximately forty-two days, he lived his life writing. He began his first jail cell letter on October 21, 1859, "with several sabre cuts in my head, & bayonet stabs in my body,"[1] and wrote his last letter to Lora Case one hour before his execution on December 2, 1859.

He awoke each morning and then moved to his desk. He dipped his pen in ink, leaned over, and wrote. The last night of his life, he wrote until midnight, and, at daybreak, he hurried to his desk one final time.[2]

To his last day, his last walk down the jail stairs, to his last wagon ride (sitting on top of his coffin to the gallows), to his last steps (up the gallows stairs), to his last breath ("Make it quick!" he said, then snap)—he lived with purpose, and sometimes eloquence. His letters, his conversations, his final words to people were often about slavery. He kept writing until the hangman came.

There was the start of a manuscript about Kansas found in the Kennedy House after the raid, along with a letter book that contained a draft of John Brown's essay "Sambo's Mistake," written in the 1840s for *The Ram's Horn*.[3] In February of 1858, in the home of Frederick Douglass in Rochester, New York, he drafted a new Constitution.

Oswald Garrison Villard felt that the jail cell letters redeemed John Brown. "The true Deliverance came with John Brown behind the bars at Charlestown," he said. It was "by words, and words, embodying his moral principles...that he stirred his Northern countrymen to their depths and won the respect even of the citizens of the South." His country would cherish most, Villard thought, "the memory of the prisoner of Charlestown in 1859 as at once a sacred, a solemn and an inspiring American heritage."[4]

I couldn't help but think that the reason Villard preferred him there was that he was caged in that jail cell—finally safe from the signature bloody acts that distressed Villard so much. The letters were certainly part of his legacy, though I don't believe, as Villard seems to, that they were what secured his reputation. Few people even know they exist.

Still, it could be argued that John Brown was in some sense a man of letters. In one fairly early letter from his jail cell, he wrote, "You know that Christ once armed Peter. So also in my case I think he put a sword into my hand, and there continued it so long as he saw best, and then kindly took it from me...I wish you could know with what cheerfulness I am now wielding the 'sword of the Spirit' on the right hand and on the left."[5]

John Brown believed in the power of language—at least, I think that's what he meant by "wielding the 'sword of the Spirit.'" So maybe he'd like my book at least well enough to think of me as a friend from the Western Reserve. I'm not worried about whether he agrees with everything I've said. He left his story to the future—the same "place" he left the country to that he loved.

In a letter written just days before his death, he imagined leaving his reputation in the hands of a tribunal. "I leave it to an impartial tribunal to decide whether the world has been the *worse* or the better of my *living* and *dying* in it,"[6] he said.

He left the matter of his good name (or ill) to all of us, so I took him at his word. Some people might feel very differently about John Brown than I do, hold other opinions, or even choose to move his story to new ground and reassemble it, like the engine house. But I think he'd welcome all our books, just as he would have welcomed all the lyrics different singers adapted to the melody of "John Brown's Song." Nobody trusted the Declaration of Independence the way John Brown did, and its words "the Right of the People" are central.

I sometimes hid from John Brown, but he would always find me. He knew I had work to do, and he wouldn't let me rest.

No, I don't know if he'll like what I've said. I'm just grateful I had the chance to say it.

Epilogue

My travels with John Brown began in 2007 and ended in 2016, just prior to the election of Donald J. Trump. I spent the next two years revising the book that grew out of that experience and thinking about what my time with John Brown had meant. During the revision period, I would occasionally incorporate information from new books I was reading or lectures I attended that clarified or extended what I'd focused on.

During final copyediting, in the midst of the pandemic and shortly after the election of Joseph Biden as president, I realized how much had changed since I traveled with John Brown. The Fire Museum in Hudson was open now and the offices in Town Hall had moved and been replaced by Destination Hudson (a greeting center). The John Brown House in Akron had its brand new roof and siding—with exhibits and sculpture busts on display inside, the National Museum of African American History and Culture in Washington had opened, and scholars and citizens throughout the country had prepared new lectures and books about John Brown, his raiders, and his world.

The broader political landscape had altered too. Donald Trump had been our president for four years (January 20, 2017–January 20, 2021); COVID-19 had killed over 500,000 Americans and transformed the way we lived; George Floyd was murdered outside a convenience store in Minneapolis; Black Lives Matter protests had begun across the nation; and New York City, Portland, Oregon, and Seattle, Washington, had been declared "anarchist jurisdictions." A viciously contested presidential election resulted in the storming of the United States Capitol on January 6, 2021, and in the second impeachment of Donald Trump.

It would be impossible for me to change the landscape of my book to include all that had happened since the end of my journey with John Brown. The particular time of his life, and of my life when we were together, had to be preserved. Context, as I'd learned, was essential. It was the atmosphere— the very air—of every story, as it was of mine.

Sometimes, I admit, it *was* very tempting to add details that occurred while the manuscript was in copyediting. Part of me, for example, wanted John Brown and Donald J. Trump to meet and talk, because race seemed central to both their lives. Important thinkers believed that Trump's election had a strong racial component that posed risks to democratic government. Toni Morrison claimed that Americans who voted for Trump were terrified of "the consequences of a collapse of white privilege," of losing "the comfort of being 'naturally better than.'"[1] Michael Eric Dyson said this: "We have, in the span of a few years, elected the nation's first Black president and placed in the Oval Office the scariest racial demagogue in a generation. The two may not be unrelated. The remarkable progress we seemed to make with the former has brought out the peril of the latter."[2]

But I decided it would be best not to do this, because so many others were waiting in the wings to tell the story of Donald Trump, and, if I'd done my job, my readers would think of John Brown without further help from me. Besides, John Brown probably would have just invited the 45th president of the United States to his jail cell and preached about the Golden Rule. I wouldn't be able to get a word in edgewise.

Incorporating all the events of recent years would not only change the emphasis of my story but leave the impression that it was possible to finish history, or know how America's story would play out, which it is not. Our country will always have new scenes to add because it is organic, struggling from its beginning to evolve into the kind of representative democracy John Brown wanted so badly for us to have.

No, it was best to leave things where they were.

The constancy of John Brown's vision of racial justice—of his *cause*—was what mattered most anyway, and what flowed beneath any time boundaries I might construct in a narrative. It's true that John Brown handed over the right to judge his life to others, but on the issue of preserving the belief that *all men are created equal,* he remained fixed. His methods were born of a very particular time of human brutality and terror in America's history, and they must never be needed again. The cause he lived for, however, is as urgent and timely as it ever was.

Acknowledgments

Michele Alston, administrative assistant, and Rev. Dr. Calvin J. McFadden Sr., senior pastor, St. John's Congregational Church, Springfield, Massachusetts; the staff of the Torrington Historical Society; Vivien Sandlund and Donald Fleming, professors of history at Hiram College; David Anderson, professor emeritus of English at Hiram College and co-editor of *Anthology of Western Reserve Literature*; Diccon Ong, chair of the History Department, and Tom Germain, digital archives library assistant, Western Reserve Academy; Joan Maher, former teacher in the Hudson Public Schools and Hudson resident who lives in Emily Metcalf's seminary on Baldwin Street; Nick Zaklanovich and Allyn Marzulla, videographers, HCTV; William Heath, writer and historian; Christopher Wood, History & Geography Department, and Terry Metter, Center for Local & Global History, Cleveland Public Library; Polly Reynolds, librarian and archival assistant, Sarah Lebovitz, adult services and archival assistant, and Derrick Ranostaj, Emerging Technologies librarian, Hudson Library & Historical Society; David Everett, former director, and Jeffery C. Wanser, former coordinator for Government Documents, Hiram College Library; Margaret Humberston, head of Library and Archives, Phyllis Jurkowski, archivist, Joanna Kiss, Collections Information and Imaging administrator, and Stephen Sullivan, assistant registrar, Springfield Museums; Patricia Boulos, Head of Digital Programs, Boston Athenæum; Amy L. Newell, John Brown expert for the Lake Erie Islands Historical Society on Put-in-Bay; Brad McKay, Richfield arborist; Carolyn Smith, archivist, and Adrien Hilton, processing archivist, Rare Book & Manuscript Library, Columbia University; Joanne Martin, co-founder, president, and CEO, and Carol Jolley, assistant to Joanne Martin, the National Great Blacks in Wax Museum, Baltimore, Maryland; Christina Kastell, curator of History and Anthropology, Putnam Museum and Science

Center, Davenport, Iowa; Annette Stransky, president of the Saratoga Historical Foundation, and Katie Alexander, volunteer at the Saratoga History Museum; Morex Arai, reference services assistant, Huntington Library; Richfield Historical Society staff members Linda Fleming, curator, Kelly E. Clark, curatorial specialist, Mark Mitchell, curator of photos, Susan Loughry, secretary, and Lynn Richardson, Oviatt Family expert with Friends of Crowell Hilaka; Rebecca Ebert, archives librarian, and Joan Wood, archives assistant, the Stewart Bell Jr. Archives, Handley Regional Library, Winchester Frederick County Historical Society; Ann Hull, executive director of the Franklin County Historical Society, which includes management of the John Brown House in Chambersburg, Pennsylvania, and Jenny Shifler, operations manager of the Society; Douglas W. Jones, Iowa Freedom Trail Grant Project manager, State Historical Society of Iowa, Des Moines; Curt Mason, communications director, Jefferson County Historical Society; Steve Strimer, director, David Ruggles Center in Florence, Massachusetts; Richard West, proprietor of Periodyssey, sellers of rare periodicals and ephemera; Ken Grossi, college archivist, Oberlin College Archives; Warren Lyons, painter and portrait artist; Jean Libby, author and curator, *John Brown Photo Chronology*; Christie Borkan, architectural historian; Rick Hanna, former pharmacist of Saywell's and co-owner of the Saywell's Building; Rebecca Larson-Troyer and Iris Bolar, Special Collections librarians at the Akron-Summit County Library; Louis A. DeCaro Jr., John Brown biographer and devoted blogger; Sara J. Keckeisen and Teresa Coble, reference services, Kansas State Historical Society; Patricia S. Eldredge, historic preservationist; Aaron P. Parsons, photo archivist, West Virginia Archives & History; Ann Sindelar, archivist at Western Reserve Historical Society; Rev. Mary L. Staley, priest-in-charge, St. Paul's Episcopal Church, Put-in-Bay; Mary Swander, former poet laureate of Iowa and expert on the state; Harry Wilkins, archivist of the Tabor Historical Society; Jeanette E. Sherbondy and Jeffrey D. Sherbondy, Sherbondy family members and genealogists; Stanley Brown, great-great-great grandson of John Brown and keeper of family records; Jeffrey A. Mills, genealogist of the family of Ruth Mills (Brown); Marty Brown, descendant of Jason Brown and transcriber of family letters (private collection of F. G. Brown); Charles Schollenberger, journalist and John Brown collector, Prairie Village, Kansas; Jamie Newhall, Senior Multimedia Producer, The University of Akron; the Ohio Arts Council.

Special gratitude must be given to Gwen Mayer, Thomas L. Vince, and, in memory, James F. Caccamo—Hudson librarians extraordinaire. And to the remarkable and supportive staff of The University of Akron Press—Jon Miller (Director), Amy Freels (Editorial & Design Coordinator), Thea Ledendecker (Editorial & Business Manager), and Julie Gammon (Marketing Manager).

Thanks to my loving Ohio family—Stephen, Melissa, Logan, and Carson Dyer—as well as other family members spread across the states. And thanks, as well, to friends and colleagues who sent constant encouragement, along with valuable tips about what John Brown was up to in their regions. Thomas and Annabelle Coyne remain, in memory, as staunchly supportive of my work as they ever were. In memory, also, is Prudence Dyer, my mother-in-law, whose contributions to my John Brown research cannot be tallied.

Most of all, thanks to Daniel Osborn Dyer, who never veered, even when I did.

Notes

PREFACE

1. Richard Holmes, "A Quest for the Real Coleridge," *The New York Review of Books*, December 18, 2014, http://www.nybooks.com/articles/2014/12/18/quest-real-coleridge/.

GLIMPSES OF JOHN BROWN IN HUDSON, OHIO

1. Thanks to contributors Debbi Classen, Liz Murphy, and Ted Olson, along with archivists Tom Vince and Gwen Mayer, for text and historical input for *A Picture of Hudson* (Hudson, OH: Destination Hudson, 2018). An especially good timeline of Hudson history provided help throughout.

2. Hudson and Akron are now both in Summit County, though the two towns were part of Portage County before portions of several counties joined in 1840 to form Summit.

3. Grace Goulder Izant, *Hudson's Heritage: A Chronicle of the Founding and the Flowering of the Village of Hudson, Ohio* (Kent, OH: Kent State University Press, 1985), 109–10.

4. Thomas L. Vince, "Surviving Two Centuries," *Inside Hudson*, September 2013, 14–17.

5. See early debate about building a hall in Hudson in "Shall We Have a Hall?," letter to the editor, *Hudson Enterprise*, September 27, 1877.

6. The first lines on the bicentennial sign are these: "On this site, the first meetinghouse owned by the Hudson Congregational Church was dedicated March 1, 1820, twenty-one years after David Hudson first came to the Hudson area. Its members met here until they completed their sanctuary on Aurora Street in 1865. In August 1835, church members unanimously adopted a resolution declaring that slavery is 'a direct violation of the law of Almighty God.'"

7. Lois Newkirk, ed., *Hudson: A Survey of Historic Buildings in an Ohio Town*, with an introduction by Thomas L. Vince (Kent, OH: Kent State University Press, 1989), 184.

8. Ann Engle, *The Judge Van Rensselaer Humphrey Home, 264 North Main Street, Hudson, Ohio*, 8–9, Hudson Heritage Association House Files, Hudson Library & Historical Society.

9. Patricia Eldredge and Thomas L. Vince, *National Trust for Historic Preservation Tour Guide to Historic Hudson Houses*, October 1973, Vertical File, History—National Register, Hudson Library & Historical Society. Descriptions of key historical houses on streets of the original village are provided. See also "Nat'l. Trust Tour Here Draws Favorable Comment," *Hudson Hub*, October 17, 1973.

10. Newkirk, ed., *Hudson: A Survey of Historic Buildings*, 87.

11. The description of the interior of the meetinghouse comes from Izant, *Hudson's Heritage*, who took the detail from a comment by the Reverend Stephen Bradstreet of Cleveland (117).

12. Henry Wadsworth Longfellow, "Haunted Houses," in *The Poetical Works of Longfellow*, with an introduction by George Monteiro, Cambridge Edition (Boston: Houghton Mifflin, 1975), 188–89.

13. John Rolfe, "20. and odd Negroes," excerpt from a letter from John Rolfe to Sir Edwin Sandys (1619/1620), *Encyclopedia Virginia*, Virginia Foundation for the Humanities, http://www.encyclopediavirginia.org/_20_and_odd_Negroes_an_excerpt_from_a_letter_from_John_Rolfe_to_Sir_Edwin_Sandys_1619_1620.

14. Listed here are the sources of the three phrases from John Brown letters in order of their mention: "To My Dear Sir [Hon. D. R. Tilden], Charlestown, Jefferson Co., Va., Monday, Nov. 28, 1859," in *A*

John Brown Reader, ed. Louis Ruchames (London: Abelard-Schuman, 1959), 154–55; "To My Dear Stedfast Friend [Rev H L Vaill], Charlestown, Jefferson Co., Va., 15th Nov. 1859," in Ruchames, *A John Brown Reader,* 135–36; "To Rev. McFarland, Jail, Charlestown, Wednesday, Nov. 23, 1859," in Ruchames, *A John Brown Reader,* 145–46. Citations to specific letters written by John Brown and collected by Ruchames or Clarence S. Gee (*John Brown Letters,* transcribed by Clarence S. Gee, Hudson Library & Historical Society) will be given only in the Notes, not the Bibliography, with the exception of his letter to Henry L. Stearns—known familiarly as his "Autobiography."

15. Roger Brooke Taney, Scott v. Sandford, Cornell University Law School, Legal Information Institute, https://www.law.cornell.edu/supremecourt/text/60/393#writing-ussc_cr_0060_0393_zo.

16. See "John Brown" [genealogy], Brown-Gee, Series II, Box #2, Folder #3, Hudson Library & Historical Society.

17. See Gerald W. McFarland, "Hudson's John Brown: The Controversy Continues," Video Recording, Vault Collection, Hudson Library & Historical Society. This address was delivered on October 24, 1985, at Hudson, OH, in celebration of the Hudson Library & Historical Society's seventy-fifth anniversary.

18. John Davey, "A Monument for John Brown, the Friend of Southern Slaves," *Cleveland Plain Dealer,* January 24, 1904. See also John Davey, "Monument for John Brown: John Davey Has Plan for Memorial and Preservation of Trees at Same Time," *Cleveland Plain Dealer,* January 24, 1904.

19. Correspondence conducted between Harlan N. Wood, acting headmaster of Western Reserve Academy, Harold T. Clark, and Clarence S. Gee from August through September of 1930 is held by the Hudson Library & Historical Society.

20. "Civil War Buffs to 'Bivouac' Here for John Brown Days," *Hudson Hub-Times,* July 3, 1985.

21. Patricia Eldredge, "Case Histories: Hudson, Ohio," in *Historic Preservation in Small Towns: A Manual of Practice,* ed. Arthur P. Ziegler Jr. and Walter C. Kidney (Nashville: American Association for State and Local History, 1980), 80.

22. James F. Caccamo, *Hudson, Ohio and the Underground Railroad* (Hudson, OH: Friends of the Hudson Library, 1992), 24.

23. "Building for Lease," *Hudson Hub-Times,* November 2, 2014.

24. The land was originally part of a vast claim deeded to the American colonies by King Charles II in 1662—initially extending to the "South Sea" (Pacific Ocean). Ten years after the Revolutionary War, the federal government adjusted Connecticut's claim, reducing it to the size of Connecticut itself— approximately 120 miles from east to west. See Western Reserve Historical Society, "What Is the Western Reserve?," http://www.wrhs.org/about/wrhs-history/.

25. Thomas L. Vince, "How Luck and Destiny Led to City's Founding" (lecture, Hudson Heritage Association, Barlow Community Center, Hudson, OH, October 8, 2015).

26. Robert A. Wheeler, ed., "Document Six: David Hudson, Sr.: An Early Settler Arrives in Northeastern Ohio, 1799," in *Visions of the Western Reserve: Public and Private Documents of Northeast Ohio, 1750–1860* (Columbus: Ohio State University Press, 2000), 57.

27. For a history of the early settlement of Hudson, see Lucius V. Bierce, *Historical Reminiscences of Summit County* (Akron, OH: T. & H. G. Canfield, 1854), 83–96, https://archive.org/details/historicalreminoobiergoog.

28. James F. Caccamo, *The Story of Kent, Ohio* (Kent, OH: Kent Historical Society, 1999), 22–23.

29. See David Ross Bennett, *The John Brown Birthplace* (Torrington, CT: Torrington Historical Society, 2002); Gerald W. McFarland, *A Scattered People: An American Family Moves West* (1985; repr., Amherst: University of Massachusetts Press, 1991).

30. Larkin Rogers, "Food of the Historic Western Reserve" (lecture, Hudson Heritage Association, Barlow Community Center, Hudson, OH, December 13, 2018).

31. Frederick Clayton Waite wrote about the chapel in *Western Reserve University, The Hudson Era: A History of Western Reserve College and Academy at Hudson, Ohio, from 1826 to 1882* (Cleveland: Western Reserve University Press, 1943).

32. Frederick Douglass spoke in front of the Western Reserve College Chapel on a platform erected under a large tent at Commencement season in 1854 (there were several days of events) on the topic "The Claims of the Negro, Ethnologically Considered, An Address Before the Literary Societies of Western Reserve College, at Commencement, July 12, 1854," The Cornell University Library Digital Collections. See also Mark J. Price, "Frederick Douglass, an Ex-Slave, Gave Moving Hudson Talk," *Akron Beacon Journal*, February 13, 2017.

33. John Brown, "To Mr. Henry L. Stearns, Red Rock, Iowa, 15th July 1857," in Ruchames, *A John Brown Reader*, 37.

34. Newkirk, ed., *Hudson: A Survey of Historic Buildings*, 27.

35. In his June 26, 1811, entry from *A Tour to New Connecticut in 1811: The Narrative of Henry Leavitt Ellsworth*, ed. Phillip R. Shriver, Vol. I of the Western Reserve History Studies Series (Cleveland: Western Reserve Historical Association, 1985), traveler Henry Leavitt Ellsworth, a cousin of the Hudson Ellsworths, wrote that many houses were framed, and the tavern was painted white (62–63).

36. Hudson's Congregationalists, along with the college community, were strongly in favor of temperance, and the town had frequent divisions between "Wet" and "Dry" throughout its early history. The fire of 1892 occurred after a vote to close the saloons, causing some to think it was set by an angry arsonist. James W. Ellsworth's commitment to revitalize the town after his return to Hudson in 1907 was dependent on a fifty-year agreement to keep the town dry. Details about the path the fire of 1892 took are included in James F. Caccamo's book *The Story of Hudson Ohio* (Hudson, OH: Friends of the Hudson Library, 1995), 25–30.

37. Alice Johnson, *Musical Chairs on Main Street: Hudson, Ohio* (self-published, 1979), 52; Newkirk, ed., *Hudson: A Survey of Historic Buildings*, 27.

38. Owen Brown, *Owen Brown's Autobiography as Written to His Daughter Marian Brown Hand, ca. 1850, Together with Family Correspondence Concerning the Autobiography*, transcribed by Rev. Clarence S. Gee, April 17, 1961, Hudson Library & Historical Society, 9.

39. Newkirk, ed., *Hudson: A Survey of Historic Buildings*; Jane Ann Turzillo, *Hudson, Ohio*, Images of America Series (Chicago: Arcadia, 2002).

40. The church bell, according to church historian Emily E. Metcalf, was purchased by Dr. Moses Thompson with a load of cheese he took to Pittsburgh in a wagon ("History of the First Congregational Church in Hudson, Ohio," *Historical Papers Delivered at the Centennial Anniversary of the First Congregational Church of Hudson, Ohio*, September 4, 1902, Hudson Congregational Church Manuscript Collection, Hudson Library & Historical Society, 8).

41. Izant, *Hudson's Heritage*, 117.

42. Izant, *Hudson's Heritage*, 90.

43. Laura Freeman, "Tour of Old Chapel Street Cemetery Uncovers Past Secrets," *Hudson Hub-Times*, October 15, 2014.

44. Emily Metcalf, "Woman's Work in the Hudson Church for a Century," *Historical Papers Delivered at the Centennial Anniversary of the First Congregational Church of Hudson, Ohio*, September 4, 1902, Hudson Congregational Church Manuscript Collection, Hudson Library & Historical Society, 21.

A LINCOLN LOOK-ALIKE

1. Some of the background about John Brown photographs comes from Jean Libby's book *John Brown Photo Chronology: Catalog of the Exhibition at Harpers Ferry 2009* (Palo Alto, CA: Allies for Freedom Publishers, 2009), as well as her supplement, *John Brown Photo Chronology Supplement; Revisions to the Catalog of the Exhibition at Harpers Ferry 2009* (Palo Alto, CA: Allies for Freedom Publishers, 2015). One insert titled "John Brown and History of Photography," in the revised edition (insert pages 90–91), is helpful in differentiating among early photographic techniques used for John Brown images—including those for replication.

2. Information about the Sharps can be found on pages 42–43 of *American Gun: A History of the U.S. in Ten Firearms* (New York: William Morrow, 2013), by Chris Kyle with William Doyle.

3. Quoted in Oswald Garrison Villard, *John Brown 1800–1859: A Biography Fifty Years After* (Boston: Houghton Mifflin, 1910), 312, 626 (note #7).

4. James Malin, "The John Brown Legend in Pictures, 2: Kissing the Negro Baby," *Kansas Historical Quarterly* 9.4 (November 1940): 339–41, Kansas State Historical Society, http://www.kshs.org/p/the-john-brown-legend-in-pictures-2/12849.

5. David S. Reynolds, *John Brown, Abolitionist: The Man Who Killed Slavery, Sparked the Civil War, and Seeded Civil Rights* (New York: Knopf, 2005), 201.

6. See Libby's *John Brown Photo Chronology Supplement* for further information about the Akron photograph (insert pages 24–25).

7. For an account of Libby's search for the Ohio origin of the 1856 photograph, see "The John Brown Daguerreotypes," *The Daguerreian Annual 2002–2003* (The Daguerreian Society, 2004), 39–41.

8. Caccamo, *Hudson, Ohio and the Underground Railroad*, 33.

9. John T. Nelson, "Lucy Markerly: A Case Study of an Englishwoman's Immigration to the Western Reserve in the 1830s," *Northeast Ohio Journal of History* 4.1 (Spring 2007), https://blogs.uakron.edu/nojh/2007/04/21/lucy-markerly-1830s/.

10. Patricia Eldredge and Priscilla Graham, *Square Dealers: A Short History of Nineteenth Century Main Street and the Commercial Buildings on the Public Square, Hudson, Ohio* (Hudson, OH: Hudson Heritage Association, 1980), #4 and #5.

11. For more about Markillie, see "John Markillie Early Well-Known Citizen," *Hudson Times*, May 28, 1931, Vertical File, Biography–Markillie, Hudson Library & Historical Society.

12. Frederick Douglass, *Life and Times of Frederick Douglass, Written by Himself*, 1893, in *Frederick Douglass: Autobiographies*, notes by Henry Louis Gates Jr. (New York: Library of America, 1994), 716.

13. William Herndon and Jesse William Weik, *Herndon's Lincoln: The True Story of a Great Life*, Vol. 3 (Chicago, New York, and San Francisco: Belford, Clarke & Company, 1889), 586, https://archive.org/stream/herndonslincolnto3inhern#page/n5/mode/2up.

14. Gwen Mayer reported that Owen Brown earned the title of veteran of the War of 1812 for his role in supplying troops with cattle. There's a metal marker by his grave with his title.

15. John Brown, "To Mr. Henry L. Stearns, Red Rock, Iowa, 15th July 1857," 38.

16. Mark J. Price, "One Last Glimpse of Lincoln," *Akron Beacon Journal*, April 13, 2015.

17. See Eugene F. Fairbanks, compiler of *Abraham Lincoln Sculpture Created by Avard T. Fairbanks* (Bellingham, WA: Fairbanks Art and Books, 2002), 146.

18. Frederick Douglass, "To William Cooper Nell, Lynn, Mass, February 5, 1848," published in *The North Star* 1.7 (February 11, 1848), Frederick Douglass Papers at the Library of Congress, 3, https://www.loc.gov/item/mfd.21017/.

19. This image was not found until 1996 at a Pennsylvania auction and "mislabeled 'Pennsylvania farmer'" (Jean Libby, "Chronology of John Brown Photo Portraits Self-Guided Tour by Jean Libby, author and curator, for teachers and researchers," http://www.alliesforfreedom.org/files/Exhibit_talking_narrative_3_.pdf).

20. Mrs. Russell, the wife of the Hon. Thomas Russell, helped house John Brown in her inconspicuous home in Boston after the Kansan trouble of 1856, saw him in the spring of 1859 when he visited the Russells after his Missouri raid, and, along with her husband, visited John Brown in his Charles Town jail cell. Katherine Mayo interviewed Mrs. Russell in 1909, and it was at that time that Mrs. Russell supposedly told the story of John Brown holding Minnie in the palm of his hand (Katherine Mayo, "Brown in Hiding and in Jail," *New York Evening Post*, October 23, 1909, in Ruchames, *A John Brown Reader*, 237).

21. Herndon and Weik, *Herndon's Lincoln: The True Story of a Great Life*, 586–87.

22. Henry Villard, *Lincoln on the Eve of '61*, ed. Harold G. and Oswald Garrison Villard (New York: Knopf, 1941), 4.

23. John Niven, *Salmon P. Chase: A Biography* (New York: Oxford University Press, 1995), 220; Harriet Taylor Upton and Harry Gardner Cutler, *History of the Western Reserve*, Vol. 3 (University City, MO: Lewis Publishing, 1910), 1670, https://books.google.com/books/about/History_of_the_Western_Reserve.html?id=L5GPjobXdWoC.

24. Marie E. Zakrzewska, who founded several women's hospitals and was trained at the Western Reserve Medical College in Cleveland, came to Hudson in 1856 to hear Ralph Waldo Emerson speak. Emerson's cousin, Professor Alfred Emerson, taught mathematics and physics at the college from 1853–1856 (*A Woman's Quest: The Life of Marie E. Zakrzewska*, ed. Agnes C. Vietor [New York: D. Appleton and Co, 1924], 160–61, http://iiif.lib.harvard.edu/manifests/view/drs:2585817$8i%20161).

25. John Brown, "Brown's Interview with Mason, Vallandigham, and Others," Harper's Ferry, Oct. 19, 1859, in Ruchames, *A John Brown Reader*, 120.

26. Quoted in John Mead, "An Insurrection of Thought: The Literature of Slave Rebellion in the Age of John Brown," master's thesis, University of Illinois at Chicago, 1998, xxv.

27. For a historical description of the radicalism of Jefferson, Ohio, and Ashtabula County, see James T. Fritsch, "Prologue: The Wonder of the Age," in *The Untried Life: The Twenty-Ninth Ohio Volunteer Infantry in the Civil War* (Athens: Swallow Press/Ohio University Press, 2012), 1–7.

28. Stephen B. Oates, *To Purge This Land with Blood: A Biography of John Brown*, Second Edition (1970; repr. Amherst: University of Massachusetts Press, 1984), 316. Reynolds in *John Brown, Abolitionist* talks about John Brown founding the Black Strings in 1858 to coordinate the activities of the Underground Railroad (273).

29. Carl E. Feather, "The John Brown Affair," *Star Beacon*, October 15, 2011, http://www.starbeacon.com/community/the-john-brown-affair/article_4a235918-9499-58d6-8baa-ab65839b459d.html.

30. Mary Land discusses at some length the numerous attempts that were made to link John Brown and Congressman Joshua Giddings ("John Brown's Ohio Environment," *Ohio State Archaeological and Historical Quarterly* 57 [January 1948]: 43).

31. James F. Caccamo, "Early Blacks in Hudson," *Ex Libris: A Publication of the Hudson Library and Historical Society* 11.1 (Winter 1990): 1–2.

32. J. Brent Morris, *Oberlin, Hotbed of Abolitionism: College, Community, and the Fight for Freedom and Equality in Antebellum America* (Chapel Hill: University of North Carolina Press, 2014).

33. Caccamo, *Hudson, Ohio and the Underground Railroad*, 13–16.

34. Tom Calarco, *Places of the Underground Railroad: A Geographical Guide* (Santa Barbara, CA: Greenwood, 2011), 137–39.

35. The Ohio legislature passed a law on January 5, 1804, titled "An Act to Regulate Black and Mulatto Persons" and renewed it with additional restrictions on January 25, 1807, and again in 1811, 1816, 1824, and 1831. It was not repealed until February 19, 1849. The specifics of the Ohio Black Laws can be found in William Cox Cochran, *The Western Reserve and the Fugitive Slave Law: A Prelude to the Civil War*, Publication No. 101 (Cleveland: Collections of the Western Reserve Historical Society, 1920), 54–77, https://archive.org/stream/cu31924017903299#page/n111/mode/2up.

36. The story of Sam and Martin and the arrest of Joseph Keeler in May 1820 was brought to light by Mae Pelster, *Abolitionists, Copperheads and Colonizers in Hudson & the Western Reserve* (Charleston, SC: The History Press, 2011), 27–35. The incident was recorded in the *Cleaveland Herald* May 9, 1820; November 14, 1820; December 12, 1820; January 2, 1821; and March 20, 1821.

37. An Akron ladies' literary magazine, *The Akron Offering*, included articles that simultaneously opposed slavery and endorsed colonization (Maud Wellington, "Slavery," *The Akron Offering: A Ladies' Literary Magazine, 1849–1850*, ed. Jon Miller [Akron, OH: The University of Akron Press, 2013], 332–36).

38. Abraham Lincoln, Speech at Elwood, Kansas, December 1 [November 30?], 1859, University of Michigan, *Collected Works of Abraham Lincoln*, Vol. 3, http://quod.lib.umich.edu/l/lincoln/lincoln3/1:164?rgn=div1;view=fulltext.

39. Abraham Lincoln, Speech at Leavenworth, Kansas, December 3, 1859, University of Michigan, *Collected Works of Abraham Lincoln*, Vol. 3, http://quod.lib.umich.edu/l/lincoln/lincoln3/1:166?rgn=div1;view=fulltext.

40. Abraham Lincoln, "Address at Cooper Institute, New York City," February 27, 1860, in *Abraham Lincoln: Speeches and Writings 1859–1865*, notes and selections by Don E. Fehrenbacher (New York: Library of America, 1989), 123.

41. Thomas Hamilton published the *Weekly Anglo-African* after the *Anglo-African Magazine* ceased publication in 1860. It continued until 1865.
42. Henry Louis Gates Jr., "Abraham Lincoln on Race and Slavery," in *Lincoln on Race & Slavery*, ed. Henry Louis Gates Jr. and Donald Yacovone (Princeton, NJ: Princeton University Press, 2009), xxv.
43. Lincoln, Speech at Leavenworth, Kansas.
44. Abraham Lincoln, "First Inaugural Address," March 4, 1861, in *Abraham Lincoln: Speeches and Writings 1859–1865*, 215.
45. James W. Loewen reviewed eighteen textbooks used in history classes of American high schools for errors, omissions, or biases. Only one of them, he found, included any of the angry phrases in Lincoln's "Second Inaugural Address" (*Lies My Teacher Told Me: Everything Your American History Textbook Got Wrong*, rev. ed. [New York: New Press, 2007], 188–89).
46. Abraham Lincoln, "Second Inaugural Address," March 4, 1865, in *Abraham Lincoln: Speeches and Writings 1859–1865*, 686–87.
47. Information about the line Akron residents rode to Hudson comes from Price, "One Last Glimpse of Lincoln."
48. Henry Villard, *Lincoln on the Eve of '61*, 86.
49. Abraham Lincoln, "Remarks at Hudson, Ohio," February 15, 1861, University of Michigan, *Collected Works of Abraham Lincoln*, Vol. 4, https://quod.lib.umich.edu/l/lincoln/lincoln4/1:336?rgn=div1;submit=Go;subview=detail;type=simple;view=fulltext;q1=hudson.
50. Additional information about Lincoln's visit to Hudson on his presidential train comes from "Lincoln in Ohio on His Way to Inauguration," Chapter 6 of Daniel J. Ryan's *Lincoln and Ohio* (1923; repr. Dover: Ohio Historical Society and Old Hundredth Press, 2008), 128; from Michele Collins' article "Observing the 150th Anniversary of the Civil War and Hudson's Role," *Hudson Life Magazine*, February 2011, 4–5; and from Laura Freeman's "Abe Was Here," *Hudson Hub-Times*, February 20, 2011.
51. Lincoln Ellsworth became a famous polar explorer and the only Hudson resident who was ever commemorated on a stamp printed by the United States Postal Service (Caccamo, *The Story of Hudson Ohio*, 38). The year of commemoration was 1988.
52. A comprehensive history of 5 East Main, old Ellsworth Hall, is provided in "The Building at 5 East Main," Vertical File, Hudson Historic Buildings, Hudson Library & Historical Society.
53. Price, "One Last Glimpse of Lincoln."
54. Fred Kaplan, "John Quincy Adams: American Visionary" (lecture, Hudson Library & Historical Society, Hudson, OH, September 22, 2014). He'd recently completed a new book with the same title (New York: Harper, 2014).
55. Joseph J. Ellis, *American Dialogue: The Founders and Us* (New York: Knopf, 2018), 46.
56. John Brown has not been alone in his criticism of the American Constitution. On the momentous 200th anniversary of the document in 1987, Supreme Court Justice Thurgood Marshall argued against a "blind pilgrimage to the shrine" of the Constitution, and against "flagwaving fervor." He asked, instead, that people "more quietly commemorate the suffering, struggle, and sacrifice that has triumphed over much of what was wrong with the original document." He said, "I plan to celebrate the bicentennial of the Constitution as a living document" (Thurgood Marshall, "The Bicentennial Speech," http://thurgoodmarshall.com/the-bicentennial-speech/); in his speech "What to the Slave Is the Fourth of July?," given on July 5, 1852, in Rochester, Frederick Douglass used "scorching irony" to insist that the "great principles" of the Declaration of Independence be extended "to the American slave" (Appendix to *My Bondage and My Freedom*, in *Frederick Douglass: Autobiographies*, 431–35).
57. Lora Case's reminiscences were first published as a series of nineteen newspaper articles in *The Hudson Independent* (February–August, 1897) and reprinted in 1963 with notes, an index, and an introduction by Frances B. B. Sumner by the Hudson Library & Historical Society. The book is now catalogued under the title *Hudson of Long Ago: Reminiscences*, and page 55 of that text records the story of John Brown's speech and his train departure.

58. John Brown, "To My Dear Sir [Lora Case Esqr], Charlestown, Jefferson, Co Va, 2d Dec. 1859," in Ruchames, *A John Brown Reader*, 158–59.

59. The ninth poem of A. E. Housman's *A Shropshire Lad* is a contemplative poem about the gallows and hangings and ill fate, and includes the image alluded to here (*The Collected Poems of A. E. Housman* [New York: Henry Holt, 1940]).

REVERIE 1

1. Mark J. Camp, *Railroad Depots of Northeast Ohio* (Charleston, SC: Arcadia, 2007), 110. Before a Pennsylvania line depot was built for elevated track, a former Pennsylvania depot sat at road level. According to Tom Vince, it was on Streetsboro Street in the area of the former Reserve Inn, now Lager & Vine (email from Thomas L. Vince, August 16, 2017).

2. Caccamo, *The Story of Hudson Ohio*, 14.

3. Turzillo, *Hudson, Ohio*, Images of America Series, 7, 115.

4. Thomas L. Vince, "Former Saloon Saved," *Inside Hudson*, March 2014, 20.

THE CASE-BARLOW FARM AND THE UNDERGROUND RAILROAD

1. Dorothy Markulis, "Historic Treasure," *Discover Hudson*, 2016, 12–16. https://issuu.com/dixcom/docs/hudson_discover_2015.

2. William Anderson, *River Boy: The Story of Mark Twain*, illustrated by Dan Andreasen (New York: HarperCollins, 2003), n.p.

3. See Ann Hagedorn, *Beyond the River: The Untold Story of the Heroes of the Underground Railroad* (New York: Simon and Schuster, 2002).

4. These particular northeastern Ohio sites are named by Caccamo in his book *Hudson, Ohio and the Underground Railroad* (17–18, 25).

5. Much of the information about the Underground Railroad in Ohio comes from Wilbur Henry Siebert, *The Mysteries of Ohio's Underground Railroads* (Columbus: Long's College Book Company, 1951). An Ohio State history professor, Siebert began his research on the Underground Railroad with a book published in 1898 called *The Underground Railroad: From Freedom to Slavery*. It was based largely on responses to inquiries (they were called "circulars"), and in it Siebert identified an elaborate network with defined stops, landmarks, and roads. His research and conclusions would begin to be challenged in the 1960s by Larry Gara.

6. Siebert, *The Mysteries of Ohio's Underground Railroads*, 13.

7. See Henry Louis Gates Jr., "Who Really Ran the Underground Railroad?," *The African Americans: Many Rivers to Cross*, https://www.pbs.org/wnet/african-americans-many-rivers-to-cross/history/who-really-ran-the-underground-railroad/.

8. Eric Foner, *Gateway to Freedom: The Hidden History of the Underground Railroad* (New York: Norton, 2015), 4.

9. The Freedom on the Move project at Cornell is a database project that focuses on ads for fugitives (http://freedomonthemove.org/).

10. Sally R. McArn, *The Underground Railroad—An American Legend* (1977), Hudson Library & Historical Society.

11. See Foner's *Gateway to Freedom* for an excellent discussion of the Underground Railroad in New York City, a work that includes one chapter on "Origins of the Underground Railroad: The New York Vigilance Committee" (63–90).

12. David W. Blight, "Why the Underground Railroad, and Why Now? A Long View," in *Passages to Freedom: The Underground Railroad in History and Memory*, ed. David W. Blight (Washington: Smithsonian, 2004), 233–47.

13. Caccamo, *Hudson, Ohio and the Underground Railroad*, 7–13, 24–26.

14. Nikki Custy, "Hudson and the Underground Railroad," *Hudson Life Magazine*, July 2013, 4–6.

15. Caccamo, *Hudson, Ohio and the Underground Railroad*, 27–29, 33.

16. Case, *Hudson of Long Ago*, 9–10, 53.

17. Gates, "Who Really Ran the Underground Railroad?"

TWENTY-FIRST-CENTURY OHIO NEIGHBORS

1. Alan Brinkley, *The Unfinished Nation: A Concise History of the American People,* 6th ed. (New York: McGraw-Hill, 2009), 307, 328.
2. George Brown Tindall and David Emory Shi, *America: A Narrative History*, Brief Ninth Edition (New York: Norton, 2012), 472–73, 481–84.
3. Patricia Eldredge, "Patricia Eldredge Papers," Box 2 of 2, in process, Hudson Library & Historical Society.
4. Laura Freeman, "An Image of Ellsworth," *Hudson Hub-Times,* July 4, 2012.
5. Eldredge and Graham, *Square Dealers,* #25.
6. Thomas L. Vince, "Mystery of House Solved," *Inside Hudson,* January 2014, 20.
7. Eldredge, "Case Histories: Hudson, Ohio," 70.
8. Thomas L. Vince, "History of the Chapel Bell" (lecture, Hudson Heritage Association, Western Reserve Academy Chapel, Hudson, OH, May 10, 2018).
9. Lincoln Ellsworth, *James William Ellsworth: His Life and Ancestry* (New York: National Americana Society, 1930).
10. Jim Cochran, letter to the editor, "Is John Brown Tribute Appropriate?," *Hudson Hub-Times,* April 5, 2009.
11. David McNees, letter to the editor, "Supports Library's Educational Efforts," *Hudson Hub-Times,* April 8, 2009.
12. Louis A. DeCaro Jr., letter to the editor, "John Brown Remarks 'Unfortunate,'" *Hudson Hub-Times,* April 12, 2009. DeCaro compiled, introduced, and published fourteen essays he'd written about John Brown's life and legacy, some from his blog, in *John Brown: The Man Who Lived (Essays in Honor of the Harper's Ferry Raid Sesquicentennial, 1859–2009).*
13. Melissa Thomson and E. Leslie Polott, letter to the editor, "Library Clarifies John Brown Events," *Hudson Hub-Times,* April 12, 2009.
14. Tim Troglen, "Great-great-grand Niece of Abolitionist John Brown to Pay Historic Church a Visit," *Hudson Hub-Times,* April 28, 2013, https://www.beaconjournal.com/story/news/local/hudson-hub-times/2013/04/28/great-great-grand-niece-abolitionst/19735677007/.
15. Thomas L. Vince, "Abraham Lincoln and John Brown" (lecture, Sons of Union Veterans of the Civil War, Cuyahoga Falls Public Library, Cuyahoga Falls, OH, July 2, 2013).
16. For a recent discovery about the bust's location since 1902 see Jess Bidgood, "A Mysterious Noseless Bust at Tufts Gets Back Its Name: John Brown," *New York Times,* October 31, 2016, http://www.nytimes.com/2016/11/01/us/a-mysterious-noseless-bust-at-tufts-gets-back-its-name-john-brown.html?_r=0.
17. Mary A. Brown, "To My Dear Mrs. Stearns, North Elba, Jan 7th, 1863," Brown-Gee, Series III, Box #2, Folder #3, Hudson Library & Historical Society.

NINETEENTH-CENTURY OHIO NEIGHBORS

1. Quoted in Bonnie Laughlin-Schultz, *The Tie That Bound Us: The Women of John Brown's Family and the Legacy of Radical Abolitionism* (Ithaca, NY: Cornell University Press, 2013), 150.
2. Manisha Sinha, *The Slave's Cause: A History of Abolition* (New Haven, CT: Yale University Press, 2016), 217.
3. Interview by Katherine Mayo with George A. Griswald, January 4, 1909, Ohio Interviews, Brown-Villard, Box #1, Hudson Library & Historical Society.
4. Interview by Katherine Mayo with Abner Caldwell, December 28, 1908, Ohio Interviews.
5. "Affidavits of John Brown's Alleged Insanity, presented at the time of his trial at Charlestown, Va., in 1859. Originals in the Congressional Library, Washington, DC," Brown-Gee, Series I, Box #12, Folder #32, Hudson Library & Historical Society.
6. Interview by Katherine Mayo with Charles Lusk, December 21, 1908, Ohio Interviews.
7. Interview by Katherine Mayo with Mrs. Porter Hall, December 22, 1908, Ohio Interviews.
8. Interview by Katherine Mayo with E. O. Randall, December 26, 1908, Ohio Interviews.
9. Interview by Katherine Mayo with Ransom M. Sanford, December 20, 1908, Ohio Interviews.

10. Interview by Katherine Mayo with Robert W. Thompson, December 20, 1908, Ohio Interviews.

11. For an account of the brief stay of John Brown, John Jr., Owen, and Jason in the Akron jail, see John Brown Jr., *Reminiscences*, in *Meteor of War: The John Brown Story*, eds. Zoe Trodd and John Stauffer (Maplecrest, NY: Brandywine Press, 2004), 65.

12. Christian Cackler, *Recollections of an Old Settler: Life in the Early Western Reserve, Hudson and Franklin Township* (1874; repr. Kent, OH: Roger Thurman, 1992), 45–48.

13. Interview by Katherine Mayo with Christian Cackler Jr., December 24, 1908, Ohio Interviews. Christian Cackler Jr. was actually the third Christian Cackler in the line.

14. Interview by Katherine Mayo with Mrs. Johnson Bartshe, December 23, 1908, Ohio Interviews.

15. Interview by Katherine Mayo with Mrs. Danley Hobart [Amelia], December 1908, Ohio Interviews.

16. Interview by Katherine Mayo with Dr. Andrew Willson, December 24, 1908, Ohio Interviews.

17. Case, *Hudson of Long Ago*, 48–56.

18. Interview by Katherine Mayo with Benjamin K. Waite, December 26, 1908, Ohio Interviews.

19. Interview by Katherine Mayo with C. H. Buss, December 25, 1908, Ohio Interviews.

20. Interview by Katherine Mayo with Henry Myers and Daniel W. Myers, December 11, 1908, Ohio Interviews.

21. Interview by Katherine Mayo with John Whedon, December 20, 1908, Ohio Interviews.

22. Interview by Katherine Mayo with Ransom M. Sanford, Ohio Interviews.

23. Cackler, *Recollections of an Old Settler*, 46.

24. Quoted in F. B. Sanborn, ed. *The Life and Letters of John Brown: Liberator of Kansas and Martyr of Virginia*, Third Edition, Classic Reprint Series, Forgotten Books (1885; repr., Concord, MA: F. B. Sanborn, Publisher, 1910), 55.

25. Reynolds talks about the muskets and mentions that John Jr. and Owen were holding them, but Jason hid in the woods (*John Brown, Abolitionist*, 76).

26. Harlan L. Trumbull, "To Mrs. Theodore S. Sprague, 45 Division Street, Hudson, Ohio, 19 Nov. 1971," Vertical File, Biography—John Brown, Hudson Library & Historical Society.

27. Many of the details about John Brown's failed business ventures of this period come from Oswald Garrison Villard, *John Brown 1800–1859*, 26–33.

28. Quoted in Sanborn, *The Life and Letters of John Brown*, 88.

29. When John Brown was in Kansas in 1857, W. A. Phillips, an antislavery journalist for the *Tribune* who conducted three interviews with John Brown, encouraged him to establish a pioneer city, another speculation scheme. Phillips reported in his second interview, "I could perceive that it did not at all harmonize with the views and purposes of Captain Brown, and I suspected that a location one hundred and eighty miles from the Missouri border was in his opinion rather remote from the scene of operations" ("Three Interviews with Old John Brown," *Atlantic Monthly*, December 1879, https://www.theatlantic.com/magazine/archive/1879/12/three-interviews-old-john-brown/589084/).

30. "Former Land Surveyor Hanged at Charlestown, Virginia—December 2, 1859," *The Empire State Surveyor* 5.2 (March, April, 1969): 3–5, Brown-Gee, Series I, Box #1, Folder #34, Hudson Library & Historical Society; Oswald Garrison Villard, *John Brown 1800–1859*, 31–33.

31. Interview by Katherine Mayo with Henry Myers and Daniel W. Myers, Ohio Interviews.

32. Quoted in Oswald Garrison Villard, *John Brown 1800–1859*, 40–41.

33. Izant, *Hudson's Heritage*, 116.

34. Karl H. Grismer, *Akron and Summit County* (Akron, OH: Summit County Historical Society, 1952), 58.

35. Grace Goulder, *Ohio Scenes and Citizens* (Cleveland: World Publishing Company, 1964), 197.

36. John Brown, "Remedy for Bots or Grubs, in the Heads of Sheep—Remarks on the Fine Sheep of Ohio and Other States," *Ohio Cultivator*, April 15, 1846, *"His Soul Goes Marching On": The Life and Legacy of John Brown*, West Virginia Archives & History, http://archive.wvculture.org/history/jbexhibit/ohiocultivator.html.

37. Quoted in James Redpath, *The Public Life of Capt. John Brown* (1860; repr., Nabu Public Domain, 2010), 57.

38. Oswald Garrison Villard, *John Brown 1800–1859*, 27.
39. Samuel A. Lane, *Fifty Years and Over of Akron and Summit County* (Akron, OH: Beacon Job Department, 1892), 840.
40. Brown and Oviatt Agreement (handwritten), January 2, 1842, Boyd B. Stutler Collection, Ms78-1, *"His Soul Goes Marching On": The Life and Legacy of John Brown*, West Virginia Archives & History, http://archive.wvculture.org/history/jbexhibit/bbsmso1-0012.html.

LOSING ALMOST EVERYTHING IN RICHFIELD, OHIO

1. John Brown Bankruptcy Inventory (handwritten), 1842, Boyd B. Stutler Collection, Ms78-1, *"His Soul Goes Marching On": The Life and Legacy of John Brown*, West Virginia Archives & History, http://archive.wvculture.org/history/jbexhibit/bbsms03-0006.html.
2. John Brown, "To George Kellogg, Esq., Richfield, Summit County, Ohio, Oct. 17, 1842," in Ruchames, *A John Brown Reader*, 49.
3. John Brown, "John Brown's Wills," Appendix F, in Oswald Garrison Villard, *John Brown 1800–1859*, 668.
4. Information about the fate of the Bibles comes from a note Clarence S. Gee appended to a letter he transcribed—Mary A. Brown, "To My Dear Friend Mrs. Stearns, North Elba, N.Y., Aug 4th, 1863," Brown-Gee, Series III, Box #2, Folder #3, Hudson Library & Historical Society.
5. Ann Duke describes John Brown's houses in Richfield in "The Underground Railroad's Tale of Deliverance Has Roots in Richfield," *The Richfield Times Magazine*, March 2013, 5.
6. "Old Buss Company Store," Vertical File, Historic Houses, Hudson Library & Historical Society.
7. John Buss, *John Buss Diaries*, John Buss Manuscript Collection, John Buss Papers, Hudson Library & Historical Society. George Leander Starr, another Hudson resident, kept a diary from the time he was a teen in the 1840s to 1920, (Diary [by year], Starr Manuscript Collection, Starr Family Papers, Starr Diaries, Hudson Library & Historical Society).
8. The actual gravestones were erected by John Brown Jr. at the close of the Civil War (Ernest C. Miller, *John Brown, Pennsylvania Citizen: The Story of John Brown's Ten Years in Northwestern Pennsylvania* [Warren: Penn State Press, 1952], 14).
9. Miller, *John Brown, Pennsylvania Citizen*.
10. Benjamin Quarles, *Allies for Freedom* (1974; repr., *Allies for Freedom & Blacks on John Brown*, Boston: DaCapo Press, 2001), 185.
11. Eunice Merton, "Friends Share John Brown's Grief," Between Nursery Rows, *The Gristmill*, ca. 1947, http://www.friendsofcrowellhilaka.org/john-browns-grief.html.
12. John Brown, "To Dear Son [John Jr.], Richfield, 25th Sept 1843," in Ruchames, *A John Brown Reader*, 50–51.
13. Izant, *Hudson's Heritage*, 135.
14. Merton, "Friends Share John Brown's Grief."
15. Merton, "Friends Share John Brown's Grief."
16. John Brown, "To Dear Son [John Jr.], Richfield, 25th Sept 1843," 50–51.
17. Merton, "Friends Share John Brown's Grief"; another column by Eunice Merton recounts the effort of Mason Oviatt to help five fugitives reach Oberlin in a false-bottomed hay wagon owned by Heman Oviatt ("Road to Freedom," Between Nursery Rows, *The Gristmill*, February 7, 1947, http://www.friendsofcrowellhilaka.org/road-to-freedom.html).
18. Additional acreage was donated by the Farnum, Brush, and Dick families. The most recent gift came from the East Ohio Gas Company—.078 acres in 1948 ("Richfield History," Richfield Historical Society, http://www.richfieldohiohistoricalsociety.org/richfield-history.html).
19. "Through all the dreary night of death / In peaceful slumbers may you rest, / And when eternal day shall dawn / And shades and death have past and gone, / O may you then with glad surprise / In God's own image wake and rise" ("Childhood and Early Adult Years," Boyd B. Stutler Collection, *"His Soul Goes Marching On": The Life and Legacy of John Brown*, West Virginia Archives & History, http://archive.wvculture.org/history/jbexhibit/jbchapter1.html).
20. John Brown, "To Dear Son [John Jr.], Richfield, 25th Sept 1843," 50–51.

21. John Whedon mentioned this to Katherine Mayo during his Ohio interview (Ohio Interviews).

REVERIE 2

1. James Redpath, in *The Public Life of Capt. John Brown* (377–78), includes several unpublished paragraphs from Rebecca Buffum Spring's November 1859 interview with John Brown.

MOTHERS AND SONS

1. The seminary was moved from its original location on North Main Street to its current location on Baldwin in 1858 (Joan Maher, "Emily Metcalf's Seminary," lecture, Hudson Heritage Association, Barlow Community Center, Hudson, OH, February 12, 2015).

2. In addition to Salmon Brown, who died in 1796 before the Browns left for Ohio, Owen and Ruth Mills Brown had an unnamed son who died at birth in the same year Salmon did ("Family of Owen Brown," Hudson Library & Historical Society, https://www.hudsonlibrary.org/historical-society/family-of-owen-brown/).

3. Edwin W. Mills, "To Miss [Ada M.] Remington, June 7, 1933," Brown-Adair, in process, Hudson Library & Historical Society.

4. John Brown, "To My Dear Friend [Rev. Luther Humphrey], Charlestown, Jefferson Co. Va., 19th Nov. 1859," in Ruchames, *A John Brown Reader*, 139–40.

5. Metcalf, "Woman's Work," 21.

6. Metcalf, "Woman's Work," 21.

7. For an interpretation of this drawing as a rendition of the story of Elisha and the Shunammite woman, see Christopher Heppner, "The Chamber of Prophecy: Blake's 'A Vision' (Butlin #756) Interpreted," *Blake/An Illustrated Quarterly* 25.3 (Winter 1991/1992), http://bq.blakearchive.org/25.3.heppner.

8. *Holy Bible*, Authorized or King James Version (Philadelphia: The John C. Winston Company, n.d), 360.

9. *Holy Bible*, 360.

10. Metcalf, "Woman's Work," 21.

11. Owen Brown, *Owen Brown's Autobiography*, 3.

12. Owen Brown, *Owen Brown's Autobiography*, 7.

13. John Brown, "To Mr. Henry L. Stearns, Red Rock, Iowa, 15th July 1857," 38.

14. According to Rebecca Buffum Spring, John Brown told her the story of sleeping with cows in a graveyard during her interview with him in his jail cell ("How I Brought First Aid to Wounded John Brown [Harper's Ferry 1859]," *The New York Press*, October 13, 1907).

15. John Brown, "To Mr. Henry L. Stearns, Red Rock, Iowa, 15th July 1857," 38.

16. America's enslaved provided not only the labor force for the South's economy, but its "capital stock" (Ned and Constance Sublette, *The American Slave Coast: A History of the Slave-Breeding Industry* [Chicago: Lawrence Hill Books, 2016], 38–39, 44).

17. Edward E. Baptist, *The Half Has Never Been Told: Slavery and the Making of American Capitalism* (New York: Basic, 2014), xxii.

18. John Brown, "To Mr. Henry L. Stearns, Red Rock, Iowa, 15th July 1857," 38.

19. James Moore, "Darwin the Abolitionist," week of February 6, 2009, interview by Bruce Gellerman, *Living on Earth*, http://www.loe.org/shows/segments.html?programID=09-P13-00006&segmentID=4.

20. See David S. Reynolds, *Mightier Than the Sword: Uncle Tom's Cabin and the Battle for America* (New York: Norton, 2011).

21. Emily Dickinson, "The Props assist the House," *The Poems of Emily Dickinson*, ed. R. W. Franklin (Cambridge, MA: Belknap Press of Harvard University, 1999), 325–26.

22. John Brown, "To My Dearly Beloved Wife, Sons: & Daughters, *Every One*, Charlestown, Prison, Jefferson Co. Va., 30th Nov 1859," in Ruchames, *A John Brown Reader*, 156–58.

23. John Brown, "To My Dear Mrs. Spring, Charlestown, Jefferson County, Va., Nov. 24, 1859," in Ruchames, *A John Brown Reader*, 146–48.

24. Two hundred and seventy free Blacks were residents of Springfield proper, and one hundred and

thirty lived other places in Hampden County (Reynolds, *John Brown, Abolitionist*, 103).

25. Reynolds, *John Brown, Abolitionist*, 106–07.

FATHERS AND SONS

1. The account of this child's birth, illness, and death are recorded in two letters from John Brown: "To Dear Children, Akron, Ohio, May 14, 1852" and "To Dear Son John, Akron, Ohio, July 20, 1852," on pages 149–50 of Sanborn, *The Life and Letters of John Brown*.
2. "Children of John Brown of Harper's Ferry," Hudson Library & Historical Society, https://www.hudsonlibrary.org/historical-society/children-of-john-brown/.
3. Owen Brown, *Owen Brown's Autobiography*, 6–8.
4. Waite, "Sources of the Present Names of Streets in Hudson," Frederick Waite Manuscript Collection, in process, Hudson Library & Historical Society, 5.
5. Waite, "Sources of the Present Names of Streets in Hudson," 5.
6. "Want Street Named for Owen Brown," *North Summit Times*, April 6, 1951, Hudson Library & Historical Society.
7. Waite, *Western Reserve University*, 27, 44.
8. Storrs had gone to Tallmadge, Ohio, in rainy weather to preach for three hours about the need for abolitionism, and the excursion weakened his already weak lungs, leading to his death from a pulmonary hemorrhage a few months later.
9. Elizur Wright proceeded to send his articles to *The Liberator* in Boston, a decision that brought him national attention.
10. The crisis over slavery at the college is discussed in detail by Waite in "Slavery: The Crisis of 1833," a section of his book *Western Reserve University* (94–111).
11. Philip Green Wright and Elizabeth Q. Wright, *Elizur Wright: The Father of Life Insurance* (Chicago: University of Chicago Press, 1937), 60.
12. Beriah Green, *Four Sermons Preached in the Chapel of the Western Reserve College: On Lord's Days, November 18th and 25th, and December 2nd and 9th, 1832,* Books on Demand from Miscellaneous Pamphlet Collection (Library of Congress).
13. Louis A. DeCaro Jr., *"Fire From the Midst of You"* (New York: New York University Press, 2002), 110–11.
14. Owen Brown, "To Rev. S. L. Adair and Family, Hudson, Sept 6th, 1842," Brown-Adair, Box #1, Folder Brown Letters 1835–1855, Hudson Library & Historical Society. The clarification in parentheses is the transcriber's.
15. *Records of the Free Congregational Church of Hudson, Organized October 7th A.D. 1842*, Hudson Congregational Church Manuscript Collection, Hudson Library & Historical Society. For a summary of the seven years the Free Church existed (1842–49), see DeCaro, *"Fire from the Midst of You,"* 185.
16. *Records of the Free Congregational Church of Hudson, Organized October 7th A.D. 1842.*
17. Case, *Hudson of Long Ago*, 49–50.
18. Charles Storrs Adair, according to Tom Vince (cc of email to Tracy Schooner, April 5, 2016), was named for Charles B. Storrs, the first President of Western Reserve College (1830–1833).
19. Owen Brown, "To Dear Gran Son Charles Adair, Hudson, Ohio, Feb. 23, 1856," Brown-Adair, in process, Hudson Library & Historical Society.
20. Quoted in Robert S. Fletcher, "John Brown and Oberlin," *Oberlin Alumni Magazine*, February 1932, 135.
21. Owen Brown, *Owen Brown's Autobiography*, 1.
22. Owen Brown, "To Rev. S. L. Adair and Family, Hudson, Sept 6th, 1842."
23. Ulysses S. Grant, *Personal Memoirs of U. S. Grant*, Vol. 1 (New York: Charles L. Webster & Co., 1885), 20; also see Ron Chernow's *Grant* (New York: Penguin Press, 2017) for information about Jesse Grant's decision to leave his half-brother's tannery in Maysville, Kentucky, after his apprenticeship because the region depended on slave labor (5).
24. Robert E. McGlone, *John Brown's War Against Slavery* (Cambridge: Cambridge University Press,

2009), 114–42, as well as Part III of the book, "Jeremiads" (145–200). See, also, McGlone's essay "John Brown, Henry Wise, and the Politics of Insanity," in *His Soul Goes Marching On: Responses to John Brown and the Harpers Ferry Raid*, ed. Paul Finkelman (Charlottesville: University Press of Virginia, 1995), 213–52.

25. John T. Hubbell, "John Brown," *Timeline Forum* (Ohio Historical Society) 9.2 (February–March 1992): 20–33. In DeCaro's book "*Fire from the Midst of You*," he titled his chapter about Pottawatomie "Pottawatomie and the Fatherless," and paired the worsening of conditions in Kansas in the spring of 1856 with the worsening of Owen's health—and eventual death. He paid attention to the possibility that learning of his father's death shortly before the attack might have added an element of desperation to John Brown's assault (223–36).

26. In his biography *John Brown and the Legend of Fifty-Six*, Malin noted that early biographers failed to include the Pottawatomie episode in their accounts—Redpath and Hinton, as well as Sanborn, for a while—and implied that, among other possibilities, they "had come to believe in their own romancing" (Philadelphia: The American Philosophical Society, 1942), 404, https://hdl.handle.net/2027/mdp.39015013278620?urlappend=%3Bseq=426.

27. John Brown, "To Dear Father, Browns Station Kansas, T, 26th March, 1856," *John Brown Letters*.

28. John Brown, "To Dear Father, Springfield, Mass, 10th Jany 1849," in Ruchames, *A John Brown Reader*, 67.

29. Jason Brown also received money from Owen Brown, his grandfather, while he was in Kansas. He wrote to thank him for his generosity in January of 1856 ("To Dear Grandfather [Owen Brown], Osawatomie K. T., Jan 23rd, 1856," Brown-Adair, in process, Hudson Library & Historical Society).

30. Reynolds, *John Brown, Abolitionist*, 132–33.

31. Jason wrote to Owen Brown, his grandfather, about his son's death with striking openness and sadness ("To Dear Grandfather, Osawatomie K.T., June 14th, 1855," Brown-Adair, in process, Hudson Library & Historical Society).

32. John Brown, "To Dear Father, Brownsville Kansas Territory, 19th Oct 1855," in Ruchames, *A John Brown Reader*, 87–88.

33. John Brown, "To Dear Father, Randolph Pa., August 11th, 1832," in Ruchames, *A John Brown Reader*, 41–42.

34. John Brown, "To My Dear Wife and Children, New Hartford, 12th June 1839," in Ruchames, *A John Brown Reader*, 44–45.

A WAREHOUSE AND A STOREFRONT CHURCH IN SPRINGFIELD, MASSACHUSETTS

1. History Committee of St. John's Congregational Church, *The History of St. John's Congregational Church, 1844–1962* (Springfield, MA: St. John's Congregational Church, 1962), 17. Another recollection of the office John Brown rented in John L. King's old warehouse was provided by E. C. Leonard, who occupied an office in the same block (quoted in Sanborn, *The Life and Letters of John Brown*, 64–65).

2. Reynolds, *John Brown, Abolitionist*, 82.

3. John Brown, "To Dear Wife, Springfield, Mass., 28th Nov. 1850," in Ruchames, *A John Brown Reader*, 71–72.

4. Jean Libby includes a picture of this Augustus Washington daguerreotype in her *John Brown Photo Chronology: Catalog of the Exhibition at Harpers Ferry 2009*, as well as her Supplement.

5. History Committee, *The History of St. John's Congregational Church*, 18.

6. Reynolds, *John Brown, Abolitionist*, 88.

7. Spring, "How I Brought First Aid to Wounded John Brown [Harper's Ferry 1859]"; Katherine Mayo, "Brown in Hiding and in Jail," 236.

8. John Brown, "Words of Advice," adopted Jan. 15, 1851, in Ruchames, *A John Brown Reader*, 76–78.

9. John Brown, "To Dear Wife, Springfield, Mass., Jan. 17, 1851," in Ruchames, *A John Brown Reader*, 75.

10. History Committee, *The History of St. John's Congregational Church*, 17–20.

11. St. John's Congregational Church website, http://sjkb.org/discover_stjohns/history.html.

12. History Committee, *The History of St. John's Congregational Church*, 39.

13. "John Brown's Wills," 668.

14. *The History of St. John's Congregational Church* says this about the window: "John Brown is not forgotten in Springfield nor will he be by the members of St. John's Church who are reminded of him by the beautiful stained-glass window in the rear of the sanctuary given in his honor" (22).

THE JOHN BROWN MONUMENT BEHIND THE AKRON ZOO

1. Katie Byard, "Public Can View Brown Memorial," *Akron Beacon Journal*, July 2, 2009.

2. Reynolds talks about the song being part of America's improvisational tradition and traces its history (*John Brown, Abolitionist*, 465–70).

3. Grismer, *Akron and Summit County*, 287.

4. Margaret Washington, *Sojourner Truth's America* (Urbana: University of Illinois Press, 2009), 222–29.

5. Mark J. Price, "Attorney Decried Bigotry in Akron," *Akron Beacon Journal*, February 24, 2014.

6. Also, in Franklin Mills bells tolled from one to two p.m., and a "great indignation meeting" was held in Ravenna, attended, Karl H. Grismer said, "by scores of persons from Franklin Township" (Grismer, *The History of Kent: Historical and Biographical*, revised edition [1932; repr., Kent, OH: Kent Historical Society, 2001], 35–36).

7. David Lieberth, email to Joyce Dyer, August 30, 2010.

8. Jim Carney, "John Brown Monument Is Out of Public View, but Never Out of Public Controversy," *Akron Beacon Journal*, December 31, 2011.

9. Peter T. Nesbett, *Jacob Lawrence: The Complete Prints (1963–2000)* (Seattle: University of Washington Press, 2001), 38–40.

REVERIE 4

1. John Brown, "To Dear Brother [Frederick], Randolph, Nov. 21, 1834," in Ruchames, *A John Brown Reader*, 42–43.

2. Oswald Garrison Villard, *John Brown 1800–1859*, 333.

3. See Melville's poem "The Portent," Louisa May Alcott's "With a Rose," William Dean Howells' "Old Brown," and John G. Whittier's "Brown of Osawatomie," all available in Ruchames, *A John Brown Reader*, 285, 271–72, 266–68, 295–96.

4. Muriel Rukeyser, *The Life of Poetry*, foreword by Jane Cooper (1949; repr., Ashfield, MA: Paris Press, 1996), 29–37.

5. Michael Gold, *Life of John Brown* (Girard, KS: Haldeman-Julius Company, 1924), 3, 39.

6. Merrill D. Peterson, *John Brown: The Legend Revisited* (Charlottesville: University of Virginia Press, 2002), 111, 153.

7. John Stauffer and Zoe Trodd, "Introduction: The Meaning and Significance of John Brown," in *The Tribunal: Responses to John Brown and the Harpers Ferry Raid*, eds. John Stauffer and Zoe Trodd (Cambridge, MA: Belknap Press of Harvard University Press, 2012), xlix.

THE ENGINE HOUSE AT HARPERS FERRY

1. Osborne P. Anderson, *A Voice from Harper's Ferry: A Narrative of Events at Harper's Ferry; with Incidents Prior and Subsequent to Its Capture by Captain Brown and His Men* (Boston: Printed for the Author, 1861), https://hdl.handle.net/2027/loc.ark:/13960/t42r3xn6t?urlappend=%3Bseq=20.

2. The final version of the Constitution was taken to printer William Howard Day in St. Catharine's, Canada West, where Day spent sixteen days secretly setting its fifteen pages, hand-stitching it, and being sure to omit a title page which could identify him or his press or the authors of the document (Morris, *Oberlin, Hotbed of Abolitionism*, 225).

3. Especially helpful for this summary have been Oates, *To Purge This Land*, 274–84; McGlone, *John Brown's War Against Slavery*, 312–18; and Reynolds, *John Brown, Abolitionist*, 239–41 and 95–137.

4. Quarles, *Allies*, 94.

5. Quarles, *Allies*, 102.

6. Quarles, *Allies*, 100–1.

7. Oswald Garrison Villard, *John Brown 1800–1859*, 496.

8. Hannah Geffert, "They Heard His Call: The Local Black Community's Involvement in the Raid on Harpers Ferry," in *Terrible Swift Sword: The Legacy of John Brown*, ed. Peggy A. Russo and Paul Finkelman (Athens: Ohio University Press, 2005), 33.

9. "HHA Meeting Explores Link Between Ellsworth, 1893 World's Fair," *Hudson Hub-Times*, March 26, 2017; Erik Larson, *The Devil in the White City* (New York: Crown, 2003), 48–52, 377.

10. Paul A. Shackel, "John Brown's Fort: A Contested National Symbol," in Russo and Finkelman, *Terrible Swift Sword*, 179–84.

11. Details about the second annual meeting of the Niagara Movement at Harpers Ferry are found in "John Brown's Day," the opening chapter of Quarles' book *Allies*, 3–14.

12. Quoted in Quarles, *Allies*, 7.

13. W. E. B. Du Bois, "The Niagara Movement's Address to the Country by W. E. B. Du Bois, 1906," *New York Times*, August 20, 1906, http://college.cengage.com/history/ayers_primary_sources/niagaramovement_address_1906.htm.

14. David Roediger, introduction to *John Brown*, by W. E. B. Du Bois (1909; repr., New York: Modern Library, 2001), xi.

15. Henry Louis Gates Jr., "The Black Letters on the Sign: W. E. B. Du Bois and the Canon," in *Black Folk Then and Now*, The Oxford W. E. B. Du Bois, ed. Henry Louis Gates Jr. (New York: Oxford University Press, 2007), n.p., https://books.google.com/books?id=23TiAgAAQBAJ.

16. Shackel, "John Brown's Fort: A Contested National Symbol," 187. Much of the history of the fort comes from Shackel's article, as well as remarks by Quarles in *Allies*.

17. In Quarles, *Allies*, 181–82.

18. In Quarles, *Allies*, 182–83.

19. Mary Johnson, "An 'Ever Present Bone of Contention': The Heyward Shepherd Memorial," *West Virginia History* 56 (1997): 1–26, http://archive.wvculture.org/history/journal_wvh/wvh56-1.html.

20. Quarles, *Allies*, 183.

21. "Monument to Heyward Shepherd," *Stone Sentinels*, http://www.stonesentinels.com/Harpers_Ferry/Heyward_Shepherd.php.

22. Edward T. Linenthal, "Healing and History: The Dilemmas of Interpretation," in *Rally on the High Ground: The National Park Service Symposium on the Civil War*, ed. Robert K. Sutton, http://www.nps.gov/parkhistory/online_books/rthg/chap3b.htm.

23. Greg Tasker, "Tribute to Victim of Brown's Raid Still Controversial," *Baltimore Sun*, September 3, 1995, https://www.baltimoresun.com/news/bs-xpm-1995-09-03-1995246078-story.html.

24. "Harpers Ferry History Marker," *Stone Sentinels*, http://www.stonesentinels.com/Harpers_Ferry/Harpers_Ferry_History.php.

25. Don Aines, "Plaque Honoring Brown Is Dedicated," Hagerstown *Herald-Mail*, July 15, 2006.

26. Brian Witte, "NAACP to Honor Abolitionist John Brown," Fox News, Associated Press, Baltimore, July 14, 2006, http://www.foxnews.com/printer_friendly_wires/2006Jul14/0,4675,AbolitionistHonored,00.html.

FREDERICK DOUGLASS AND JOHN BROWN

1. Lerone Bennett, "Tea and Sympathy: Liberals and Other White Hopes" (extract), in *Blacks on John Brown*, 140.

2. Ezra Greenspan, *William Wells Brown: An African American Life* (New York: W.W. Norton, 2014), 491.

3. William Wells Brown, "John Brown and the Fugitive Slave Law," in *William Wells Brown: Clotel & Other Writings*, ed. Ezra Greenspan (New York: Library of America, 2014), 917–18.

4. Nell Irvin Painter, "Truth Be Told," review of *William Wells Brown: An African American Life*, by Ezra Greenspan, *New York Times Book Review*, November 16, 2014, 14.

5. William Wells Brown, "John Brown and the Fugitive Slave Law" (917–22) contains John Brown's

"Words of Advice," but was not published by William Wells Brown until March 10, 1870, in *The New York Independent*.

6. Frederick Douglass, "John Brown: An Address by Frederick Douglass at the Fourteenth Anniversary of Storer College," Harper's Ferry, West Virginia, May 30, 1881 (Dover, NH: Morning Star Job Printing House, 1881), 9, https://archive.org/details/johnbrownaddress00doug.

7. Frederick Douglass, "Letter from Frederick Douglass to Harriet Tubman, 1868," Harriet Tubman Historical Society, http://www.harriet-tubman.org/letter-from-frederick-douglass/.

8. Douglass, "To William Cooper Nell, Lynn, Mass, February 5, 1848," 3.

9. Lerone Bennett, "Tea and Sympathy: Liberals and Other White Hopes," 139–40.

10. James McBride, *The Good Lord Bird* (New York: Riverhead, 2013).

11. Ira Berlin, *The Long Emancipation: The Demise of Slavery in the United States* (Cambridge, MA: Harvard University Press, 2015), 8.

12. Freedmen and Southern Society Project (http://www.freedmen.umd.edu/), Freedom on the Move Project, and other organizations work to these ends.

13. Hannah Geffert (with Jean Libby), "Regional Black Involvement in John Brown's Raid on Harpers Ferry," in *Prophets of Protest: Reconsidering the History of American Abolitionism*, eds. Timothy Patrick McCarthy and John Stauffer (New York: New Press, 2006), 165–79.

14. Fred Landon, "Canadian Negroes and the John Brown Raid," *The Journal of Negro History* (April 1, 1921): 174–82, https://archive.org/details/jstor-2713730.

15. Du Bois, *John Brown*, 210–14. See also Geffert, "They Heard His Call," 35–36.

16. See Virginia Ott Stake, *John Brown in Chambersburg* (Chambersburg, PA: Franklin County Heritage, 1977).

17. Douglass, *Life and Times of Frederick Douglass*, 758–60.

18. Frederick Douglass, "To the Editor, *Rochester Democrat and American*, October 31, 1859," in *Life and Times of Frederick Douglass*, 751–53.

19. Annie Brown Adams, John E. Cook, and Jeremiah G. Anderson all believed that Douglass had pledged to join the group. Louis A. DeCaro Jr. talked about the curious absence of personal letters between Douglass and any member of the Brown family after 1859. "Such historical silence may be very significant indeed," he said ("John Brown: The Empty Coffin and Philadelphia," presentation at the Historical Society of Pennsylvania, Philadelphia, PA, December 2, 2009, 9).

20. McBride, *The Good Lord Bird*, 328–32.

21. David Blight, *Frederick Douglass: Prophet of Freedom* (New York: Simon and Schuster, 2018), 295.

22. DeCaro, "John Brown: The Empty Coffin," 9.

23. Blight, *Frederick Douglass: Prophet of Freedom*, 309.

24. Du Bois, *John Brown*, 205–6.

25. Jeanette E. Sherbondy's essay "Sherbondy Hill of Akron, Ohio" is about a section of Akron still named for the Sherbondy family (July 2007, http://sherbondy.org/Sherbondy%20Hill%20pdf.pdf).

26. Warren Lyons, email to Joyce Dyer, October 26, 2015.

27. Lyons, email to Joyce Dyer, November 9, 2015.

28. McBride also said, "I had some fun with Frederick Douglass' character... You know, serious students of African American history might not be pleased" (NPR Staff, "'Good Lord Bird' Gives Abolitionist Heroes Novel Treatment," August 17, 2013, http://www.npr.org/2013/08/17/212588754/good-lord-bird-gives-abolitionist-heroes-novel-treatment).

REVERIE 5

1. Lyons, email to Joyce Dyer, March 12, 2017.

2. Lyons, email to Joyce Dyer, October 9, 2015.

3. Lyons, email to Joyce Dyer, February 21, 2017.

4. Lyons, email to Joyce Dyer, March 12, 2017.

5. Paul Finkelman, "A Look Back at John Brown," *Prologue Magazine*, Spring 2011, National Archives, https://www.archives.gov/publications/prologue/2011/spring/brown.html.

NORTH ELBA AND TIMBUCTO

1. See DeCaro for an excellent timeline of John Brown's movement during the Springfield and North Elba years (*"Fire from the Midst of You,"* 136–215).

2. Oswald Garrison Villard, *John Brown 1800–1859*, 83–88.

3. John Brown, "To Dear Wife, Springfield, Mass., 28th Nov. 1850," 71–72; "To Dear Wife, Albany, New York, 31st Dec. 1850," *John Brown Letters*.

4. Oswald Garrison Villard, *John Brown 1800–1859*, 73.

5. John Brown, "To Dear Father, Springfield, Mass, 10th Jany 1849," 67.

6. In a letter to two of Mary Ann Brown's daughters, Thomas Wentworth Higginson tried to assure them that their mother was safe in his company. In passing, he told them, "One thing we have ascertained: *the prison is not hard to get out of.* But Captain John Brown doesn't wish to come out, at present, and sends the most earnest messages begging us not to attempt it" ("To Dear friends [Annie and Sarah Brown], Worcester, Nov. 4, 1859," Brown-Adair, in process, Hudson Library & Historical Society).

7. Thomas Wentworth Higginson, "A Visit to John Brown's Household in 1859," in *Contemporaries* (1900; repr., Upper Saddle River, NJ: Literature House, 1970), 220.

8. A detailed study of the history of this stone is provided by Clarence S. Gee in his article "The Stone on John Brown's Grave," *New York History*, April 1961.

9. Reynolds, *John Brown, Abolitionist*, 20; Quarles, *Allies*, 191.

10. "John Brown Farm Cemetery," *Northern New York Tombstone Transcription Project*, https://www.nnytombstoneproject.net/essex/north_elba/john_brown.htm.

11. Clarence S. Gee, "Watson Brown, 1835–1859," Brown-Gee, Series III, Box #1, Folder #11, Hudson Library & Historical Society.

12. Quoted in Oswald Garrison Villard, *John Brown 1800–1859*, 553.

13. A "John Anderson," identified as "Negro," is also in this list on the stone.

14. J. Max Barber, Address by J. Max Barber, May 9, 1935 (Lake Placid, New York), in *Blacks on John Brown*, 109–15.

15. The intentions of Lyman Epps Sr. (who died in 1897) to accompany John Brown to Harpers Ferry are discussed by his son (and namesake) in "Lyman Epps, 79, Recalls Day His Father Promised to Join John Brown Raid," *Saranac Lake Enterprise*, March 4, 1933, Brown-Gee, Series III, Box #4, Folder #8, Hudson Library & Historical Society.

16. For the history of the John Brown Memorial Association see Edwin N. Cotter Jr., "The John Brown Memorial Association and the John Brown Farm," *John Brown the Abolitionist—a Biographer's Blog*, August 26, 2010, http://abolitionist-john-brown.blogspot.com/2010/08/john-brown-memorial-association-and.html.

17. John Brown, "To Dear Brother [Frederick], Randolph, Nov. 21, 1834," 42–43.

18. *Copperhead Voters List of 1863*, Newspaper Collection, Miscellaneous Loose Editions, Hudson Library & Historical Society.

19. Buss, *John Buss Diaries*, December 4, 1859.

20. Thomas Drew, compiler, *The John Brown Invasion: An Authentic History of the Harper's Ferry Tragedy with Full Details of the Capture, Trial, and Execution of the Invaders, and of all the Incidents Connected Therewith* (Boston: James Campbell, 1860), 63, https://archive.org/details/johnbrowninvasioo0drew/page/62/mode/2up.

21. Drew, *The John Brown Invasion*, 79.

22. Details about the funeral trip are taken primarily from Joshua Young, "The Funeral of John Brown," *New England Magazine* (April 1904): 229–43, https://books.google.com/books?id=v69JAQAAMAAJ; Reynolds, *John Brown, Abolitionist*, 398–401; DeCaro, "John Brown: The Empty Coffin and Philadelphia"; and Oswald Garrison Villard, *John Brown 1800–1859*, 558–62.

23. One newspaper reported that the decoy coffin was actually taken to the Walnut Street wharf to make the crowd think it was the real coffin on the way to Manhattan (DeCaro, "John Brown: The Empty Coffin and Philadelphia," 10).

24. Joshua Young, "The Funeral of John Brown," 232.

25. J. M. Hopper, Bill of the Undertaker for the Body of John Brown (handwritten), December 5, 1859, Boyd B. Stutler Collection, *"His Soul Goes Marching On": The Life and Legacy of John Brown*, West Virginia Archives & History, http://archive.wvculture.org/history/jbexhibit/bbsms12-0054.html.

26. Quoted in Joshua Young, "The Funeral of John Brown," 234.

27. Joshua Young, "The Funeral of John Brown," 236.

28. Joshua Young, "The Funeral of John Brown," 237–38.

29. See the eulogy of Wendell Phillips, "Burial of John Brown," in *John Brown: The Making of a Revolutionary*, ed. Louis Ruchames (New York: Universal Library, 1969), 266–69.

30. Joshua Young, "The Funeral of John Brown," 240.

THE UNBURIED

1. Alice Keesey Mecoy, "Please Do Not Move Owen Brown's Gravesite," *John Brown the Abolitionist— a Biographer's Blog*, June 21, 2011, http://johnbrownkin.blogspot.com/2011/06/please-do-not-move-owen-browns.html?m=1.

2. Oswald Garrison Villard, *John Brown 1800–1859*, 558.

3. W. P. McGuire, Editorial on Winchester Medical College, *Virginia Medical Monthly*, 48.1 (April 1924): 45–47, Winchester Medical College Collection, 190 THL/WFCHS, Stewart Bell Jr. Archives, Handley Regional Library, Winchester, Virginia.

4. Abner H. Cook, "The Winchester Medical College, Winchester, Virginia, 1827–1862," *The Medical Pickwick* 4.1 (January 1918): 3–7, Winchester Medical College Collection, 190 THL/WFCHS, Stewart Bell Jr. Archives, Handley Regional Library, Winchester, Virginia.

5. Jerry W. Holsworth, *Civil War Winchester* (Charleston: The History Press, 2011), 21, 65.

6. A. Bentley Kinney, "A Skeleton's Revenge: The Burning of the Winchester Medical College," Winchester Medical College Collection, 190 THL/WFCHS, Stewart Bell Jr. Archives, Handley Regional Library, Winchester, Virginia.

7. Clarence S. Gee, note appended to a letter from Mary A. Brown, "To My Dear Friend Mrs. Stearns, North Elba, Mar 3, 1863," Brown-Gee, Series III, Box #2, Folder #3, Hudson Library & Historical Society.

8. J. J. Johnson, "To the Editor of the *Chicago Tribune*, Martinsville, Indiana, August 27, 1882," Brown-Gee, Series III, Box #1, Folder #11, Hudson Library & Historical Society.

9. Laughlin-Schultz, *The Tie That Bound Us*, 114–22.

10. John Brown, "To Dear Mary, Springfield, 29th Nov 1846," in Ruchames, *A John Brown Reader*, 57–58.

11. Mary A. Brown, "To Dear Salmon and Family, Put in Bay, Sept. 16th, 1882," Brown-Gee, Series III, Box #2, Folder #3, Hudson Library & Historical Society.

12. Quarles, *Allies*, 173.

13. Thomas Featherstonhaugh, "The Final Burial of the Followers of John Brown," *New England Magazine* (April 1901): 133.

14. Featherstonhaugh, "The Final Burial of the Followers of John Brown," 134.

15. Quoted in Quarles, *Allies*, 174.

16. Quarles, *Allies*, 173.

17. Quarles, *Allies*, 137.

18. Steven Lubet, *The "Colored Hero" of Harper's Ferry: John Anthony Copeland and the War Against Slavery* (New York: Cambridge University Press, 2015), 202.

19. McGuire, Editorial, 46–47.

20. Paul Finkelman, "Manufacturing Martyrdom: The Antislavery Response to John Brown's Raid," in Finkelman, *His Soul Goes Marching On*, 49.

21. Quarles, *Allies*, 138.

22. Quoted in Quarles, *Allies*, 139.

23. Quoted in Fletcher, "John Brown and Oberlin," 139.

24. Quarles, *Allies*, 137.

25. James Monroe, "A Journey to Virginia in December, 1859," a Thursday lecture by Prof. James Monroe (1897), Electronic Oberlin Group Documents, http://www.oberlin.edu/external/EOG/ HistoricalDocuments.html.

26. Monroe, "A Journey to Virginia in December, 1859."

27. Quarles, *Allies*, 142.

28. Quarles, *Allies*, 142.

29. Fletcher, "John Brown and Oberlin," 141.

30. Quarles, *Allies*, 149.

31. The bronze marker beside the cenotaph reads: "This marble cenotaph, erected by the citizens of Oberlin in 1860 in Westwood Cemetery, was moved to this site [Martin Luther King Memorial Park] by the Neighborhood Youth Corps. in 1971. The original inscription on the marble follows: 'These Colored Citizens of Oberlin, the Heroic Associates of the immortal John Brown, gave their lives for the slave. Et nunc servitudo etiam mortua est, laus Deo. S. Green, died at Charleston, Va., Dec. 16, 1859, age 23 years. J. A. Copeland, died at Charleston, Va., Dec. 16, 1859. L. S. Leary, died at Harper's Ferry, Va., Oct. 20, 1859, 24 years.'"

32. Mary Shelley, *Frankenstein; or, the Modern Prometheus* (1818; repr., London: William Pickering, 1996), 35.

33. Mark Twain, "Jim and the Dead Man," *New Yorker*, June 26, 1995. From first half of a handwritten manuscript of *The Adventures of Huckleberry Finn* found in an attic in 1990.

34. Tim Marshall, *Murdering to Dissect: Grave-robbing, Frankenstein and the Anatomy Literature* (Manchester, UK: Manchester University Press, 1995).

35. Robert J. Christie, *The Memoirs of Dr. Robert J. Christie*, Chapter V, http://flanaganfamily.net/genealo/memoirs.htm#chV.

NATIONAL GREAT BLACKS IN WAX MUSEUM

1. Solomon Northup, *Twelve Years a Slave* (Auburn, NY: Derby and Miller, 1853), Project Gutenberg 2014, http://www.gutenberg.org/files/45631/45631-h/45631-h.htm.

2. Marcus Rediker, *The Slave Ship: A Human History* (New York: Viking, 2007), 354.

3. Charles Johnson, *Middle Passage* (New York: Atheneum, 1990), 74.

4. Ta-Nehisi Coates, "The Case for Reparations," *Atlantic*, June 2014, https://www.theatlantic.com/magazine/archive/2014/06/the-case-for-reparations/361631/.

5. Ta-Nehisi Coates, "Notes from the Sixth Year," in *We Were Eight Years in Power: An American Tragedy* (New York: One World, 2017), 151–61.

6. Jean Toomer, *Cane* (New York: Liveright, 1923), Project Gutenberg 2019, http://www.gutenberg.org/files/60093/60093-h/60093-h.htm. The story of the Turners is in the "Kabnis" section of the novel.

7. A historical marker to the memory of "Mary Turner and the Lynching Rampage of 1918" was placed near the lynching site in South Georgia in May of 2010.

8. Sarah Kaplan, "For Charleston's Emanuel AME Church, Shooting Is Another Painful Chapter in Rich History," *The Washington Post*, June 18, 2015, http://www.washingtonpost.com/news/morning-mix/wp/2015/06/18/for-charlestons-emanuel-a-m-e-church-one-of-the-oldest-in-america-shooting-is-another-painful-chapter-in-long-history/.

9. Annie (Mrs. Annie Brown Adams), John Brown's daughter who stayed at the Kennedy Farmhouse for a while, said that her father's beard at the time of Harpers Ferry was short, "an inch or an inch and a half long" (quoted in Oswald Garrison Villard, *John Brown 1800–1859*, 419).

10. Libby, *John Brown Photo Chronology Supplement*, insert pages 54–55.

11. Joanne Martin, email to Joyce Dyer, March 21, 2013.

12. Martin, email to Joyce Dyer, April 15, 2015.

13. In addition to Freddie Gray, young Black men killed by police during the years of this project included, among others, Trayvon Martin in Florida; Eric Garner in New York; Michael Brown in Ferguson, Missouri; Tamir Rice (just twelve years old) in Cleveland; Walter Scott in North Charles-

ton; Alton Sterling in Baton Rouge; Philando Castile of Falcon Heights, Minnesota; and Terence Crutcher in Tulsa.

14. Ta-Nehisi Coates, *Between the World and Me* (New York: Spiegel and Grau, 2015), 7–17.

REVERIE 6

1. John Brown, "Brown's Interview with Mason, Vallandigham, and Others," 121.

2. Quarles, *Allies*, 179.

3. Peterson, *John Brown: The Legend Revisited*, 155.

4. Barack Obama, "Remarks by the President on the Economy in Osawatomie, Kansas," December 6, 2011, https://obamawhitehouse.archives.gov/the-press-office/2011/12/06/remarks-president-economy -osawatomie-kansas; see also a speech Obama referred to given by Theodore Roosevelt at Osawatomie in 1910, "New Nationalism Speech," August 31, 1910, TeachingAmericanHistory.org, http://teachingamericanhistory.org/library/document/new-nationalism-speech.

5. David Anderson, authority on the Western Reserve, believes that Garfield might have been staying at the time at a home built for Amos Sutton Hayden, the school's first principal, which was just a short walk from the "Garfield House," and also on Hinsdale Street. Or, he suggests, the Garfields might have been living with his wife's family in a large Hiram house razed in 1967 (David Anderson, email to Joyce Dyer, October 8, 2015).

6. David Anderson provided detail about the séance conducted in Bonney Castle (Facebook, March 4, 2017).

7. John Brown, "To Frederick Douglass, the Negro leader, Akron, O., Jan. 9, 1854," in Ruchames, *A John Brown Reader*, 84–85.

8. See, for example, John Brown, "John Brown to Joshua Giddings, July 04, 1848," Kansas State Historical Society, https://www.kshs.org/km/items/view/308358 and Joshua R. Giddings, "Joshua R. Giddings to John Brown, March 17, 1856," Kansas State Historical Society, http://www.kansas-memory.org/item/4258.

9. James Redpath, "James Redpath to Elias Nason, April 10, 1874," West Virginia Memory Project, John Brown/Boyd B. Stutler Collection, http://archive.wvculture.org/history/wvmemory/jbdetail. aspx?Type=Text&Id=1023.

10. James A. Garfield, *The Diary of James A. Garfield*, ed. with an introduction by Harry James Brown and Frederick D. Williams, Vol. I.: 1848–1871 (East Lansing: Michigan State University Press, 1967), 344–45. A note about the inscription in his pocket diary was added by the editors under this entry.

11. Eyal Naveh, "John Brown and the Legacy of Martyrdom," in Russo and Finkelman, *Terrible Swift Sword*, 89.

12. Oswald Garrison Villard, *John Brown 1800–1859*, 187–88.

DANGER FOR THE SECRET SIX

1. Morris, *Oberlin, Hotbed of Abolitionism*, 229–30.

2. Quoted in Reynolds, *John Brown, Abolitionist*, 341.

3. Edward J. Renehan Jr., *The Secret Six: The True Tale of the Men Who Conspired with John Brown* (Columbia : University of South Carolina Press, 1997), 224.

4. Reynolds, *John Brown, Abolitionist*, 341.

5. Elaine Showalter, *The Civil Wars of Julia Ward Howe* (New York: Simon & Schuster, 2016), 156–58.

6. Steven Lubet, *John Brown's Spy: The Adventurous Life and Tragic Confession of John E. Cook* (New Haven, CT: Yale University Press, 2012), 143–64, 252–56.

7. Lubet, *John Brown's Spy*, 251.

8. Brenda Wineapple, *White Heat: The Friendship of Emily Dickinson & Thomas Wentworth Higginson* (New York: Knopf, 2008), 92–93.

9. Thomas Wentworth Higginson, *Letters and Journals of Thomas Wentworth Higginson 1846–1906*, ed. Mary Potter Thacher Higginson (New York: Houghton Mifflin, 1921), 84–85, https://archive. org/details/lettersandjourno1higggoog.

DANGER FOR JOHN BROWN'S FAMILY

1. John Brown, "To My Dearly Beloved Wife, Sons: & Daughters, *Every One*, Charlestown, Prison, Jefferson Co. Va., 30th Nov. 1859," 156–58.

2. John Brown, "To My Dearly Beloved Sisters Mary A, & Martha, Charlestown, Jefferson Co. Va., 27th Nov. 1859. Sabbath," in Ruchames, *A John Brown Reader*, 152–53.

3. John Brown, "To Dear Children, All, Charlestown, Jefferson County, Va., Nov. 22, 1859," in Ruchames, *A John Brown Reader*, 142–43.

4. John Brown, "To Dear Children, Charlestown, Jefferson County, Va., Nov. 22, 1859," in Ruchames, *A John Brown Reader*, 143–44.

5. Laughlin-Schultz, *The Tie That Bound Us*, 137.

6. John Brown, "To My Dearly Beloved Wife, Sons: & Daughters, *Every One*, Charlestown, Prison, Jefferson Co. Va., 30th Nov. 1859," 156–58.

7. Salmon Brown, "My Father, John Brown, by Salmon Brown, the Only Survivor of Twenty Children," in Ruchames, *A John Brown Reader*, 189. When the article appeared in *Outlook* in 1913, three children of John Brown in addition to Salmon were still living—Annie, Sarah, and Ellen (Laughlin-Schultz, *The Tie That Bound Us*, 175).

8. Katherine Mayo interviewed Salmon Brown in 1909. At the time of the interview, Salmon and his wife were living with their daughter Agnes (Mrs. Evans) in a suburb of Portland, Oregon ("Sturdy Children of John Brown," *The New York Evening Post*, November 6, 1909, [Supplement], 3).

9. Clarence S. Gee, "Eulogy for Mrs. Lucy Brown Clark," February 26, 1934, Brown Family Reunion Papers, Box #1, Folder 1930–1935 (1934A), Hudson Library & Historical Society.

10. Laughlin-Schultz, *The Tie That Bound Us*, 137.

11. Oswald Garrison Villard, *John Brown 1800–1859*, 166–67, 193–97.

12. Ralph Keeler, "Owen Brown's Escape from Harper's Ferry," *Atlantic Monthly*, March 1874, 344, https://hdl.handle.net/2027/uc1.b000780624?urlappend=%3Bseq=354.

13. Keeler, "Owen Brown's Escape," 344–65.

14. Keeler, "Owen Brown's Escape," 365.

15. Lydia Jane Ryall, *Sketches and Stories of the Lake Erie Islands* (Norwalk, OH: American Publishers, 1913), 334.

16. Although Jason's reason for leaving Akron and his wife, Ellen, to live in California with Owen has never been fully discovered, letters in the private collection of F. G. Brown, provided by Marty Brown, direct descendant of Jason Brown, indicate that Jason returned to Akron in 1894, just prior to Ellen's death (John Brown Jr., "Dear Nephew [Charles P. Brown], Put-in-Bay, May 6, 1894"), but then relocated to Ben Lomond, California, for several years before coming back to Akron again, this time permanently, around 1908 (Jason Brown, "Dr. Soper, Akron, Ohio, Jan 2nd, 1896"; Jason Brown, "Dear Grandsons [Gerald & Jay Brown], Ben Lomond Cal, May 23, 1900"; Jason Brown, "Dear Jay, Ben Lomond Cal., June 19, 1900"; Jason Brown, "Dear Gerald, Ben Lomond Calif., April 30th, 1903").

17. Tom Chester provided the annotated obituary "Funeral of Owen Brown—The Last Survivor of John Brown's Historic Raid on Harpers Ferry, Va., in 1859," from the *Pasadena Standard*, January 12, 1889, http://tchester.org/sgm/msc/brown_funeral_notice.html.

18. Charles E. Frohman, *Put-in-Bay: Its History* (Columbus: Ohio Historical Society, 1971); Robert J. Dodge, *Isolated Splendor: Put-in-Bay and South Bass Island* (Hicksville, NY: Exposition Press, 1975).

19. John Brown Jr., "To Dear Friend [Frank B. Sanborn], Put-in-Bay, February 26, 1883," Brown-Gee, Series III, Box #4, Folder #12, Hudson Library & Historical Society.

20. Reynolds, *John Brown, Abolitionist*, 48.

21. Bonnie Laughlin-Schultz, "How John Brown Smashed the Whisky Barrel," *California History*, 92.3 (Fall 2015): 16.

22. Amy L. Newell, *The Caves of Put-in-Bay* (Columbus: Greyden Press, 1995), 30.

23. Nora Marks, reprinted 1889 interview, in Frohman, *Put-in-Bay: Its History*, 53.

24. For an account of a visit with Jay Cooke and Salmon Chase, see *The Journal of Jay Cooke* or *The Gibraltar Records, 1865-1905*, ed. James E. Pollard (Columbus: Ohio State University Press, 1935), 35, 120–22; details about his work surveying and mining for gold in the Black Hills can be found in Newell, *The Caves of Put-in-Bay*, 30, 36.

25. Newell, *The Caves of Put-in-Bay*, 32–36.

26. Interview with Rev. Mary L. Staley, priest-in-charge, St. Paul's Episcopal, Put-in-Bay, October 4, 2012.

27. Mary A. Brown, "To Mr. Sewall Dear Friend [Samuel E. Sewall], North Elba, Feb 13, 1861," Brown-Gee, Series III, Box #2, Folder #3, Hudson Library & Historical Society.

28. Mary A. Brown, "To Dear Son Owen, Decorah Iowa, Jan. 31st 1864," Brown-Gee, Series III, Box #2, Folder #3, Hudson Library & Historical Society.

29. Mary A. Brown, "To My Dear Friend Mrs. Stearns, North Elba, N.Y., Aug 4th, 1863."

30. Laughlin-Schultz, *The Tie That Bound Us*, 97.

31. Gee, "Watson Brown," Brown-Gee, Series II, Box #2, Folder #4, Hudson Library & Historical Society.

32. Mary A. Brown, "To Dear Friend [George L. Stearns], North Elba, Jan 7, 1860," Brown-Gee, Series III, Box #2, Folder #3, Hudson Library & Historical Society. A notation is provided that the letter is misdated by a month.

33. Tony Horwitz, *Midnight Rising: John Brown and the Raid That Sparked the Civil War* (New York: Henry Holt, 2011), 168.

34. Mary A. Brown, "To Dear Friend Mr. McKim, North Elba, Mar 6, 1860," Brown-Gee, Series III, Box #2, Folder #3, Hudson Library & Historical Society.

35. A note about the death of "Little Freddie" is typed on the back of a summary sheet about Watson Brown's life prepared by Gee ("Watson Brown"). It reads: "North Elba Cemetery / Gone Home / Frederick W. / Son of / W & I Brown / Died Aug. 1, 1863."

36. Mary A. Brown, "To Dear Friend [Mr. J. M. McKim], North Elba, Sept 2, 1863," Brown-Gee, Series III, Box #2, Folder #3, Hudson Library & Historical Society.

37. Daniel Rosenberg, *Mary Brown: From Harpers Ferry to California*, Occasional Papers Series Number Seventeen (New York: American Institute for Marxist Studies, 1975), 18, https://archive.org/details/MaryBrown/page/n11/mode/2up.

38. Laughlin-Schultz, *The Tie That Bound Us*, 94–96.

39. Everyone, except Bronson's daughter Louisa May Alcott, seemed happy about the daughters of John Brown staying in the Alcott home. Louisa made a notation in April of 1861 when the girls came to board, saying they "upset my plans of rest and writing when the report and the sewing were done. I had my fit of woe up garret" (*Louisa May Alcott: Her Life, Letters, and Journals*, ed. Ednah D. Cheney [Boston: Roberts Brothers, 1889], 127, University of North Carolina at Chapel Hill, https://archive.org/details/louisamayalcotthalco).

40. Damon G. Nalty, *The Browns of Madronia: Family of Abolitionist John Brown Buried in Madronia Cemetery Saratoga, California* (Saratoga, CA: Saratoga Historical Foundation, 1996), 32; April Hope Halberstadt, "Sarah Brown, Artist and Abolitionist," July 2006, Saratoga Historical Foundation, http://www.saratogahistory.com/History/sarah_brown.htm. During the time that Ellen (Brown) and James Fablinger were managing a farm in Saratoga, they became friends with neighbors named the Cunninghams. Florence Cunningham, the young daughter of Amanda and Ebenezer, grew up with the Fablinger children and became a passionate local historian. The Browns left many family relics with Florence Cunningham for safekeeping, including Sarah's paintings of her parents. When Florence Cunningham died in 1965, she left her entire estate, including all the items she'd safeguarded over the years, to create a museum.

41. Rosenberg, *Mary Brown*, 19.

42. Most of the detail about the adventures between Decorah, Iowa, and Red Bluff, California, comes from Rosenberg and Nalty.

43. "The Passing of Sarah Brown, Daughter of John Brown of Harper's Ferry: A Pioneer of Saratoga," *Saratoga Record* 3.22 (July 7, 1916): 1–2, Brown-Gee, Series II, Box #2, Folder #6, Hudson Library & Historical Society.

44. Nalty, *The Browns of Madronia*, 10.

45. George Hamlin Fitch, "The Santa Clara Valley and Santa Cruz Mountains," in *Picturesque California: The Rocky Mountains and the Pacific Slope; California, Oregon, Nevada, Washington, Alaska, Montana, Idaho, Arizona, Colorado, Utah, Wyoming, Etc.*, ed. John Muir (New York: J. Dewing, 1888), 250–51.

46. "John Brown's Widow: A Visit to Her Mountain Home," *San Francisco Sunday Chronicle*, April 10, 1881, Kent Historical Society.

47. Rosenberg, *Mary Brown*, 26.

48. Nalty, *The Browns of Madronia*, 7.

49. Rosenberg, *Mary Brown*, 28.

50. Mary A. Brown, "To Dear Brother [Jeremiah Root Brown], Rohnerville, Jan. 21st, 1873," Brown-Gee, Series III, Box #2, Folder #3, Hudson Library & Historical Society.

51. Laughlin-Schultz, *The Tie That Bound Us*, 107.

52. Rosenberg, *Mary Brown*, 28

53. James Townsley, "The Potawatomie Tragedy: John Brown's Connection with It, Statement of James Townsley, an Eye-Witness," Lawrence (Kansas) *Daily Journal* December 10, 1879, in Ruchames, *A John Brown Reader*, 197–203.

54. Halberstadt, "Sarah Brown, Artist and Abolitionist."

55. Laughlin-Schultz, *The Tie That Bound Us*, 114–33.

56. John Brown, "To Dear Wife and Children, Every One, Charlestown, Jefferson County, Va., Nov. 8, 1859," in Ruchames, *A John Brown Reader*, 132–33.

REVERIE 7

1. Helen Macdonald, *H Is for Hawk* (New York: Grove Press, 2014), 85.

2. William Shakespeare, "Sonnet 27," *The Arden Shakespeare Complete Works*, revised edition, ed. Richard Proudfoot, Ann Thompson, David Scott Kastan, and H. R. Woudhuysen (London: Arden Shakespeare, 2001), 22.

ACROSS ALL OF IOWA

1. William Blake, "The Tyger," in *Songs of Innocence and of Experience* (1794; repr., London: Oxford University Press, 1977).

2. William C. Cutler, *History of the State of Kansas* (Chicago: A. T. Andreas, 1883), 171, http://www.columbia.edu/cu/lweb/digital/collections/cul/texts/ldpd_8627113_001/ldpd_8627113_001.pdf.

3. The print of John Brown in Missouri is #16 of twenty-two (Nesbett, *Jacob Lawrence*, 10, 40).

4. Louis A. DeCaro Jr. explored the possible connection between real people and John Brown's choice of particular noms de guerre in "Notes on John Brown's Names of War," *John Brown the Abolitionist— a Biographer's Blog*, August 5, 2009, http://abolitionist-john-brown.blogspot.com/2009/08/notes-on-john-browns-names-of-war.html.

5. *The Interpreter's Dictionary of the Bible*, Vol. 4, R–Z (Nashville: Abingdon Press, 1962), 312.

6. Morris, *Oberlin, Hotbed of Abolitionism*, 226–27.

7. Quarles, *Allies*, 184–85; Erik Anderson, "John Brown's Farm Opens to the Public for the First Time Since the '60s," *The Frederick News-Post*, November 4, 2017.

8. The Kansas State Historical Society (Kansapedia) explained the objections to the paintings this way in "Kansas State Capitol—Curry murals": "There were controversies over his use of fanatical abolitionist John Brown as a focal point, the color of the Hereford bull, the length of the woman's skirt, and the curling pig's tail" (https://www.kshs.org/kansapedia/kansas-state-capitol-curry-murals/16864).

9. Kevin Young, "American Bison," in *Brown* (New York: Knopf, 2018), 38.

10. In an essay adapted from N. P. Willis, Edgar Allan Poe described the scenery at Harpers Ferry as "perhaps the most picturesque in America" ("Harper's Ferry," *Graham's Magazine* 20.2 [February 1842], http://www.eapoe.org/rejected/essays/hrpfry01.htm).

11. Oswald Garrison Villard, *John Brown 1800–1859*, 367.

12. McGlone, *John Brown's War Against Slavery*, 211.

13. Lowell J. Soike, *Busy in the Cause: Iowa, The Free-State Struggle in the West, and the Prelude to the Civil War* (Lincoln: University of Nebraska Press, 2014), 139.

14. Quoted in Sanborn, *The Life and Letters of John Brown*, 487.

15. Oswald Garrison Villard provided both commentary and primary documents that were extremely helpful to forming the narrative of the Iowa segment in *John Brown 1800–1859* (346–90).

16. John Brown, "Old Brown's Parallels," Trading Post, Kansas, Jan., 1859, in Ruchames, *A John Brown Reader*, 114–15.

17. Berlin, *The Long Emancipation*, 32–36.

18. "Brown's Rescued Negroes Landed in Canada," *New-York Semi-Weekly Tribune*, March 19, 1859, *"His Soul Goes Marching On": The Life and Legacy of John Brown*, West Virginia Archives & History, http://archive.wvculture.org/history/jbexhibit/tribune021159.html.

19. Soike, *Busy in the Cause*, 128–35.

20. Louis A. DeCaro Jr., "Brown's Flaws, and the Flaws of His Critics Too," *John Brown the Abolitionist—a Biographer's Blog*, July 22, 2012, http://abolitionist-john-brown.blogspot.com/2012_07_01_archive.html.

21. "John Brown's Colony, Windsor, Upper Canada, November 6, 1859," in Redpath, *The Public Life of Capt. John Brown*, 228.

22. Richard J. Hinton, *John Brown and His Men* (1894; repr., New York: Arno Press, 1968), 227.

23. "Iowa and the Underground Railroad," https://iowaculture.gov/sites/default/files/History%20-%20Education%20-%20Lifelong%20-%20Learning%20-%20Iowa%20Underground%20Railroad%20%28PDF%29.pdf.

24. Michael Shermer, *The Moral Arc: How Science and Reason Lead Humanity Toward Truth, Justice, and Freedom* (New York: Henry Holt, 2015), 192–207.

25. William Wells Brown, *Narrative of William W. Brown, A Fugitive Slave. Written by Himself*, in *William Wells Brown: Clotel & Other Writings*, ed. Ezra Greenspan (New York: Library of America, 2014), 49–52.

26. Keeler, "Owen Brown's Escape from Harper's Ferry," 364.

27. Lydia Maria Child, "Mrs. Child to John Brown, Wayland, Mass., Oct. 26, 1859," Boyd B. Stutler Collection, *"His Soul Goes Marching On": The Life and Legacy of John Brown*, West Virginia Archives & History, http://archive.wvculture.org/history/jbexhibit/bbspr02-0016.html.

28. Neil Henderson, "Markillie Cemetery," *The Hudson Green: Newsletter of Hudson Genealogical Study Group* 18.2 (June 2007): 1–3, http://www.rootsweb.ancestry.com/~ohhudogs/GreenJun2007.pdf.

29. A handwritten copy of the St. Catharines, Canada West, letter, addressed to his son John Jr., is reproduced in Beverly Lowry, *Harriet Tubman: Imagining a Life* (New York: Doubleday, 2007), 237–38.

30. Dan Swanson, "Historical Society Published Map of Civil Bend," *Nebraska City News-Press*, January 18, 2012.

31. Andrew Delbanco, *The War Before the War: Fugitive Slaves and the Struggle for America's Soul from the Revolution to the Civil War* (New York: Penguin, 2018), 2.

32. David Stark, "Lesser Known Jesse James Gunfight at Civil Bend," *Gallatin North Missourian*, April 4, 1993, Daviess County Historical Society, http://daviesscountyhistoricalsociety.com/2004/05/01/lesser-known-jesse-james-gunfight-at-civil-bend/.

33. George Washington Doane, "The Dead in Christ," in *"Songs by the Way": The Poetical Writings of the Right Rev. George Washington Doane*, arranged and edited by William Croswell Doane (New York: D. Appleton, 1860), http://anglicanhistory.org/usa/gwdoane/songs1860/.

34. The words "fat dirt" appear on a tile about land and rural life on the inside wall of the Grinnell I-80 rest stop and are attributed to Paul Engle (Iowa Department of Transportation, https://iowadot.gov/maintenance/rest_areas/posters/i8ogrinnell.pdf).

35. Oswald Garrison Villard, *John Brown 1800–1859*, 369.

36. Oswald Garrison Villard, *John Brown 1800–1859*, 369.

37. Soike, *Busy in the Cause*, 134.

38. John Brown, "Old Brown's Parallels," 115.

39. Marilynne Robinson, *Gilead* (New York: Farrar, Straus and Giroux, 2004).

40. Quoted in Oswald Garrison Villard, *John Brown 1800–1859*, 384–85.

41. John Brown, "Old Brown's Parallels," 115.

42. Soike, *Busy in the Cause*, 149

43. Quoted in Hinton, *John Brown and His Men*, 226.

44. The Grinnell I-80 rest stop features decorative tiles on the inside walls commemorating Iowa life, land, art, and history.

45. Some of the detail in this section comes from "Iowa and the Underground Railroad."

46. Lowell J. Soike, *Necessary Courage: Iowa's Underground Railroad in the Struggle against Slavery* (Iowa City: University of Iowa Press, 2013), 148–49.

47. The sign on the Grinnell Green provides a footnote indicating the source of Amos Bixby's words: Letter from A. Bixby to Lewellyn Bixby, February 22, 1859.

48. From the sign on the Grinnell Green.

49. "Grinnell, Josiah Bushnell," *The Biographical Dictionary of Iowa*, University of Iowa Press Digital Editions, http://uipress.lib.uiowa.edu/bdi/DetailsPage.aspx?id=146.

50. Ransom Langdon Harris, "John Brown and His Followers in Iowa," *Midland Monthly*, October 1894, 266–67; Narcissa Macy Smith, "Reminiscences of John Brown," *Midland Monthly*, September 1895, 231–33.

51. John Brown, "Provisional Constitution and Ordinances for the People of the United States," adopted at a convention in Chatham, Canada West, May 8–10, 1858, in Ruchames, *A John Brown Reader*, 111–12.

52. H. Scott Wolfe, "Farmer Maxson's Newel Post: A Piece of History," *John Brown the Abolitionist—a Biographer's Blog*, June 2, 2011, http://abolitionist-john-brown.blogspot.com/2011/06/from-field-farmer-maxsons-newel-post.html.

53. John Greenleaf Whittier based the doctor in his poem "Snow-Bound" on Dr. Elias Weld and also dedicated his poem "The Countess" to him. Weld originally lived in Haverhill, Massachusetts (Whittier's hometown), moved to Hallowell, Maine, about 1820, and spent the last years of his life residing in the home of Myron Tracy at 42 Aurora Street, Hudson, OH (the home burned to the ground in 1866, three years after Weld died). The connection between Whittier and the Hudson family of Myron Tracy was explained to me by Gwen Mayer, who wrote the entry "Aurora Street #42" in the Houses of Hudson Collection compiled for the database Summit Memory (http://www.summitmemory.org/cdm/singleitem/collection/hudson/id/478/rec/3). Information about the relationship of Whittier and Weld is also available in *The Letters of John Greenleaf Whittier*, ed. John B. Pickard, Vol. I, 1828–1845 (Cambridge, MA: Belknap Press of Harvard University Press, 1975), 9–11.

54. James Malin, "The John Brown Legend in Pictures: Kissing the Negro Baby," *Kansas Historical Quarterly* 8.4 (November 1939): 339–41, Kansas State Historical Society, http://www.kancoll.org/khq/1939/39_4_malin.htm.

55. Oates, *To Purge This Land*, 242.

56. Benjamin F. Gue, *Biographies and Portraits of the Progressive Men of Iowa: Leaders in Business, Politics and the Professions, Together with an Original and Authentic History of the State* (Des Moines, IA: Conway and Shaw, 1899), 73, https://archive.org/details/biographiesandpo3shamgoog/page/n6/mode/2up.

57. Oswald Garrison Villard, *John Brown 1800–1859*, 388.

58. Mrs. E. S. Butler, "A Woman's Recollections of John Brown's Stay in Springdale," *Midland Monthly*, July 1898, 576.

59. Nathaniel Philbrick, *In the Hurricane's Eye* (New York: Viking, 2018), 22–25.

60. John Brown Jr., quoted in Sanborn, *The Life and Letters of John Brown*, 494; Stake, *John Brown in Chambersburg*, Chapter IV.

61. Soike, *Busy in the Cause*, 120.

62. C. B. Galbreath, "Edwin Coppoc" and "Barclay Coppoc," *Ohio Archaeological and Historical Publications* 30 (Columbus: Ohio State Archaeological and Historical Society, 1921): 397–451, 459–82, https://www.google.com/books/edition/_/T4QUAAAAYAAJ?hl=en&gbpv=0.

63. Louis Thomas Jones, *The Quakers of Iowa* (Iowa City: State Historical Society of Iowa, 1914), 196, https://archive.org/details/quakersofiowa00jonerich.

64. Jones, *The Quakers of Iowa*, 197.

65. Just five days after John Brown was hanged, at the conclusion of numerous accusations about the role of the Springdale Quakers, the group itself prepared a reply: "While we believe that our principals of peace were never dearer to most of our members than now, we feel it to be cause of deep regret that those engaged in the late deplorable outbreak at Harpers Ferry, have been entertained, & otherwise encouraged by some of our members" (Jones, *The Quakers of Iowa*, 195–96).

66. Two letters, mailed from two different places, were drafted by Benjamin Gue, his brother David Gue (who made the painting of the Markillie daguerreotype of John Brown, unveiled in 1915), and A. L. Smith (Soike, *Necessary Courage*, 160–61; Jean Libby, *John Brown Photo Chronology*, 30).

67. Gue, *Biographies and Portraits of the Progressive Men of Iowa*, 73–74.

68. Hinton, *John Brown and His Men*, 227.

69. Soike, *Busy in the Cause*, 154.

70. For the volatile history of this bridge, see David A. Pfeiffer, "Bridging the Mississippi: The Railroads and Steamboats Clash at the Rock Island Bridge," *Prologue Magazine*, Summer 2004, National Archives, http://www.archives.gov/publications/prologue/2004/summer/bridge.html.

REVERIE 8

1. John Brown, "Reception of John Brown & Party at Grinnell, Iowa" (handwritten), February 26, 1859, Kansas State Historical Society, http://www.kansasmemory.org/item/5269.

2. Paul Auster and J. M. Coetzee, *Here and Now: Letters 2008–2011* (New York: Penguin, 2013), 6.

BREAKING THE GOLDEN RULE

1. John Brown, "Brown's Interview with Mason, Vallandigham, and Others," 121.

2. Russell Banks, *Cloudsplitter* (New York: HarperCollins, 1998).

3. John Brown, "To My Dear Mrs. Spring, Charlestown, Jefferson County, Va., Nov. 24, 1859," 146–48.

4. John Brown, "To Dear Son John, Akron, Ohio, Aug. 6, 1852," in Sanborn, *The Life and Letters of John Brown*, 150–51.

5. John Brown, "To My Dear Mrs. Spring, Charlestown, Jefferson County, Va., Nov. 24, 1859," 146–48.

6. John Brown, "To My Dear Afflicted Wife & Children, Springfield, 8th Nov 1846," in Ruchames, *A John Brown Reader*, 56.

7. John Brown, "To Dear Mary, Springfield, 29th Nov 1846," 57–58.

8. John Brown, "To Dear Friend E. B. of R.I., Charlestown, Jefferson County, Va., Nov. 1, 1859," in Ruchames, *A John Brown Reader*, 129–30.

9. John Brown, "To Dear Brother Jeremiah, Charlestown, Jefferson County, Va., Nov. 12, 1859," in Ruchames, *A John Brown Reader*, 134.

10. The 1860 census showed that 12.57% of the total population of the US were enslaved. There were, in other words, 3,953,760 enslaved people at this time in the United States. The category of "Free Colored" on the census included 488,070 individuals (United States Census Bureau, "1860 Census: Population of the United States," https://www2.census.gov/library/publications/decennial/1860/population/1860a-02.pdf).

11. John Brown, "To Dear Wife and Children, Every One, Charlestown, Jefferson County, Va., Nov. 8, 1859," 132–33.

12. A letter to Mary Ann Brown's children in late November of 1859 begins with the lines, "I am here with Mrs. Lucretia Mott (sic) where I expect to stay until your dear father is disposed of. O what a terrible thought" ("To Dear Children One & All, Near Philadelphia, Nov 28, 1859," Brown-Gee, Series III, Box #2, Folder #3, Hudson Library & Historical Society).

13. John Brown, "To Dear Wife, Charlestown, Jefferson Co. Va., 26th Nov. 1859," in Ruchames, *A John Brown Reader*, 151–52.

14. Interview by Katherine Mayo with Mrs. Danley Hobart [Amelia], December 1908, Ohio Interviews.

15. Quoted in Oswald Garrison Villard, *John Brown 1800–1859*, 50.

16. Interview by Katherine Mayo with Mrs. Rebecca Spring, 547 DeSoto Street, Los Angeles, September 1908, John Brown Manuscripts, Box #16, Folder #7, Rare Book and Manuscript Library, Columbia University Library.

17. Mary A. Brown, "To My Dear Friend Mrs. Stearns, North Elba, N.Y., Aug 4th, 1863."

18. In a note Gee appended to a letter from Mary to Mrs. George L. Stearns ("To My Dear Friend Mrs. Stearns, North Elba, Aug 4th, 1863"), he wrote this: "After the period of treatment at David Riggles' [sic] water cure establishment at Northampton, Mass., in 1849, Mrs. Brown became a convert to the water cure. Note above on treating diphtheria. After removal to California she served the neighborhood as a practical nurse—using the water treatment when the patients would stand for it."

19. DeCaro, *"Fire from the Midst of You,"* 171–85. Many details about Ruggles and his establishment, as well as Mary's trip to Northampton, come from DeCaro's work.

20. Quoted in Washington, *Sojourner Truth's America*, 177.

21. DeCaro, *"Fire from the Midst of You,"* 183.

22. The Committee, along with its successor, the New York State Vigilance Committee, helped between 3,000 and 4,000 fugitives from 1835 through 1860 (Foner, *Gateway to Freedom*, 2–11, 61–62, 238); Graham Russell Hodges, "The Hazards of Anti-Slavery Journalism," *Media Studies Journal* 14.2 (Spring/Summer 2000), http://www.hartford-hwp.com/archives/45a/394.html. See Sinha, *The Slave's Cause*, for a description of Black vigilance committees throughout the North that were inspired by Ruggles' organization (388).

23. Dorothy B. Porter, "David Ruggles, 1810–1849; Hydropathic Practitioner," *Journal of the National Medical Association* 49.1 & 2 (January and March, 1957, two-part article); Hodges, "The Hazards of Anti-Slavery Journalism."

24. The dominant Democratic party of New York kept close ties with the South even after 1827, helping slave catchers return fugitives. Approximately one-third of voters in New York City voted for Lincoln in 1860 (Foner, *Gateway to Freedom*, 9); Sven Beckert, *Empire of Cotton: A Global History* (New York: Knopf, 2014), 110.

25. Washington, *Sojourner Truth's America*, 176–77.

26. DeCaro, *"Fire from the Midst of You,"* 182–85.

27. John Brown, "To My Dear Wife, Charlestown, Jefferson Co Va., 16 Nov. 1859," in Ruchames, *A John Brown Reader*, 137–38.

28. Nalty, *The Browns of Madronia*, 26.

29. John Brown, "To Mr. Henry L. Stearns, Red Rock, Iowa, 15th July 1857," 38.

30. Soike, *Busy in the Cause*, 140–42.

31. Soike lists nineteenth-century sources that document the kidnapping, including one that provides names of captives (*Busy in the Cause*, 247, footnote 42).

32. John Doy, *The Narrative of John Doy, of Lawrence, Kansas* (1860; repr., University of Michigan University Library: Michigan Historical Reprint Series, 2005), 22–24.

33. Doy, *The Narrative of John Doy*, 25.

34. Doy, *The Narrative of John Doy*, 54.

35. Doy, *The Narrative of John Doy*, 123.

36. Oswald Garrison Villard, *John Brown 1800–1859*, 380.

37. Doy, *The Narrative of John Doy*, 123.

38. George B. Gill, "To My Dear Friend [Richard J. Hinton], Milan, Sumner Co., Kan., July 7, 1893," in Ruchames, *John Brown*, 239–42; interview with Mrs. Rebecca Spring (by Katherine Mayo).

39. DeCaro, "John Brown Remarks 'Unfortunate,'" 9.

TERROR ON POTTAWATOMIE CREEK

1. Reynolds, *John Brown, Abolitionist*, 309.

2. Nora Titone, *My Thoughts Be Bloody: The Bitter Rivalry Between Edwin and John Wilkes Booth That Led to an American Tragedy* (New York: Free Press, 2010), 208–14.

3. Abraham Lincoln, "Last Public Address," April 11, 1865, *Abraham Lincoln Online*, http://www.abrahamlincolnonline.org/lincoln/speeches/last.htm.

4. In an introduction to *President Lincoln Assassinated!!: The Firsthand Story of the Murder, Manhunt, Trial and Mourning*, a compilation published by the Library of America in 2014, historian Harold Holzer explains Booth's true intent to "decapitate" on April 14, 1865, "the executive branch of the federal government" (xxii).

5. Macdonald, *H Is for Hawk*, 202.

6. Quoted in Reynolds, *John Brown, Abolitionist*, 340.

7. Oswald Garrison Villard, *John Brown 1800–1859*, 187–88.

8. Report of the Special Committee Appointed to Investigate the Troubles in Kansas, with the Views of the Minority of Said Committee, University of Michigan Library, http://quod.lib.umich.edu/cgi/t/text/text-idx?c=moa;idno=AFK4445.

9. Howells, "Old Brown," 266–68.

10. William Dean Howells, "John Brown after Fifty Years," in Ruchames, *A John Brown Reader*, 358.

11. Oswald Garrison Villard, *John Brown 1800–1859*, 85, 153; see also, for biographical detail on Lucius V. Bierce, Grismer, *Akron and Summit County*, 665.

12. Bierce served as commander in chief of the Patriot Army of the West during the Canada Patriot War of 1837–1839.

13. Oates, *To Purge This Land with Blood*, 130.

14. Lucius V. Bierce, "Address Delivered at Akron, Ohio, on the Evening of the Execution of John Brown," December 2, 1859 (Columbus: Ohio State Journal Steam Press, 1865), 9, https://hdl.handle.net/2027/loc.ark:/13960/t6d221k4k?urlappend=%3Bseq=7.

15. DeCaro, *"Fire from the Midst of You,"* 230–31.

16. Cutler, *History of the State of Kansas*, 131.

17. Quoted in Oswald Garrison Villard, *John Brown 1800–1859*, 160.

18. Townsley, "The Potawatomie Tragedy," 200.

19. Quoted in Oswald Garrison Villard, *John Brown 1800–1859*, 162.

20. Quoted in Oswald Garrison Villard, *John Brown 1800–1859*, 163–64.

21. Andrew Johnson, "Remarks to the Senate," December 12, 1859, in *The Tribunal: Responses to John Brown and the Harpers Ferry Raid*, 306.

22. James Baldwin, "The Creative Process," in *Baldwin: Collected Essays*, selected by Toni Morrison (New York: Library of America, 1998), 669–72.

23. Quoted in Oswald Garrison Villard, *John Brown 1800–1859*, 163.

24. Reynolds, *John Brown, Abolitionist*, 147.

25. Quoted in Oates, *To Purge This Land with Blood*, 141, 257–58.

26. Reynolds, *John Brown, Abolitionist*, 221–24.

27. Henry David Thoreau, "A Plea for Captain John Brown," in *Thoreau: Collected Essays and Poems*, selections by Elizabeth Hall Witherell (New York: Library of America, 2001), 407.

28. Townsley, "The Potawatomie Tragedy," 197–203.

29. Quoted in Louis A. DeCaro Jr., *John Brown, The Cost of Freedom: Selections from His Life & Letters* (New York: International Publishers, 2007), 50.

30. Quoted in Oswald Garrison Villard, *John Brown 1800–1859*, 165.

31. Quoted in *John Brown in Akron: A 150th Anniversary Commemoration* (brochure, Akron, OH: Summit County Historical Society, 2009), 10.

32. Quoted in Oswald Garrison Villard, *John Brown 1800–1859*, 152.

33. Salmon Brown, "John Brown and Sons in Kansas Territory," in Ruchames, *A John Brown Reader*, 194.

34. Karl Gridley transcribes John Brown's speech "Idea of Things in Kansas" (with John Brown's notations) and provides background information to the speech in "An 'Idea of Things in Kansas': John Brown's 1857 New England Speech," *Kansas History: A Journal of the Central Plains* 27 (Spring–Summer 2004): 76–85, https://www.kshs.org/publicat/history/2004spring_gridley.pdf.

35. John Brown, "Brown's Interview with Mason, Vallandigham, and Others," 125.

36. Quoted in Oswald Garrison Villard, *John Brown 1800–1859*, 179.

37. Reynolds, *John Brown, Abolitionist*, 177.

38. John Brown, "To Dear Wife and Children, Every One, Near Brown's Station, K. T., June, 1856," in Ruchames, *A John Brown Reader*, 94–97.

39. Oates, *To Purge This Land with Blood*, 384–85.

40. Samuel Lyle Adair, "To Bro. & Sis. Hand & Other Friends, Osawatomie, K. T., May 28, 1856," Brown-Gee, Series I, Box #1, Folder #28, Hudson Library & Historical Society.

41. Gold, *Life of John Brown*, 17, 34–35, 37.

42. George MacDonald Fraser, *Flashman and the Angel of the Lord* (New York: Knopf, 1995), 91.

43. Louis A. DeCaro Jr., "The Pottawatomie Killings and Popular Culture," *John Brown the Abolitionist—a Biographer's Blog*, December 9, 2011, http://abolitionist-john-brown.blogspot.com/2011/12/from-hell-on-wheels-to-midnight-rising.html.

44. DeCaro, "John Brown: The Empty Coffin and Philadelphia," 4.

45. DeCaro, *"Fire from the Midst of You,"* 236.

46. Salmon Brown, "John Brown and Sons in Kansas Territory," 191; see also Patrick Chura, *Thoreau the Land Surveyor* (Gainesville: University Press of Florida, 2010), 135–54.

47. James N. Gilbert, "A Behavioral Analysis of John Brown: Martyr or Terrorist?" in Russo and Finkelman, *Terrible Swift Sword*, 115.

48. Finkelman, "A Look Back at John Brown."

49. Reynolds, *John Brown, Abolitionist*, 451.

50. Quoted in Oswald Garrison Villard, *John Brown 1800–1859*, 455.

51. Katie Byard, "Past Being Preserved," *Akron Beacon Journal*, December 23, 2017.

REVERIE 9

1. Guy Gugliotta, "New Estimate Raises Civil War Death Toll," *New York Times*, April 2, 2012, https://www.nytimes.com/2012/04/03/science/civil-war-toll-up-by-20-percent-in-new-estimate.html.

2. "Civil War Battles," HistoryNet, https://www.historynet.com/civil-war-battles.

3. Du Bois, *John Brown*, 206.

4. John Brown, "Charlestown, Va, 2d December 1859," in Ruchames, *A John Brown Reader*, 159. Note to guards.

5. Finkelman, "A Look Back at John Brown."

6. Townsley, "Potawatomie Tragedy," 200; Salmon Brown, "John Brown and Sons in Kansas Territory," 193.

7. Reynolds, *John Brown, Abolitionist*, 167.

8. Douglass, *Life and Times*, 744.

9. Thomas Hamilton, "Brown and Nat Turner: An Editor's Comparison," in *Blacks on John Brown*, 37–39; T. Thomas Fortune, "'John Brown and Nat. Turner,' January 12 and 29, 1889," in *The Tribunal*, 515–17; George Washington Williams, *History of the Negro Race in America from 1619 to 1880: Negroes as Slaves, as Soldiers, and as Citizens*, Vol. II (1800–1880) (New York: G. P. Putnam's Sons, 1883), https://books.google.com/books?id=TR-hGrKdr7QC.

10. *The Confessions of Nat Turner, the Leader of the Late Insurrection in Southampton, Va.*, as made to Thomas R. Gray, http://docsouth.unc.edu/neh/turner/turner.html.

11. Berlin, *The Long Emancipation*, 31.

12. James Baldwin, *No Name in the Street* (1972; repr., New York: Vintage, 2007), 54.

13. John Brown, "To Dear Wife, Springfield, Mass., Jan. 17, 1851," 75.

AFTERWORD

1. John Brown, "To Dear Sir [Hon Thos. Russell], Charlestown Jefferson County Va, Oct. 21, 1859," in Ruchames, *A John Brown Reader*, 127.

2. Drew, *The John Brown Invasion*, 66.

3. For the manuscript about Kansas see Oswald Garrison Villard, *John Brown 1800–1859*, 86–88, 354–56. The essay "Sambo's Mistakes" (in Ruchames, *A John Brown Reader*, 61–64) was retrieved right after the raid by a soldier and journalist named Clifton W. Tayleure, who later donated it to the Maryland Historical Society (see Maryland Center for History and Culture, "The Tale of John Brown's Letter Book," including donation letter from Clifton W. Tayleure, November 3, 1883, https://www.mdhistory.org/the-tale-of-john-browns-letter-book/); in this essay, Reynolds suggests, "Brown entered sympathetically into Black culture to a degree unmatched by any other white person of his day" (*John Brown, Abolitionist*, 119–21).

4. Oswald Garrison Villard, *John Brown 1800–1859*, 588–89.

5. John Brown, "To Dear Friend E. B. of R. I., Charlestown, Jefferson County, Va., Nov. 1, 1859," 129–30.

6. John Brown, "To My Dear Sir [Hon. D. R. Tilden], Charlestown, Jefferson County, Va., Monday, Nov. 28, 1859," 154–55.

EPILOGUE

1. Toni Morrison, "Making America White Again," *New Yorker*, November 21, 2016, http://www.newyorker.com/magazine/2016/11/21/making-america-white-again.

2. Michael Eric Dyson, *Tears We Cannot Stop: A Sermon to White America* (New York: St. Martin's Press, 2017), 3.

Bibliography

Adair, Samuel Lyle. "To Bro. & Sis. Hand & Other Friends, Osawatomie, K. T., May 28, 1856."
Brown-Gee, Series I, Box #1, Folder #28. Hudson Library & Historical Society.

"Affidavits of John Brown's Alleged Insanity, presented at the time of his trial at Charlestown, Va., in 1859. Originals in the Congressional Library, Washington, D.C." Brown-Gee, Series I, Box #12, Folder #32. Hudson Library & Historical Society.

Aines, Don. "Plaque Honoring Brown Is Dedicated." *Herald-Mail*, Hagerstown, MD, July 15, 2006.

Alcott, Louisa May. *Louisa May Alcott: Her Life, Letters, and Journals*. Edited by Ednah D. Cheney. Boston: Roberts Brothers, 1889. https://archive.org/details/louisamayalcotthalco.

———. "With a Rose, That Bloomed on the Day of John Brown's Martyrdom." In Ruchames, *A John Brown Reader*, 271–72.

Anderson, Erik. "John Brown's Farm Opens to the Public for the First Time Since the '60s." *Frederick News-Post*, November 4, 2017.

Anderson, Osborne P. *A Voice from Harper's Ferry: A Narrative of Events at Harper's Ferry; with Incidents Prior and Subsequent to Its Capture by Captain Brown and His Men*. Boston: Printed for the Author, 1861. https://hdl.handle.net/2027/loc.ark:/13960/t42r3xn6t?urlappend=%3Bseq=20.

Anderson, William. *River Boy: The Story of Mark Twain*. Illustrated by Dan Andreasen. New York: HarperCollins, 2003.

Auster, Paul and J. M. Coetzee. *Here and Now: Letters 2008–2011*. New York: Penguin, 2013.

Baldwin, James. "The Creative Process." In *Baldwin: Collected Essays*, selected by Toni Morrison, 669–72. New York: Library of America, 1998.

———. *No Name in the Street*. 1972. Reprint, New York: Vintage, 2007.

Banks, Russell. *Cloudsplitter*. New York: HarperCollins, 1998.

Baptist, Edward E. *The Half Has Never Been Told: Slavery and the Making of American Capitalism*. New York: Basic, 2014.

Barber, J. Max. Address by J. Max Barber, Lake Placid, NY, May 9, 1935. In Quarles, *Blacks on John Brown*, 109–15.

Beckert, Sven. *Empire of Cotton: A Global History*. New York: Knopf, 2014.

Bennett, David Ross. *The John Brown Birthplace*. Torrington, CT: Torrington Historical Society, 2002.

Bennett, Lerone. "Tea and Sympathy: Liberals and Other White Hopes." In Quarles, *Blacks on John Brown*, 139–43.

Berlin, Ira. *The Long Emancipation: The Demise of Slavery in the United States*. Cambridge, MA: Harvard University Press, 2015.

Bidgood, Jess. "A Mysterious Noseless Bust at Tufts Gets Back Its Name: John Brown." *New York Times*, October 31, 2016. http://www.nytimes.com/2016/11/01/us/a-mysterious-noseless-bust-at-tufts-gets-back-its-name-john-brown.html?_r=0.

Bierce, Lucius V. "Address Delivered at Akron, Ohio, on the Evening of the Execution of John Brown." December 2, 1859. Columbus: Ohio State Journal Steam Press, 1865. https://hdl.handle.net/2027/loc.ark:/13960/t6d221k4k?urlappend=%3Bseq=7.

———. *Historical Reminiscences of Summit County.* Akron, OH: T. & H. G. Canfield, 1854. https://archive.org/details/historicalreminoobiergoog.

Blake, William. "The Tyger." In *Songs of Innocence and of Experience.* 1794. Reprint, London: Oxford University Press, 1977.

Blight, David W. *Frederick Douglass: Prophet of Freedom.* New York: Simon & Schuster, 2018.

———. "Why the Underground Railroad, and Why Now? A Long View." In *Passages to Freedom: The Underground Railroad in History and Memory,* edited by David W. Blight, 233–47. Washington, DC: Smithsonian, 2004.

Brinkley, Alan. *The Unfinished Nation: A Concise History of the American People.* 6th ed. New York: McGraw-Hill, 2009.

Brown and Oviatt Agreement (handwritten). January 2, 1842. Boyd B. Stutler Collection, Ms 78-1, *"His Soul Goes Marching On": The Life and Legacy of John Brown.* West Virginia Archives & History. http://archive.wvculture.org/history/jbexhibit/bbsms01-0012.html.

Brown, Jason. "Dear Gerald, Ben Lomond Calif., April 30th, 1903." Private collection of F. G. Brown.

———. "To Dear Grandfather [Owen Brown], Osawatomie K. T., Jan 23rd, 1856." Brown-Adair, in process. Hudson Library & Historical Society.

———. "To Dear Grandfather [Owen Brown], Osawatomie K.T., June 14th, 1855." Brown-Adair, in process. Hudson Library & Historical Society.

———. "Dear Grandsons [Gerald & Jay Brown], Ben Lomond Cal, May 23, 1900." Private collection of F. G. Brown.

———. "Dear Jay, Ben Lomond Cal., June 19, 1900." Private collection of F. G. Brown.

———. "Dr. Soper, Akron, Ohio, Jan 2nd, 1896." Private collection of F. G. Brown.

Brown, John. "Brown's Interview with Mason, Vallandigham, and Others." Harper's Ferry, Oct. 19, 1859. In Ruchames, *A John Brown Reader,* 118–25.

———. "An 'Idea of Things in Kansas': John Brown's 1857 New England Speech," edited by Karl Gridley. *Kansas History: A Journal of the Central Plains* 27 (Spring–Summer 2004): 76–85. https://www.kshs.org/publicat/history/2004spring_gridley.pdf.

———. *John Brown Letters.* Transcribed by Clarence S. Gee. Hudson Library & Historical Society.

———. "John Brown to Joshua Giddings, July 04, 1848." Kansas State Historical Society. https://www.kshs.org/km/items/view/308358.

———. "John Brown's Wills," Appendix F. In Villard, *John Brown 1800–1859,* 667–70.

———. "Old Brown's Parallels." Trading Post, Kansas, Jan., 1859. In Ruchames, *A John Brown Reader,* 114–15.

———. "Provisional Constitution and Ordinances for the People of the United States." Adopted at a Convention in Chatham, Canada West, May 8–10, 1858. In Ruchames, *A John Brown Reader,* 111–13.

———. "Reception of John Brown & Party at Grinnell, Iowa" (handwritten). February 26, 1859. Kansas State Historical Society. http://www.kansasmemory.org/item/5269.

———. "Remedy for Bots or Grubs, in the Heads of Sheep—Remarks on the Fine Sheep of Ohio and Other States." *Ohio Cultivator,* April 15, 1846. *"His Soul Goes Marching On": The Life and Legacy of John Brown.* West Virginia Archives & History. http://archive.wvculture.org/history/jbexhibit/ohiocultivator.html.

———. "Sambo's Mistakes." *Rams Horn,* between January 1847 and June 1848. In Ruchames, *A John Brown Reader,* 61–64.

———. "To Mr. Henry L. Stearns, Red Rock, Iowa, 15th July 1857." In Ruchames, *A John Brown Reader,* 35–41.

———. "Words of Advice." Adopted Jan. 15, 1851. In Ruchames, *A John Brown Reader,* 76–78.

Brown, John, Jr. "To Dear Friend [Frank B. Sanborn], Put-in-Bay, February 26, 1883." Brown-Gee, Series III, Box #4, Folder #12. Hudson Library & Historical Society.

———. "Dear Nephew [Charles P. Brown], Put-in-Bay, May 6, 1894." Private collection of F. G. Brown.

———. *Reminiscences*. In *Meteor of War: The John Brown Story*, edited by Zoe Trodd and John Stauffer, 63–66. Maplecrest, NY: Brandywine Press, 2004.

Brown, Mary A. "To Dear Brother [Jeremiah Root Brown], Rohnerville, Jan. 21st, 1873." Brown-Gee, Series III, Box #2, Folder #3. Hudson Library & Historical Society.

———. "To Dear Children One & All, Near Philadelphia, Nov 28, 1859." Brown-Gee, Series III, Box #2, Folder #3. Hudson Library & Historical Society.

———. "To Dear Friend [George L. Stearns], North Elba, Jan 7, 1860 [misdated, should be Feb. 7 or Feb. 8]." Brown-Gee, Series III, Box #2, Folder #3. Hudson Library & Historical Society.

———. "To Dear Friend [Mr. J. M. McKim], North Elba, Sept 2, 1863." Brown-Gee, Series III, Box #2, Folder #3. Hudson Library & Historical Society.

———. "To Dear Friend Mr. McKim, North Elba, N.Y., Mar 6, 1860." Brown-Gee, Series III, Box #2, Folder #3. Hudson Library & Historical Society.

———. "To Dear Salmon and Family, Put in Bay, Sept. 16th, 1882." Brown-Gee, Series III, Box #2, Folder #3. Hudson Library & Historical Society.

———. "To Dear Son Owen, Decorah Iowa, Jan. 31st, 1864." Brown-Gee, Series III, Box #2, Folder #3. Hudson Library & Historical Society.

———. "To Mr. Sewall Dear Friend [Samuel E. Sewall], North Elba, Feb 13, 1861." Brown-Gee, Series III, Box #2, Folder #3. Hudson Library & Historical Society.

———. "To My Dear Friend Mrs. Stearns, North Elba, Mar 3, 1863." Brown-Gee, Series III, Box #2, Folder #3. Hudson Library & Historical Society.

———. "To My Dear Friend Mrs. Stearns, North Elba, N.Y., Aug 4th, 1863." Brown-Gee, Series III, Box #2, Folder #3. Hudson Library & Historical Society.

———. "To My Dear Mrs. Stearns, North Elba, Jan 7th, 1863." Brown-Gee, Series III, Box #2, Folder #3. Hudson Library & Historical Society.

Brown, Owen. *Owen Brown's Autobiography as Written to His Daughter Marian Brown Hand, ca. 1850, Together with Family Correspondence Concerning the Autobiography*. Transcribed by Rev. Clarence S. Gee, April 17, 1961. Hudson Library & Historical Society.

———. "To Dear Gran Son Charles Adair, Hudson, Ohio, Feb. 23, 1856." Brown-Adair, in process. Hudson Library & Historical Society.

———. "To Rev. S. L. Adair and Family, Hudson, Sept 6th, 1842." Brown-Adair, Box #1, Folder Brown Letters 1835–1855. Hudson Library & Historical Society.

Brown, Salmon. "John Brown and Sons in Kansas Territory." In Ruchames, *A John Brown Reader*, 189–97.

———. "My Father, John Brown, by Salmon Brown, The Only Survivor of Twenty Children." In Ruchames, *A John Brown Reader*, 182–89.

"Brown's Rescued Negroes Landed in Canada." *New-York Semi-Weekly Tribune*, March 19, 1859. *"His Soul Goes Marching On": The Life and Legacy of John Brown*. West Virginia Archives & History. http://archive.wvculture.org/history/jbexhibit/tribune021159.html.

Brown, William Wells. "John Brown and the Fugitive Slave Law." In *William Wells Brown: Clotel & Other Writings*, edited by Ezra Greenspan, 917–22. New York: Library of America, 2014.

———. *Narrative of William W. Brown, A Fugitive Slave*. In *William Wells Brown: Clotel & Other Writings*, edited by Ezra Greenspan, 9–54. New York: Library of America, 2014.

"The Building at 5 East Main." Vertical File. Hudson Historic Buildings. Hudson Library & Historical Society.

"Building for Lease." *Hudson Hub-Times*, November 2, 2014.

Buss, John. *John Buss Diaries*. John Buss Manuscript Collection, John Buss Papers. Hudson Library & Historical Society.

Butler, Mrs. E. S. "A Woman's Recollections of John Brown's Stay in Springdale." *Midland Monthly*, July 1898.

Byard, Katie. "Past Being Preserved." *Akron Beacon Journal*, December 23, 2017.

———. "Public Can View Brown Memorial." *Akron Beacon Journal*, July 2, 2009.

Caccamo, James F. "Early Blacks in Hudson." *Ex Libris: A Publication of the Hudson Library & Historical Society* 11.1 (Winter 1990): 1–2.

———. *Hudson, Ohio and the Underground Railroad*. Hudson, OH: Friends of the Hudson Library, 1992.

———. *The Story of Hudson Ohio*. Hudson, OH: Friends of the Hudson Library, 1995.

———. *The Story of Kent, Ohio*. Kent, OH: Kent Historical Society, 1999.

Cackler, Christian. *Recollections of an Old Settler: Life in the Early Western Reserve, Hudson and Franklin Townships*. 1874. Reprint, Kent, OH: Roger Thurman, 1992.

Calarco, Tom. *Places of the Underground Railroad: A Geographical Guide*. Santa Barbara, CA: Greenwood, 2011.

Camp, Mark J. *Railroad Depots of Northeast Ohio*. Charleston, SC: Arcadia, 2007.

Carney, Jim. "John Brown Monument Is Out of Public View, but Never Out of Public Controversy." *Akron Beacon Journal*, December 31, 2011.

Case, Lora. *Hudson of Long Ago: Progress of Hudson During the Past Century, Personal Reminiscences of an Aged Pioneer*. Introduction by Frances B. B. Sumner. Originally published as *Reminiscences*, 1897. Reprint, Hudson, OH: Hudson Library & Historical Society, 1963.

Chernow, Ron. *Grant*. New York: Penguin Press, 2017.

Chester, Tom. Annotation of "Funeral of Owen Brown—The Last Survivor of John Brown's Historic Raid on Harpers Ferry, Va., in 1859." Obituary from the *Pasadena Standard*, January 12, 1889. Reprinted online at http://tchester.org/sgm/msc/brown_funeral_notice.html.

Child, Lydia Maria. "Mrs. Child to John Brown, Wayland, Mass., Oct. 26, 1859." Boyd B. Stutler Collection, *"His Soul Goes Marching On": The Life and Legacy of John Brown*. West Virginia Archives & History. http://archive.wvculture.org/history/jbexhibit/bbspr02-0016.html.

"Childhood and Early Adult Years." Boyd B. Stutler Collection. *"His Soul Goes Marching On": The Life and Legacy of John Brown*. West Virginia Archives & History. http://archive.wvculture.org/history/jbexhibit/jbchapter1.html.

"Children of John Brown of Harper's Ferry." Hudson Library & Historical Society. https://www.hudsonlibrary.org/historical-society/children-of-john-brown/.

Christie, Robert J. *The Memoirs of Dr. Robert J. Christie*. Chapter V. http://flanaganfamily.net/genealo/memoirs.htm#chV.

Chura, Patrick. *Thoreau the Land Surveyor*. Gainesville: University Press of Florida, 2010.

"Civil War Battles." HistoryNet. https://www.historynet.com/civil-war-battles.

"Civil War Buffs to 'Bivouac' Here for John Brown Days." *Hudson Hub-Times*, July 3, 1985.

Coates, Ta-Nehisi. *Between the World and Me*. New York: Spiegel and Grau, 2015.

———. "The Case for Reparations." *Atlantic*, June 2014. https://www.theatlantic.com/magazine/archive/2014/06/the-case-for-reparations/361631/.

———. *We Were Eight Years in Power: An American Tragedy*. New York: One World, 2017.

Cochran, Jim. "Is John Brown Tribute Appropriate?" Letter to the Editor, *Hudson Hub-Times*, April 5, 2009.

Cochran, William Cox. *The Western Reserve and the Fugitive Slave Law: A Prelude to the Civil War*. Publication No. 101. Cleveland: Collections of the Western Reserve Historical Society, 1920. https://archive.org/details/cu31924017903299.

Collins, Michele. "Observing the 150th Anniversary of the Civil War and Hudson's Role." *Hudson Life Magazine*, February 2011.

Cook, Abner H. "The Winchester Medical College, Winchester, Virginia, 1827–1862." *The Medical Pickwick* 4.1 (January 1918): 3–7. Winchester Medical College Collection, 190 THL/WFCHS, Stewart Bell Jr. Archives. Handley Regional Library, Winchester, Virginia.

Cooke, Jay. *The Journal of Jay Cooke or The Gibraltar Records, 1865–1905*. Edited by James E. Pollard. Columbus: Ohio State University Press, 1935.

Copperhead Voters List of 1863. Newspaper Collection, Miscellaneous Loose Editions. Hudson Library & Historical Society.

Cotter, Edwin N., Jr. "The John Brown Memorial Association and the John Brown Farm." *John Brown the Abolitionist—a Biographer's Blog*, August 26, 2010. http://abolitionist-john-brown.blogspot.com/2010/08/john-brown-memorial-association-and.html.

Custy, Nikki. "Hudson and the Underground Railroad." *Hudson Life Magazine*, July 2013.

Cutler, William C. *History of the State of Kansas*. Chicago: A. T. Andreas, 1883. http://www.columbia.edu/cu/lweb/digital/collections/cul/texts/ldpd_8627113_001/ldpd_8627113_001.pdf.

Davey, John. "A Monument for John Brown, the Friend of Southern Slaves." *Cleveland Plain Dealer*, January 24, 1904.

———. "Monument for John Brown: John Davey Has Plan for Memorial and Preservation of Trees at Same Time." *Cleveland Plain Dealer*, January 24, 1904.

Delbanco, Andrew. *The War Before the War: Fugitive Slaves and the Struggle for America's Soul from the Revolution to the Civil War*. New York: Penguin, 2018.

DeCaro, Louis A., Jr. "Brown's Flaws, and the Flaws of His Critics Too." *John Brown the Abolitionist—a Biographer's Blog*, July 22, 2012. http://abolitionist-john-brown.blogspot.com/2012_07_01_archive.html.

———. *"Fire from the Midst of You."* New York: New York University Press, 2002.

———. "John Brown Remarks 'Unfortunate.'" Letter to the Editor, *Hudson Hub-Times*, April 12, 2009.

———. *John Brown the Abolitionist—a Biographer's Blog*. http://abolitionist-john-brown.blogspot.com.

———. *John Brown, the Cost of Freedom: Selections from His Life & Letters*. New York: International Publishers, 2007.

———. "John Brown: The Empty Coffin and Philadelphia." Presentation at The Historical Society of Pennsylvania, Philadelphia, December 2, 2009.

———. *John Brown: The Man Who Lived* (*Essays in Honor of the Harper's Ferry Raid Sesquicentennial, 1859–2009*). Morrisville, NC: Lulu, 2009.

———. "Notes on John Brown's Names of War." *John Brown the Abolitionist—a Biographer's Blog*, August 5, 2009. http://abolitionist-john-brown.blogspot.com/2009/08/notes-on-john-browns-names-of-war.html.

———. "The Pottawatomie Killings and Popular Culture." *John Brown the Abolitionist—a Biographer's Blog*, December 9, 2011. http://abolitionist-john-brown.blogspot.com/2011/12/from-hell-on-wheels-to-midnight-rising.html.

Dickinson, Emily. "The Props assist the House." In *Poems of Emily Dickinson*, edited by R. W. Franklin, 325–26. Cambridge, MA: Belknap Press of Harvard University, 1999.

Doane, George Washington. "The Dead in Christ." In *"Songs by the Way": The Poetical Writings of the Right Rev. George Washington Doane*, arranged and edited by William Croswell Doane. New York: D. Appleton, 1860. http://anglicanhistory.org/usa/gwdoane/songs1860/.

Dodge, Robert J. *Isolated Splendor: Put-in-Bay and South Bass Island*. Hicksville, NY: Exposition Press, 1975.

Douglass, Frederick. "The Claims of the Negro, Ethnologically Considered, An Address Before the Literary Societies of Western Reserve College, at Commencement, July 12, 1854." Cornell University Library Digital Collections.

———. "John Brown: An Address by Frederick Douglass at the Fourteenth Anniversary of Storer College." Harper's Ferry, West Virginia, May 30, 1881. Dover, NH: Morning Star Job Printing House, 1881. https://archive.org/details/johnbrownaddress00doug.

———. "Letter from Frederick Douglass to Harriet Tubman, 1868." Harriet Tubman Historical Society. http://www.harriet-tubman.org/letter-from-frederick-douglass/.

———. *Life and Times of Frederick Douglass, Written by Himself*. 1893. In *Frederick Douglass: Autobiographies*, notes by Henry Louis Gates Jr., 453–1045. New York: Library of America, 1994.

———. "To the Editor, *Rochester Democrat and American*, October 31, 1859." In *Life and Times of Frederick Douglass, Written by Himself*. 1893. In *Frederick Douglass: Autobiographies*, notes by Henry Louis Gates Jr., 751–53. New York: Library of America, 1994.

———. "To William Cooper Nell, Lynn, Mass, February 5, 1848." *The North Star*, 1.7 (February 11, 1848). Frederick Douglass Papers at the Library of Congress. https://www.loc.gov/item/mfd.21017/.

———. "What to the Slave Is the Fourth of July?" Appendix to *My Bondage and My Freedom*. In *Frederick Douglass: Autobiographies*, notes by Henry Louis Gates Jr., 431–35. New York: Library of America, 1994.

Doy, John. *The Narrative of John Doy, of Lawrence, Kansas*. 1860. Reprint, University of Michigan University Library: Michigan Historical Reprint Series, 2005.

Drew, Thomas, compiler. *The John Brown Invasion: An Authentic History of the Harper's Ferry Tragedy with Full Details of the Capture, Trial, and Execution of the Invaders, and of All the Incidents Connected Therewith*. Boston: James Campbell, 1860. https://archive.org/details/johnbrowninvasio00drew.

Du Bois, W. E. B. *John Brown*. Edited by David Roediger. 1909. Reprint, New York: Modern Library, 2001.

———. "The Niagara Movement's Address to the Country by W. E. B. Du Bois, 1906." *New York Times*, August 20, 1906. http://college.cengage.com/history/ayers_primary_sources/niagaramovement_address_1906.htm.

Duke, Ann. "The Underground Railroad's Tale of Deliverance Has Roots in Richfield." *The Richfield Times Magazine*, March 2013.

Dyson, Michael Eric. *Tears We Cannot Stop: A Sermon to White America*. New York: St. Martin's Press, 2017.

Eldredge, Patricia. "Case Histories: Hudson, Ohio." In *Historic Preservation in Small Towns: A Manual of Practice*, edited by Arthur P. Ziegler Jr. and Walter C. Kidney, 69–82. Nashville: American Association for State and Local History, 1980.

———. "Patricia Eldredge Papers." Box 2 of 2, in process. Hudson Library & Historical Society.

Eldredge, Patricia, and Priscilla Graham. *Square Dealers: A Short History of Nineteenth Century Main Street and the Commercial Buildings on the Public Square, Hudson, Ohio*. Hudson, OH: Hudson Heritage Association, 1980.

Eldredge, Patricia, and Thomas L. Vince. *National Trust for Historic Preservation Tour Guide to Historic Hudson Houses*. October 1973. Vertical File. History—National Register. Hudson Library & Historical Society.

Ellis, Joseph J. *American Dialogue: The Founders and Us*. New York: Knopf, 2018.

Ellsworth, Henry Leavitt. *A Tour to New Connecticut in 1811: The Narrative of Henry Leavitt Ellsworth*. Edited by Phillip R. Shriver. Vol. I of the Western Reserve History Studies Series. Cleveland: Western Reserve Historical Society, 1985.

Ellsworth, Lincoln. *James William Ellsworth: His Life and Ancestry*. New York: National Americana Society, 1930.

Engle, Ann. *The Judge Van Rensselaer Humphrey Home, 264 North Main Street, Hudson, Ohio*. Hudson Heritage Association House Files. Hudson Library & Historical Society.

Fairbanks, Eugene F., compiler. *Abraham Lincoln Sculpture Created by Avard T. Fairbanks*. Bellingham, WA: Fairbanks Art and Books, 2002.

"Family of Owen Brown." Hudson Library & Historical Society. https://www.hudsonlibrary.org/historical-society/family-of-owen-brown.

Feather, Carl E. "The John Brown Affair." *Star Beacon*, October 15, 2011. http://www.starbeacon.com/community/the-john-brown-affair/article_4a235918-9499-58d6-8baa-ab65839b459d.html.

Featherstonhaugh, Thomas. "The Final Burial of the Followers of John Brown." *New England Magazine* (April 1901): 128–34.

Finkelman, Paul, ed. *His Soul Goes Marching On: Responses to John Brown and the Harpers Ferry Raid*. Charlottesville: University Press of Virginia, 1995.

———. "A Look Back at John Brown." *Prologue Magazine*, Spring 2011. National Archives. https://www.archives.gov/publications/prologue/2011/spring/brown.html.

———. "Manufacturing Martyrdom: The Antislavery Response to John Brown's Raid." In Finkelman, *His Soul Goes Marching On*, 41–66.

Fitch, George Hamlin. "The Santa Clara Valley and Santa Cruz Mountains." In *Picturesque California: The Rocky Mountains and the Pacific Slope; California, Oregon, Nevada, Washington, Alaska, Montana, Idaho, Arizona, Colorado, Utah, Wyoming, Etc.*, edited by John Muir. New York: J. Dewing, 1888.

Fletcher, Robert S. "John Brown and Oberlin." *Oberlin Alumni Magazine*, February 1932.

Foner, Eric. *Gateway to Freedom: The Hidden History of the Underground Railroad*. New York: Norton, 2015.

"Former Land Surveyor Hanged at Charlestown, Virginia—December 2, 1859." *The Empire State Surveyor* 5.2 (March, April, 1969): 3–5. Brown-Gee, Series I, Box #1, Folder #34. Hudson Library & Historical Society.

Fortune, T. Thomas. "'John Brown and Nat Turner,' January 12 and 29, 1889." In Stauffer and Trodd, *The Tribunal*, 515–17.

Fraser, George MacDonald. *Flashman and the Angel of the Lord*. New York: Knopf, 1995.

Freedmen and Southern Society Project. http://www.freedmen.umd.edu/.

Freedom on the Move Project. https://freedomonthemove.org/.

Freeman, Laura. "Abe Was Here." *Hudson Hub-Times*, February 20, 2011.

———. "An Image of Ellsworth." *Hudson Hub-Times*, July 4, 2012.

———. "Tour of Old Chapel Street Cemetery Uncovers Past Secrets." *Hudson Hub-Times*, October 15, 2014.

Fritsch, James T. "Prologue: The Wonder of the Age." In *The Untried Life: The Twenty-Ninth Ohio Volunteer Infantry in the Civil War*, 1–7. Athens: Swallow Press/Ohio University Press, 2012.

Frohman, Charles E. *Put-in-Bay: Its History*. Columbus: Ohio Historical Society, 1971.

Galbreath, C. B. "Edwin Coppoc" and "Barclay Coppoc." *Ohio Archaeological and Historical Publications* 30 (Columbus: Ohio State Archaeological and Historical Society, 1921): 397–451, 459–82. https://www.google.com/books/edition/_/T4QUAAAAYAAJ?hl=en&gbpv=1.

Garfield, James A. *The Diary of James A. Garfield*. Vol. I: 1848–1871. Edited and introduced by Harry James Brown and Frederick D. Williams. East Lansing: Michigan State University Press, 1967.

Gates, Henry Louis, Jr. "Abraham Lincoln on Race and Slavery." In *Lincoln on Race & Slavery*, edited by Henry Louis Gates Jr. and Donald Yacovone, xvii–lxviii. Princeton, NJ: Princeton University Press, 2009.

———. "The Black Letters on the Sign: W. E. B. Du Bois and the Canon." In *Black Folk Then and Now. The Oxford W. E. B. Du Bois*, edited by Henry Louis Gates Jr. New York: Oxford University Press, 2007. https://books.google.com/books?id=23TiAgAAQBAJ.

———. "Who Really Ran the Underground Railroad?" *The African Americans: Many Rivers to Cross*. https://www.pbs.org/wnet/african-americans-many-rivers-to-cross/history/who-really-ran-the-underground-railroad/.

Gee, Clarence S. "Eulogy for Mrs. Lucy Brown Clark." February 26, 1934. Brown Family Reunion Papers, Box #1, Folder 1930–1935 (1934A). Hudson Library & Historical Society.

———. Note appended to a letter from Mary A. Brown. "To My Dear Friend Mrs. Stearns, North Elba, Mar 3, 1863." Brown-Gee, Series III, Box #2, Folder #3. Hudson Library & Historical Society.

———. Note appended to a letter from Mary A. Brown. "To My Dear Friend Mrs. Stearns, North Elba, NY, Aug 4th, 1863." Brown-Gee, Series III, Box #2, Folder #3. Hudson Library & Historical Society.

———. "The Stone on John Brown's Grave." *New York History*, April 1961.

———. "Watson Brown." Brown-Gee, Series II, Box #2, Folder #4. Hudson Library & Historical Society.

———. "Watson Brown, 1835–1859." Brown-Gee, Series III, Box #1, Folder #11. Hudson Library & Historical Society.

Geffert, Hannah. "They Heard His Call: The Local Black Community's Involvement in the Raid on Harpers Ferry." In Russo and Finkelman, *Terrible Swift Sword*, 23–45.

Geffert, Hannah (with Jean Libby). "Regional Black Involvement in John Brown's Raid on Harpers Ferry." In McCarthy and Stauffer, *Prophets of Protest*, 165–79.

Giddings, Joshua R. "Joshua R. Giddings to John Brown, March 17, 1856." Kansas State Historical Society. http://www.kansasmemory.org/item/4258.

Gilbert, James N. "A Behavioral Analysis of John Brown: Martyr or Terrorist?" In Russo and Finkelman, *Terrible Swift Sword*, 107–17.

Gill, George B. "To My Dear Friend [Richard J. Hinton], Milan, Sumner Co., Kan., July 7, 1893." In Ruchames, *John Brown*, 239–42.

Gold, Michael. *Life of John Brown*. Girard, KS: Haldeman-Julius, 1924.

Goulder, Grace. *Ohio Scenes and Citizens*. Cleveland: World Publishing, 1964.

Grant, Ulysses S. *Personal Memoirs of U. S. Grant*. Vol. 1. New York: Charles L. Webster, 1885.

Green, Beriah. *Four Sermons Preached in the Chapel of the Western Reserve College: On Lord's Days, November 18th and 25th, and December 2nd and 9th, 1832*. Books on Demand from Miscellaneous Pamphlet Collection (Library of Congress).

Greenspan, Ezra. *William Wells Brown: An African American Life*. New York: W. W. Norton, 2014.

"Grinnell, Josiah Bushnell." *The Biographical Dictionary of Iowa*. University of Iowa Press Digital Editions. http://uipress.lib.uiowa.edu/bdi/DetailsPage.aspx?id=146.

Grismer, Karl H. *Akron and Summit County*. Akron, OH: Summit County Historical Society, 1952.

———. *The History of Kent: Historical and Biographical*. 1932. Revised Edition. Reprint, Kent, OH: Kent Historical Society, 2001.

Gue, Benjamin F. *Biographies and Portraits of the Progressive Men of Iowa: Leaders in Business, Politics and the Professions, Together with an Original and Authentic History of the State*. Des Moines, IA: Conway and Shaw, 1899. https://archive.org/details/biographiesandpo3shamgoog/page/n6/mode/2up.

Gugliotta, Guy. "New Estimate Raises Civil War Death Toll." *New York Times*, April 2, 2012. https://www.nytimes.com/2012/04/03/science/civil-war-toll-up-by-20-percent-in-new-estimate.html.

Hagedorn, Ann. *Beyond the River: The Untold Story of the Heroes of the Underground Railroad*. New York: Simon and Schuster, 2002.

Halberstadt, April Hope. "Sarah Brown, Artist and Abolitionist." July 2006. Saratoga Historical Foundation. http://www.saratogahistory.com/History/sarah_brown.htm.

Hamilton, Thomas. "Brown and Nat Turner: An Editor's Comparison." In Quarles, *Blacks on John Brown*, 37–39.

"Harpers Ferry History Marker." *Stone Sentinels*. http://www.stonesentinels.com/Harpers_Ferry/Harpers_Ferry_History.php.

Harris, Ransom Langdon. "John Brown and His Followers in Iowa." *Midland Monthly*, October 1894.

Henderson, Neil. "Markillie Cemetery." *The Hudson Green: Newsletter of Hudson Genealogical Study Group* 18.2 (June 2007): 1–3. http://www.rootsweb.ancestry.com/~ohhudogs/GreenJun2007.pdf.

Heppner, Christopher. "The Chamber of Prophecy: Blake's 'A Vision' (Butlin #756) Interpreted." *Blake/An Illustrated Quarterly* 25.3 (Winter 1991/1992). http://bq.blakearchive.org/25.3.heppner.

Herndon, William, and Jesse William Weik. *Herndon's Lincoln: The True Story of a Great Life*. Vol. 3. Chicago, New York, and San Francisco: Belford, Clarke & Company, 1889. https://archive.org/details/herndonslincolnto3inhern.

"HHA Meeting Explores Link Between Ellsworth, 1893 World's Fair." *Hudson Hub-Times*, March 26, 2017.

Higginson, Thomas Wentworth. "To Dear Friends [Annie and Sarah Brown], Worcester, Nov. 4, 1859." Brown-Adair, in process. Hudson Library & Historical Society.

———. *Letters and Journals of Thomas Wentworth Higginson 1846–1906*. Edited by Mary Potter Thacher Higginson. New York: Houghton Mifflin, 1921. https://archive.org/details/lettersandjourno1higggoog.

———. "A Visit to John Brown's Household in 1859." In *Contemporaries*. 1900. Reprint, Upper Saddle River, NJ: Literature House, 1970.

Hinton, Richard J. *John Brown and His Men*. 1894. Reprint, New York: Arno Press, 1968.

History Committee of St. John's Congregational Church. *The History of St. John's Congregational Church, 1844–1962*. Springfield, MA: St. John's Congregational Church, 1962.

Hodges, Graham Russell. "The Hazards of Anti-Slavery Journalism." *Media Studies Journal* 14.2 (Spring/Summer 2000). http://www.hartford-hwp.com/archives/45a/394.html.

Holmes, Richard. "A Quest for the Real Coleridge." *The New York Review of Books*, December 18, 2014. http://www.nybooks.com/articles/2014/12/18/quest-real-coleridge/.

Holsworth, Jerry W. *Civil War Winchester*. Charleston, SC: The History Press, 2011.

Holy Bible. Authorized or King James Version. Philadelphia: The John C. Winston Company, n.d.

Holzer, Harold. "Introduction." In *President Lincoln Assassinated!!: The Firsthand Story of the Murder, Manhunt, Trial, and Mourning*, compiled and introduced by Harold Holzer, xv–xxxiii. New York: Library of America, 2014.

Hopper, J. M. Bill of the Undertaker for the Body of John Brown (handwritten). Brooklyn, December 5, 1859. Boyd B. Stutler Collection, *"His Soul Goes Marching On": The Life and Legacy of John Brown*. West Virginia Archives & History. http://archive.wvculture.org/history/jbexhibit/bbsms12-0054.html.

Horwitz, Tony. *Midnight Rising: John Brown and the Raid That Sparked the Civil War*. New York: Henry Holt, 2011.

Housman, A. E. Poem IX from *A Shropshire Lad*. In *The Collected Poems of A. E. Housman*. New York: Henry Holt, 1940.

Howells, William Dean. "John Brown after Fifty Years." In Ruchames, *A John Brown Reader*, 356–64.

———. "Old Brown." In Ruchames, *A John Brown Reader*, 266–68.

Hubbell, John T. "John Brown." *Timeline Forum* (Ohio Historical Society) 9.2 (February–March 1992): 20–33.

The Interpreter's Dictionary of the Bible. Vol. 4, R–Z. Nashville: Abingdon Press, 1962.

"Iowa and the Underground Railroad." https://iowaculture.gov/sites/default/files/History%20-%20Education%20-%20Lifelong%20Learning%20-%20Iowa%20Underground%20Railroad%20%28PDF%29.pdf.

Izant, Grace Goulder. *Hudson's Heritage: A Chronicle of the Founding and the Flowering of the Village of Hudson, Ohio*. Kent, OH: Kent State University Press, 1985.

John Brown Bankruptcy Inventory (handwritten). 1842. Boyd B. Stutler Collection, Ms78-1, *"His Soul Goes Marching On": The Life and Legacy of John Brown*. West Virginia Archives & History. http://archive.wvculture.org/history/jbexhibit/bbsms03-0006.html.

"John Brown Farm Cemetery." *Northern New York Tombstone Transcription Project*. https://www.nnytombstoneproject.net/essex/north_elba/john_brown.htm.

"John Brown" [genealogy]. Brown-Gee, Series II, Box #2, Folder #3. Hudson Library & Historical Society.

John Brown in Akron: A 150th Anniversary Commemoration. Brochure. Akron, OH: Summit County Historical Society, 2009.

"John Brown's Colony." Windsor, Upper Canada, November 6, 1859. In Redpath, *The Public Life of Capt. John Brown*, 228.

"John Brown's Widow: A Visit to Her Mountain Home." *San Francisco Sunday Chronicle*, April 10, 1881. Kent Historical Society.

"John Markillie Early Well-Known Citizen." *Hudson Times*, May 28, 1931. Vertical File. Biography—Markillie. Hudson Library & Historical Society.

Johnson, Alice. *Musical Chairs on Main Street: Hudson, Ohio*. Self-published, 1979.

Johnson, Andrew. "Remarks to the Senate." December 12, 1859. In Stauffer and Trodd, *The Tribunal*, 303–7.

Johnson, Charles. *Middle Passage*. New York: Atheneum, 1990.

Johnson, J. J. "To the Editor of the *Chicago Tribune*, Martinsville, Indiana, August 27, 1882." Brown-Gee, Series III, Box #1, Folder #11. Hudson Library & Historical Society.

Johnson, Mary. "An 'Ever Present Bone of Contention': The Heyward Shepherd Memorial." *West Virginia History* 56 (1997): 1–26. http://archive.wvculture.org/history/journal_wvh/wvh56-1.html.

Jones, Louis Thomas. *The Quakers of Iowa*. Iowa City: State Historical Society of Iowa, 1914. https://archive.org/details/quakersofiowa00jonerich.

"Kansas State Capitol—Curry murals." Kansas State Historical Society (Kansapedia). https://www.kshs.org/kansapedia/kansas-state-capitol-curry-murals/16864.

Kaplan, Fred. "John Quincy Adams: American Visionary." Lecture, Hudson Library & Historical Society, Hudson, Ohio. September 22, 2014.

———. *John Quincy Adams: American Visionary*. New York: Harper, 2014.

Kaplan, Sarah. "For Charleston's Emanuel AME Church, Shooting Is Another Painful Chapter in Rich History." *The Washington Post*, June 18, 2015. https://www.washingtonpost.com/news/morning-mix/wp/2015/06/18/for-charlestons-emanuel-a-m-e-church-one-of-the-oldest-in-america-shooting-is-another-painful-chapter-in-long-history/.

Keeler, Ralph. "Owen Brown's Escape from Harper's Ferry." *Atlantic Monthly*, March 1874. https://hdl.handle.net/2027/uc1.b000780624?urlappend=%3Bseq=354.

Kinney, A. Bentley. "A Skeleton's Revenge: The Burning of the Winchester Medical College." Winchester Medical College Collection, 190 THL/WFCHS, Stewart Bell Jr. Archives. Handley Regional Library, Winchester, Virginia.

Kyle, Chris, with William Doyle. *American Gun: A History of the U.S. in Ten Firearms*. New York: William Morrow, 2013.

Land, Mary. "John Brown's Ohio Environment." *The Ohio State Archaeological and Historical Quarterly* 57 (January 1948): 24–47.

Landon, Fred. "Canadian Negroes and the John Brown Raid." *The Journal of Negro History* (April 1, 1921): 174–82. https://archive.org/details/jstor-2713730.

Lane, Samuel A. *Fifty Years and Over of Akron and Summit County*. Akron, OH: Beacon Job Department, 1892.

Larson, Erik. *The Devil in the White City*. New York: Crown, 2003.

Laughlin-Schultz, Bonnie. "How John Brown Smashed the Whisky Barrel." *California History* 92.3 (Fall 2015): 16–36.

———. *The Tie That Bound Us: The Women of John Brown's Family and the Legacy of Radical Abolitionism*. Ithaca, NY: Cornell, 2013.

Libby, Jean. "Chronology of John Brown Photo Portraits Self-Guided Tour by Jean Libby, author and curator, for teachers and researchers." http://www.alliesforfreedom.org/files/Exhibit_talking_narrative_3_.pdf.

———. "The John Brown Daguerreotypes." *The Daguerreian Annual 2002–2003*. The Daguerreian Society, 2004: 31–50.

———. *John Brown Photo Chronology: Catalog of the Exhibition at Harpers Ferry 2009*. Palo Alto, CA: Allies for Freedom Publishers, 2009.

———. *John Brown Photo Chronology Supplement; Revisions to the Catalog of the Exhibition at Harpers Ferry 2009*. Palo Alto, CA: Allies for Freedom Publishers, 2015.

Lincoln, Abraham. "Address at Cooper Institute." February 27, 1860. In *Abraham Lincoln: Speeches and Writings 1859–1865*, notes and selections by Don E. Fehrenbacher, 111–30. New York: Library of America, 1989.

———. "First Inaugural Address." March 4, 1861. In *Abraham Lincoln: Speeches and Writings 1859–1865*, notes and selections by Don E. Fehrenbacher, 215–24. New York: Library of America, 1989.

———. "Last Public Address." April 11, 1865. Abraham Lincoln Online. http://www.abrahamlincolnonline.org/lincoln/speeches/last.htm.

———. "Remarks at Hudson, Ohio." February 15, 1861. University of Michigan, *Collected Works of Abraham Lincoln*, Vol. 4. https://quod.lib.umich.edu/l/lincoln/lincoln4/1:336?rgn=div1;submit=Go;subview =detail;type=simple;view=fulltext;q1=hudson.

———. "Second Inaugural Address." March 4, 1865. In *Abraham Lincoln: Speeches and Writings 1859–1865*, notes and selections by Don E. Fehrenbacher, 686–87. New York: Library of America, 1989.

———. Speech at Elwood, Kansas. December 1 [November 30?], 1859. University of Michigan, *Collected Works of Abraham Lincoln*, Vol. 3. http://quod.lib.umich.edu/l/lincoln/lincoln3/1:164?rgn=div1;v iew=fulltext.

———. Speech at Leavenworth, Kansas. December 3, 1859. University of Michigan, *Collected Works of Abraham Lincoln*, Vol. 3. http://quod.lib.umich.edu/l/lincoln/lincoln3/1:166?rgn=div1;view=fullt ext.

Linenthal, Edward T. "Healing and History: The Dilemmas of Interpretation." In *Rally on the High Ground: The National Park Service Symposium on the Civil War*, edited by Robert K. Sutton. http://www.nps.gov/parkhistory/online_books/rthg/chap3b.htm.

Loewen, James W. *Lies My Teacher Told Me: Everything Your American History Textbook Got Wrong*. Rev. ed. New York: New Press, 2007.

Longfellow, Henry Wadsworth. "Haunted Houses." In *The Poetical Works of Longfellow*, 188–89. Introduction by George Monteiro. Cambridge Edition. Boston: Houghton Mifflin, 1975.

Lowry, Beverly. *Harriet Tubman: Imagining a Life*. New York: Doubleday, 2007.

Lubet, Steven. *The "Colored Hero" of Harper's Ferry: John Anthony Copeland and the War Against Slavery*. New York: Cambridge University Press, 2015.

———. *John Brown's Spy: The Adventurous Life and Tragic Confession of John E. Cook*. New Haven, CT: Yale University Press, 2012.

"Lyman Epps, 79, Recalls Day His Father Promised to Join John Brown Raid." *Saranac Lake Enterprise*, March 4, 1933. Brown-Gee, Series III, Box #4, Folder #8. Hudson Library & Historical Society.

Macdonald, Helen. *H Is for Hawk*. New York: Grove Press, 2014.

Maher, Joan. "Emily Metcalf's Seminary." Lecture, Hudson Heritage Association. Barlow Community Center, Hudson, OH. February 12, 2015.

Malin, James C. *John Brown and the Legend of Fifty-Six*. Philadelphia: The American Philosophical Society, 1942. https://hdl.handle.net/2027/mdp.39015013278620?urlappend=%3Bseq=426.

———. "The John Brown Legend in Pictures. Kissing the Negro Baby." *Kansas Historical Quarterly* 8.4 (November 1939): 339–41. Kansas State Historical Society. http://www.kancoll.org/ khq/1939/39_4_malin.htm.

———. "The John Brown Legend in Pictures, 2: Kissing the Negro Baby." *Kansas Historical Quarterly* 9.4 (November 1940): 339–41. Kansas State Historical Society. https://www.kshs.org/p/the-john-brown-legend-in-pictures-2/12849.

Marks, Nora. Reprint interview from 1889 with John Brown Jr. In *Put-in-Bay: Its History*, by Charles E. Frohman, 46–54. Columbus: Ohio Historical Society, 1971.

Markulis, Dorothy. "Historic Treasure." *Discover Hudson*, 2016, 12–16. https://issuu.com/dixcom/docs/ hudson_discover_2015.

Marshall, Thurgood. "The Bicentennial Speech." http://www.thurgoodmarshall.com/speeches/ constitutional_speech.htm.

Marshall, Tim. *Murdering to Dissect: Grave-robbing, Frankenstein and the Anatomy Literature*. Manchester, UK: Manchester University Press, 1995.

Maryland Center for History and Culture. "The Tale of John Brown's Letter Book," including donation letter from Clifton W. Tayleure, November 3, 1883. https://www.mdhistory.org/the-tale-of-john-browns-letter-book/.

Mayer, Gwen. "Aurora Street #42." Houses of Hudson Collection. Summit Memory. http://www. summitmemory.org/cdm/singleitem/collection/hudson/id/478/rec/3.

Mayo, Katherine. "Brown in Hiding and in Jail." *New York Evening Post*, October 23, 1909. In Ruchames, *A John Brown Reader*, 234–40.

———. Interview with Mrs. Rebecca Spring, 547 DeSoto Street, Los Angeles, September 1908. John Brown Manuscripts. Box #16, Folder #7. Rare Book and Manuscript Library, Columbia University Library.

———. Ohio Interviews. Brown-Villard, Box #1. Hudson Library & Historical Society.

———. "Sturdy Children of John Brown." *The New York Evening Post*, November 6, 1909, (Supplement), 3.

McArn, Sally R. *The Underground Railroad—An American Legend.* 1977. Hudson Library & Historical Society.

McBride, James. *The Good Lord Bird.* New York: Riverhead, 2013.

McCarthy, Timothy Patrick, and John Stauffer, eds. *Prophets of Protest: Reconsidering the History of American Abolitionism.* New York: New Press, 2006.

McFarland, Gerald W. "Hudson's John Brown: The Controversy Continues." October 24, 1985. Video Recording. Vault Collection. Hudson Library & Historical Society.

———. *A Scattered People: An American Family Moves West.* 1985. Reprint, Amherst: University of Massachusetts Press, 1991.

McGlone, Robert E. "John Brown, Henry Wise, and the Politics of Insanity." In Finkelman, *His Soul Goes Marching On*, 213–52.

———. *John Brown's War Against Slavery.* Cambridge: Cambridge University Press, 2009.

McGuire, W. P. Editorial on Winchester Medical College. *Virginia Medical Monthly* 48.1 (April 1924): 45–47. Winchester Medical College Collection, 190 THL/WFCHS, Stewart Bell Jr. Archives. Handley Regional Library, Winchester, Virginia.

McNees, David. "Supports Library's Educational Efforts." Letter to the Editor, *Hudson Hub-Times*, April 8, 2009.

Mead, John. "An Insurrection of Thought: The Literature of Slave Rebellion in the Age of John Brown." Master's thesis, University of Illinois at Chicago, 1998.

Mecoy, Alice Keesey. "Please Do Not Move Owen Brown's Gravesite." *John Brown the Abolitionist—a Biographer's Blog*, June 21, 2011. http://johnbrownkin.blogspot.com/2011/06/please-do-not-move-owen-browns.html?m=1.

Melville, Herman. "The Portent." In Ruchames, *A John Brown Reader*, 285.

Merton, Eunice. "Friends Share John Brown's Grief." Between Nursery Rows. *The Gristmill*, ca. 1947. http://www.friendsofcrowellhilaka.org/john-browns-grief.html.

———. "Road to Freedom." Between Nursery Rows. *The Gristmill*, February 7, 1947. http://www.friendsofcrowellhilaka.org/road-to-freedom.html.

Metcalf, Emily. "History of the First Congregational Church in Hudson, Ohio." *Historical Papers Delivered at the Centennial Anniversary of the First Congregational Church of Hudson, Ohio.* September 4, 1902. Hudson Congregational Church Manuscript Collection. Hudson Library & Historical Society.

———. "Woman's Work in the Hudson Church for a Century." *Historical Papers Delivered at the Centennial Anniversary of the First Congregational Church of Hudson, Ohio.* September 4, 1902. Hudson Congregational Church Manuscript Collection. Hudson Library & Historical Society.

Miller, Ernest C. *John Brown, Pennsylvania Citizen: The Story of John Brown's Ten Years in Northwestern Pennsylvania.* Warren: Penn State University Press, 1952.

Mills, Edwin W. "To Miss [Ada M.] Remington, June 7, 1933." Brown-Adair, in process. Hudson Library & Historical Society.

Monroe, James. "A Journey to Virginia in December, 1859," a Thursday lecture by Prof. James Monroe (1897). Electronic Oberlin Group Documents. http://www.oberlin.edu/external/EOG/HistoricalDocuments.html.

"Monument to Heyward Shepherd." *Stone Sentinels.* http://www.stonesentinels.com/Harpers_Ferry/Heyward_Shepherd.php.

Moore, James. "Darwin the Abolitionist." Week of February 6, 2009. Interview by Bruce Gellerman. Living on Earth. http://www.loe.org/shows/segments.html?programID=09-P13-00006&segmentID=4.

Morris, J. Brent. *Oberlin, Hotbed of Abolitionism: College, Community, and the Fight for Freedom and Equality in Antebellum America.* Chapel Hill: University of North Carolina Press, 2014.

Morrison, Toni. "Making America White Again." *New Yorker*, November 21, 2016. http://www.newyorker.com/magazine/2016/11/21/making-america-white-again.

Nalty, Damon G. *The Browns of Madronia: Family of Abolitionist John Brown Buried in Madronia Cemetery Saratoga, California.* Saratoga, CA: Saratoga Historical Foundation, 1996.

"Nat'l. Trust Tour Here Draws Favorable Comment." *Hudson Hub*, October 17, 1973.

Naveh, Eyal. "John Brown and the Legacy of Martyrdom." In Russo and Finkelman, *Terrible Swift Sword*, 77–90.

Nelson, John T. "Lucy Markerly: A Case Study of an Englishwoman's Immigration to the Western Reserve in the 1830s." *Northeast Ohio Journal of History* 4.1 (Spring 2007). https://blogs.uakron.edu/nojh/2007/04/21/lucy-markerly-1830s/.

Nesbett, Peter T. *Jacob Lawrence: The Complete Prints (1963–2000).* Seattle: University of Washington Press, 2001.

Newell, Amy L. *The Caves of Put-in-Bay.* Columbus: Greyden Press, 1995.

Newkirk, Lois, ed. *Hudson: A Survey of Historic Buildings in an Ohio Town.* Introduction by Thomas L. Vince. Kent, OH: Kent State University Press, 1989.

Niven, John. *Salmon P. Chase: A Biography.* New York: Oxford University Press, 1995.

Northup, Solomon. *Twelve Years a Slave.* Auburn, NY: Derby and Miller, 1853. Project Gutenberg 2014. https://www.gutenberg.org/files/45631/45631-h/45631-h.htm.

NPR Staff. "'Good Lord Bird' Gives Abolitionist Heroes Novel Treatment," August 17, 2013. http://www.npr.org/2013/08/17/212588754/good-lord-bird-gives-abolitionist-heroes-novel-treatment.

Oates, Stephen B. *To Purge This Land with Blood: A Biography of John Brown.* 1970. 2nd ed. Reprint, Amherst: University of Massachusetts Press, 1984.

Obama, Barack. "Remarks by the President on the Economy in Osawatomie, Kansas," December 6, 2011. https://obamawhitehouse.archives.gov/the-press-office/2011/12/06/remarks-president-economy-osawatomie-kansas.

"Old Buss Company Store." Vertical File. Historic Houses. Hudson Library & Historical Society.

Painter, Nell Irvin. "Truth Be Told." Review of *William Wells Brown: An African American Life*, by Ezra Greenspan. *New York Times Book Review*, November 16, 2014.

"The Passing of Sarah Brown, Daughter of John Brown of Harper's Ferry: A Pioneer of Saratoga." *Saratoga Record* 3.22 (July 7, 1916): 1–2. Brown-Gee, Series II, Box #2, Folder #6. Hudson Library & Historical Society.

Pelster, Mae. *Abolitionists, Copperheads and Colonizers in Hudson & the Western Reserve.* Charleston, SC: History Press, 2011.

Peterson, Merrill D. *John Brown: The Legend Revisited.* Charlottesville: University of Virginia Press, 2002.

Pfeiffer, David A. "Bridging the Mississippi: The Railroads and Steamboats Clash at the Rock Island Bridge." *Prologue Magazine*, Summer 2004. National Archives. http://www.archives.gov/publications/prologue/2004/summer/bridge.html.

Philbrick, Nathaniel. *In the Hurricane's Eye.* New York: Viking, 2018.

Phillips, W. A. "Three Interviews with Old John Brown." *Atlantic Monthly*, December 1879. https://www.theatlantic.com/magazine/archive/1879/12/three-interviews-old-john-brown/589084/.

Phillips, Wendell. "Burial of John Brown." In Ruchames, *John Brown*, 266–69.

A Picture of Hudson. Hudson, OH: Destination Hudson, 2018.

Poe, Edgar Allan (adapted from N. P. Willis). "Harper's Ferry." *Graham's Magazine* 20.2 (February 1842). http://www.eapoe.org/rejected/essays/hrpfry01.htm.

Porter, Dorothy B. "David Ruggles, 1810–1849; Hydropathic Practitioner." *Journal of the National Medical Association* 49.1 & 2 (January and March, 1957, two-part article).

Price, Mark J. "Attorney Decried Bigotry in Akron." *Akron Beacon Journal*, February 24, 2014.

———. "Frederick Douglass, an Ex-Slave, Gave Moving Hudson Talk." *Akron Beacon Journal*, February 13, 2017.

———. "One Last Glimpse of Lincoln." *Akron Beacon Journal*, April 13, 2015.

Quarles, Benjamin. *Allies for Freedom*. 1974. Reprint, *Allies for Freedom & Blacks on John Brown*. Boston: Da Capo Press, 2001.

———, ed. *Blacks on John Brown*. 1972. Reprint, *Allies for Freedom & Blacks on John Brown*. Boston: Da Capo Press, 2001.

Records of the Free Congregational Church of Hudson, Organized October 7th AD 1842. Hudson Congregational Church Manuscript Collection. Hudson Library & Historical Society.

Rediker, Marcus. *The Slave Ship: A Human History*. New York: Viking, 2007.

Redpath, James. "James Redpath to Elias Nason, April 10, 1874." West Virginia Memory Project, John Brown/Boyd B. Stutler Collection. http://archive.wvculture.org/history/wvmemory/jbdetail.aspx?Type=Text&Id=1023.

———. *The Public Life of Capt. John Brown*. 1860. Reprint, Nabu Public Domain, 2010.

Renehan, Edward J., Jr. *The Secret Six: The True Tale of the Men Who Conspired with John Brown*. Columbia: University of South Carolina Press, 1997.

Report of the Special Committee Appointed to Investigate the Troubles in Kansas, with the Views of the Minority of Said Committee. University of Michigan Library. http://quod.lib.umich.edu/cgi/t/text/text-idx?c=moa;idno=AFK4445.

Reynolds, David S. *John Brown, Abolitionist: The Man Who Killed Slavery, Sparked the Civil War, and Seeded Civil Rights*. New York: Knopf, 2005.

———. *Mightier Than the Sword: Uncle Tom's Cabin and the Battle for America*. New York: Norton, 2011.

"Richfield History." Richfield Historical Society. http://www.richfieldohiohistoricalsociety.org/richfield-history.html.

Robinson, Marilynne. *Gilead*. New York: Farrar, Straus and Giroux, 2004.

Roediger, David, ed. Introduction to *John Brown*, by W. E. B. Du Bois, xi–xxii. 1909. Reprint, New York: Modern Library, 2001.

Rogers, Larkin. "Food of the Historic Western Reserve." Lecture, Hudson Heritage Association. Barlow Community Center, Hudson, OH. December 13, 2018.

Rolfe, John. "20. and odd Negroes." Excerpt from a letter from John Rolfe to Sir Edwin Sandys (1619/1620). *Encyclopedia Virginia*. Virginia Foundation for the Humanities. http://www.encyclopediavirginia.org/_20_and_odd_Negroes_an_excerpt_from_a_letter_from_John_Rolfe_to_Sir_Edwin_Sandys_1619_1620.

Roosevelt, Theodore. "New Nationalism Speech," August 31, 1910. TeachingAmericanHistory. http://teachingamericanhistory.org/library/document/new-nationalism-speech/.

Rosenberg, Daniel. *Mary Brown: From Harpers Ferry to California*. Occasional Papers Series Number Seventeen. New York: American Institute for Marxist Studies, 1975. https://archive.org/details/MaryBrown/page/n11/mode/2up.

Ruchames, Louis. *John Brown: The Making of a Revolutionary*. Introduction by Louis Ruchames. New York: Universal Library, 1969.

———, ed. *A John Brown Reader: The Story of John Brown in His Own Words, in the Words of Those Who Knew Him, and in the Poetry and Prose of the Literary Heritage*. Introduction by Louis Ruchames. London: Abelard-Schuman, 1959.

Rukeyser, Muriel. *The Life of Poetry*. 1949. Reprint, with a new foreword by Jane Cooper, Ashfield, MA: Paris Press, 1996.

Russo, Peggy A., and Paul Finkelman, eds. *Terrible Swift Sword: The Legacy of John Brown.* Athens: Ohio University Press, 2005.

Ryall, Lydia Jane. *Sketches and Stories of the Lake Erie Islands.* Norwalk, OH: American Publishers, 1913.

Ryan, Daniel J. *Lincoln and Ohio.* 1923. Reprint, Dover, OH: Ohio Historical Society and Old Hundredth Press, 2008.

St. John's Congregational Church Website. http://sjkb.org/discover_stjohns/history.html.

Sanborn, F. B., ed. *The Life and Letters of John Brown: Liberator of Kansas and Martyr of Virginia.* 1885. Third Edition. Classic Reprint Series, Forgotten Books. Concord, MA: F. B. Sanborn, 1910.

Shackel, Paul A. "John Brown's Fort: A Contested National Symbol." In Russo and Finkelman, *Terrible Swift Sword*, 179–89.

Shakespeare, William. "Sonnet 27." In *The Arden Shakespeare Complete Works.* Revised Edition. Edited by Richard Proudfoot, Ann Thompson, David Scott Kastan, and H. R. Woudhuysen, 22. London: Arden Shakespeare, 2001.

"Shall We Have a Hall?" Letter to the Editor, *Hudson Enterprise*, September 27, 1877.

Shelley, Mary. *Frankenstein; or, the Modern Prometheus.* 1818. Reprint, London: William Pickering, 1996.

Sherbondy, Jeanette E. "Sherbondy Hill of Akron, Ohio." July 2007. http://sherbondy.org/Sherbondy%20Hill%20pdf.pdf.

Shermer, Michael. *The Moral Arc: How Science and Reason Lead Humanity Toward Truth, Justice, and Freedom.* New York: Henry Holt, 2015.

Showalter, Elaine. *The Civil Wars of Julia Ward Howe.* New York: Simon & Schuster, 2016.

Siebert, Wilbur Henry. *The Mysteries of Ohio's Underground Railroads.* Columbus: Long's College Book Company, 1951.

Sinha, Manisha. *The Slave's Cause: A History of Abolition.* New Haven, CT: Yale University Press, 2016.

Smith, Narcissa Macy. "Reminiscences of John Brown." *Midland Monthly*, September 1895.

Soike, Lowell J. *Busy in the Cause: Iowa, the Free-State Struggle in the West, and the Prelude to the Civil War.* Lincoln: University of Nebraska Press, 2014.

———. *Necessary Courage: Iowa's Underground Railroad in the Struggle against Slavery.* Iowa City: University of Iowa Press, 2013.

Spring, Rebecca Buffum. "How I Brought First Aid to Wounded John Brown (Harper's Ferry 1859)." *The New York Press*, October 13, 1907.

Stake, Virginia Ott. *John Brown in Chambersburg.* Chambersburg, PA: Franklin County Heritage, 1977.

Staley, Mary L. Interview by Joyce Dyer. St. Paul's Episcopal, Put-in-Bay. October 4, 2012.

Stark, David. "Lesser Known Jesse James Gunfight at Civil Bend." *Gallatin North Missourian*, April 4, 1993. Daviess County Historical Society. http://daviesscountyhistoricalsociety.com/2004/05/01/lesser-known-jesse-james-gunfight-at-civil-bend/.

Starr, George Leander. Diary [by year]. Starr Manuscript Collection, Starr Family Papers, Starr Diaries. Hudson Library & Historical Society.

Stauffer, John, and Zoe Trodd. "Introduction: The Meaning and Significance of John Brown." In Stauffer and Trodd, *The Tribunal*, xix–lix.

———, eds. *The Tribunal: Responses to John Brown and the Harpers Ferry Raid.* Cambridge, MA: Belknap Press of Harvard University Press, 2012.

Sublette, Ned and Constance. *The American Slave Coast: A History of the Slave-Breeding Industry.* Chicago: Lawrence Hill Books, 2016.

Swanson, Dan. "Historical Society Published Map of Civil Bend." *Nebraska City News-Press*, Jan. 18, 2012.

Taney, Roger Brooke. Scott v. Sandford. Cornell University Law School, Legal Information Institute. https://www.law.cornell.edu/supremecourt/text/60/393#writing-USSC_CR_0060_0393_ZO.

Tasker, Greg. "Tribute to Victim of Brown's Raid Still Controversial." *The Baltimore Sun*, September 3, 1995. https://www.baltimoresun.com/news/bs-xpm-1995-09-03-1995246078-story.html.

Thomson, Melissa, and E. Leslie Polott. "Library Clarifies John Brown Events." Letter to the Editor, *Hudson Hub-Times*, April 12, 2009.

Thoreau, Henry David. "A Plea for Captain John Brown." In *Thoreau: Collected Essays & Poems*, selected by Elizabeth Hall Witherell, 396–417. New York: Library of America, 2001.

Tindall, George Brown, and David Emory Shi. *America: A Narrative History*. Brief Ninth Edition. New York: Norton, 2012.

Titone, Nora. *My Thoughts Be Bloody: The Bitter Rivalry Between Edwin and John Wilkes Booth that Led to an American Tragedy*. New York: Free Press, 2010.

Toomer, Jean. *Cane*. New York: Liveright, 1923. Project Gutenberg 2019. http://www.gutenberg.org/files/60093/60093-h/60093-h.htm.

Townsley, James. "The Potawotomie Tragedy: John Brown's Connection with It, Statement of James Townsley, an Eye-Witness." Lawrence (Kansas) *Daily Journal*, December 10, 1879. In Ruchames, *A John Brown Reader*, 197–203.

Trodd, Zoe, and John Stauffer, eds. *Meteor of War: The John Brown Story*. Maplecrest, NY: Brandywine Press, 2004.

Troglen, Tim. "Great-great-grand Niece of Abolitionist John Brown to Pay Historic Church a Visit." *Hudson Hub-Times*, April 28, 2013. https://www.beaconjournal.com/story/news/local/hudson-hub-times/2013/04/28/great-great-grand-niece-abolitionst/19735677007/.

Trumbull, Harlan L. "To Mrs. Theodore S. Sprague, 45 Division Street, Hudson, Ohio, Nov. 19, 1971." Vertical File. Biography—John Brown. Hudson Library & Historical Society.

Turner, Nat. *The Confessions of Nat Turner, the Leader of the Late Insurrection in Southampton, Va.*, as made to Thomas R. Gray. http://docsouth.unc.edu/neh/turner/turner.html.

Turzillo, Jane Ann. *Hudson, Ohio*. Images of America Series. Chicago: Arcadia, 2002.

Twain, Mark. "Jim and the Dead Man." *New Yorker*, June 26, 1995.

United States Census Bureau. "1860 Census: Population of the United States." https://www2.census.gov/library/publications/decennial/1860/population/1860a-02.pdf.

Upton, Harriet Taylor, and Harry Gardner Cutler. *History of the Western Reserve*. Vol. 3. University City, MO: Lewis Publishing, 1910. https://books.google.com/books/about/History_of_the_Western_Reserve.html?id=L5GPjobXdWoC.

Villard, Henry. *Lincoln on the Eve of '61*. Edited by Harold G. and Oswald Garrison Villard. New York: Knopf, 1941.

Villard, Oswald Garrison. *John Brown 1800–1859: A Biography Fifty Years After*. Boston: Houghton Mifflin, 1910.

Vince, Thomas L. "Abraham Lincoln and John Brown." Lecture, Sons of Union Veterans of the Civil War. Cuyahoga Falls Public Library, Cuyahoga Falls, OH. July 2, 2013.

———. "Former Saloon Saved." *Inside Hudson*, March 2014.

———. "History of the Chapel Bell." Lecture, Hudson Heritage Association. Western Reserve Academy Chapel, Hudson, OH. May 10, 2018.

———. "How Luck and Destiny Led to City's Founding." Lecture, Hudson Heritage Association. Barlow Community Center, Hudson, OH. October 8, 2015.

———. "Mystery of House Solved." *Inside Hudson*, January 2014.

———. "Surviving Two Centuries." *Inside Hudson*, September 2013.

Waite, Frederick Clayton. "Sources of the Present Names of Streets in Hudson." Frederick Waite Manuscript Collection, in process. Hudson Library & Historical Society.

———. *Western Reserve University, The Hudson Era: A History of Western Reserve College and Academy at Hudson, Ohio, from 1826 to 1882*. Cleveland: Western Reserve University Press, 1943.

"Want Street Named for Owen Brown." *North Summit Times*, April 6, 1951. Hudson Library & Historical Society.

Washington, Margaret. *Sojourner Truth's America*. Urbana: University of Illinois Press, 2009.

Wellington, Maud. "Slavery." In *The Akron Offering: A Ladies' Literary Magazine, 1849–1850*, edited by Jon Miller, 332–36. Akron, OH: The University of Akron Press, 2013.

Western Reserve Historical Society. "What Is the Western Reserve?" http://www.wrhs.org/about/wrhs-history/.

Wheeler, Robert A., ed. "Document Six: David Hudson, Sr.: An Early Settler Arrives in Northeastern Ohio, 1799." In *Visions of the Western Reserve: Public and Private Documents of Northeast Ohio, 1750–1860*, 57–63. Columbus: Ohio State University Press, 2000.

Whittier, John Greenleaf. "Brown of Osawatomie." In Ruchames, *A John Brown Reader*, 295–96.

———. *The Letters of John Greenleaf Whittier*. Edited by John B. Pickard. Vol. I, 1828–1845. Cambridge, MA: Belknap Press of Harvard University Press, 1975.

Williams, George Washington. *History of the Negro Race in America from 1619 to 1880: Negroes as Slaves, as Soldiers, and as Citizens*. Vol. II (1800–1880). New York: G. P. Putnam's Sons, 1883. https://books.google.com/books?id=TR-hGrKdr7QC.

Wineapple, Brenda. *White Heat: The Friendship of Emily Dickinson & Thomas Wentworth Higginson*. New York: Knopf, 2008.

Witte, Brian. "NAACP to Honor Abolitionist John Brown." Fox News, Associated Press, Baltimore, July 14, 2006. http://www.foxnews.com/printer_friendly_wires/2006Jul14/0,4675,AbolitionistHonored,00.html.

Wolfe, H. Scott. "Farmer Maxson's Newel Post: A Piece of History." *John Brown the Abolitionist—a Biographer's Blog*, June 2, 2011. http://abolitionist-john-brown.blogspot.com/2011/06/from-field-farmer-maxsons-newel-post.html.

Wright, Philip Green and Elizabeth Q. Wright. *Elizur Wright: The Father of Life Insurance*. Chicago: University of Chicago Press, 1937.

Young, Joshua. "The Funeral of John Brown." *New England Magazine* (April 1904): 229–43. https://books.google.com/books?id=v69JAQAAMAAJ.

Young, Kevin. "American Bison." In *Brown*. New York: Knopf, 2018.

Zakrzewska, Marie E. *A Woman's Quest: The Life of Marie E. Zakrzewska*. Edited by Agnes C. Vietor. New York: D. Appleton and Co, 1924. http://iiif.lib.harvard.edu/manifests/view/drs:2585817$8i.

Photo Credits

BOSTON ATHENÆUM
John Brown after battles in Kansas (Item: UTB-6, 5.4, broj (no. 1). John Brown, 1 photograph : sixth plate daguerreotype, b&w, [ca. 1856].)

CHICAGO HISTORY MUSEUM
Akron portrait of John Brown (Chicago History Museum, IChi-022207)

KANSAS STATE HISTORICAL SOCIETY
John Brown's Fort rebuilt for the 1893 Columbian Exposition in Chicago (Kansas State Historical Society, 220343)
John Steuart Curry standing on a ladder by the *Tragic Prelude* mural in the Kansas State Capitol (Kansas State Historical Society, 784)
John Brown supporters, including Jacob Willetts, standing on far left (Kansas State Historical Society, 207817)
Augustus Wattles (Kansas State Historical Society, 90680)
Stone house built by Augustus Wattles in Linn County, where John Brown wrote "Parallels" (or, possibly, in a log cabin on this site before this structure was built) (Kansas State Historical Society, 228901)
Sam and Jane Harper (1894), former enslaved people from Missouri farms who were liberated by the parties of John Brown and Aaron Stevens in 1858 (courtesy Kansas State Historical Society, 208796)
Dutch Henry's cabin site in Franklin County, showing old settlers standing nearby (Kansas State Historical Society, 215985)

LIBRARY OF CONGRESS
Abraham Lincoln, candidate for US president, before delivering his Cooper Union address, New York, NY, on Feb. 27, 1860, photo by Mathew Brady (Brady-Handy Collection, Prints & Photographs Division, LC-USZ62-1891)
William Lloyd Garrison, ca. 1870 (Liljenquist Family Collection of Civil War Photographs, Prints & Photographs Division, LC-DIG-ppmsca-53260)
Gerrit Smith, between 1855 and 1865 (Prints and Photographs Division, LC-DIG-cwpbh-02631)
Colonel Simon Perkins Mansion, photo by Carl F. Waite, 1934 (Prints & Photographs Division, HABS OHIO,77-AKRO,1-)
Stereograph of Harpers Ferry and railroad bridge, 1865 (Prints & Photographs Division, LC-DIG-stereo-1s01839)
Interior of the engine house just before it was stormed, wood engraving, 1859 (Prints and Photographs Division, LC-USZ62-132541)
John Brown lying wounded, beside son (Prints and Photographs Division, LC-USZ62-44565)
John Brown's Fort, ca. 1885 (Liljenquist Family Collection of Civil War Photographs, Prints and Photographs Division, LC-DIG-ppmsca-40573)

Cook Hall, on grounds of Storer College, founded 1867 (Prints and Photographs Division, HABS WVA,19-HARF,32-E—5)

Niagara Movement founders, middle row showing W. E. B. Du Bois second from the right and J. Max Barber third from the right, superimposed over an image of Niagara Falls, 1905 (Prints and Photographs Division, LC-DIG-ppmsca-37818)

Julian Bond (Prints and Photographs Division, LC-DIG-ds-05289)

Head-and-shoulders portrait of Frederick Douglass, photo by J. W. Hurn, 1862 (Prints and Photographs Division, LC-DIG-ds-07422)

Harriet Tubman, portrait by Benjamin F. Powelson, 1868 or 1869 (Prints and Photographs Division, LC-DIG-ppmsca-54230)

John Brown's grave and the "Big Rock," North Elba, photo by S. R. Stoddard, ca. 1896 (Prints and Photographs Division, LC-USZ62-107590)

John Brown riding on his coffin to his execution, *Frank Leslie's Illustrated Newspaper* (Prints and Photographs Division, LC-USZ62-79479)

Charles Town street scene, showing back of courthouse (Prints and Photographs Division, LC-USZ62-74889)

State Hospital, Utica, New York, ca. 1905 (formerly State Lunatic Asylum) (Detroit Publishing Company Collection, Prints and Photographs Division, LC-D4-18751 [P&P])

Thomas Wentworth Higginson, photo by William Notman (William A. Gladstone Collection of African American Photographs, Prints and Photographs Division, LC-DIG-ppmsca-11424)

Mary Ann Brown with daughters Annie (left) and Sarah (right) (Prints & Photographs Division, LC-USZ62-24743)

James Buchanan, 15th President of the United States (1857–1861) (Prints & Photographs Division, LC-DIG-pga-13395)

Lydia Maria Child (Prints & Photographs Division, LC-DIG-ppmsca-54178)

Jesse James dead in his coffin (Prints & Photographs Division, LC-USZ62-26562)

Josiah Bushnell Grinnell, between 1855 and 1865 (Brady-Handy Collection, Prints & Photographs Division, LC-BH82- 5370 A)

William Maxson House, photo by C. C. Woodburn, 1934 (Prints & Photographs Division, HABS IOWA,16-SPRING.V,1—4)

John Wilkes Booth with the Richmond Grays at the hanging of John Brown, left of Caskie (man at center with goatee), photo by Lewis Graham Dinkle (Prints & Photographs Division, LC-USZ62-8908)

SPRINGFIELD MUSEUM

31 Franklin Street by Unknown Photographer [SPC-06-002884.03] (Courtesy of the Springfield Photo Collection, The Lyman & Merrie Wood Museum of Springfield History, Springfield, MA)

Sketch of Eli Baptist by Unknown Artist [SPC-04-0088.2-02] (Courtesy of the Springfield Photo Collection, The Lyman & Merrie Wood Museum of Springfield History, Springfield, MA)

Thomas Thomas by Unknown Photographer [SPC-04-0350.01-01] (Courtesy of the Springfield Photo Collection, The Lyman & Merrie Wood Museum of Springfield History, Springfield, MA)

Sanford Street Church by Unknown Photographer [SPC-02-0060-05](Courtesy of the Springfield Photo Collection, The Lyman & Merrie Wood Museum of Springfield History, Springfield, MA)

WEST VIRGINIA STATE ARCHIVES

John Brown holding Subterranean Pass banner, photo by Augustus Washington (Boyd B. Stutler Collection of John Brown, West Virginia State Archives, PH01-0001)

Painting of John Brown in Kansas by Daniel Beard from a photo taken by Colonel John Bowles (Boyd B. Stutler Collection of John Brown, West Virginia State Archives, PH01-0074)

Governor Henry Wise of Virginia (tall hat, third from left) examining wounded Harpers Ferry prisoners, sketch by Alfred Berghaus, *Leslie's Illustrated Newspaper* (Boyd B. Stutler Collection of John Brown, West Virginia State Archives, PH06-0010)

Oswald Garrison Villard (Boyd B. Stutler Collection of John Brown, West Virginia State Archives, PH04-0081)

Henry Thompson, married to John Brown's daughter Ruth (Boyd B. Stutler Collection of John Brown, West Virginia State Archives, PH02-0043)

Dangerfield Newby (Boyd B. Stutler Collection of John Brown, West Virginia State Archives, PH05-0042)

Hugh Forbes (Boyd B. Stutler Collection of John Brown, West Virginia State Archives, PH05-0019)

Osborne Perry Anderson (Boyd B. Stutler Collection of John Brown, West Virginia State Archives, PH05-0044)

Lewis W. Washington, great-grandnephew of George Washington (Boyd B. Stutler Collection of John Brown, West Virginia State Archives, PH05-0068)

Lewis Sheridan Leary (Boyd B. Stutler Collection of John Brown, West Virginia State Archives, PH05-0035)

Sketch of burial of John Brown at North Elba, *New York Illustrated News* (Boyd B. Stutler Collection of John Brown, West Virginia State Archives, PH06-0066)

John Brown headstone, North Elba farm, photo by S. R. Stoddard, 1888 (Boyd B. Stutler Collection of John Brown, West Virginia State Archives, PH02-0083)

Annual pilgrimage to John Brown gravesite by John Brown Memorial Association, May 9, 1930 (Boyd B. Stutler Collection of John Brown, West Virginia State Archives, PH03-0249)

Lyman Epps Sr. (Boyd B. Stutler Collection of John Brown, West Virginia State Archives, PH04-0030)

Sheriff James Campbell, who hanged John Brown (Boyd B. Stutler Collection of John Brown, West Virginia State Archives, PH04-0020)

Arrival of John Brown's body at the North Elba farm, sketch by Thomas Nast, *New York Illustrated News* (Boyd B. Stutler Collection of John Brown, West Virginia State Archives, PH06-0064)

Final viewing of John Brown's body, sketch by Thomas Nast, *New York Illustrated News* (Boyd B. Stutler Collection of John Brown, West Virginia State Archives, PH06-0065)

Jeremiah Goldsmith Anderson (Boyd B. Stutler Collection of John Brown, West Virginia State Archives, PH05-0003)

Watson Brown (Boyd B. Stutler Collection of John Brown, West Virginia State Archives, PH02-0038)

Horatio N. Rust (Boyd B. Stutler Collection of John Brown, West Virginia State Archives, PH04-0075)

Oliver Brown (Boyd B. Stutler Collection of John Brown, West Virginia State Archives, PH02-0022)

Burial of Oliver Brown and his fellow raiders at North Elba in 1899, Rev. Joshua Young standing far left and Col. Richard Hinton next to him (Boyd B. Stutler Collection of John Brown, West Virginia State Archives, PH03-0244)

Shields Green, hanged December 16, 1859 (Boyd B. Stutler Collection of John Brown, West Virginia State Archives, PH05-0023)

John Anthony Copeland Jr., hanged December 16, 1859 (Boyd B. Stutler Collection of John Brown, West Virginia State Archives, PH05-0007)

John Avis, John Brown's jailer (Boyd B. Stutler Collection of John Brown, West Virginia State Archives, PH04-0006)

The Secret Six (Boyd B. Stutler Collection of John Brown, West Virginia State Archives, PH04-0076)

Four sons of John Brown, clockwise, Salmon, John Jr., Owen, Jason (Boyd B. Stutler Collection of John Brown, West Virginia State Archives, PH02-0051)

Two-story house incorporated into Mary Ann Brown's original cabin home in Saratoga, California (Boyd B. Stutler Collection of John Brown, West Virginia State Archives, PH03-0140)

John Henry Kagi (Boyd B. Stutler Collection of John Brown, West Virginia State Archives, PH05-0029)

George B. Gill (Boyd B. Stutler Collection of John Brown, West Virginia State Archives, PH06-0078)

Aaron Dwight Stevens (Boyd B. Stutler Collection of John Brown, West Virginia State Archives, PH05-0055)

Edwin and Barclay Coppoc, dual image (Boyd B. Stutler Collection of John Brown, West Virginia State Archives, PH05-0011)

Charles Town jail, where John Brown stayed, razed in 1930 (Boyd B. Stutler Collection of John Brown, West Virginia State Archives, PH06-0127)

Mary Ann Brown arriving in Charles Town to visit her husband, December 1, 1859, sketch by Alfred Berghaus, *Leslie's Illustrated Newspaper* (Boyd B. Stutler Collection of John Brown, West Virginia State Archives, PH06-0047)

The Last Supper, John and Mary Ann Brown in the parlor of jailer John Avis the evening before his execution, sketch by David C. Hitchcock, *New York Illustrated News* (Boyd B. Stutler Collection of John Brown, West Virginia State Archives, PH06-0030)

Artificially created photograph of John Brown with John Doy (Boyd B. Stutler Collection of John Brown, West Virginia State Archives, PH01-0129)

Joyce Dyer is Professor Emerita of English at Hiram College. She was the first director of the Lindsay-Crane Center for Writing and Literature at Hiram, where she held the John S. Kenyon Chair in English. Before Hiram, she taught twelve years at Western Reserve Academy.

Her essays have appeared in magazines such as *North American Review, Writer's Chronicle*, and the *New York Times*, as well as numerous anthologies.

Dyer is the author of *In a Tangled Wood: An Alzheimer's Journey, Gum-Dipped: A Daughter Remembers Rubber Town*, and *Goosetown: Reconstructing an Akron Neighborhood*. She edited *Bloodroot: Reflections on Place by Appalachian Women Writers* and *From Curlers to Chainsaws: Women and Their Machines* (co-editor).

She received the 1998 Appalachian Book of the Year Award, the 2009 David B. Saunders Award in Creative Nonfiction, Ohio Arts Council Individual Excellence Awards (in nonfiction), and a Gold Medal in the category of anthology in the 2016 Independent Publisher Book Awards contest.

She lives in Hudson, Ohio, with her husband, Daniel, approximately one hundred feet from the spot where John Brown made a vow in 1837 to destroy slavery.